SINDH
UNDER THE
MUGHALS

Origin and Development of Historiography
(1591–1737 CE)

SINDH
UNDER THE
MUGHALS

Origin and Development of Historiography
(1591–1737 CE)

HUMERA NAZ

Foreword by
MICHEL BOIVIN

OXFORD
UNIVERSITY PRESS

Oxford University Press is a department of the University of Oxford.
It furthers the University's objective of excellence in research, scholarship,
and education by publishing worldwide. Oxford is a registered trade mark of
Oxford University Press in the UK and in certain other countries

Published in Pakistan by
Oxford University Press
No. 38, Sector 15, Korangi Industrial Area,
PO Box 8214, Karachi-74900, Pakistan

© Oxford University Press 2023

The moral rights of the author have been asserted

First Edition published in 2023

All rights reserved. No part of this publication may be reproduced, stored in
a retrieval system, or transmitted, in any form or by any means, without the
prior permission in writing of Oxford University Press, or as expressly permitted
by law, by licence, or under terms agreed with the appropriate reprographics
rights organization. Enquiries concerning reproduction outside the scope of the
above should be sent to the Rights Department, Oxford University Press, at the
address above

You must not circulate this work in any other form
and you must impose this same condition on any acquirer

ISBN 978-0-19-070128-4

Typeset in Times New Roman
Printed on 55gsm Book Paper

Printed by Delta Dot Technologies (Pvt.) Ltd, Karachi

Acknowledgements
Cover Images: Mughal flower border © M.K Studios / Shutterstock
Mughal colourful decorative plant illustration for
wall painting © artistsayeed / Shutterstock

I humbly dedicate this work to my mother
Anis Parveen
without whose courage, support, and prayers,
I could not have achieved anything.

Contents

Foreword ix
Acknowledgements xii
Glossary xiv
Transliteration System xvii
Introduction xviii

1. **Indian Historiography in Retrospect** 1
   - History and Historiography 1
   - The Ancient Indian Historiography: Traditions and Characteristic 4
   - Early Indo-Muslim Historiography: Its Genesis and Major Trends (1206–1526 CE) 13
     - Origin and Development of Historiographical Tradition in India 16
     - Major Trends and Traditions of Early Indo-Muslim Historiography 28
   - Indo-Mughal Historiography: Its Development, Major Traditions, and Characteristic 31
     - Major Traditions and Characteristics of Indo-Mughal Historiography 33

2. **Mughal Rule in Sindh: The Period of Origin and Development of Historiographical Trends** 40
   - *Nusrat Nama-i-Tarkhan*—The First Political History Compiled in Sindh 48
   - Genres of Non-Political Historical Literature: *Tadhkiras*, *Malfuzat*, and *Insha* 59
     - *Tadhkirat al-Murad:* The First Hagiographic Account (Biography Including *Malfuz* Literature) Compiled in Sindh 62
     - *Tadhkira Rawzat al-Salatin:* The Earliest Biographical Account (*tadhkira*) of the Poets Compiled in Sindh 69

viii CONTENTS

- *Jawahir al-Aja'ib* (The Wonderful Jewels): The First 75
  Tadhkira of the Poetesses Compiled in Sindh

3. **Political Literature/Chronicles** 81
   - *Tarikh-i-Sindh* alias *Tarikh-i-Masumi* 82
   - *Beglar Nama* (The Book of Beglar) 93
   - *Tarikh-i-Baldah-i-Thatta* alias *Tarikh-i-Tahiri* 100
   - *Mazhar-i-Shahjahani* (The Manifestation of the Emperor 115
     Shah Jahan): The First Manual on Mughal Administration
     in Sindh
   - *Tarkhan Nama*, or *Tarikh-i Sind Dar Zamana-i Arghun* 126
     Wa Tarkhan (The History of Sindh During the Reign of
     the Arghuns and Tarkhans)
   - *Intikhab-i-Muntakhib*, or *Intikhab-i-Muntakhib* 134
     al-Tawarikh (*Intikhab Nama*)

4. ***Tadhkira*** **and** ***Malfuz*** **Literature** 140
   - *Hadiqat al-Awliya-i-Sindh:* The First Biographical 144
     Directory of the Sufi Saints of Sindh
   - *Tadhkira Mashayikh-i-Sewistan:* The Biographical 150
     Directory of the Sufi Saints of Sewistan
   - *Dhakhirat al-Khawanin:* The Earliest Biographical 156
     Directory of the Mughal Nobility

5. ***Insha*** **Literature (Epistolography)** 168
   - *Munshat-i-Namakin* (The Epistles of Namakin) 171
   - *Aadab-i-Alamgiri/Munshat-i-Alamgiri* 181
     (The Letters of Aurangzeb)
   - *Raqa'im-i-Kara'im* (The Notations of Greatness) 187

6. **Conclusion** 193

Notes 212
Selected Bibliography 242
Index 251

Foreword

The Mughal dynasty marked the history of all South Asia, and of the whole world. In particular, the monuments it left behind remain among the gems of humanity's heritage. The most famous of them is undoubtedly the Taj Mahal, the magnificent tomb that the Mughal emperor Shah Jahan (1592–1658) had built for his deceased wife Mumtaz Mahal (1593–1631). The Mughals have added to the development of architecture on a wide scale, in the different capitals they have created over the centuries. They were also patrons of the arts, whose support allowed the development of many masterpieces, starting with miniature painting. The importance of the Mughals in the history of South Asia is reflected in the innumerable books and studies that have been devoted to them, and that researchers still devote to them.

However, these works are largely dominated by a conventional representation of history, one that focuses on the places of power, the imperial cities, the court, and the exercise of power within these capitals. The numerous achievements of the emperors have generally been projected to highlight the greatness of these sovereigns. This is so because the reign of the Mughals corresponds to an apogee, that is to say one of the rare moments in history when South Asia was almost unified. The Mughal Empire was gigantic, and the great diversity of its components led the emperors into warfare at the four corners of the empire to try to maintain its unity.

However, one Mughal ruler embodies more than any other the splendours of the empire: Akbar. Born in Umerkot in Sindh in 1542, he succeeded his father Humayun in 1555 at the age of 14 for a reign that would last half a century. The many facets of Akbar's reign have been the subject of much work, but among the areas that have been left unexplored is the impact of his rule on the outlying regions that made up his empire. In 1591, Akbar conquered a new province in the west of the empire: Sindh. The history of Sindh itself has been studied by many scholars, including the Mughal period. One example is the work of Ansar Zahid Khan titled *History and Culture of Sind* (1980). This book was devoted to a study of socio-economic organization and institutions during the sixteenth and seventeenth centuries.

Dr Humera Naz's book focuses on the epistemological, concentrating on the birth of a historiography in Sindh that occurred during this Mughal period. Her erudition regarding first-hand sources is apparent from the great variety of these sources, which are almost all in Persian. Nonetheless, it should be mentioned that Dr Naz's book's importance goes far beyond the political perspective. She sifts through works written in Persian during this period, and extracts numerous lessons about the religious and social life of Sindh under the Mughals. But what are the factors that produced this renewal of historiography in Sindh in this period? The historiography of the Persian language was certainly not created during the Mughal period. The author recalls in this regard that she has relied on oral traditions transmitted by bards, such as *charan*s.

However, the Mughal period will produce both a renewal and a consequent expansion of historiography. The author explains with the greatest clarity that this epistemological development is mainly due to the patronage of the Mughals, through their governors and other administrators. This does not mean that there was no Persian-language historiographical tradition in Sindh; the famous *Chach Namah* attests otherwise. However, before the arrival of the Mughal emperor Akbar, who was himself a native of Sindh, the territory had been subject to great instability as a result of countless invasions and wars. By seizing Sindh, Akbar brought the region into the *pax mogholica*. Furthermore, it has been clearly demonstrated that the rise of historiography in Mughal Sindh was a direct result of Akbar's efforts to strengthen this type of work throughout his empire.

After tracing the emergence of historiography, Dr Naz reviews different types of literary traditions: political chronicles, writings about saints, and those concerning epistolography. A considerable contribution to the research concerns two specific types of literature: *malfuzat*s and *tadhkira*s, which are the subject of Chapter 4. Taking up Carl Ernst's observation that this literature must be analysed according to several criteria, Dr Naz constructs a specific methodology to get as close as possible to the historical truth contained in the proposals of the authors on which it is based. To really appreciate the quality of her work, it is important to observe in detail how she does it. Dr Naz begins by defining this literature as non-political. She classifies these sources as 'alternative sources' which can corroborate the events narrated in political chronicles. Nonetheless, the main contribution these sources bring is that they allow us to touch the lives of the common people about whom history has generally not been written.

Regarding this kind of literature, Dr Naz is quite aware that it is often neglected by historians, who see political sources as the main, if not the sole, source for studying history. The *Tadhkira* literature traces back to an Arabic genre known as *asm'a al-rijal*, in which poets used to collect biographies of heroes and famous men. Later, it was also used in Persia, and finally in India, with Awfi's *Lubab al-Albab* (The Quintessence of the Hearts), written in 1221–1222 CE at Uch (in the Middle Ages, Southern Punjab was included in present day Sindh). In what is the oldest available book of this kind composed in India, Dr Naz stresses upon the important data that can be collected. Another genre is the *malfuzat*, which is free from any political influence, and provides information gathered from mystic records; this presents a very different perspective to the notions formed and perpetuated by the political chronicles. For this reason, as stated by Dr Naz, *malfuzat* literature has great value in understanding important fragments of medieval Indian society.

Dr Humera Naz's book is a major contribution to the history of Sindh, and consequently to that of Pakistan and South Asia. Beyond the excellence of the research, it must be emphasized that, if the reign of the Mughal rulers has been studied in detail, it is mainly in the imperial context, namely from the centres of power they had created and developed in northern India. In publishing this book, Dr Naz has shifted the focus, producing an innovative perspective on how the Mughals exercised power in territories relatively far from the imperial centres, but above all she reveals the leading role they played in developing historiography through the spread of several literary genres. Thus, Dr Naz's work renews the field of Mughal studies, but at the same time, it is much more than that.

MICHEL BOIVIN
Director, Centre for South Asian Studies
CNRS-EHESS
PARIS

Acknowledgements

I developed an interest in the history of Sindh in my early years at university when I contributed a research paper titled 'The Soomra period in Sindh' at a conference. Later, I found opportunities to conduct further research on different topics related to Sindh. As my area of focus is medieval Indian history, I chose a topic connected to medieval Sindh for my work. The main purpose of this research is to analyse the historical sources of medieval Sindh from a fresh perspective. In this respect, emphasis is laid on the circumstances that led to the rise, growth, and development of historiography in Sindh during Muslim rule—the Mughal period in particular. Mughal rule in Sindh witnessed the emergence of new trends of historiographical interest in the region, which gradually strengthened and crystallised the perceptions of scholarly activities and the volume of knowledge in this regard.

I would like to express my reverent and profound gratitude to Dr Nasreen Afzal, for her able guidance, invaluable advice, and encouragement in completing this research work. I am also grateful to professor Dr Rehana Afsar for encouraging and supporting me in my endeavour.

I am particularly grateful to the eminent scholar and researcher, Dr G.M. Lakho, Chairman of the Department of General History at the University of Sindh, for his continuous and caring guidance, and well-timed advice, which helped me through a number of stages in the process of completing this work. He generously gave me access to rare manuscripts, original sources, newly published source books, and photocopies of some material, the original copies of which were unavailable. I owe him a heartfelt thanks for the kindness and consideration he always showed me. Likewise, I wish to offer my thanks to Dr Ansar Zahid Khan, Secretary, Pakistan Historical Society, for his continuous guidance, assistance and support from the beginning to the end of my research journey and for giving me access to his personal collection and the library of the Pakistan Historical Society.

I am also indebted to Dr Nawaz Ali Shoq, for providing me with some unpublished manuscripts and other rare primary sources from his collection. I am also grateful to Dr M. Saleem Akhtar, a distinguished scholar of Persian and History, for his guidance and his generosity in supplying me with valuable material. Dr Akhtar introduced me to the oriental section of the library at the University of the Punjab, Lahore.

I owe thanks to my esteemed friend and colleague, Dr Faezeh Zehra Mirza, for her valuable assistance in translating extracts from classical Persian to English. I am also indebted to Fakhar Bilal, teaching faculty, department of History, Quaid-i-Azam University, Islamabad for arranging my visit and access to the Syed Hussamuddin Rashidi Collection, located in the library of Quaid-i-Azam University and the library of the University of the Punjab, Lahore.

I am also thankful to Mr Muhammad Hasan for supplying me with some rare material from the collection of the National Institute of Historical and Cultural Research (NIHCR), Islamabad. I would be failing in my duty if I was not to record my profound thanks and gratitude to Dr Iqbal Chawla, Chairman of the Department of History at the University of the Punjab, who facilitated my research by allowing me complete access to the libraries of the University of the Punjab and the Research Society of Pakistan, Lahore.

I want to pay my special thanks to Dr Azizudin Hussain, Director, Rampur Rada Library, India, for providing me with an opportunity to access the rare collection of the institute, particularly the manuscript section. I am also thankful to the librarian of Sahitya Academy, New Delhi, Mr Sufian Ahmad, for the extra support and help he provided in searching and obtaining copies of some required material.

I would like to express my gratitude to the directors and librarians of the Persian Research Centre of Iran and Pakistan, Islamabad; Sindh Archives; Institute of Sindhology; Sindhi Adabi Board; National Museum Library; Shah Abdul Latif Bhitai Chair, University of Karachi; and Dr Mahmud Hussain Library, University of Karachi.

Glossary

A'immah	Members of the House of the Holy Prophet (PBUH)
Abhinaya	A traditional actor who performed through body language
Abiyat	Poems
Akhyana	A grand narrative to be presented through recitation of a text
Amil	Revenue collector
Amin	Land surveyor/assessor
Amir	Nobleman or an official of high rank
Amir al-Umara	Head of the *amirs*
Ansab	Genealogies
Arbab	Record keeper of revenue
Ard-dashts	Petitions
Asm'a al-rijal	The biographies of transmitters of *hadiths*
Awliyas	Saints
Ayyam al-Arab	The battle memories of the Arabs
Bakhshi	Military pay-master in a province and/or an intelligence officer
Bhrigvangirases	Officials assigned to record and keep the traditional genealogies of the royal families
Ba'it	Oath of fealty
Dabir	Secretary
Dastak	Payment orders
Dastan	Epic
Dastur al-Amals	Manuals of administration
Diwan	Collection of poems chiefly *ghazals*
Diwans	Official archives (lit. a list or register)
Farmans	Royal orders
Fawjdar	Commandant of a territory
Fiqh	Muslim jurisprudence
Futuh	Unsolicited charity
Gathas	Hindu religious songs
Hadith	Speeches and actions of the Holy Prophet (PBUH)
Hafiz	Reciter of the Holy Quran

xiv

GLOSSARY

Haji	A pilgrim
Harem	Female quarter in the palace
Hikayat	Stories often told and heard orally
Ilm al-Rijal	Science of biography
Insha/insha pardazi	Epistolography
Isnad	Chain of transmission
Itihasa	Tradition which comprised of the second order of religious literature
Jagir	Land grant
Jagirdar	Holder/owner of a specific territory
Karoris	Revenue collectors
Khalifa	Deputy
Khanqahs	Monasteries
Latifas	Anecdotes
Madrasa	Educational institution
Maghazis	Material expeditions of the Holy Prophet (PBUH)
Majalis	Spiritual gatherings
Maktubat	Epistles
Malfuzat	Collection of discourses or utterances of Sufi saints
Manaqib	Prose eulogies generally concerning to a ruler, noble, saint, or learned man
Mansab	Rank/position
Mansabdar	Rank-holder
Mathnawi	A poetical expression
Mufti	Title given to a recognized theologian
Muhtasib	The regulator of public business who controlled trade and enforced Islamic injunctions
Munshi	Draftsman of imperial letters, edicts and documents
Murshid	Spiritual guide
Muwarrikhin	Historians
Narasamsis	Poetic forms of eulogies
Qazi	Muslim judge who renders decisions according to the Sharia
Qasidas	Eulogistic odes
Qissa-khwans	Story tellers
Risalat	Prophethood of the Holy Prophet (PBUH)
Sadr	Chief ecclesiastical officer and supervisor of the endowments of land reserved for charity
Sama	Musical session for mystical poetry
Sanads	Royal decrees

Sandhivigrahikas	The salaried court poets
Sawar	Horseman
Shaykh	Spiritual mentor
Shaykh al-Islam	The chief jurist-consult of a city or realm
Sirah	Biography of the Holy Prophet (PBUH)
Sunnah	Traditions of the Holy Prophet (PBUH)
Sutas	The minstrels or bards
Tadhkiras	Hagiography or biographical directories or anthologies of Sufis or literary personalities
Tafsir	Transliteration/interpretation
Tariqat	Mystic rule of life
Tasawwuf	Mysticism
Tashbih	A poetic imaginary characteristic
Tawhid	Oneness of God
Thanah	Police station
Ulema	Learned men or scholars
Umara	Rank-holders
Urs	The death anniversary of a Sufi saint
Usul-i-Isnad	Veracity of the statement
Vamsas	The Buddhist religious books
Vamsavalis	The traditional genealogies
Wakil-i-Mutlaq	Regent of Mughal affairs
Wali	Saint
Waqa'i-nawis	News-writer/royal reporter or secret agent
Wazir	Prime minister

Transliteration System

All the medieval Muslim names, terms, and words in Persian and Arabic used in this book are literally transliterated. The transliteration system is as below:

ا	a		ص	s
ال	al-		ض	d
او	aw		ط	t
ای	ay		ظ	z
ب	b		ع	a'a
ت and ٹ	t		غ	gh
ث	th		ف	f
ج	j		ق	q
چ	ch		ک	k
ح	h		گ	g
خ	kh		ل	l
د	d		م	m
ذ	dh		ن	n
ر	r		و	u:w:aw
ز	z		ه	h
س	s		ء	ʾ
ش	sh		ی	i:y

Introduction

This book covers a century-and-a-half of Mughal rule (the Timurids) in Sindh, starting with the occupation of Sindh by Emperor Akbar in 1591 CE and up until the end of the Mughal supremacy in Sindh in 1737 CE, brought about by the Kalhoras (r. 1737–1783 CE). This period witnessed the main currents and cross-currents in the development of historiography, in terms of introducing trends, traditions, and methodology. The book's main aim is to analyse the trends and major characteristics in the field of historiography during the Mughal rule in Sindh.

Historiography covers historical narratives and creates awareness, among scholars, of the experiments undertaken by past historians. It is, in fact, the art of communicating knowledge of the past. It is a work of subjective creativity that is directed by the contemporary socio-cultural and intellectual environment, which inevitably moulds and drives the historians' perspectives. According to E. Sreedharan:

> Historiography tells us the story of the successive stages of evolution or development of historical writings. It has come to include the evolution of the ideas and techniques associated with the writing of history and changing attitudes towards the nature of history itself. Ultimately, it comprises the study of the development of the human sense for the past.[1]

While it is a relatively modern trend, some techniques of recording events and personal accounts have been around since the inception of recorded history. In short, various types of methodologies have been deliberately or conversely, unwittingly or unconsciously, used by historians since time immemorial. But only in the nineteenth century did a consciousness of these trends and traditions develop and evolve into a scientific discipline studied to gain a greater understanding of history.

It is a well-known fact that the Greeks are the first who developed the art of writing history. Greek historiography dates back more than 2500 years. Then, it was in the form of mythical tales.[2] In Greek culture, these tales were first transmitted orally and later this became the basis of its literature. The earliest Greek historical literature adopted the form of mythological songs and poetic stories designated as '*Epos*'.[3] It created a sense of the past and enabled the underprivileged classes to forge a connection with history. While the fifth century BCE witnessed remarkable development by the Greeks in the art of narrating contemporary and past events, it seems that afterwards a decisive transition occurred from depicting theocratic and mythical history, to authentic historical literature. Post-sixth century BCE was an epoch of transition for the Greeks. They adopted a more reflective rather than imaginative approach in recording historical accounts, as is evinced by Herodotus (484–425 BCE) and Thucydides (460–400 BCE).[4]

This development was an important influence on the writing of history elsewhere around the Mediterranean region. The Greek historians greatly contributed to the development of a historical methodology, which was subsequently followed by the Romans.[5] The main feature of Greco-Roman historiography is the humanistic element; it is a narrative of human history. From Herodotus and Thucydides, history was now the reconstruction of man's deeds, purposes, successes, and failures, while the gods had no place in human affairs. Man (and woman) themselves were responsible for their actions and fate. This concept of free will and the driving force behind their achievement and failure was a philosophical idea. The tendency to learn about human activities of the past was grounded in the desire to understand the consequences of one's actions.

The nature, quality, and quantity of historical literature have always varied among different generations and nations. This variation reflects the social life and beliefs of the people of different regions and ages. As such, this applies to Greco-Roman's European counterparts and to the early Muslim or Arab civilisation, with its historical traditions and the use of sophisticated methods of historiography that they initiated. The beginning of Muslim historiography actually meant the beginning of historiography among the Arabs.

However, history had always been a decisive factor in the outlook of the Arabs.[6] It is not possible to disregard the role of the pre-Islamic period in the incipient development of historiography from both historical and cultural perspectives. However, a definite transition took place from the pre-Islamic to the Islamic period in terms of literary and cultural developments. Historical and cultural developments are interdependent and naturally contributed to enabling the pre-Islamic historical consciousness among the Arabs to evolve into the historiography of the Islamic era.

The early Arab historians of the Islamic era considered the Quran and the Prophet's traditions (*sunnah*) as their main sources.[7] In the early phase, there was no difference between hadith[8] scholars and *muwarrikhin* (historians). Authentication of events and facts regarding *hadith*—termed as *isnad*—and the biographies of the narrators of traditions (*asm'a al-rijal*), were given so much importance that historiography entered a new phase that gradually became a full-fledged discipline of knowledge.

The Arab historiography was based on the analysis, evaluation, and examination of authentic primary sources and organisation of these sources into a narrative timeline. Muslim historical traditions first began developing from the earlier seventh century with the reconstruction of the *Sirah*[9] literature. In order to evaluate the sources, various methodologies were developed, such as the 'science of biography', 'science of *hadith*', and *isnad* (chain of transmitters). These methodologies were later applied to other historical figures in terms of *ilm al-rijal* (science of biography). Validating the *hadith* or *isnad* was a major study among the Arabs. The Arab historians were meticulous in authenticating these historical records for which they used eyewitnesses, oral traditions, and official archives (the diwans) as their sources.

The Arabs were the first who combined history with scientific geography on a larger scale, consequently, history assumed a broader outlook in terms of world histories. The Arabs had a genius for history and gradually evolved some techniques in this particular field. The Abbasid period (r. 750–1258 CE) is particularly significant for unique achievements in the realm of the intellectual and cultural development of Muslim thoughts and ideas, including history writing. Some new trends and traditions were introduced, and historiography became a part of religious studies with certain doctrinal guidelines, principles, and values.

Arab historiography adopted a broader, more democratic scope and was not confined to rulers, dynasties, conquests, and court affairs. Instead, it included the history of working-class people in its ambit. Historians also turned their attention to urban history and the history of the newly conquered cities and towns. Arab historiography played a significant and dominant role in the intellectual culture of that epoch, through its chronicles on different themes and subjects, such as cities, families, dynasties, and even some other less consequential matters and personalities. It somehow preserved the 'values' of history in addition to adopting new scientific methods for interpreting it. Though some historians advocated an approach to copying the past with no modification; they also made attempts to use the scholarly tools of rationalism, or the causation theory in their interpretation of the past.

It is also evident that during the Abbasid Caliphate (r. 750–1258 CE), Arab historiography gradually became dominated by Persian influence besides other intellectual activities and a large co-existent Arabic literature produced by the Persians. The impetus provided by the Persians was essential not only for the development of the Islamic civilization, but also for the early Muslim historiography. At the time, the Persian language and mindset had gained a preeminent position in compiling historical literature and Persian historiography was able to pursue its course to a certain extent.[10] Early Muslim historiography is indebted to the Persians for introducing some new trends and features such as the history of dynasties and political institutions. Later, the eleventh century witnessed a new emerging trend; the origin and growth of official history writing by historians of royal courts, who were employed to glorify the life and times of the rulers.[11]

The Persian-speaking Turks brought this tradition of history writing with them when they established the Muslim rule in India under the Sultanate of Delhi (r. 1206–1526 CE). Consequently, a continuous chronological record of major events in Indo-Muslim history is available to us in a series of works ranging from the thirteenth to the nineteenth century, covering both dynasties and regions.

Unfortunately, we have not found any written records of Indian history prior to Muslim rule (r. 1206–1857 CE). Early Brahman religious literature—including the *Ramayana*, *Mahabharata*, and *Puranas*—provides records of some historical events, but these cannot be considered authentic and reliable, as they are hyperbolic in nature. The *Rajatarangini* by Kalhana (a Kashmiri historian) is regarded as the earliest historical source in India, compiled in Sanskrit in 1148 CE. This book comprises the history of Kashmir and is a reliable historical account.

It is evident that all early Indo-Muslim historiography was in the Persian language, since Persian was the language of the court as well as the official language of the Sultanate of Delhi. Persian-language scholarship received a setback when Timur invaded India in 1398 CE and destroyed the Delhi Sultanate. But it soon revived and expanded exponentially during the years of the Timurid-Mughal dynasty (r. 1526–1857 CE). During this period, Indo-Persian historiography became a vibrant, multi-faceted tradition of scholarship, including *tuzuk*s (autobiography/ biographical memoirs), *diwan*s (collections of poetry), *akhlaq* (ethical treatises), *manaqibs* (didactic history), *nasihat* (advice literature), *hikayat* (anecdotes), *insha* (belles-lettres/epistolography), *dasturs* and *manshoors* (manifestoes/gazetteers and manuals of technical prose and administration), *malfuzat* (conversational discourses of Sufis, mystics, and saints), *tadhkiras*[12] (biographical directories and hagiographical accounts) and innumerable political histories. These works were produced in the Timurid-Mughal court in Agra and Delhi, as well as at the independent courts of Persian-speaking rulers of semi-autonomous Timurid–Mughal provinces in Bengal, Bihar, Gujarat, Sindh, the Deccan, Madras, etc.

Prior to the Mughal period, Sindh also had a rich body of historical records in the form of folkloric tales, romantic poems, epics, and ballads of local bards and *charans*. In this way, the historical narratives and anecdotes were transmitted orally from one generation to another, though in this process bards and *charans* indulged in gross exaggerations, especially while describing the exploits of their patrons. However, the beauty of their work lies in the fact that these chroniclers also often dared to utter truths that sometimes were unpalatable to their masters.[13]

Oral accounts in the form of folklore found their shape in Sindh during the last days of the Arab rule and the Soomra period (1058–1349 CE). The folklore of Sindh, like all other folklore, is the result of an interaction of cultural, geographical, and religious factors and offers valuable historical evidence of cultural influence.[14] Apparently, it was a very important historical source in a region such as Sindh, where we found no written records till the middle of the sixteenth century.[15]

The earliest record of the history of the Arab conquest of Sindh was written outside India in the ninth century, when an anonymous writer compiled *Minhaj al-Din Wa'l Mulk* (The Way towards Religion and the World) in Arabic, most probably between 830 and 868 CE. Though, some scholars referring to certain internal evidences infer that the work must have been written earlier than 753 CE.[16] However, this book was subsequently translated into Persian under the title of the *Fateh-Nama-i-Sindh* (The History of the Conquest of Sindh), better known as the *Chach Nama*, by Ali bin Hamid bin Abi Bakr Al-Kufi (d. 1220 CE) in 1216 CE at Bhakkar.[17] In fact, no work written prior to the *Chach Nama* is extant. This book deals not only with the history of Sindh, but that of India as well.

The Mughal rule in Sindh played a dynamic role in literary and scholarly development, including history writing, which is almost entirely in Persian. In fact, the historians of Mughal Sindh were not devoid of concepts of history. Their emphasis varied, and their aims differed, but they viewed history as an exploration of investigating facts. In an environment where they were bound not to use their own judgement and had to restrain themselves according to the wishes of their patron rulers, they tried to convey what they really wanted to. On the other hand, some of these chroniclers would use exaggerated hyperbolic language for praising something or someone, when the main objective was to condemn.

Some of them believed silence to be the best option in such circumstances, but they overlooked the fact that often 'omission of facts sometimes did greater harm to history than exaggeration or overstatement'.[18]

In this way, we see a considerable quantity of authentic historical literature in the history of India as well as the history of Sindh after the time of the Arab conquest. With the commencement of the Mughal rule in Sindh, official and non-official chroniclers produced works dealing with the ruling dynasties. Some scholars compiled works of a non-political genre also. In this regard, Mughal Emperor Akbar's period bore the torch and lit the path for subsequent historians. Scholars from Persia migrated and settled in India and Sindh because the Mughal emperors offered strong inducements in the form of robes of honour, titles, ranks, land grants, and cash rewards. Due to the involvement of the Safavids of Persia in patronising various other activities, particularly industrial arts, architecture, theology, and sectarian philosophy, the prospects of literary writers were limited in Persia.

Compared to this, in India, poetry, prose, arts, and architecture all enjoyed court patronage, and 'any man could profess anything whether the religion allowed it or not.'[19] The sovereignty of Mughal emperors, such as Akbar, Jahangir, Shah Jahan, and Aurangzeb also shows to its credit a fairly long list of nobles, court historians, poets, and epistolographers. We can judge this based on the number of works compiled during this period. The literary output of this period, not just in its quantity but in its literary excellence too, surpasses all former periods.

The present volume comprises six chapters; a summary of each chapter is given below.

Chapter 1 traces the concept of history and historiography, and the correlation between the two. It briefly describes the origin and development of the art of writing history which originated among the Greco-Romans and developed its major characteristics. It further provides a detailed critical review of ancient Indian historical literature, which is based mainly on the Brahman religious epics and how no written record of the history of India is found till the beginning of Muslim rule in 1206 CE. Briefly addressing traditions and methods in early Muslim historiography (Arab historiography), provides a strong basis for early Indian historiography. The emergence of Indo-Persian traditions of historiography titled 'early Indo-Muslim historiography', commenced with Turkish rule in India, after a number of scholars, men of letters, and artists, migrated from Persia and Central Asia, and settled in India. It traces the significant impact of the Muslim legacy of intellectual development in India and attempts to understand its genesis and identify its major trends. Historiography during the Mughal period in India along with its traditions and trends is also a sub-topic of this chapter. This is indispensable because in order to understand these trends, traditions, and characteristics of Mughal historiography in Sindh, it is necessary to trace their development from early Indo-Muslim historiography.

Chapter 2 focuses on the evolution of historical traditions in Sindh from ancient times. It provides the historical background of the shift of power from the native rule of the Sammas to the emergence of a new foreign power in the region, the Mughals (the Arghuns and the Tarkhans) in 1519–1520 CE. Later, power was transferred into the hands of the Great Timurids in 1591 CE. This chapter elaborates on the accounts of the commencement of a new era of literary and scholarly activities under royal patronage and its impact on the intellectual development and social life in the region. In particular, it highlights the origin and development of the art of writing history in terms of political chronicles such as the *Nusrat Nama-i-Tarkhan* (The Book of the Victories of the Tarkhans) by Muhammad bin Bayazid Purani (*c.* 1560 CE), which is regarded as the earliest work compiled in Sindh as well as some other genres of historiography in terms of non-political literature, for instance, *hikayats*, *tadhkiras*, *malfuzat*, *insha*, etc. This non-political literature also includes *Tadhkirat al-Murad*, the first hagiographic account; *Rawzat al-Salatin*, the foremost biographical account of the Persian poets; and the *Jawahir al-Aja'ib*, the first biographical directory of Persian poetesses compiled in Sindh.

Chapter 3 discusses in detail the historical works compiled during the Timurid-Mughal period in Sindh (r. 1591–1737 CE). The literature written in this period formed a substantial number of political chronicles on Sindh, particularly about dynastic histories. Each of the books is critically analysed under the purview of biographical sketches and the choice of subjects of the author, description of the title, its sources, authenticity, assessment of historical value, and its contribution to the transformation and evolution of historiography. The *Tarikh-i-Sindh* alias *Tarikh-i-Masumi* (*c.* 1600 CE) of Mir Muhammad Masum seems to be one of the earliest, and the most authentic and basic sources of the history of Sindh, which was compiled during the Timurid-Mughal period. The other historical compilations discussed are the *Beglar Nama* (1608 CE); the *Tarikh-i-Tahiri* (1621 CE); *Tarik Mazhar-i-Shahjahani* (1628 CE); *Tarikh-i Sind dar Zamana-i Arghun wa Tarkhan* also called the *Tarkhan Nama* (*c.* 1654 CE); and the *Intikhab-i-Muntakhib*, also known as the *Intikhab-i-Muntakhib-*

ut-Tawarikh, or *Intikhab Nama* (*c.* 1673–1674 CE). The authenticity and value of these works are assessed in terms of corroboration of their records with the other contemporary works. Consequently, this chapter furnishes the significant features of the historiographical outlook during the Mughal era that shaped the earliest historiographical trends in Sindh during the seventeenth century. The *tadhkira* is a unique genre of Muslim historiography, which is a combination of biography and a directory or anthology of the works of Sufi saints, poets, scholars, and other eminent personalities.

Chapter 4 critically examines the historical writings of a non-political genre comprising the *tadhkira* (biographical memoirs) cum *malfuz* (discourses of Sufi saints) literature, compiled during the Mughal period. The chapter includes three major works, such as the *Hadiqat al-Awliya*, also known as the *Hadiqat al-Awliya-i-Sindh* (The Garden of the Sufi Saints of Sindh) (*c.* 1607–1608 CE); the *Tadhkira Mashayikh-i-Sewistan* (The Biographical Directory of the Saints of Sewistan) (*c.* 1632 CE); and the *Dhakhirat al-Khawanin* (The Biographical Directory of the Mughal Nobility) (*c.* 1650–1651 CE). This chapter focuses on the critical examination of the sources in terms of the lives, and notably the miracles and virtues of the Sufi saints and Shaykhs of Sindh. It offers a record of institutional and regional history, and touches upon the popular cults, customs, and traditions; elucidating the relationships of these Sufis with the elites as well as the common people it explores their effect on contemporary politics and society. It is true that the court historians often ignored the 'spirit of the age', social forces, or causation in history, but on the other hand, the *malfuz* and *tadhkira* literature of varied types are full of information about the lives of common people and discussions over the cause-and-effect factor of the historical events.

Chapter 5 explains the *insha* literature compiled in Sindh during the Mughal period. This literature includes the *Munshat-i-Namakin* (the epistles of Namakin) (*c.* 1598 CE); the *Aadab-i-Alamgiri* or the *Munshat-i-Alamgiri* (*c.* 1703–1704 CE); and the *Raqa'im-i-Kara'im* (the epistles of Emperor Aurangzeb) (*c.* 1718–1719 CE). This chapter presents comprehensive accounts of such works as important sources of the political and social history of Sindh and its adjoining regions, including describing the topography, the origin of different native tribes, crops, climate, and conditions of trade and commerce. These collections of official letters of the reign of Shah Jahan and Aurangzeb have also facilitated in providing an analysis of their reigns in a fresh perspective of Medieval Indian history. This chapter further offers interesting details regarding the administrative set-up, bureaucracy, and economic conditions during the Mughal rule in Sindh.

Chapter 6 sums up the trends and traditions of Mughal historiography in Sindh. While analyses of the historiographical trends and traditions are usually based on political chronicles, contemporary historians well acquainted with the knowledge of techniques and approaches of modern European historiography, emphasise the need to consult non-political literature: the *tadhkiras*, the *malfuzat*, the *insha*, the *manshoors*, etc., for reinterpreting the political and social history. A considerable amount of new and interesting information about all aspects of history such as politics, society, culture, religion, economy, etc., can be found in these sources. They also offer a valuable record of institutional and regional history, and knowledge about popular cults, customs, and traditions.

This book is a preliminary inquiry, and it is hoped that it might lead to further research by scholars into the process of acculturation and the pivotal role played by Sindh in this regard.

CHAPTER 1

Indian Historiography in Retrospect

History and Historiography

History as 'the study of man's dealings with other men and the adjustment of working relations between human groups',[1] usually refers to the sum total of human activities of the past, but also covers thoughts, hopes, and feelings.[2] According to E.H. Carr:

> The historian distils from the experience of the past [from the parts that are accessible to him] which he recognizes as amenable to rational explanation and interpretation and from it draws conclusions which may serve as a guide to action.[3]

The study of history in particular affords a mental discipline that helps meet contemporary challenges soberly and intelligently. It brings into view the strengths and weaknesses of different cultures and societies, and an understanding of their national ideals and traditions.

Historiography, or 'the art of writing history', is a discipline that deals with historical narratives and increases awareness among research scholars of the experiments conducted by past historians. It has also been termed as the 'history of history writing'.[4] The word historiography implies historical consciousness. Human beings have always had an awareness of humanity's constant evolution and its dependence upon its actions and passions. Yet historiography is also a discipline of knowledge—historical knowledge—and can also be seen as a form of written expression, a 'literary genre' of sorts.[5] It is, in fact, the art of communicating the knowledge of the past to younger generations in order to build up a sense of continuity.

As historiography is a work of subjective creativity, it is directed by the contemporary social and intellectual environment that drives the historians' thinking. It tells the story of the successive stages of development in historical writings, including the evolution of ideas and techniques and the changing attitudes towards the nature of history itself. It is, in other words, a study of the development of our sense of the past.[6]

During its initial phases, history writing was like story-writing and very little care was taken regarding the authenticity of what was being recorded.[7] As the art of historiography developed, it led to a more accurate analysis of literary sources, and the separation of fact from fiction. Also, historiography sought a better comprehension of the writers and the events that they chronicled, to overcome, as far as possible, the distortion that contemporary ideals and sensibilities inevitably impose on historians.

Historiography provides an opportunity for the historian to examine his scholarly conscience in the mirror of past scholarship. In this way, a historian is concerned with the recreation of the significant features of the past, with the help of numerous fragmentary evidences as sources.

With this discerning outlook, historical writing has witnessed different phases of transition and evolution during various periods of history. This evolution is experienced both in quality and quantity. The reason behind this diversity in trends and traditions was the social environment and religious beliefs of the people and their historical conscience and consciousness—or the lack thereof. For this reason, the stimulating force (based on imaginary ideas like myths and epics) working behind the Greek and Roman historians was fundamentally different from the force that inspired the Christian historians of the Middle Ages or the Arabs of the early Muslim period. However, religion was the main motive behind history writing in many civilisations.

As the study of history progressively came under the influence of diverse ideas, it began to change more rapidly. Historiography, as a special branch of history, traces these changes through the centuries. The reason behind one of the changes can be traced back to the work of ancient and medieval historians who were salaried and obliged, or under compulsion, to please their patrons. These historians produced 'a local saga' which was a collection of myths, epics, hymns, and folklore sung in praise of great heroes on ceremonial occasions.[8] However, some genuine scholars were sifting facts throughout history and compiled their work while being mindful of the authenticity and assessment of the sources they consulted. Still, in some works, exaggeration and misinformation have certainly compromised the integrity of the work.

Historical writing first emerged in Ancient Egypt and then in the form of Babylonian epigraphy, as evinced from remains that are almost 5,000 years old.[9] While such historical narratives are not considered to be historiography, these archaeological remains of early human settlers help give us an idea about their way of life. However, no far-reaching testimony of these early periods existed until the invention of written expression, that is, until the art of writing had been invented.

The invention of writing was a revolutionary step in the history of human development. In the beginning, it adopted a primitive and obscure form of pictograms, which were inscribed on the implements and cave walls during the middle and later Palaeolithic periods. By *c.* 3000 BCE, the Egyptians made remarkable progress by inventing almost twenty-four hieroglyphic signs to indicate as many consonantal sounds as are present in the modern alphabet. Once maritime trade started, the Phoenicians devised a regular script and rough alphabet, around 1300 BCE. This alphabet had twenty-two signs that were all consonants.

It was the Greeks who completed the formation process of the alphabet invented by the Phoenicians. After some modifications, the Romans disseminated this Greek alphabet to the Western Empire and through the Byzantines, this alphabet reached Eastern Europe.[10] Gradually, people started to record historical chronicles besides adopting other literary activities. This practice spread to Palestine, Babylon, and Syria. The earliest chronologies date back to Mesopotamia and ancient Egypt, though no historical writers in these early civilisations were known by name.

In pre-classical times, about 2500 BCE, in the Mesopotamian civilisation, history writing did not acquire a scribed form. It was but a quasi-history. This quasi-history of the pre-classical period lacked critical examination and research. It was merely a record of events already known to a writer, or the deeds of divine powers such as gods and monarchs. Such history is also known as 'theocratic history'; in which human action is completely absent.

Another sort of quasi-history is known as the 'myth'[11] which deals with legends, people and events, though not all of it is about human activities. The Hebrew Scriptures (the Old Testament) contain both theocratic history and myth. However, the theocratic element tends to be universalistic, as God was considered as the Divine Head of all mankind instead of any specific community.[12] The ancient Hebrews led the way as they fashioned national history out of thirty-nine books of the Hebrew scripture, out of which only seventeen can be considered historical. The Hebrews tried to describe the history of mankind from what they believed to be the 'creation'. They were the first to create the idea of a universal history. But these too were quasi-historical in nature.[13]

In this manner, the craft of recording contemporary and past events developed quite early in a handful of civilisations. Thus, the credit for the origin and development of early historiography goes to the Greeks, who were also the inventors of many other literary and scientific activities.

R.G. Collingwood states that pre-classical history founded its ground on theocracy and myth that made the history of this era a quasi-history. He emphasised four characteristics of history that were absent in pre-classical history: (1) science, (2) the humanistic element, (3) method of inquiry, and (4) purpose.[14]

Consequently, understanding the past appears to be a universal human need, and the telling of history has emerged independently in civilisations around the world. It is evident that historiography formally has its roots in Greece, Rome, and China.[15]

The Ancient Indian Historiography: Traditions and Characteristics

Unlike China, Greece, and Rome, the literature of ancient Indian history is not extant. Most modern scholars hold the view that before the dawn of the modern age, the people of India did not have a sophisticated approach to history writing.[16] Rather, its accounts seem to be merged with a particular form of religious literature that was not very authentic. Some historians are of the view that the people of India did not pay much attention to compiling historical writings in a proper manner, because of their lack of curiosity about secular affairs; the influence of fatalist doctrines; the absence of dynamic history, and a sense of homogeneity; the lack of interest in a scientific outlook; and various other factors.[17]

On the other hand, however, some scholars assert that in ancient times Indians did not neglect the important discipline of historiography. In fact, they were good writers of history. Although ancient India did not produce a Thucydides, there is considerable evidence to suggest that every important Hindu court might have maintained archives and genealogies of its rulers, such as the court of Samudragupta (r. 335–375 CE), who was the famous ruler of the Gupta dynasty (r. 335–375 CE).[18]

Perhaps, the basic philosophy of the people of India, according to which the ultimate purpose of life was to liberate the soul from the chain of birth and death, diminished interest in keeping a historical account in ancient India. Moreover, the lack of contact of Indian people with the outside world, particularly in the realm of ideas may have been another factor that created barriers in writing history. Conceivably, the motivational force that stimulated the Greco-Romans, the Church, and the Arab historiography was absent in India. However, the twelfth century Kashmiri poet, Kalhana, compiled the *Rajatarangini* (The River of Kings). As a native of Kashmir, which had relations with China and the Islamic world, it is highly likely that he was influenced by their cultural history. On the other hand, some scholars are of the opinion that 'ancient India did have a sizeable volume of historical literature, but that it all perished because of the ravages of time, or invasions.'[19]

No matter what the actual circumstances, ancient India has not bequeathed to us any authentic historical work. History is a weak spot in Indian literature, in fact, it is practically non-existent. But if history is considered to be a record of the evolution of the human mind, India surely has a history, even if its pattern and mode of expression do not conform to the conventional definition of history. Undoubtedly, in the legends, myths, traditions, anecdotes, epics, *Puranas*, and other literary records, an unbounded history does emerge. And while it may not be categorised as history in its traditional sense, historical material can nonetheless be gleaned from it.

The historical traditions of ancient India are bound closely with the arrival of the Aryans in around 1500 BCE. Evidence of the Vedic Sanskrit language is found from this time. The sparse and inferential ancient Indian historical literature is mainly based upon the Vedic, epic, Puranic, Jain, and Buddhist traditions and testimonies, written in Sanskrit, Parakrit, and Pali languages.[20] The early Brahman Sanskrit literature, including the *Ramayana*, *Mahabharata*, and *Puranas*, is considered to be religious literature. It provides us with a record of some historical events, but cannot be considered authentic, or reliable, as the accounts are hyperbolic in nature. The total lack of historical coherence in it is characteristic of Sanskrit literature as a whole and there is an absence of chronology in the entire corpus of ancient Indian literature.

However, the *Puranas* (Hindu religious texts) and the *Vamsas* (Buddhist religious texts) help us in tracing a definite order of antecedence and sequence through the jumble of the names of emperors and princes in ancient India. But these sources require a careful and critical examination in order to arrive at any conclusive facts. The *Puranas* suffer from a Brahmanical bias; while the *Vamsas* obviously have a Buddhistic narrative, so much so that the worth of these works for providing historical facts is vitiated.[21] This religious literature, however, may not have sufficient utility value for verifying political history, but certain sections of it contain an amount of historical information of a non-political nature. On the other hand, the secular literature, excluding biographies, is useful for understanding the social and economic conditions of the times and can be helpful in constructing a strictly historical narrative. This, along with religious and ritualistic literature, does provide some information on the prevailing trends and customs of ancient India.

Our knowledge of the ancient times in India rests mainly on oral traditions. It has earlier been stated that Brahmanic literature, the *Vedas*, and the *Puranas* are neither books of historical purpose, nor do they deal with history, but are semi-historical and the only real source is that which was transmitted by word of mouth. This oral tradition of history from the later Vedic age, had five distinct forms, namely *gathas*, *narasamsis*, *akhyana*, *Itihasa*, and *Purana*. Basically, these were the songs and the epics that were sung on various occasions.

The four *Vedas* are the holiest scriptures in the Hindu religious tradition. The oldest is the *Rig Veda*. It is a collection of hymns along with commentary dating back to the period between 1500 and 1200 BCE. It is clear that these scriptures originated in oral form. The *Rig Veda* contains historical allusions, of which some are about contemporary people and events of its time, but most refer to bygone times and persons. Thus, the most primitive recognised form of the historical tradition in India are the verses and compositions of the *Rig Veda*. The poetic forms of the hymns are known as *gathas* and *narasamsis*. Originally, the word *gatha* simply meant a song, but gradually it came to signify a distinct genre of literary composition. It occurs only in the later strata of the *Rig Veda* and is associated with the *Kanva* priests of the *Bhrigvangiras* group.[22]

A few examples of *gathas* and *narasamsis*, which were preserved in Vedic literature, explicitly purport their historical nature. The term '*narasamsi-gatha*' refers to a form of story, or legend, that existed in the Vedic age, which was when some of the heroes of these sagas lived. The *Mahabharata*, the *Puranas*, and the *Ramayana* are some of the historical works that contain numerous *gathas*.[23] The *narasamsi-gathas* were usually sung to celebrate the heroic deeds of ancient rulers and deities.[24] The references in the *Rig Veda* to royal eulogies, *gathas* and *narasamsis*, indicate the existence of an oral tradition of historical compositions that sometimes influenced the fixed and written religious tradition. However, it was not separate from the ritualistic tradition.

The *gathas* and the *narasamsis* are distinguished from the religious hymns and assumed a purely ritualistic approach developed by the priests of the time. Both of these are generally associated with the *Itihasa* and the *Puranas* and purport their affiliation with the historical tradition. *Itihasa* in Sanskrit means history and consists of the *Mahabharata* and the *Ramayana*, and sometimes parts of the *Puranas*.

The *Ramayana* is all about Rama and the earliest parts were composed around 700, or 400 BCE. The *Mahabharata* is the epic about the Kurukshetra War and is believed to have been composed around 400 BCE, though it is highly likely that it is far older. The *Puranas* are religious texts that contain knowledge about mythology, cosmology, philosophy, and all things theocratic. The historical nature of *gathas* and the *narasamsis* is further evinced by the injunction that during the Ashvamedha (horse-sacrifice) ritual, the Kshatriya minstrel would sing the *gathas*, celebrating the heroic deeds of the one who performs the sacrifice. These songs were also sung at weddings.

An *akhyana* has been defined as a grand narrative presented through recitation of a text and songs by *abhinaya* (the art of expression through body gestures). The *akhyanas* were already in existence in the Vedic period. Several hymns of the *Rig Veda* allude to *akhyana*. The earliest reference to the word *akhyana* denotes a story illustrating a moral concept, but later it was considered as a form of historical composition allied to *Itihasa* and the *Purana*. Both the *Ramayana* and *Mahabharata* illustrate a good example of *akhyana*, as both were presented through a recitation of the text and songs performed by an *abhinaya*.[25] The *Nirukta* and *Bṛhaddevatā* include references to *akhyana* and *Itihasa* in the *Rig Veda*. The *Rig Veda* assumes a semi-dramatic and semi-epic nature, which became a source for the style of the later historical dramas and epics. Nevertheless, the *akhyanas* were gradually assimilated in the *Itihasa-Purana* tradition.

Both, the *Mahabharata* and *Ramayana*, came into existence during the later *Vedic* period (1100–500 BCE). These are epics written in the form of poems and are good illustrations of the *Itihasa*. The *Itihasa* traditions were further described as *Itihasa-Veda* in the *Brahmanas* and *Upanishads*, which are considered to be a more traditional form of recorded history.[26]

The *Itihasa* tradition, which initially comprised the second order of religious literature, eventually came to the forefront. Religion standardised the *Itihasa* tradition, but it also destroyed the historical character of the tradition. On the other hand, the antiquity of the *Puranas* goes back to the Vedic age, between 500 BCE and 500 CE. The word *Purana* literally means that 'which has lived from ancient times', or 'a work contains records of past events.'[27] It contains genuine historical traditions that to some extent find corroboration in archaeology. The *Mahabharata* is said to be composed by Vyasa. He is also supposed to be the scribe of the *Vedas* and *Puranas*.[28] The word Vyasa actually means 'compiler' in Sanskrit and is a central figure in Hinduism.

As a work of sacred studies, *Itihasa* and *Purana* occur together in the *Brahmanas* and the *Upanishads* and occasionally they are merged together which indicates their close association in a singular and similar content. Thus, in keeping with the religious genre, the *Itihasa-Purana* literature was designated a fixed literary form.[29] Later on, *gathas*, *narasamsis*, and *akhyana* were absorbed in *Itihasa* and *Puranas*, as the three constituent elements of the *Puranas*. However, these traditions did not receive a predetermined literary form, and this eventually resulted in the two gigantic traditions of the *Itihasa* and *Purana*.

Notwithstanding, the *Puranas*, the *Mahabharata* and, to a lesser degree, the *Ramayana*, profess to be genuine historical accounts of the traditions and earliest occurrences in this region.[30] The *Vedas*, the *Brahmanas*, and other Brahmanic literature, also provide information about the past, which is evidently based upon traditions.

The oral tradition, which flourished in the early Vedic age and communicated a mass of religion, knowledge, history, and legends to the people, began to become formalised and assumed a fixed literary form in the concluding phase of the later Vedic age, between 400 BCE and 400 CE. The literature on the *Itihasa* and *Purana* developed significantly. It crystallised into several works. The *Vamsa* (dynastic tradition), a subject of many hymns and references in the text of the *Puranas*, flourished during this period. This development is characterised by the emergence of new ruling dynasties. They patronised notable Brahmans in their kingdoms in order to keep their hold on the body politics and developed a strong connection with them. Subsequently, the historical tradition metamorphosed into the form of official history.

The tradition of compiling official records was developed in the royal courts and its rise and development was associated with the politico-economic environment of the era. The Sutas, custodians of scripture, and the Bhrigvangirases, who were responsible for the development of the *Puranic-Vamsa* tradition, survived because of the favour of their masters and patrons. The Bhrigvangirases were officially assigned to record and keep the *Vamsavalis* (the traditional genealogies) of the royal families. In the early medieval age, when the heroic tradition of history changed into the courtly one, the wandering Sutas and the Bhrigvangirases were replaced by the Sandhivigrahikas, salaried court poets, who were responsible for glorifying the king and his royal deeds.[31] However, members of the Bhrigvangiras family (Brahmans by caste) were closely associated with the *Itihasa-Purana* tradition. Thus, they also played a significant role in composing the *Ramayana*.[32]

The court of historiography, however, developed under the influence of the later Bhrigvangirases and mainly focused on the glorification of royalty instead of the compilation of the *Vamsa* that the early Bhrigvangirases had hitherto composed. The early Bhrigvangirases served tribes and thus told tales of the wisdom and customs of tribal people. Later, the tribal character of society altered, and dynasties of kings began to rule people.

During this period, the Bhrigvangirases depended on the rulers and not tribes for survival. Historiography became dependent on the organisation of the court, which brought the prince and the poet much closer together. This created a relationship between the prince, poet, courtier, and the chronicles. Naturally, the historical tradition adapted to the new social structure; it became an effective medium for expressing aspects of the king's life and courtly culture. It disseminated the new social values of chivalry, heroism, and loyalty. While it provides some facts and accounts of events, it is largely considered to be primarily mythological and dogmatic in nature.

Besides the Bhrigvangirases, the institution of the Sutas was another factor that contributed to the development of the historical traditions in ancient India. The word *suta* appears in religious literature such as the *Samhitas* and the *Brahmanas*. In the later Vedic period, the word *suta* meant a minstrel, or bard. Its origins are uncertain, but the Sutas nevertheless became one of the most important officials of the court in the later Vedic age. They were mostly drawn from the Bhrigvangiras families.[33]

The Suta's main responsibility was to compile chronicles of important events and keep a record of royal and ecclesiastical genealogies, and all the important royal and religious activities. However, their approach was practically lacking in objectivity. Their main purpose was to please their rulers by praising their conduct and manners. Despite these unsound traits, they are credited for introducing the earliest ancient Indian historical traditions.

The tradition of panegyric biographies assumed greater political and historical significance when the tradition of compiling biographies of the kings was started. This change in the historical tradition occurred because the Bhrigvangirases had to follow the changing trends to keep their position. Therefore, as tribal values decreased and the culture of the courts developed, highlighting heroic deeds in history was replaced by recording events and the political achievements of the existing ruler. With time, the wandering Sutas and Bhrigvangirases were substituted by paid court poets who received royal patronage. They were known as the Sandhivigrahikas and were closely associated with the Sutas and Bhrigvangirases.

Vamsa literature was produced in bulk in this period, to record and glorify the reigns of the many ruling families that were emerging at the time. This literature comprised dynastic genealogies and records of important events. However, the *Vamsa* form developed a vast body of quasi-historical literature, freed from the more eulogising *suta* tradition. The Buddhist *Rajavamsa*, *Dipavamsa*, and the *Mahavamsa*, the Jain

Harivamsa, the Hindu *Raghuvamsa*, *Sasivamsa*, and the *Parthivivali* of the Helarji, are some of the examples of the *Vamsa* genre of a vast body of semi-historical literature.[34]

The second phase of historical traditions was developed in the surroundings of royal courts which includes historical epics, generally known as *chitras* or biographies of the rulers composed during the early medieval period of Indian history.[35] This semi-historical work also includes the biographical accounts of the saints, prophets, and religious men. One of such works is known as the *Buddhacarita*[36] written by Ashvaghosha, who was a Buddhist teacher and compiled the religious conversations of Buddha in the second century CE. This earliest biographical literature provides the chronicles about the rulers and the wars in the form of myths and hymns. Such sort of writings can also be traced in the *Ramayana* and the *akhyanas* of Vedic literature.

It is observed that by the end of the seventh century, some of the ancient works tried to provide a matter-of-fact rendering of certain events but they are embellished with much legendary matter. Hence the important stage in the development of Indian historiography started in the first quarter of the seventh century with the *Harshacharita*, which is a biography of the last ruler of the Pushyabhuti dynasty King Harshavardhana (r. 606–647 CE)[37] written by Banabhatta.[38] This book is regarded as a pioneering work in Indian history. Harsha was the patron of the author. Banabhatta was a Bhargava and due to his family tradition, was inclined towards history. However, his work is not of a purely historical character but of a literary category known as *kavya*,[39] which lacks in a chronological narrative of events. Besides, historical evidence has shown that some parts of the book are fictitious—mainly those recording the heroic deeds of his patron. This compilation is full of rhetorical descriptions and literary embellishments. It covers just a few months of Harsha's reign.

Another significant contribution to early Indian historiography is the biography of Vikramaditya VI, titled *Vikramankadeva Charita*, written by Bilhana, a Kashmiri Brahman born in 1040 CE. He was patronised by Someshvara I, father of Vikramaditya VI, the Chalukya king of Kalyani. This book helps in verifying certain historical facts about Vikramaditya VI.[40]

Another early historian is Sandhyakar Nandi. He was a court poet who compiled the events of the reign of the Pala King Rampala (1082–1124 CE). He included a small part of Rampala's autobiography in his epic poem, *Ramacharitam*, based on the *Ramayana*.

Manasollasa is another historical work of the early period written by Someshvara III (1126–1138 CE), the son and successor of Vikramaditya VI.

Manasollasa was an encyclopaedia on royal duties and pleasures and an incomplete biography of his father entitled *Vikramankabhyudaya*.

Jayanaka was another important writer who wrote his epic *Prithviraja Vijaya* in praise of the gallant deeds of the Chauhan-Rajput ruler of northern Rajasthan, sometime between 1191–1193 CE, after the two wars of Tarain.[41] Prithviraj (r. 1166–1192 CE) fought two battles against Mohammad Ghori; in the first battle (1191 CE) Mohammad Ghori was injured and retreated, while in the second (1192 CE) Prithviraj was killed.

Chand Bardai, a poet at Prithviraj III's court composed a separate epic, *Prithviraj Raso*. The work gives an account of the origin of the Chahamana (Chauhan) dynasty[42] and is present in its original form, along with the additional material which was incorporated into it in the years that followed.

Nayachandra Suri, a Jain writer of the fifteenth century, wrote *Hammira Mahakavya*, which deals with the legendary story of the heroic and tragic thirteenth century Chauhan king, Hammira. He was betrayed by his trusted generals and Alauddin Khilji defeated him. Nayachandra also traces the early history of the Chauhan dynasty, which is not as extensive as the one provided by Jayanaka.

Padmagupta (alias Parimala) wrote an epic on the Paramara King Sindhuraja of Avanti titled *Nava-sahasanka-charita*. The work is based on real events, but factual occurrences are transmuted into a romantic legend.

However, the *Rajatarangini*, the chronicle of the kings of Kashmir by Kalhana, is considered as the earliest best-known history of India, compiled in Sanskrit in 1148 CE. Kalhana, a historian-poet of the twelfth century, was a Brahman from Kashmir and the son of Kanpaka, a minister of King Harshadeva of Kashmir. The *Rajatarangini* is a general history of Kashmir that does not follow any particular dynasty. Kalhana used primary sources such as past archives, official documents, royal edicts, inscriptions, numismatics, and archaeological evidence while compiling his work. He used the fundamental principles of modern historiography consulting eleven existing historical books on Kashmir and pointing out errors in them. It consists of almost 800 Sanskrit verses. This work shows the notable influence of Chinese and Muslim historiography because there were centuries-old cultural links between Kashmir and these two empires. Following the practice in China, some of the Hindu states in India had begun to appoint court historians since early medieval times. The tradition of compiling dynastic annals found in the *Rajatarangini* was so new to Indian practice that one is tempted to attribute this to Chinese influence. The tradition of such annals had developed in China since very early times and, as can be seen by the above narrative, it was later adopted by the outlying kingdoms of India like Kashmir.[43] On the other hand, Kashmir also had cultural relations with Persia from ancient times.[44] It seems clear from the *Rajatarangini* that the Kashmiri traditions of historiography were also influenced by Persian trends, since it describes events in chronological order. However, sparing in dates, it follows the reigns of the different dynasties and describes rebellions, wars and conquests, and the rise and fall of the dynasties. It was composed in verses like the *Shah Nama*[45] (The Book of Kings) of Firdausi and is mostly based on legend.

Out of all the above-mentioned historical works on ancient Indian history, only the *Rajatarangini* has been given the status of an authentic and reliable source, though its author was not above the traditional Indian outlook on life, steeped in theological and metaphysical concepts. According to Arthur L. Basham, 'Kalhana's attitude to history was the general trend of the entire period'.[46] In short, it can be said that Kalhana's rendition of historiography was a clear improvement on romantic chronicles like those of Bana, Bilhana, Jayanaka etc.

At the time when a historical consciousness was developing in the north, in the south, including the kingdoms of Andhra, Karnataka, Kerala, Tamil Nadu, and a few southern districts of Maharashtra, the approach to history was not very different. In terms of historical background, it follows the precedence of the north, however, it did not lack in historical ideas. Tamil Nadu was rich in the *sangam* classics, which are the poetic works of early Tamils, beginning in *c.* 500 BCE. Among other subjects, they contain a magnificently rich variety of historical literature.[47] The *sangams* were compiled in Pali, the language of Buddhist literature which later more or less ceased to exist as an important language of creative writing in the south.

The Sangam Age in Tamil literature was a period of great literary splendour, when Tamil poetry reached its pinnacle. The first *sangam* had its sect in old Madura, under the patronage of the Pandyan kings, and the poems included eulogies of famous personalities.[48] The *sangams* elucidate the social, economic, cultural, religious, and political conditions of the people, though they too lack in chronology, genealogy, and authenticity. They cover the period from 500 BCE to 500 CE and in the seventh century Sangam literature took on its final shape.

Thus, we find that while ancient Indian historiography includes an enormous quantity of historical literature, there is hardly any worthwhile record of history except Kalhana's *Rajatarangini*, and even this is defective in several respects. Historical writing appeared only in the latter part of this period. Historical traditions found in ancient India are vastly different from the modern concepts of history. These works do not provide facts gleaned from reliable sources. 'Their chief sources were the Vedico-Agamic culture based upon the intrinsic authority of the revealed word.'[49] The ancient Indians did not organise or express their ideas in a methodical way; they did not draw appropriate conclusions; did not show relevant connections between events; and did not archive records in any particular framework of time and space. But regardless of these inadequacies, the great advantages of their treatment of history cannot be denied. Ancient India did not produce any historians, only philosophers of history.

Early Indo-Muslim Historiography: Its Genesis and Major Trends (1206–1526 CE)

It is a well-known fact that after the Greco-Romans, the second phase of historiography takes its birth from Islam. History had always been a discipline of knowledge among the Muslims, since they had their own historical traditions from the pre-Islamic era, such as *Ayyam al-Arab* (The Battle Memories of the Arabs), *ansab* (genealogies), and *qasidas* (eulogistic odes).[50] The origin of historiography during the early Muslim era is significant, as it drew from the scriptural writings that were based on the Holy Quran and the *hadith* of Prophet Muhammad (PBUH). The *sirah*, or the biography of the Prophet (PBUH), the *hadith*, and the *maghazis* (his material expeditions), are all significant as supplementary historical material to the Quranic revelations and as a source for documentation of the early events of Muslim history. The Muslim historical consciousness was motivated by the development of the science of *hadith*.[51]

In common parlance, early Muslim historiography refers to the study of early origins of Muslim religious learning, based on a critical analysis, evaluation, and examination of authentic primary source material, and the organisation of these sources into a narrative chronology.[52] The early Muslim historians developed various methodologies, such as the 'Science of *hadith*' and *isnad* (chain of transmission), in order to evaluate these sources. Apart from *hadith*, these methodologies were further applied to other historical works and *ilm al-rijal* (the science of biography) practiced among the Muslims. The modern practice of scientific citation and historical method is greatly in debt to the rigor of the *isnad* tradition of the early Muslims.

The Arabs extensively contributed to the origin and growth of early Muslim historiography. Even though historiography in its true sense developed during the Abbasid period, some historical literature had already been composed during the Umayyad reign. While most of the works have survived only in the form of fragments in the classical sources, they spanned the transition of the 'history tradition' from the pre-Islamic era, to their own times in a continuous manner. There was an emphasis on the evaluation and authentication of the sources and internal and external criticism. They relied on eyewitnesses, oral traditions, and official archives (the *diwans*) as their sources[53] and have the distinction of introducing the practice of date-mark and chronology in their work. This literature recorded historical anecdotes with particular emphasis on date and year—a practice that was as yet unknown to other contemporary nations. The earliest Muslim literature provides significant evidence of historical consciousness as well as a sense of scientific treatment in the compilation of source material.

The Arab historians are unique in comparison to all their contemporaries due to the unusual form of their compositions. They adopted a 'narrative style' for history writing. Arab historiography dealt with subjects like data about cities, families, dynasties, events, and sometimes less consequential matters and personalities. They maintained a chronological order and had an innovative approach to historical laws such as causation and periodicity. Since they had no precedent in the technical development of historiography, some flaws and shortcomings can be found in their work. But there is no doubt that in the field of historiography, the early Muslims established high standards in determining the authenticity of the information; the compilation of historical data; and the administration of a chronological approach.

The early Muslim historians were not all Arabs—most of them were Persians and by no means inferior to the native Arab writers. Initially, they did not delve deeply into the historiographical methodologies that they were introduced to and took very little interest in their work. Generally, they merely applied the method handed down by the prevailing Islamic tradition. Only in later times, when the Persian language and culture had established its ascendant position in literature, was Persian historiography able to pursue its own course.[54] However, during the first two centuries of the Islamic era, there are no traces of Persian historiographical influence on Arab history writing.

Persian influence significantly increased during the eighth century (the Abbasid period), not only in political, cultural, and literary activities, but in every sphere of life. The intelligentsia of Persian origin held a notable status among historians of the classical period, which started from the ninth century. Their work in terms of content may be categorised as the histories of the world, or universal history; monographs about a certain period, dynasty, or person; and histories of various countries, or cities.⁵⁵ Similar to other narrative types of Persian literature, these accounts are written in the simple, strictly objective style of the old Arabic histories. The Persians introduced some new trends in early Muslim historiography regarding dynastic, socio-religious and official histories, and the history of political institutions. With time, more and more trends were introduced by them.⁵⁶

However, prior to examining the emerging trends and characteristics of the early Indo-Muslim historiography, it would be essential to get an idea of the cultural environment of the era and the political background in which historiography originated and was further nurtured in South Asia.

Muslim rule in India rightly claims to have produced an abundant quantity of historical literature on Medieval India. The early Muslim rule in India, as generally believed, started in the wake of Muhammad bin Qasim's invasion of Debal (Sindh) in 712 CE. However, the Muslims had already started their encroachments on Indian territory during the caliphate of Hazrat Umar (RA). After the annexation of Persia and Makran, they invaded Sindh.⁵⁷ The earliest reference to the Muslim presence in the Bannu region is made in the *Futuh al-Buldan*, which provides evidence of the al-Muhallab ibn Abi Sufra's invasion of this region during the reign of the Umayyad caliph Muawiyah bin Abi-Sufyan, in 664 CE.⁵⁸ It is also a well-known fact that Muslim rule existed in certain parts of Makran and present-day Balochistan, prior to the Arab invasion of Debal.

Arab rule in Sindh continued till the eleventh century CE when Mahmud of Ghazni conquered some parts of India in 1001 CE.⁵⁹ Mahmud of Ghazni (r. 998–1030 CE) succeeded in laying the foundation of a new empire that encompassed Sindh, Punjab, and the north-western region of India.⁶⁰ In fact, this period is significant for the development of the Persian language and literature. Arabic, the former official language—the language of the rulers and the court—was replaced by Persian. The Ghaznavid court was a centre of great Persian poets and scholars. The Turko-Persian culture in India prospered during this period. Amongst literary men, Al-Biruni was the first who came to India during the early years of eleventh century and made a comprehensive study of Indian culture. He wrote the *Tarikh al-Hind* or *Kitab al-Hind* (A History of India), which mainly deals with the socio-cultural and religious conditions of the people of India.⁶¹ Richard N. Frye praised Al-Biruni, 'the contributions of Al-Biruni and other Persians towards mathematical knowledge in the Muslim world are astonishing'.⁶²

After the Ghaznavids, another Turkish Muslim dynasty from Central Asia, the Ghorids, from Ghor, Afghanistan, entered the subcontinent and captured Ghazni and Lahore. The founder of the Ghorid dynasty, Shihab al-Din Muhammad Ghori, penetrated further into the subcontinent in 1192 CE. Soon after, he left his deputy Qutub al-Din Aibak (r. 1206–1210 CE) behind in India and returned home. Qutub laid the foundation of the Slave Dynasty (1206–1290 CE) and established the Muslim rule under the Sultanate of Delhi. He is regarded as the first Sultan who established Muslim polity with the central authority in India.[63]

The rule of the Umayyads, Abbasids, and Ghaznavids was limited to Sindh, Punjab, and the north-western parts of India that had no established authority in the rest of northern India. In order to understand the long-lasting and decisive influence of the Muslim period, it would be more appropriate if the Muslim period is considered to have commenced with the foundation of the Turkish slave dynasty. With the commencement of this rule, a new era of historiographical traditions came into existence as the Ghorids and the Sultans of Delhi were also great patrons of the Persian language, culture, and literature.

During this period, Thatta, Sehwan, Multan, Uch, Pakpattan, and Lahore became important centres of learning. A great number of Persian scholars and partisans migrated and settled in India due to the Mongol devastation of Transoxiana and Khurasan. They enriched society with their great contributions in the field of scholarly and cultural activities. At the time, Delhi had become the most important cultural centre of the Muslims in the East after the devastation of Baghdad by the Mongols in 1258 CE.[64] Like the Ghaznavids and the Ghorids, the Sultans of Delhi also adopted Turkish and Persian culture and traditions in every field of their lives. They patronised literary activities and introduced and the custom of history writing.

Origin and Development of Historiographical Tradition in India

Historiography is generally considered to have existed in India for a millennium; ever since the Muslim rule started. That was the beginning of a new era in scholarship in the region. During the early Muslim period, historiography was introduced and developed in India with a particular form and set of rules. It was purposely instituted by the Muslims 'as a deliberate form of cultural expression' reinforced by the Arabian, Persian, and Turkish sources that were available to the authors.[65]

The Muslims established the normal parameters and premises of history writing in India in order to develop the discipline in an empirical manner. Muslim rule produced a succession of historical accounts that were, according to Professor Dodwell, 'far superior to the English chronicles of the medieval period'.[66] However, we find a detailed record of the earliest arrival of the Muslims in South Asia (eighth century CE) in the *Fath Nama-i-Sindh* (alias *Chach Nama*), which is in sharp contrast to the mythical accounts prevalent at that time among the local people.[67]

Subsequently, there is a marked increase in quantity and improvement in the quality of historiography here. For this reason, the whole period of Muslim rule in India is well documented. Historians were attached to the royal courts and were patronised by the rulers. Following the Persian courtly tradition, a number of historical accounts that were produced were eulogistic, celebrating the achievements of the monarch and written from the standpoint of the ruling class. On the other hand, numerous works presented accounts of people other than rulers, scholars, mystics, etc. This was literature in the form of *tadhkiras*, *malfuzat*, and *insha*.

As mentioned earlier, the prevailing historiographical trends in India during the Sultanate of Delhi were strongly influenced by the Persian and Central Asian traditions from which the ruling dynasties migrated.[68] India and Persia in particular share a long history of social-cultural interchange, due to their geographical proximity and political goodwill. The cultural links between them were renewed with the advent of Islam. A mass migration from Persia to India is not a phenomenon specific to a certain period. However, the trend appears to have increased significantly after the establishment of Muslim rule in India. The Persia-based elite played important roles in the court of the Sultanate of Delhi by the thirteenth and fourteenth centuries.[69] Muhammad Yasin writes:

> During the early period of Muslim conquest, the Turks and the Afghans were the muscle; whereas the Persians supplied the brain of the ruling aristocracy of India.[70]

The Persians who came and settled in India were many and varied: administrators, officials, scholars, poets, mystics, craftsmen, artisans, artists, traders, etc. Their refined culture, which was rooted in the Persian language and culture, afforded them certain advantages as they sought patronage in the royal courts of the Sultans of Delhi in northern India, and the Adil Shahis and the Qutub Shahis in the South. Most of them were welcomed by these courts and attained important posts there. Thus, Persia played a dominant role in India, not only in the field of politics and religion, but also socially in the form of subjects such as literature, architecture, miniatures, manuscripts, calligraphy, coinage, etc.[71] Moreover, the Persian style of history writing also influenced the pattern of historiography in India. All the contemporary chronicles confirm the continuous presence of the Persians and their ideas at the Indian courts.[72]

Historians of the Muslim world, including India, generally followed two major traditions: the Arab and the Persian. Arab historiography included a wide spectrum covering society, institutions, politics, and culture, reflecting the history of the era. Persian historiography, on the other hand, only offered the history of the rulers as 'the Persians were the courtly flatterer of their patrons'.[73] The Arab technique of ascertaining the truth was by taking the testimony of an event from an eyewitness and checking the *isnad*, that is, assessing various factors, including the character of the eye-witness and judging if he was a genuine eyewitness or not, to ensure the reliability of the information. The Arabs gave a lot of importance to this aspect of historiography. However, this approach was not strictly followed throughout India. The Persian practice that was adopted by these historians depended only on the authority or the reliability of the source that passed on the information, without questioning the data much. Some of the histories tend to only present the authors' own ideas or are repetitions of what is already written or said about an event.

Further, Arab historiography provides a picture of every sphere of human society and its entire related phenomenon, without distinguishing between a common person and a ruler, which was also absent in Indian Muslim history writing. Despite the traditions of Persian historiography, where the king and his actions were the focus of the narrative and the activities of the masses were completely ignored. Not giving proper regard to critical evaluation of sources and eyewitnesses; lack of an overall view, and not bothering about sifting sources and searching for the original author were deviations from the correct traditions in the history written by these scholars; still it met certain basic standards of writing chronicles on politics and society, which defines the outline of historical literature.

V.N. Rao, in *Textures of Time*, discussed Peter Hardy's classificatory scheme for Persian histories, written during the Sultanate period that remains a dominant paradigm in the field.[74] Hardy drew on H.A.R. Gibb to argue that with the passing of the golden age of Arabic historical writing (such as al-Tabari's work), Muslim historiography in India became 'theocratic rather than humanistic', with no sense of the immediate past, concerned solely with the history of the *ummah* and without any progressive world view.[75]

To Hardy, most of the genres emerging in Persian India (universal history, hagiography, advice, or 'artistic forms'), either had 'facts subordinated to effect', or simply had a 'great disinclination for facts'.[76] For Hardy, this meant an overarching theory of history and historical writing in Muslim India; once history writing left Arabia (and the Arabic language) the historic content deteriorated quickly. Consequent to this, Hardy argues that the historical understanding of this period is 'literally composed of strata upon strata of frozen narratives', where historical tropes continue to reign.[77] The 'frozen' narratives make the task of pre-Mughal historiography more dependent on making sense through classifying genres, which was what Hardy did.

The early medieval Indo-Muslim historiography mainly flourished under the Turko-Persian tradition, which encouraged historical writings in Persian. It was a projection of the overall Muslim historiography that evolved beyond India. Peter Hardy refers to the period of the Sultanate of Delhi (1206–1440 CE) as 'a colonial period in Indo-Muslim historiography—a period when Muslim historians remained aloof within the "civil lines" of Muslim historical writings'.[78] Almost all the Indo-Muslim historians, apart from Isami,[79] compiled historical works covering all aspects of the incumbent ruler including issues and events of political significance. In these works, the dynastic periodisation was deficient in dates, overlapping of events, and involved much repetition. The works of Barani[80] and Isami also suffer from chronological inaccuracy.

Nevertheless, the Indo-Muslim historians showed a highly developed taste and innate talent for the historiography of their own. This voluminous amount of historical literature has long served as the main source for the history of medieval India. With all its faults, it is more rational, secular, objective, and authoritative as compared to the mythological, theological, and legendary style of ancient Indian historical literature. The early Indo-Muslim historiography abounds in *mathnawis* (poetical expressions), biographies, and local and general universal histories.[81] It also influenced the minds of contemporary scholars like Ziya al-Din Barani, Shams Siraj Afif, Minhaj-us-Siraj Juzjani, Abdul Malik Isami, Yahya bin Ahmad Sirhindi, Amir Khusro, Muhammad Qasim Firishta, Ain al-Mulk Mahru, etc., who gave an organised shape to history as an independent discipline. General histories followed the pattern of universal histories in the form of genealogy, chronology of political events, and eulogy of the reigning sultans; as well as stating the dictums of virtuous rulers and giving numerous cosmological, geographical, and ethnographical data.

Drawing genealogical charts was a major historiographical tradition of that era. The earliest compilation of this kind was the *Shajara-i-Ansab-i-Mubarakshahi*[82] by Fakhar al-Mudabbir Mubarak Shah. The main part of the work comprised 137 genealogies. It is also religious and didactic in character. This chronicle was transcribed and kept in the royal library. Regardless of its historical value, it lacks a critical approach to sources that, since the earliest times, had been an integral part of Muslim historiography, known as the *isnad*.

Since most historians were court employees, their works primarily concerned their royal patrons and never gave any details about the rest of society, least of all the underprivileged. Consequently, a compilation of dynastic history was the most prominent trend. However, notwithstanding their eulogistic approach and tendency to seek royal favour, the historians were very strict about Islamic practices and ready to check any deviation in this regard by the rulers.

The historians of the Sultanate period critically examined the activities of the rulers in accordance with the injunctions of Islam. Thus, a general statement of the ruler being a good Muslim is to be found in virtually all the narratives of the sultans. Of course, other character traits vary from sultan to sultan. On the face of it, it is quite unthinkable that an Islamic ruler should not seek to be called a good Muslim, though in this regard it may be mentioned that Ala al-Din Khilji (r. 1296–1316 CE) did consider the possibility of founding a new religion.

Thus, the general sequence of the historians (except Minhaj's *Tabaqat*)[83] was, on the whole, critical of sultans as far as religion was concerned. In fact, they were full of denunciation of the whole Turkish Sultanate as they felt that the people were no longer as orthodox as they ought to be. This attitude was reflected in a biased tendency that coloured their narratives. They felt particularly justified in this view, because there was no tradition of historiography in India prior to their arrival and they indigenised this learning with its Persian characteristics.

Still, the main motive behind their work was personal gain. Whether they were associated with the court or not, common values and historiographical premises were the thread that linked historians such as Barani, Minhaj, and Sirhindi.[84] The distinctive historical events they witnessed, and the diversity of their individual lives and temperament resulted in the distinct aspects of their approach to history.[85]

Historians of the early Muslim period in India, including Minhaj, benefited from reliable sources and eyewitness accounts, but their work is nevertheless deficient in its critical evaluation of the authenticity of the sources and contains some unauthentic accounts. The work of Minhaj is so broad in its scope that it covers more than twenty Muslim dynasties across the globe. Despite the shortcoming regarding its sources, this book is considered a very important source on the Mongol invasions of the thirteenth century, as well as the accounts of the Ghaznavids, the Ghorids, and the Slave Dynasty, since the author was an eyewitness to these events.

The historians introduced eulogistic histories, including *manaqib* (eulogies) and *fada'il*. As a general rule, the authors started their narration with a statement in praise of God, generally in verse (referred to as *hamd*) or prose, followed by praise of Prophet Muhammad (PBUH) in prose or verse (referred as *na'at*). Then, they acknowledged debts of gratitude and showered words of praise and reverence for those whom the author honoured. Mostly, this included sultans, *umara* (nobility), *ulema* (religious scholars and religious leaders) and Sufis, some of whom the work would be dedicated to. In the introductory remarks or preface, the author usually highlights the aims and objectives of the work.

A didactic aspect of history was another new feature introduced in early Indo-Muslim historiography. The compilation of poems as a *qasida* (panegyric) in praise of the sultan was considered the most interesting and passionate form of a work of history during the Sultanate period. The main purpose was to educate the sultans on their duties through the historian's philosophy. Badr al-Din alias Badre Chach (d. 1346 CE), a courtier of Sultan Muhammad bin Tughluq, composed the *Shah Nama*[86] which consists of 30,000 verses. This work sheds light on the social and cultural life of the era of Sultan Muhammad bin Tughluq, besides giving an account of his leading campaigns.[87] The author provides valuable information that helps in confirming accurate dates of some important events. But as far as authenticity of events and facts are concerned, this book does not have much historical value. Overall, it represents a really good example of Turkish influence on Persian literature.[88]

The panegyric *manaqib* is a form of highly refined literature dedicated to a ruler, a noble, a saint, or a learned man. Utb'i's *Tarikh-i-Yamini* is considered as the first attempt in this regard, which was composed in praise of Mahmud of Ghazni and his father Subaktigin.[89] Afterwards, some historians in India also followed this style of narration.

A prominent historian of the Sultanate period who is considered to be the first one to use this form, is Shams Siraj Afif. His father Shams-i-Afif held various important positions under the reign of Sultan Feroz Shah Tughluq (1351–1388 CE). Afif produced a number of worthy books in eulogistic form, such as *Manaqib-i-Ala'i* (The Virtues of Ala al-Din Khilji); *Manaqib-i-Sultan Ghiyas al-Din Tughluq Shah* (The Great Qualities of Sultan Ghiyas al-Din Tughluq); *Manaqib-i Sultan Muhammad* (The Great Qualities of Sultan Muhammad bin Tughluq); *Dhikr-i Kharab-i Delhi* (The Accounts of the Sack of Delhi); and *Tarikh-i-Ferozshahi* (The History of Sultan Feroz Shah Tughluq). The first three works deal with the periods of Ala al-Din Khilji (r. 1296–1316 CE), Ghiyas al-Din Tughluq (r. 1320–1325 CE), and Muhammad bin Tughluq (r. 1325–1351 CE) respectively.

The fourth one, meanwhile, reproduces the accounts of Timur's sack of Delhi in 1398 CE. Timur (1336–1405 CE) was a great Central Asian conqueror who led numerous successful expeditions in West, South, and Central Asia and founded the Timurid dynasty.

Nevertheless, these four works are not extant and the *Tarikh-i-Ferozshahi* is the only existing and the most important work produced by Shams Siraj Afif. He composed this book in the first decade of the fifteenth century, honouring Sultan Feroz Shah and providing a very good supplement to Barani's *Tarikh-i-Ferozshahi*. It provides a reflection of the socio-cultural and spiritual life of the common masses.[90] While this work too has some flaws, including religious prejudices, and tends to exaggerate his patron's achievements, its historical value and genuineness cannot be denied.

Since the historians of this age were usually well-versed in many subjects, such as theology, philosophy, and jurisprudence, their intellectual capacity was not narrow. Consequently, they often drew conclusions from past events in order to guide the rulers in the consequence of their actions. They would try to enlighten them about the logic of history. The historians performed not only their duties as narrators of events, but also as philosophers, teachers, and guides to the rulers as well as the community. The most illustrious example of such a historian is Ziya al-Din Barani (d. 1359 CE). He wrote eight books but most of them are untraceable. Two of his most remarkable works are the *Tarikh-i-Ferozshahi* and *Fatawa-i-Jahandari*.

Tarikh-i-Ferozshahi was completed in 1357 CE and comprises information about the period of Ghiyas al-Din Balban (r. 1266–1287 CE) till the sixth regal year of Feroz Shah, to whom this work is dedicated. In it, Barani dwells on the uses of history, its methods of composition, and its place in the field of knowledge. He also mentions in the introductory chapter, the qualities that make a good historian. In order to comprehend its contents, it is quite necessary to understand the expressions, connotations, and terminologies that Barani uses in the text. According to N.K. Singh:

> Barani is one of those historians who refuse to enlighten a reader unless he has thoroughly familiarized himself with the basic categories of his thought and the chief characteristics of his personality.[91]

Though this work has historical worth of the period of Muhammad bin Tughluq, it lacks in sequence of the events. Barani himself confessed this shortcoming of his work as he writes:

I have written in this history the principles of Sultan Muhammad's administration and have paid no heed to the sequence and order of events.[92]

Both of Barani's works, the *Tarikh-i-Ferozshahi* and *Fatawa-i-Jahandari*, subscribe to the genre of historical literature that provides guidelines on the qualities, virtues, and talents that a good monarch should possess. He also expresses the principles of administration and ideals of government, citing examples from the history of Iran and other Muslim nations. In *Tarikh-i-Ferozshahi*, the author gives details about the sultans, their courts, policies, and contemporary conditions. This account is also a valuable source of the socio-economic conditions of the era.[93] Despite the fact that the main intention of the author in both these biographies was to extol the virtues of his patron, Sultan Feroz Shah, the works are flawed because he paints an unrealistic portrait of the ruler's character. As Peter Hardy says, 'a tailor's dummy garbed in ideal attributes.'[94]

Compilation of history in the form of poetic and literary artifice was another emerging historiographical trend of this era. Some of the historical compositions of this period partially adopt the style of Livy and Tacitus, whose main purpose of writing history was to thrill and amuse, and to instruct and refresh the readers by adopting an exceedingly polished style. Despite the more prosaic and straightforward text of Sirhindi and Afif, the historians of this period did not view history writing as a non-literary activity. It was their endeavour to create an image whereby they could express themselves hyperbolically in a poetic idiom. For instance, the poetic style of the story of the depopulation of Delhi during the reign of Muhammad bin Tughluq, appealed to their senses. These accounts may not be considered literal or factual depictions, but a dramatization of events, aiming to make an impact on the reader. Thus, these works can be considered as being partly journalistic and partly historical.

History was considered an essential subject for the elite, especially princes, nobles, etc. As a result, historians had an honoured status in the royal court alongside the *ulema* and the poets. It was their function to provide a form of literature that was panegyric and expressed in an exceedingly polished style. The *Taj al-Ma'athir* of Hassan Nizami is believed to be the first attempt in this regard; 'in [its] style or narration is singular; meagre in meanings and intricate on artistic prose...it is an example of a deficiency in history but fertility in elaborate and stylized language. This is why historians have ignored it.'[95] This composition of Nizami is also regarded as the first official history of the Sultanate period that focuses on political events from 1192 to 1228 CE. The *Taj al-Ma'athir* is in fact considered partly historical and partly fiction. The author uses both the Arabic and Persian languages, and prose and poetry styles side-by-side as his medium of expression.[96]

The next development in this historical genre is Amir Khusro's work. While Khusro is regarded foremost as a poet, he contributed significantly to medieval historiography. He enjoyed the patronage of almost all the Khilji Sultans. Due to his proximity to them, he was a close witness to the political events of the age. For this reason, his literary work, including his *mathnawis* and *diwans* (collections of poetry), sheds light on historical events. He composed almost ninety-two compilations, but most of his work has been lost and only a few important pieces are available to us.[97] His most noteworthy historical compilation is *Qiran-us-Sa'dain*, which was composed in 1289 CE. This book deals with the memorable event of the meeting of Bughra Khan (governor of Bengal 1281–1287 CE) and his son Mu'iz al-Din Kaiqbad (1287–1290 CE), the last of the Mamluk Sultans of Delhi. It not only provides a picture of the character of Bughra Khan but also depicts the socio-political and cultural conditions that prevailed at the time.[98]

In the *Miftah al-Futuh* (The Treasures of Victory), which he wrote in 1291 CE, Khusro provided a detailed account of the military campaigns of Sultan Jalal al-Din Khilji (the founder of the Khilji dynasty, 1290–1296 CE) during the first year of his reign. In another poetical work titled *Ashiqa* (To Love) and composed in 1316 CE, Khusro presents an account of the love affair and marriage of the prince to the daughter of Raja Karan of Gujarat. In *Nuh Sipihr* (A New Afternoon), composed in 1319 CE, Khusro provides a descriptive and authentic record of the social, philosophical, and cultural conditions of India at the time. The work also deals with the military achievements of Sultan Mubarak Shah.[99] In the *Tughluq Nama*, composed during the last year of Khusro's life, he details an account of the events leading to the accession of Sultan Ghiyas al-Din Tughluq, his victory over Khusro Shah, and a few other developments of the early years of the Tughluq reign.

There is another leading work of Khusro, titled the *Khaza'in al-Futuh* (The Treasure of Victories), or *Tarikh-i-Ala'i*, that was completed in 1311 CE. This work is considered the most valuable and authentic record of the first sixteen years of Ala al-Din Khilji's reign. It also provides a detailed account of the Deccan campaign of Malik Kafur besides Ala al-Din Khilji's military expeditions and conquests of Gujarat, Chittor, and Malwa.[100] It is considered to be an authorised account, written on the orders of the ruler.

Khawaja Abdul Malik Isami wrote a historical epic entitled the *Futuh-us-Salatin* (The Victories of the Sultans) that sheds light on the deeds of the Muslims in India from the time of Mahmud of Ghazni, till the date of its compilation in 1350 CE. As a historian of the Tughluq period, Isami occupied a unique position, being the only writer above fear or favour of Sultan Muhammad bin Tughluq. The work is composed on the pattern of Firdausi's *Shah Nama*, which consists of almost 12,000 verses.[101] It basically consists of stories, legends, anecdotes, and oral testimonies gathered from the author's friends and associates besides some eyewitness accounts. It reveals some unknown facts about Ala al-Din's Deccan campaign in 1296 CE and the Mongol invasions during the Khilji period.[102] The author's main interests were the wars and conquests and he made no attempt to provide any detailed account of the economic and administrative policies of Ala al-Din Khilji. His testimony of Muhammad bin Tughluq's complicity in his father's murder also seems to be a myth; Isami had fabricated this story.[103]

However, the accounts related to the atrocities and cruelty of Muhammad bin Tughluq during the shift of the capital to Daulatabad, contains biases and exaggerations. Isami enjoys a unique position among all other historians of the time, because he seems to be free from any fear of the Tughluq sultans. In fact, he was criticised for his bias against Sultan Muhammad bin Tughluq because he and his family suffered at the sultan's hands. Despite these issues, the value and importance of his work cannot be diminished. N.K. Singh opines on this aspect:

> Isami has written his historical work in short and swift verse. He indulged neither in the rhetoric of Amir Khusro, nor in the abstruseness of Badre Chach, but writes in a lucid graphic and simple style. But he has his own shortcomings and defects.[104]

The *Futuh-us-Salatin* may not be an authority or source for political events, but it is an account of the cultural history of the era.

Apart from many other features of writing history, a new outstanding innovation in the field of the medieval historiography of India is known as the *insha* or the official letters as a source of history. The governor of Multan, Ain al-Mulk Mahru who is also known as Malik al-Sharq, compiled the *Insha-i-Mahru* (A Work of Epistolography), a collection of 123 letters as official documents drafted by the author for the Tughluq sultans and other officials. This is considered the earliest source compiled in this regard. These letters are very authentic and a useful source of information about the period of Sultan Muhammad bin Tughluq and

Feroz Shah Tughluq.[105] This work is valuable as being the sole authority of the military expeditions of Feroz Shah to Lakhnoti and Thatta. It also gives us detailed information about the machinery of statecraft under the Tughluq sultans and the prevailing social, political, and religious conditions of the time.

Besides the traditional sources, one may also come across some new genres that emerged in Indo-Persian literature, produced during the period of the Sultanate of Delhi that can provide historical insight. In addition to the translations into Persian of Arabic and Sanskrit classics, a pioneering effort in terms of Sufi *malfuzat* (collections of discourses or utterances of saints) captured the attention of present-day historians. This literature possessed historical significance as it portrayed a picture of the social, cultural, religious, and economic conditions of the common people. Although the works of the courtly chronologists do provide general information or inferential knowledge of this aspect, but the information is merely incidental, fragmentary, and disjointed. We find no other source apart from this religious literature that deals with this aspect of history in a clear and significant manner.

This new genre inspired Persian writers in other Persian-speaking countries as well. It commenced with the compilation of *Fawa'id al-Fuad* (Morals for the Heart) by Mir Hassan Sijzi, the disciple of Shaykh Nizam al-Din Chishti (Awliya).[106] Next to him was Hamid Qalandar, who noted down the utterances of Shaykh Nasir al-Din Chiragh Delhvi and titled this work *Khair al-Majalis* (Auspicious Assemblies).[107] *Siyar al-Auliya* (The Biographical Directory of the Saints) of Mir Khurd provides insightful comments about the various projects of Sultan Muhammad bin Tughluq.[108] However, in as far as its treatment of spiritual themes is concerned, this sort of literature is unique and must be analysed through a different lens.

At this time, a number of historians were compiling a history of the rulers in Delhi, while others were compiling the history of some regional ruling dynasties of the South. The rulers of these dynasties wanted their historians to follow the same trends of writing history as the illustrious scholars of the North. These rulers patronised and nurtured the production of fine historical compilations in the Persian style and collected a large number of works of history in Arabic and Persian, from many other corners of the Turko-Persian world. Most of the regional historians migrated from other regions of India, Iran, and Central Asia and settled in the Deccan states under royal patronage.

In Kashmir, the *Rajatarangini* of Kalhana had already set up precedence for coming historians as far as style and methodology were concerned. Kashmir was the only region in India that showed any signs of history writing prior to the commencement of Muslim rule. However, after 200 years of the *Rajatarangini*, a well-known Hindu scholar of Kashmir named Jauaraja compiled an account of the events till the period of Sultan Ghiyas al-Din Zain al-Abidin (r. 1418–1419 CE and 1420–1470 CE),[109] a great patron of learning, and gave it the title, *Rajatarangini Dvitiya*. In 1459 CE, after the death of Jauaraja, Srivara, one of his pupils composed a work of contemporary history, covering the events till 1486 CE; it was titled *Rajatarangini Tritiya*. Another historian, Prajya Bhatta, carried on the work and wrote the *Rajiya Woopstak*, which covered the events from 1517 to 1596 CE.[110] This chronicle is considered to be the last attempt at writing history in Sanskrit, though Persian language and literature had been adopted during the period of Zain al-Abidin (1420–1470 CE) after which Persian replaced Sanskrit.

Subsequently, two works were written by the court poets Mulla Ahmad and Mulla Nadri, in Persian. Unfortunately, these works have been lost. Similarly, Qazi Ibrahim and Mulla Hassan Qadri, notable historians of Kashmir, also compiled chronicles in Persian during the second period of Sultan Fath Shah (1493–1505 CE) and the Chak rulers (1566–1588 CE) respectively, but these also could not stand the test of time and have long been lost. The only existing book from the pre-Mughal era is Syed Ali's *Tarikh-i-Kashmir*, which was written during the period of Sultan Yousuf Shah, who ascended the throne in 1578 CE. However, *Baharistan-i-Shahi* (The Royal Garden) enjoys the status of being the first fully detailed history of Kashmir, written anonymously in 1614 CE.[111]

In the South, Syed Ali bin Aziz Allah Tabatabai migrated from Iraq in 1550 CE. He first served in the court of Sultan of Golkonda and later joined Burhan Nizam Shah II of Ahmadnagar, where he undertook to compile the *Burhan-i-Ma'asirin* (The History of the Bahmani and Nizamshahi Dynasty).[112] This book was completed in 1596 CE and gives us an authentic and detailed explanation of the history of the Bahmani dynasty. Tabatabai extensively benefitted from Isami's work the *Futuh-us-Salatin* for the history of the period of Ala al-Din Hassan, the first Bahmani ruler.[113] This book also provides some records regarding the sultans of Gulbarga and Bidar besides the Nizamshahi dynasty of Ahmadnagar. However, the work suffers from some defects due to the praise it lavishes on the author's patron, which was a normal feature in medieval Muslim historiography.

Another Central Asian immigrant was Abdul Razzaq, who came from Herat. He entered the court of King Deva Raya II of Vijayanagar in the Deccan and wrote a noteworthy account of the state of Vijayanagar in his book entitled the *Matla-us-Sa'adain wa Majma al-Bahrain* (The Rising of the Two Fortunate Stars and the Meeting of the Two Seas).[114] The work narrates the history of Central Asian dynasties and the Trans-Indus region from 1335 to 1468 CE.[115]

Major Trends and Traditions of Early Indo-Muslim Historiography

The most important objective of the historiography of this era was to record the events, wars, and campaigns and describe the court, conduct, activities, and affairs of the rulers. There was little effort at investigating or collecting sources, or analyses, of wider historical processes.

One of the major trends in early Indo-Muslim historiography was divine intercession, which was a predominant trait brought forward from the early phase of the Indo-Muslim historiography and seems to be the guiding philosophy in these works. God is seen as working through individuals, particularly the ruler; not through classes, social forces, or the spirit of the age. This significant feature of the historiography of the era was based on the conviction that there was a Divine force behind historical processes.[116] This sort of philosophy is similar to church transcendentalism and Hindu fatalism, and hence it did not believe that actions result in reactions, nor that these determine the course of history.

In this way, the historiography of this period shows an inclination towards the providential theory. The work, to some extent, lacks in authenticity of the sources. Limitations of accuracy were normally expressed in the term 'and God knows the truth of the matter'.[117] According to this concept, the principal function of governance was the fulfilment of the Divine covenant, which dictated the terms of the ruler's contract with God. It was also a tool to glorify Muslim rule. Fundamentally, the Sultanate of Delhi was a theocracy in which the sultans were endowed with both religious and temporal powers. Most of the sultans considered themselves to be the deputies of the Abbasid caliph of Baghdad and received investitures from them. They nominally acknowledged the overlordship of the caliph,[118] asserting that they would enforce the tenets of Islam to their rule. For this reason, history that was more or less official and became, to a large extent, theocratic and not humanistic; it was purposeful and direct but not interrelated, or progressive.

One more noteworthy contribution of the Muslims to Indian historiography was more clearly defining the concept of chronology by adopting the Hijra calendar to denote dates, which were fixed and determined. As mentioned earlier, Hazrat Umar (RA) introduced a lunar Hijri calendar[119] for the Muslim world. The adoption of a single standardised calendar kept Muslims away from any confusion of chronology that had prevailed, particularly in ancient Indian and Christian chronology. It was a great step forward in Indian historiography.

However, the accounts sometimes had shortcomings and flaws in chronological sequence, due to certain limitations and constraints faced by the writers, but their efforts are worthy of appreciation. All these historical accounts on the whole complement each other and provide a fairly realistic record of the pre-Mughal period. Two famous scholars, Minhaj-us-Siraj and Ziya al-Din Barani, were quite careless in specifying dates in their works. Sirhindi shows greater circumspection in this regard, even though he is at the same time guilty of inaccuracies. However, he is less casual than the others. He carefully gives the dates of events along with the year.[120] The reason may be that neither Barani nor Minhaj were historians by profession, in fact, Barani claims that he is not. They relied on memory for the narration of events. Thus, they failed to recollect dates and the names of several individuals on many occasions.

Even though history had become a professional subject in the hands of secular scholars who were under royal patronage, there was another form of literature from which historiographical information could be gleaned, i.e., the writings and discourses of the *ulema* and Sufis. This genre of historical literature provides records of socio-religious movements and the development of thought. Their letters, the metaphysical and ethical writing, and the records of the speeches and views (termed as *malfuzat*) of these religious luminaries, are a great source of knowledge regarding the intellectual history of the era. In this literature, we find three basic components that may be termed as pure history, pure fiction, and pure ethics. A renowned work titled, *Khair al-Majalis* (The Best Gatherings) is one such example.[121] The book also sheds light on the character of famous contemporary personalities like Minhaj-us-Siraj and the socio-political and economic conditions during the period of Muhammad bin Tughluq. Such books are worthy for reconstructing the social and economic life of the Muslims in India and their contribution to the Indian culture. Most of Shams Siraj Afif's work also abounds with religious and moral precepts.

The *ulema* and the Sufis, who played a very important role in the socio-cultural setup under the Sultanate of Delhi, were mainly inspired by Iranian and Turkish (Central Asian) traditions. This tendency resulted in the need for the sultans to seek endorsement and verification of their deeds from the *ulema*.[122] Thus, the rulers sought their ideals of governance from the *ulema* on the one hand and the best practices of Persian, Greek, and Turkish norms, as well as of the first four caliphs, on the other.[123] The historians of the Sultanate, therefore, critically evaluated the activities of the rulers in the light of the dictates of religion and the best norms of ruling. They also conformed to the social concept of *murawwat* (compassion or generosity) and the religious norm of joining *ihsan* (beneficence) with *adl* (justice).[124] In this regard, history was regarded as the main source to impart moral education.

Thus, usually, we find that historians would not criticise any personality entirely on the basis of character but would rather confine themselves to any positive statements that could be attributed to that person. One statement found in virtually all narratives on the sultans describes them as good Muslims, while other character traits could vary from person to person. The tendency of these historians to not criticise individuals and personalities directly, despite critically evaluating their actions, was based on the practice of identifying the strength of the religious beliefs of the person rather than his character and the obligation of the author to uphold religious values.

Generally, the historians of the period did not consider historiography as a non-literary activity. They portrayed and depicted the events in a proverbial and poetic style and for this purpose they used exaggerated statements, for instance, Isami in his description of the depopulation of Delhi during the reign of Sultan Muhammad bin Tughluq maintained that the sultan's decision was motivated by petty revenge and that he completely depopulated the city of Delhi with this irrational decision (he uses the phrase 'destruction [*takhrib*] of Delhi').[125] It can be said that such statements were partly journalistic and partly historical if viewed in reference to modern times. Thus, one of the objectives of historiography was journalistic. Since there was no public media, victories of the Muslims were considered newsworthy by the ruling class and they had to be highlighted.

Historiography during the Sultanate period was bound within the parameters of the objectives of governance and the position of the rulers and the subjects in the scheme of society generally, and politics particularly. As most of the historians were under royal patronage and assigned the task to record the glorious deeds of their patrons, this was reflected in their compilations in terms of bias or hyperbole, if not outright fiction.

The object of writing history was largely concerned with creating an awareness of historical events among the aristocracy and arbiters of the Divine Will and with the journalistic objective of keeping the population informed of the state's developments and progress in the recent past. Another trend in contemporary historiography was to make an effort to inform the sultan, the *ulema*, and the nobles of the consequences of past rulers' actions and policies. In this capacity, they also served as something of a guidebook.

Besides, another purpose was to make public the achievements and failures of historical personalities. On this basis, the people could admire, recognise, and acknowledge benefactors and scorn and identify oppressors, as identified by historians.[126] There were, in other words, two major objectives of writing history: to broaden the vision of the sultan through a thorough analysis and to familiarise people with the actions of past rulers.

Indo-Mughal Historiography: Its Development, Major Traditions, and Characteristics

The Mughals, who succeeded the Sultanate of Delhi, continued the previous traditions of early Indo-Muslim historiography, but at the same time introduced some new trends. The mass influx from Iran and Central Asia provided an opportunity for the intermingling of different historical traditions. The *Dabistan-i-Herat* (The Herat School) of Khwand Mir, which followed the ornate style of writing of Samarqand, was established in India. This school was primarily founded by Amir Timur as the Timurid School in 1375 CE, at Samarqand, Bukhara, and Herat, in Central Asia. Timurid writers developed a specific genre of local historiography: topographical descriptions and pilgrimage guides to local shrines, coupled with biographical information on the saintly people buried there. Timurid historiography re-invented the literary *tadhkira* and opened the field of historiography to non-official writings, including personal memoirs and autobiographies. It carried out its activities till 1500 CE and gradually merged into the Safavid school of Persia, the main feature of which was its dynastic or official outlook.[127] One of the most marked differences in both of the schools is the relative absence of historical biography in the latter. Timurid historiography was firmly rooted in the Persian literary tradition of official court histories of the post-Mongol period and was also nourished by local traditions of regional history.

The Mughal period in India is significant for introducing a remarkable change in Indian historiography. In terms of source material, there was a great deal of historical works compiled by contemporary authors and scholars which was relatively more authentic and reliable than the previous ones, since these writers were either eyewitnesses or heard about the events from those who had seen or participated in them. On the other hand, while the historians of the Mughal period mainly concentrated on political history, they differed from their predecessors in terms of their social outlook, ideals, and approach.[128]

The Mughals were Persianized Turks from Central Asia. They asserted descent from both Timur and Genghis Khan. Besides Persian nobles, administrators, and soldiers; there were painters, calligraphers, architects, musicians, poets, physicians, and historians, who also displayed other diverse skills. They hailed from Tabriz, Shiraz, Herat, and other cities of the Iranian plateau, the residents of whom had accompanied the army during their flight to India. The Mughal emperors further established Persian culture, language, and literature in India, which had already been introduced during the reign of the Sultanate of Delhi. They also cultivated historiographical traditions in the Persian style.[129]

The Mughal period is striking for making impressive progress in almost every sphere of life. The cultural development was accompanied by substantial growth of all forms of art. The Mughal culture reflected the versatile impact of 'Turko-Persian' cultivation, which was linked to the culture of Bukhara and Samarqand, Babur's homeland. The Mughals had already spent sufficient time in Transoxiana and Persia and acquired all the refinement of these civilisations. Subsequently, they carried with them the full benefit of Persian arts and knowledge when they established themselves in India.[130] Therefore, they combined the local traditions with the culture of Central Asia, especially Persia; this hybridisation also affected the historiographical traditions.

The restoration of the Mughal Empire after Humayun's return from Persia in 1554 CE, established a tradition of migration from Persian territories, which continued until the Muslim states of India could no longer offer prospects of employment. Humayun's stay in Persia not only established a diplomatic relationship between the Safavid and Mughal courts, but also led to closer contact between Persia and India. This cordial relation contributed a good deal to the Indo-Muslim cultural heritage; its share among the immigrants was significant. Professor Sukumar writes:

> ... the exile of Humayun in Iran, though humiliating and painful, was not altogether barren in its results. When Emperor Humayun went to Persia after his dethronement by the hands of Sher Shah Suri in 1540 CE, he created cordial relations with the Persians. This was followed by the visit of Persian scholars to India.[131]

During Akbar's reign (1555–1605 CE) when the Mughal Empire had been consolidated, a general immigration of nobles and generals, as well as men of arts and letters from Persia, further moulded the Indo-

Muslim civilisation. These ties between India and Persia were not only political, but remarkably cultural. One such influence was the Persian language, which was the official language of the Mughal court.[132] Like his predecessors, Akbar also patronised literature and the arts. His court was a place for gathering renowned scholars who delivered erudite lectures and exchanged intellectual conversations and discourses with the emperor. Akbar's favourite leisure pursuit was history as well as philosophy. He had a perceptive approach towards the purpose and scope of history and the efficacy of a historian. Historical narrations were read out to him daily. He comprehended them and assimilated the facts with sharp and critical insight. These regular discussions had given him a rare vision into the discipline of history and he could contribute unique and knowledgeable ideas in the field too.[133]

Mughal historiography assumed a more mature, sober, dignified, and objective stature than it had in the Sultanate period. History, which previously had dealt only with royal activities, now also turned to the affairs of the people and the progress of civilisation, resulting in the emergence of the growth of ideas. History was as varied in its contents as the social status and background of those who wrote it. The Mughals, particularly Akbar, provided such a liberal environment without interference to scholars that they could even pass critical remarks against the emperor himself, as Mulla Abdul Qadir Badayuni would do, and not suffer penalties.

Major Traditions and Characteristics of Indo-Mughal Historiography

During Akbar's reign, historians began to use previously compiled works of history as their source material. It may rightly be stated that 'the study of [the] history of medieval Muslim India has been primarily the study of historians by historians.'[134] In their reconstruction of Indo-Muslim history before their own time, these historians did not go to the historical source material, old documents, inscriptions, or even the general evidence of their own intellect. They exclusively relied on the works of their predecessors as historians. In the Mughal period, it seemed that historians were not too concerned about personal gain, getting a reward, or repaying a debt of gratitude to royalty, as they had been in the previous period.

In addition, native Hindu scholars also contributed a massive share in history writing from the beginning of the seventeenth century. For example: *Chahar Chaman* (The Square Garden) by Chandar Bhan

Brahman; *Futuhat-i-Alamgiri* (The Victories of Alamgir) by Isar Das Nagir; *Gawaliyar Nama* by Munshi Hira Man; *Ibrat Nama* (The Book of Warnings) by Kamraj; *Khulasat al-Tawarik* (The Summary of the Histories) by Subhan Rai Batalwi; *Lubb al-Tawarikh* (The Quintessence of the Histories) by Bandra Ban Das; *Muntakhib al-Tawarikh* (Selective Histories) by Jagjiwan Das; *Naqsh-i-Dil Kusha* (The Impressions of a Happy Heart) by Bhim Sen; *Raja Wali* by Banwali Das Wali; *Shahjahan Nama* by Bhagwant Das; *Tarikh-i-Kashmir* (The History of Kashmir) by Nara'in Kol Aajiz; and *Tarikh-i-Maratha* (The History of Marathas) compiled by Munshi Dhokal Singh.[135]

This new trend of adopting more inclusive native historiographical traditions with a broader more humanistic scope, continued and gave rise to well-known scholars, both Muslims and Hindus writing in Persian. The contribution of the non-Muslim scholars infused a non-religious, or secular element in history writing, which developed as a significant feature of Indo-Mughal historiography.[136] However, the divine element was still present though the humanistic ambit seems to be more prominent. Mohibbul Hasan remarks in this regard that 'when we come to the Mughal period, we find a qualitative change in historical writings.'[137]

The historiographical literature produced during the Mughal period is incredibly valuable and presents a comprehensive picture of the political, religious, social, commercial, and agricultural institutions of Mughal India. The *A'in-i-Akbari* of Abu al-Fazl may be regarded as a very good example of such works. The introduction of biographies of eminent personalities was another significant feature of Indo-Mughal historiography. Some of the emperors introduced a new form of historical literature, autobiographies which are regarded as a most authentic and valuable record, for instance the *Tuzuk-i-Jahangiri* (The Autobiography of Emperor Jahangir), etc.

Mughal historiography not only includes biographies, autobiographies, and diaries, but specialised and general histories besides copious records, official documents, coins, inscriptions, private letters, royal decrees, and orders. Apart from these, there are voluminous and vivid accounts of foreign travellers who visited India. All this constitutes a rich treasure of knowledge for subsequent generations. The historiography during the Mughal period may be categorised into different parts such as official histories, government records, biographies and memoirs, non-official histories, local and provincial histories, collections of letters, gazetteers and official manuals, and literary works. The Mughal period was not only prolific in historical literature, but along with the broader trends there is an explicit growth in the medieval historiographical traditions. Thus, it provides not only the imperial point of view, but also a more generalised perspective, which may even reflect a sectarian or feminine point of view as well, for a number of religious personalities and the royal ladies also contributed their share in the compilation works on history.[138]

Besides wars, campaigns, and events of political significance, the contemporary cultural, economic, and geographical conditions also captured the attention of historians. Besides the political chronicles, there is non-political literature of a different variety, such as mystic literature (including *malfuzat* and *makubat*), poetical works, general treatises, geographical accounts, autobiographies, *tadhkiras*, manuals of book-keeping and revenue records, and theological works. The core language of all this historical literature is Persian, but some records are also found in regional languages like Marathi, Rajasthani, Bengali, Punjabi, and Sindhi and also in some foreign languages, like French, Portuguese and Dutch.[139]

The *malfuz* literature (the discourses and remarks of Sufi saints) provides very interesting information about the life and conditions of the common man. This literature is distinct from other types of historical literature in spirit, methodology, and treatment. Sufi literature had gained prominence since the Sultanate period. During the Mughal period, the Sufi literature narrated by Dara Shikoh, Sarmad, and others in prose and poetry, is considered to be important. The accounts of Sufi Shah Madar Baba and Nur al-Din Kashmiri are significant because they present a composite and united angle of vision by combining *Bhagti* and *Tasawwuf* (the movements of Hindu and Muslim mystic revivalism).[140]

Tadhkira literature is another category that furnishes interesting insights into society and the prominent people of that time. It comprises mainly of accounts by poets, but also includes the lives of *ulema*, Sufis, literati, and artists. The *Nafa'is al-Ma'asir* (The Riches of Glorious Traditions) of Ala al-Daula Qazwini was compiled in 1565–1566 CE, following this tradition and it includes biographical sketches of the famous poets of the Mughal period from Babur to Akbar.[141] Another significant tradition of Mughal historiography was the manuals, or narratives on the actual working of the administration, which were known as *Dastur al-Amals*. They constituted a reliable source of information in this regard. During the Mughal period, a large number of *Dastur al-Amals* were compiled[142] to guide the government on every aspect of the administrative machinery.

Insha (epistolography) was another source found in Mughal historiography that was one of the most exuberant expressions of personal literature of the time. Drafting letters and documents was considered to be a sign of good learning and a scholarly art. The *insha* collections of the Mughal period are also copious and valuable. They are so numerous starting from *Bada'i al-Insha* (Rare Epistles) of Hakim Yousufi, which was compiled in 1533 CE to *Nigar Nama-i-Munshi* (The Compendium of the Compilers of Letters) of Munshi Malikzada, compiled in 1683 CE.

A thorough analysis of all this literature reveals that Indo-Mughal historiography generally followed two major trends in its nature and outlook: the Arab and the Persian. These had opposite ideals to one another and different methods of handling and presenting historical data. The Arab tradition followed democratic ideals and treated history as a biography of a nation. On the other hand, the Persian tradition considered history as a biography of kings and the affairs of the court. Arab historiography with its democratic approach presented a record of political, military, social, economic, and cultural activities in chronological order. The Persian historical approach was limited to the actions of the monarch, the life of royalty, and the governing class, and excluded all other sections of the population.

Indo-Mughal historiography was also obliged to the trends and traditions set by its Central Asian precursors, where the art of historiography was well developed in its own right. The Turks brought with them a new sense of history to India. Although all the credit for the progress and development of history writing in India is given to medieval Indo-Iranian historiography traditions, the Central Asian contribution cannot be denied, as it was modern enough to believe that historians are the custodians of mankind's collective memory.

The art of historiography had always been appreciated and valued by Central Asian scholars. Hyder Dughlat in his prologue of the history of the Mughals of Central Asia titled the *Tarikh-i-Rashidi* (*c.* 1546 CE) explains the significance of this science of history.[143] The *Tarikh-i-Guzida* (The Select History) of Hamid Ullali Mustaufi compiled in 1330 CE, had also expressed such a view earlier. The Mughals borrowed the style of history writing from their Central Asian predecessors, who usually started history from the time of Hazrat Adam (AS) and included every significant historical event till this preliminary narrative reached the contemporary era. This exercise of tracing back the legendary origins of historical accounts was known as *Tarikh-i-Peshin-i-Turk* (The Earlier History of the Turks). The Turks and the Mughal dynasty carefully recorded the genealogy and history of their predecessors (*urugh/uruq*).[144] Over the years, the traditions of writing history kept on changing and the Central Asians continued to produce histories of all kinds. The Central Asian historiography possessed all the features of Perso-Arab traditions and contributed the same traits to enrich the Indian art of history writing.

Consequently, the mythological, theological, and legendary style of ancient Indian historiography evolved into a more rational, secular, and authoritative one under the Mughals.[145] It was due to the Arab influence that the scholars of medieval India enthusiastically produced works on the geography of different regions. The urge to check the veracity of the statement (*usul-i-isnad*) and emphasise the truthful presentation of facts was a rule which was also borrowed from Arabic historiography. Medieval Indian historians emphasised historical inevitability, or the providential theory as guiding the course of history—everything happens at God's Will. However, though this concept is near 'Church transcendentalism'[146] and 'fatalism',[147] these courtly historians avoided the usual formulae that are envisioned in these spiritual ideas, which were characteristic features of *malfuzat* literature only. The Sufi ideology with its metaphysical and moral views provided grounds for socio-religious movements. Works like *Munis al-Arwah* (The Confidant of Spirits), *Khair al-Majalis*, *Gulzar-i-Abrar* (The Garden of the Pious), *Mirat al-Asrar* (The Mirror of Mysteries), and others were compiled in Mughal India.

Generally, the medieval court historians ignored the 'spirit of the age', 'social forces', or 'causation in history', but the *tadhkiras* of varied types, *malfuz* literature and geographical works were full of information about the life of the 'lesser mortals' and discussions regarding the causes and effects of historical events. The *malfuz* literature, which forms an integral part of historical literature, treats history as being pre-eminently spiritual. Every action of the king is judged according to a biased principle based on his relations with saints and dervishes. The downfall or disgrace of any form was inevitable if some ruler was not amenable towards dervishes and the saints or if he had humiliated them on occasion. The angle of vision of medieval Indian historians was bound to be affected by the spiritual atmosphere in which they lived. For this reason, imperialistic wars that have religious significance were regarded as Jihad (holy war) and were faithfully recorded and were a regular feature in the Mughal sources.[148]

In Mughal historiography, historians made attempts to merge the Arab and the Persian traditions, particularly Abu al-Fazl, who is regarded as being instrumental in the advancement of the conspectus and perception of history in his time. Later, it became a tradition to also give accounts of other prominent literary and religious personalities in conjunction with narrations of the rulers. However, the mention of underprivileged members of society remained a lesser priority. This style did not follow the Arab tradition of historiography in its true spirit.

The Mughal reign is regarded as the prime period for compiling court histories. The tradition of having the official history of the empire written by royal historians was started by Akbar. It continued down to the reign of Aurangzeb. Akbar assigned the task of writing the official history to

Abu al-Fazl in 1595 CE. He wrote *Akbar Nama* (The Chronicle of Akbar) and *A'in-i-Akbari* (The Regulations of Akbar), which was completed after five revisions in 1602 CE. It is quite significant that Akbar assigned this work to Abu al-Fazl at the peak of his glory. Akbar's historian explains the method of writing his official history in *Akbar Nama* and *A'in-i-Akbari*. *Akbar Nama* is technically a history book, while *A'in-i-Akbari* is a comprehensive work to record all matters concerning Akbar's rule: the system of governance, objectives, the rules framed by Akbar, the entire set up of the administration, social commentary, and cultural overview. The whole Mughal archives were placed at the disposal of the author. His source material consisted of accounts of events written by eyewitnesses. Reports, memoranda, reports about military campaigns, minutes prepared by the officers, royal edicts (*farmans*), and other records were carefully consulted by Abu al-Fazl.[149] He had discussions with the principal officers, grandees, well-informed dignitaries, and old members of the Mughal royal family. He was not satisfied with the oral records which were often contradictory, so he asked these to be written. He checked the authenticity and reliability of the sources, critically examined them, and made necessary corrections after consultation with the emperor.

Through this process of investigation, the truth was ascertained and recorded. But Abu al-Fazl rarely acknowledged the sources from which he derived a specific piece of information. The *A'in-i-Akbari* (*c.* 1601 CE) of Abu al-Fazl is regarded as the first gazetteer of India. It also marks a new pattern in historiography.[150] This model of historical literature was largely ignored by subsequent historians, who mostly followed the strictly narrative style of *Akbar Nama*.

The compilation of provincial histories also marked a high-water mark in Indo-Mughal historiography. These too first started to be written during Akbar's reign. Numerous books in this regard were compiled: *Mirat-i-Sikandari* (History of Gujarat); *Tarikh-i-Sindh* alias *Tarikh-i-Masumi* (History of Sindh); *Tarikh-i-Hyder Malik* (History of Kashmir); *Baharistan Ghaib'i* (History of Bengal); and *Tarikh-i-Assam* (History of Assam). However, the *Tarikh Tabaqat-i-Bahadurshahi* (History of the Stages of the Bahadurshahi Dynasty), which was compiled in 1536 CE by Hussam Khan about the ruler of Gujarat, was the first such provincial history to feature chapters on several regional histories from the ancient times and a general history of India during the Mughal period apart from that of Gujarat. The complete text of this book is not extant, and we find its references only in the other sources. This pattern of compiling regional histories was later followed by Nizam al-Din Ahmad Harawi in his *Tabaqat-i-Akbari*, and others.[151] He was Akbar's *Mir Bakhshi* or head of the military. His work, the *Tabaqat-i-Akbari*, is a comprehensive work on general history covering the time from the Ghaznavids up to 1593–1594 CE.

During the period of anarchy that followed the reign of Alamgir (d. 1705 CE), three major works were compiled in terms of regional histories. These included the *Mirat-i-Ahmadi* (The Mirror of Ahmad) of Ali Muhammad Khan, which is a Persian history of Gujarat; Ghulam Husain Salim's *Riyaz-us-Salatin* (The Gardens of the Sultans) compiled in 1788 CE is a very brief account limited to the dynasties in Bengal; and the *Tarikh-i-Kirpa Ram* (The History of Kirpa Ram) is the history of Kashmir written on the pattern of *A'in-i-Akbari*. The author, Diwan Kirpa Ram, was the prime minister of the Maharaja of Kashmir. He was a great scholar of Persian.[152] Among all of these, the *Mirat-i-Ahmadi* is of a very high standard. Regional histories possess different features from national ones: national history describes the historical facts about the nation and its seat of power while other regions remain on the periphery and do not get that much importance. Whereas the history of the centre will deal with the whole country; the scope of regional histories centres mainly on the particular region.

CHAPTER 2

Mughal Rule in Sindh: The Period of Origin and Development of Historiographical Trends

Unlike most other regions of India, Sindh has, historically and geographically, maintained a distinct identity from time immemorial and this made it a unique region in India. If we consider its political and economic conditions, Sindh had remained a prosperous, peaceful, fertile, and resourceful region through the centuries. For this reason, it had always been the target for raids by foreign invaders. The people of the land withstood such aggressions and usually defeated the intruders. On the other side, they embraced people who migrated there from other regions, in keeping with their tradition of hospitality. Consequently, the political history of Sindh is a record of a region that has been governed by rulers of different races from time to time and subjected to constant strife between the sovereigns of varied origins in order to rule the region.

Different ruling dynasties, both foreign and local, left their inimitable impact on the development of historiographical traditions in Sindh. When Cyrus conquered some parts of Balochistan in 545–505 BCE and Darius I (550–486 BCE) laid the foundation of an empire that included Sindh, they introduced Aramaic[1] as the official language. Darius' officers and soldiers spoke Avasti (old Persian). At the time of Alexander's invasion (329–325 BCE), the whole Indus Valley[2] was governed by local chiefs, and Persian, which was the official language, seemed to have declined. During the Mauryan rule (321–184 BCE), Persian declined further and Pali, as well as Sanskrit, developed as the religious and official languages. The religious literature which was recorded in Sanskrit, Persian, and Pali, offered a few glimpses of the political state of the country.

The source material for the history of ancient Sindh comprises of some ancient scripts and epilogues of this period, records of Alexander's advent and travelogues, *Vedas*, *Puranas*, and mythological stories of the *Mahabharata* and the *Ramayana*.[3] The earliest mention of Sindh is found in the *Rig Veda*, which was written 1000 years after the reign of the Indus Valley Civilization (1500–1200 BCE). The *Vedas* were written on the banks of Sindhu (River Indus). The *Rig Veda* admires the Sindhu, the cradle of civilization:

> Sindhu in might surpasses all the streams that flow…
> His roar is lifted up to heaven above the earth;
> he puts forth endless vigour with a flash of light…
> Even as cows with milk rush to their calves,
> so other rivers roar into the Sindhu.
> As a warrior-king leads other warriors,
> so, does Sindhu lead other rivers…
> Rich in good steeds is Sindhu,
> rich in gold, nobly fashioned, rich in ample wealth.[4]

In this hymn, Sindhu, unlike other rivers, is considered masculine. When the Vedic seer invokes Heaven and Earth, he also invokes the Sindhu River. The *Veda* refers to the Ganges only twice, but it makes as many as thirty references to the Sindhu.[5] This is the Great Sindhu that gave Sindh its name.

The *Rig Veda* is written in a semi-dramatic and semi-epic style, which became the prototype for the later historical dramas and epics. Some royal eulogies and divine hymns are also presented in the *Rig Veda*. The work includes numerous compositions and brief metrical accounts of the ruling dynasties. It seems the *Rig Veda* is a composition in the oral tradition that is also ritualistic. This form of historical composition has sometimes influenced the fixed and written religious tradition.

The *Vedas* did not mention the political conditions of Sindh, but they did provide an outline about the social and cultural life of the people. It would be interesting to know what the *Mahabharata* says of the kingdom in old Sindhi during the period before 1000 BCE. H.T. Lambrick writes that the *Mahabharata* speaks of the kingdom of Sindh as a cultured and civilised land.[6]

> King Jayadratha of Sindh was married to Kaurava prince Duryodhan's sister, Dushhala. He was, therefore, all along on the side of the Kauravas and against the Pandavas. However, be it said to the credit of Jayadratha that he, like Dhritarashtra and Bhishma, opposed the disastrous game of dice between the Pandavas and the Kauravas. Gandhari, a prominent character of the *Mahabharata* and the mother of Kauravas was a princess of Sindh.

The *Mahabharata* was later associated or summarised in a Persian work titled the *Majma al-Tawarikh* (Compendium of Histories), which mainly consists of three parts—the first of which describes the history of Sindh prior to Sindh's seizure by the *Mahabharata* heroes.[7]

For whatever reasons, ancient Sindh has bequeathed to us no authentic historical work or history. This is an omission in its literature. However, undoubtedly, in the form of legends, myths, traditions, anecdotes, epics, *Puranas*, and other literary records, there is an unbounded legacy of history lying concealed. It may not be considered history in its true sense, but historical material can be gleaned from it.

The early Brahman Sanskrit literature, including the *Ramayana*, *Mahabharata*, and *Puranas*, are considered religious literature that provides records of some historical events, but cannot be considered authentic and reliable as they are hyperbolic in nature. The total lack of historical sense is characteristic of the whole of Sanskrit literature. There is a complete absence of chronology in the whole corpus of ancient Indian historical records. Besides religious classical Sanskrit, travellers' accounts, folklore, legends, and ballads of *bhats* and *charans* (professional bards and storytellers) are also regarded as semi-historical sources of ancient and pre-Mughal Sindh.[8] The history written so far deals excessively with the role of the rulers, wars, expeditions, tombs, palaces, etc.; there is very limited information about the socio-cultural life of the common people. These legends only comprise the actions of a few leading figures, heroes, and their wives, that represent the mythical self-appreciation of the upper classes. The only early historical record found about Sindh entitled the *Chach Nama* is after the Arab invasion, it mentions only very brief accounts of pre-Arab Sindh.

Arab rule in Sindh (r. 712–1058 CE) left a rich legacy of learning, education, and literature. The record of the British government also shows that intellectual development during Muslim rule in Sindh had produced a great number of scholars. After the Arab conquest of the region, Arabic became the official and court language and one in which most of the literary work was written. The traditional Muslim learning of logic, grammar, *hadith*, *tafsir* (interpretation of the Holy Quran), history, and biography, developed during this period. Highly devotional poetry in Sindhi dialects was composed during the Isma'ili rule (r. 960–1026 CE) in Multan and Mansura by Pir Shams al-Din and Pir Sadr al-Din, which replaced most of the hymns and songs of the pre-Muslim era. Philosophy and other intellectual sciences were encouraged as well. Later, Multan became the centre of literary activities during the reign of Nasir al-Din Qabacha (r. 1205–1228 CE), the governor of Sindh under the Sultanate of Delhi, who greatly patronised the scholars and the literary men of his times, who had migrated here from Central Asia and Persia due to the Mongol invasion. They settled mainly in his capital at Uch.[9]

The intelligentsia of medieval Sindh played a dynamic role in the origin and development of the Persian language and literature including history writing. The earliest record of the history of the Arab conquest of Sindh was written outside India in the ninth century CE, when an anonymous writer compiled the *Minhaj Al-Din Wa'l Mulk* (The Pathway of Faith and Rulership) in Arabic, most probably between the years 830 and 868 CE—though some scholars, referring to some evidence in the narratives, infer that the work must have been written earlier than 753 CE.[10] This book was subsequently translated into Persian and titled the *Fath Nama-i-Sindh* (The History of the Conquest of Sindh), better known as the *Chach Nama*, by Ali bin Hamid bin Abi Bakar al-Kufi (d. 1220 CE) in 1216 CE, at Bhakkar.[11] This was the time when Sultan Nasir Al-Din Qabacha was ruling Sindh and the adjacent south-west Punjab (1205–1228 CE) with his capital at Uch under the Sultanate of Delhi. Luminaries like Awfi (who completed his *Lubab al-Albab*) and Juzjani (who began his *Tabaqat-i-Nasiri* there) used to gather in his court.

The *Chach Nama* of Ali Kufi appeared as the first book on the history of Sindh and perhaps one of the earliest historical works compiled in India, written in the thirteenth century.[12] This book is known by numerous titles such as the *Tarikh Minhaj al-Masalik*,[13] *Kitab Futuh-us Sindh wal-Hind*,[14] and *Tarikh-i Hind*,[15] etc. The author has given the reasons for undertaking the difficult task of its translation in its preface, but he has neither mentioned the specific title of the original Arabic work, nor the name of its actual author; instead, he frequently mentions its title as the *Fath Nama-i-Sindh*.[16] At two different places in the text, the author referred to it as *Tarikh-i-Hind wa Fath-i-Sindh* (The History of India and Conquest of Sindh) or *Fath Bilad-i-Hind wa Fath-i-Sind* (The Conquest of India and Sindh). Some evidences mentioned in the text, which are mainly based on the authority of Al-Mada'ini (752–839 CE),[17] can be compared with the chapter entitled *Futuh al-Sind* (The Conquests of Sindh) in Baladhuri's *Futuh al-Buldan* (History of the Muslim Conquests)[18] and this indicates that the original in Arabic was either authored by Mada'ini or was based mainly on his works entitled the *Kitab Thaghar al-Hind* (The Book of Region of India) and the *Fath Makran* (The Conquest of Makran). Unfortunately, these two books are no longer extant. It resembles the *Futuh al-Buldan* and the *Tarikh-i-Yaqubi*[19] in its subject matter, which is quite authentic and reliable. On the other hand, some of the information is derived from oral evidence, particularly from Qazis of Aror and Bhakkar.[20]

It is evident that Ali Kufi's narration is richer than that of al-Baladhuri. The text precisely labels itself to be a *hikayat* (a story, often told and heard orally), a *tarikh* (history), and a *dastan* (epic) and the text follows these narrative styles accordingly. Kufi shows his command over the methods and theories of historiography. For instance, he uniquely blends two major components of historiography; he takes the cyclical universe of Firdausi in which the rise and fall of rulers is based on their moral qualities and infuses the concept of al-Tabari of history having a purpose of being guided by righteousness.[21] According to him, the progression of time is linear and the teleology is directly focused towards the Prophet (PBUH) and then away from the Prophet (PBUH), with the moral universe expanding and contracting according to the chronological distance from him.[22]

Nevertheless, the legendary and mythological accounts of *Chach Nama* such as the story of Rai Dahir bin Chach and the infatuation of Rani Suhandi for Chach seem more like a romantic tale than a history based on oral testimonies.[23] The romantic element of myth and folklore in the text detracts from the historic worth of the text. The first part of the *Chach Nama* is mostly filled with legendary matter that is more useful for a historian to sift out historical truth than any other early form of narration. Shahpurshah Hormasji Hodivala opines that the description of Chach's conquest was a '*rifaccimento* in Persian prose of a poetical *Digvijaya*' and 'every whit as unhistorical as similar lucubration of Sanskrit poets and Rajput bards'.[24]

Despite being mythological in its outlook, the *Chach Nama* provides valuable information and detail of the logistics and strategy of the Arabs in the battles mentioned above. The main purpose of compiling such a *magnum opus* was to provide a guideline for the administration of the newly established Muslim polity. The records of regular communications, calling for and receiving regular day-to-day reports from Muhammad bin Qasim (the Arab commander who conquered Sindh in 712 CE) and instructions sent by Hajjaj bin Yousuf (the viceroy of Iraq during the reign of the Umayyad caliph, Walid bin Abdul Malik, who sent the military expedition to Sindh), are also reproduced in the book. Ali Kufi tries to make *Chach Nama* an interesting and valuable source for Muslims rulers and conquerors. The *Chach Nama* presents the beginnings of a new political theology. The author intended the work as a guide for later generations of Muslims engaged in government and war. Kufi describes it as a '*Dastan-i-dini*' (A Holy Tale) that is firmly based on a foundation of the principles of statesmanship and government.[25] The author counsels members of the ruling elite to adopt the right sort of attitude towards members of the religious class, not forcing them to abandon their lives of devotion to suit the ruler's own convenience, but making appropriate appointments. He cites quotations from ethno-political literature in this regard, most prominently from Ibn al-Muqaffa's the *Kitab Adab al-Kabir* (The Major Work on Secretarial Etiquette).[26]

The *Chach Nama* serves as a valuable source of the political theory of the era. The approach of the author seems to be quite critical when he examines the causes of the fall and decline of a ruler and dynasty. The author suggests that it is the duty of a ruler to command the world according to the will of God; he provides a clear picture of what happens when a ruler does not perceive his rightful duty, or ignores it.[27] The structure of the *Chach Nama* implicitly affirms the concept of balance, of moderation, and a bias towards accommodation between different elements in the body politic. It signifies the importance of the role of a wise counsellor to the king and commander. Counsel is depicted as an essential element of polity. Another theme in the *Chach Nama* relates to the control and the welfare of the agents of the ruler or commander.

The *Chach Nama* was the first compilation that set forth the earliest trends and traditions of historiography in Sindh, which were followed by later historians for centuries. The writing style used by the author was didactic prose. This did not give an impression of disjunction, discord, or disharmony in the historical tradition of the period of Chach's rule and Al-Kufi's own time. The book begins with the customary ascription to God, the Beneficent and Merciful followed by salutations and reverence to the Holy Prophet (PBUH)—all books by Muslim scholars begin like this. The author mentions no reference books that he consulted at the time of its compilation. The language of the text is complex and ornate with elaborate words and expressions. The style is straightforward, and the author maintains the flow of language throughout the text. However, the language of the text is Persian, but it may be noticed that Arabic words, maxims, and idiomatic expressions of Arab origin are commonly employed by the author.[28] Indeed, the author displays his eloquence and excellent command over the Arabic idiom. The reason behind this use of Arabic may be because the book was reproduced from an Arabic version. On the other hand, this was a transitory period when the Persian language had not completely replaced Arabic, which was still being commonly used and thus resulted in hybridisation in the diction.

It is interesting to know that Ali Kufi could not restrain himself from merely making a translation from the original Arabic text; he included some additional information of marginal nature and some oral testimonies.

He exhibits his eloquence in Persian in a fine literary style, investing it with romantic content in truly Persian tradition, in order to create interest and delight his readers.[29] For this purpose, he gives a brief introduction to the different sections with poetic imagery, characteristic of the *tashbih* (simile) in a *qasida* (eulogy); he has also adorned the text by occasionally using self-composed odes and couplets of other poets, and improvised titles for Muhammad bin Qasim and others following the contemporary literary trend.[30] It is interesting to note that Ali Kufi uses Persian-Islamic idioms, particularly when recounting the events of Chach's time. For instance, although Chach was a Hindu, he warns Chandra of his accountability to God in an Islamic fashion.

The author puts prudent advice and warnings in the mouths of ministers and courtiers, in accordance with his own theory of statecraft. He inscribes elaborate conversations between different characters and at times even invests the simple business-like correspondence between Hajjaj and Muhammad bin Qasim through rhetoric. He occasionally allows his imagination to run wild and conjures up romanticised or humorous tales. The story of the two daughters of Dahir succeeding in their conspiracy to bring about the downfall and death of Muhammad bin Qasim is one of the examples of the exaggerated and hyperbolic writing style of the book.[31] The aim of the author seems to be to produce a 'popular Persian edition' of the original Arabic text, in which he was successful. Thus, the *Chach Nama* is regarded as a popular Persian version of the original, which has its own merits and demerits. *Chach Nama* concludes abruptly followed with just a short dedication and a prayer from Ali Kufi.

The multi-genre text of the *Chach Nama* catering to both Islamic norms and a local pre-Islamic past, may be considered to exemplify the formation of a distinctive sort of Muslim state at the frontier of the Muslim Empire. In the province and milieu of its production, the *Chach Nama* represents the beginnings of a new political theology. Long understood as a translation of an earlier text, it is actually a rendition with a lot of imaginative additions and embellishments that have found political and romantic resonance in the histories of Uch and Sindh, through the centuries.[32] Ali Kufi suitably adorned the text with numerous Arabic odes, maxims, and dictums. This ornate and over-elaborate writing style demonstrates the influence of Muslim culture on the author. Ali Kufi transformed the simple objective narrative into a Persian romantic version of historiography.

It is a known fact that we have no authentic and reliable written record of the successive Soomra (r. 1024–1351 CE) and Samma (r. 1351–1520 CE) periods. During the 500 years of Soomra and Samma rule, it seems that

Persian and Sindhi literature and historiography would have developed to some extent. It is widely believed that some such traditions had evolved, but must have somehow been destroyed by some upheaval, with only the *Chach Nama* and a few Sindhi poems of a dozen poets surviving.[33] The historical references of this period are meagre; rather historical records were derived from the folk-lore stories, romantic poems, epics, and ballads of local *bhats* and *charans*.[34] All these semi-historical sources contribute to the history of Sindh during that era.

Such oral recitals were introduced in Sindh during the last days of Arab rule and the subsequent Soomra period. The folklore of Sindh, like all other folklore, is the result of an interaction of cultural, geographical, and religious factors and that offers valuable historical evidence of cultural influence.[35] A number of folk tales became popular among the people, including the tales Umar-Marui/Marvi; Moomal-Rano; Sohni-Mahiwal; Saif al-Maluk-Badi al Jamal; Leela/Lilan-Chanesar; Sorath-Rai Diyach; Sassui-Pannu; and Noori-Jam Tamachi. Also, there are some other famous epics and ballads about the battles of the Soomras with the Gujjars and Ala al-Din Khilji and the Jams.[36] There are also some local ballads, such as that of Dodo-Chanesar. These are important semi-historical sources in Sindh, where no written history has been found until the fifteenth century.[37]

After the fall of the Sammas, the foreign Arghun and Tarkhan dynasties (r. 1529–1591 CE) ruled over Sindh. They were originally from Mughal stock and Persian speaking, who possessed literary taste and pursued learning. Their courts naturally attracted Persian scholars and intellectuals. During their period, the development of Persian literature in prose and poetry began and its correlation with Sindhi increasingly influenced the literature that was produced. Sindhi folklore was translated into Persian. Mir Abu al-Qasim Sultan ordered Idraki Beglari to compile the story of Leela/Lilan-Chanesar into verse, which was titled the *Chanesar Nama* (The Book of Chanesar).[38]

Hence, after the *Chach Nama*, the next piece of literature seems to have appeared after a lapse of almost four centuries. The *Nusrat Nama-i-Tarkhan* (The Book of the Victories of the Tarkhans) (*c.* 1560 CE) is regarded as the second among all the histories written in Sindh, after the *Chach Nama*, but as the latter was principally a translation of an Arabic text, the *Nusrat Nama-i-Tarkhan* is rightly designated as the earliest historical account compiled in Sindh. It falls in the category of dynastic history.

Nusrat Nama-i-Tarkhan—The First Political History Compiled in Sindh

The *Nusrat Nama-i-Tarkhan* was written by Abu Sa'id Muhammad bin Bayazid Purani, on the achievements and conquests of the Tarkhans, in 1560 CE. It is an authentic and the most valuable source of the history of the Arghuns and the Tarkhans.[39] The author and most of his family members enjoyed important and prestigious positions under the Arghun and the Tarkhan rulers. This close relationship continued for almost fifty years and then the author decided to compile a history of his benefactor.[40] For this reason, most of the events are eyewitness accounts and therefore reliable. Dr Ansar Zahid Khan, who edited this volume, opines that 'perhaps this is the old *Tarkhan Nama* that was said to have been lost in the time of Shah Jahan, or it may be a separate work'.[41]

The author's grandfather, Shaykh Jalal al-Din Abu Sa'id, belonged to an influential family of Puran, a small village situated in the northern vicinity of Herat in Afghanistan. The members of this Purani Syed family had had close associations with the Arghuns for a long time. A number of Afghanis migrated and settled in Sindh during this period. Shaykh Jalal al-Din Abu Sa'id and his family were among them. His eldest son, Syed Mahmud alias Shaykh Mirak Mahmud was close to Shah Beg Arghun (r. 1524–1556 CE), who appointed him as the *Shaykh al-Islam* (superior authority on the tenets of Islam) of Thatta. He died in 1555 CE and was buried in the Makli graveyard.[42] His youngest son Mirak Bayazid was the author's father. He was an influential personality of Bhakkar in Sindh, where he had settled. He was an esteemed poet and calligrapher. He soon gained prestige and fame among the aristocracy of Bhakkar. The author of the *Nusrat Nama-i-Tarkhan*, Abu Sa'id Muhammad bin Bayazid Purani was his youngest son.[43]

There seems inadequate information about the author's life, works, and career in contemporary literary sources. However, the succeeding compilations such as the *Tarikh-i-Masumi* (Masumi's History of Sindh, *c.* 1600 CE), *Maqalat al-Shuara*, a book of biographical treatises of poets of Sindh (*c.* 1761 CE), and *Tuhfat al-Kiram* (The Gift of the Nobles, *c.* 1767 CE) provide some references about his life and times. The *Nusrat Nama-i-Tarkhan* and the *Shajrah Sadat-i-Purani* (Genealogy of the Syeds of Puran) written by Mir Murtada, furnish some biographical accounts of the author. Mir Ali Sher Qani, (1727–1789 CE), a famous historian of the Kalhora period (r. 1701–1783 CE) mistakenly refers authorship of the *Jami Fatawa-i-Purani* (The Comprehensive Book on the Judgements of

Purani) to Abu Sa'id,[44] while it was actually compiled by Abu Sa'id's brother Syed Abdul Wahab.

Apparently, the author himself mentions that his uncle waited upon Shah Hasan at Nasarpur just after his triumph over Jam Feroz, the last Samma ruler. The author sought his approval to go to Thatta in 1524 CE. But it is not evident whether he was coming from Qandahar, Sukkur, or Bhakkar. It seems possible that he might have left Qandahar accompanying his uncle, Mirak Mahmud, after the death of his grandfather, Shaykh Jalal al-Din, when Qandahar was occupied by Babur.

The esteemed status that the author and his family assumed, provided him with an opportunity to cultivate amicable relations with the members of the ruling Arghun and Tarkhan families. According to Dr Ansar Zahid Khan, 'Most of the author's family members were noted for their excellence of character, perfection in knowledge and in spite of meagre resources at their disposal maintained fully the tradition of hospitality, hallmark of their family dating back to the days of Puran'.[45] However, when the Purani family settled in Sindh, they got divided into two main branches: the Puranis of Thatta, who were the descendants of Mirak Mahmud and Puranis of Sukkur, the descendants of Mirak Bayazid.

Though the author was the son of Mirak Bayazid, he is associated with the former branch of the family, because Shah Hasan Arghun sent him to Thatta, probably just after his migration from Qandahar in 1524 CE. He settled there permanently and enjoyed a notable professional career and made profound contributions to literary activities. He was a distinguished poet of the Persian language, in which he achieved fluency in a style like that of the *Shah Nama* of Firdausi. Syed Mir Muhammad Bayazid Purani along with his brothers secured prestigious official ranks and participated in many campaigns against the local tribes of Sindh. They played a conciliatory role in pacifying internal disputes of the ruling dynasty.

There seem contradictory accounts regarding the date of Syed Mir Muhammad Bayazid Purani's death. Three dates are mentioned in this regard, 1590 CE, 1583 CE, and 1562 CE.[46] On the other hand, the most authentic reference from the *Shajrah Sadat-i Purani* (which has been referred to above) indicates that he died in 1564 CE in Thatta at the age of seventy and was buried in the famous graveyard of Purani Sadat on the Makli hills.[47] However, Dr Riazul Islam does not agree with any of these statements and documents the year 1562 CE/970 AH as the year of his death.[48]

Evidences in the book indicate that Syed Mir Muhammad Bayazid Purani compiled his *magnum opus*, *Nusrat Nama-i-Tarkhan* in 1560 CE, during the reign of Mirza Isa Tarkhan I (r. 1554–1567 CE) with his capital at Thatta. The author also elucidates the reason for its compilation. He illustrates the usefulness and significance of historical literature. He opines that rulers generally desire to read books on history to keep themselves well-informed about the accounts of the past rulers, Prophets, celebrities, etc., to gain benefit from this knowledge and draw lessons from their experiences. The wish of the rulers to have a book on the history of Sindh led the author to compile this work. Historians and their compilations are treated as the repositories of knowledge and the means of commemorating the deeds and achievements of rulers for future generations. The fame and glory of all the kings and rulers always rest upon the works of historians and poets, and the author of the *Nusrat Nama-i-Tarkhan* beautifully summarises this notion in a stanza[49]:

سلاطین که روی زمین داشتند   متاعی بجز نام نگذاشتند
کیانی و ساسانی پیش داد   گفتار فردوسی آمد بیاد

Translation: The kings, who controlled the world, did not leave any wealth behind except their names (such as) Kiyanis, Sassanids, and Pish Dads. Firdausi's sayings will always be remembered.

The Tarkhans were a senior branch of the Arghuns. When the author's benefactor, Mirza Isa Tarkhan I came to know about his intention of compiling such a work on the history of the Tarkhans, he requested the author to include the accounts of the Arghuns[50] as well. The author writes: 'His Highness, the Nawab, whose abode is heaven also encouraged me and he uttered a praiseworthy speech saying that it is virtuous to write about the life of the previous Arghun rulers.'[51]

However, five major parts based on previously surviving works are eliminated from the text.[52] The first section of this part gives a short account about the changes in the nations and religions of the world, and destruction of heretic dogmas after the emergence of the prophets during various epochs. It also includes their brief biographical accounts starting from Hazrat Adam (AS), till the last Prophet Muhammad (PBUH). The author gives a description of a supernatural occurrence on the night of his birth. He mentions the year of his birth by referring to the futile attack of Abraha on Makkah. It also relates the history of the descendants of Japheth (in Hebrew, Yafet or Yefet), son of Prophet Nuh (AS), who is said to be the forefather of the Turks and Mongols. Further, he traces the genealogy of the Mongols, particularly the house of Genghis Khan. Following the tradition used in *Zafar Nama-i Yazidi* (The Book of Victories of Yazid) he highlights the Mongols growth into different tribes and clans and states the origin and purpose of their names. Similarly, the author also traces the history of the Arghuns and the Tarkhans from Japheth.

The first twenty pages of the book comprised of a *muqaddima* or preface stating the reason for its compilation and organisation of the contents. In the beginning, the author also discusses the organisation and methodology of the book. Its plan clearly mentions that this might be the first volume of the book but due to the murder of the author's patron, Mirza Salih, and the death of the author himself in 1564 CE, he could not complete its second volume. The book runs into two *maqalas* or parts with four chapters or sections that the author calls *maqsads* dealing with the accounts of Dhu al-Nun Arghun (r. 1489–1507 CE), Shah Beg Arghun (r. 1507–1524 CE), Shah Hasan Arghun (r. 1524–1554; d. 1556 CE) and Mirza Isa Khan Tarkhan I's (r. 1554–1567 CE) period respectively up to the time of completion of this book. All the subsequent chapters are divided into sub-headings, which may refer to *abwab*. According to its organisation, the whole text may be distributed into three major categories: the accounts of the Samma rulers and their struggle against the foreign assault of the Arghuns, accounts of the Arghuns and the Tarkhans, and lastly a record of the author's family.

The author starts the text with the traditional doxological invocation, subsequently there is a discussion on *tawhid* (belief in the oneness of God); followed by one on *risalat* (Prophethood of Muhammad [PBUH]); the merits of the four pious caliphs and the *a'immah* (plural of imam) which means the descendants of Prophet Muhammad (PBUH), such as Hazrat Hasan (AS) and Hazrat Hussain (AS), etc. The text is also elaborated with frequent use of verses from the Holy Quran.[53] The book is a durable monument of the author's command over the Arabic language. Writing in Arabic was a major trend in Muslim historiography of that time.

The author recounts the stories of the prophets of Islam, for example the following verse refers to the story of Prophet Ibrahim (AS):

قال هذا ربى فلما افل قال لا احب الافلين

Translation: He said, 'this [the sun] is my Lord.' But when it set, he said: 'I worship not that which sets'.

The author embellishes the text with massive use of poetic expressions in terms of the *mathnawis*, *nazms*, *abiya't*, etc., almost on every page of the book. Such a work shows an excellent command of the author over Arabic as well as Persian prose and poetry. The word الافلين is followed by poetical verses like a *mathnawi* in the text,[54] such as:

الافلین مثنوی:

بقدرت انجمن افروز انجم   بحکمت مردمی آموز مردم

The author also mentions his own name and the title of the book as the *Nusrat Nama-i-Tarkhan*:

در ذکر اموری که بعد ازین سمت ظهور یا بدواین کتاب را به 'نصرت نامه ترخان' مسمی گردانید و من الله الاعانة وا لتوفیق.[55]

> Translation: Reading the affairs which took place after this designation and he named this book as the *Nusrat Nama-i-Tarkhan* and all the help and success comes from God.

Syed Mir Muhammad Bayazid Purani also embellishes his accounts with chronograms[56] for special events.

For the most part, the accounts of the *Nusrat Nama-i-Tarkhan* are based upon the evidences of eyewitnesses. However, the author draws accounts of the life and times of Holy Prophet (PBUH) largely from three books entitled the *Tadhhar al-Abrar wa Tajziyah al-Akhbar* (probably *Tadhkira al-Abrar*),[57] the *Nafa'is al-Fanun fi 'Ara'is al-'Uyun* (c. 1335–1342 CE) of Shams al-Din Muhammad Amili, and the *Jami' al-Ma'arif*; the accounts of the Turks and Mongols are constructed upon the *Zafar Nama-i-Yazidi* of Shaykh Sharf al-Din Yazdi and *Mathnawi Jush wa Kharush* (Effervescence, c. 1403 CE) of Shaykh Mahmud Zingi, etc.[58] The *Mathnawi Jush wa Kharush* is a poetical expression of some events of historical significance, which elaborate on the history of the Timurids. Its author was a courtier of Amir Timur, who accompanied him in his campaign to Gurjistan (Georgia) and compiled this *mathnawi* based upon his memoirs and eyewitness accounts.[59]

The author embellishes the text with beautiful couplets according to the prevailing literary trend. The writing style of the author is complex and florid. This rhetorical style was a dominant trend in Persian historiography during the beginning of the fourteenth century. Writers of that time considered it essential to adorn their compositions with such complex rhetoric phrases, that even scholars needed lexicons to comprehend the text. The style obfuscated the sense of the historical text. Almost every page contains verses, mostly composed by the author himself, or the poetry of Firdausi, Nizami, Attar, Jami, and other celebrated classical Persian poets to emphasise his statements.[60] The use of poetic expressions is so predominating that from pages 328 to 335, there are more than eighty odes under one title. For this reason, Dr Ansar Zahid Khan states,

'... deciphering and editing was a nightmarish job'.[61] Probably only a very small class of erudite scholars and men of letters enjoyed this sort of style, whereas it obscured the true purpose of historiography. In this book, the style and arrangement of the facts were often more important than the historical truth.[62]

It may be noted that unlike other compilations including the *Tarikh-i-Masumi*, or the *Tuhfat al-Kiram*, the *Nusrat Nama-i-Tarkhan* does not elucidate events of the Samma period. The author makes fleeting references to the era during detailed descriptions of the career and activities of the Arghuns in Sindh, including Dhu al-Nun, Shah Beg, and Shah Hasan Arghun. He highlights the disastrous conditions of the famine that struck during Mirza Shah Hasan Arghun's siege of Multan. He writes:

> The tenth bird flew high in search of food but could not find a single grain of wheat, and the swift courier flew with a single thought like a deer at night in a desert, who did not pay heed to any other greenery except green pastures.[63]

The author of the *Nusrat Nama-i-Tarkhan* was a contemporary of the last Samma ruler Jam Feroz (r. 1508–1524 CE) and offers a first-hand account of this period, particularly of the Battle of Siwi (Sibbi), which was fought between the Samma ruler Jam Nizam al-Din Nanda (r. 1461–1508 CE) and the Timurid Sultan of Herat, Husayn Bayqara (r. 1469–1506 CE). This account is of great historical significance as it is eyewitness testimony. The author gives a full description of this battle. He first mentions Sindh in regard to an uprising in Siwi. He states that when Sultan Husayn Bayqara heard the grievances of the local merchants, he focused his attention on Siwi in 1489 CE and attacked and subjugated it. After a year, the Sindhi forces counterattacked and Shah Beg's brother was killed. Subsequently, Jam Nizam al-Din Nanda sent an emissary to the court of Sultan Hussain for reconciliation.[64] Afterwards, the Arghuns continued ravaging the regions of Siwi, Kahan, and Sewistan. When Shah Beg conquered Thatta and Darya Khan, the general of the Sindhi army was captured and brought before him, he slew the general on the spot. The author writes:

> And when his...sight fell upon the *gahani* friend of the Arghuns, who was there in the time of the rulers; he said that this person is Mubarak Khan and when they inquired 'are you Mubarak Khan?' In reply, he said 'ji' which means 'yes' in Sindhi language. The Sultan recalled the murder of his brother and he himself killed him with a sword.[65]

The author adds some accounts of the unique nature of the Arghun-Samma contest for supremacy in Sindh during 1489–1520 CE, which haven't been mentioned by other historians of that period, like Mir Masum, a Sindhi Muslim historian and pharmacist from Bhakkar. He is renowned for writing a detailed compilation, *Tarikh i-Sind* (History of Sindh) in *c.* 1600 and Mir Ali Sher Qani. Although both of these historians have also written about this conflict in their books, their versions are inadequate. The renowned scholar and an authority on the history of Sindh, Syed Hussamuddin Rashidi has shed considerable light on this period in his research on Qani's book, titled *Makli Nama*,[66] completed in 1760 CE. Rashidi drew up references mainly from the *Fath Nama-i Sindh*.[67] On the other hand, Syed Mir Muhammad Bayazid Purani was a devotee of the Arghuns, so his version sometimes comes across as one-sided. He overstates the achievements of his masters—while elaborating on Shah Hasan's triumphant march towards Thatta, the capital of Samma kingdom and Jam Feroz's flight to the village of Chach Khan (now Badin), he writes:

> The condition of Jam Feroz bin Jam Nizam al-Din was so pitiful that when he heard about Nawab Mirza Shah Hasan's arrival in the magnificent city of Thatta with all his great chiefs and helpful military men, he fled to Gujarat and stayed there.[68]

However, the main objective of compiling this account seems to be to record the success story of the Tarkhans over their native rivals, the Arghuns. As mentioned earlier it was at the instance of Mirza Isa I, who actually seems to be the main figure of the book, the author incorporated the history of the Arghuns. He also provides evidences regarding the internal conflicts of the ruling dynasty. As the author had a close association and affection with the Arghuns and Tarkhans, he is biased against the indigenous Sindhi people. In numerous places, he uses indecent words and expressions for them. For instance, he writes: 'In Sindh, falsehood and use of hemp is mostly practiced'.[69] He further calls the native people '*na-dan*' (ignorant),[70] '*be-din*' (infidels),[71] and advises that 'from thousands of slaves, never choose a Sindhi'.[72] At another place he makes a disgraceful statement about Sindhi women too.[73]

During the last days of Shah Hasan Arghun, the Tarkhans rebelled against him. In order to suppress this insurrection, Shah Hasan asked the native Sindhi tribes to support him. Expressing this episode, Syed Muhammad did not even bother to hide his animosity and rancour. He writes:

...anxiety aroused for the Arabs as times brought misfortune from the straw pulling nation of slaves of the masters of Thatta, and the authority of all affairs is related to his [Shah Hasan] impure qualities.[74]

Not just this work, but all the books on the history of Sindh compiled during Mughal rule show this biased and critical disposition towards native resistance against the foreign rule. The worst example of such compilations is *Mazhar-i-Shahjahani* (Manifestation for Emperor Shah Jahan) written by Yousuf Mirak, who was a Mughal official of Sindh.[75]

Despite some shortcomings, the *Nusrat Nama-i-Tarkhan* is significant since it is the earliest history compiled in Sindh that provides the most authentic, eyewitness and comprehensive accounts of not only Sindh and India, but also of Persia, Khurasan, Afghanistan, and the region of Transoxiana during the late fifteenth and early sixteenth centuries. The author had access to all the important official documents due to his own and his family's close association with the Arghun and Tarkhan rulers. They also took part and played a vital role in most of the events of historical significance.

The close associations with the Arghuns and the Tarkhans originated in the period of Sultan Husayn Bayqara of Herat, when the Arghuns gave full support and patronage to Shaykh Abu Sa'id of Puran. This was the time when Dhu al-Nun Arghun was rapidly rising as the chief noble of the Sultan in Qandahar. The fact that the Shaykh's family was overthrown by the Uzbeks in Puran, brought them closer to the Arghuns in Qandahar. This close association between the two continued unceasingly for almost fifty years, till the Tarkhans met their end at the hands of the Great Timurids. The *Nusrat Nama-i-Tarkhan* represents extensive eyewitness accounts of this whole period.

However, the exhaustive accounts of the entire story of the rise of the Arghun power and their struggle against Babur in Southern Afghanistan, is the main theme of the book. Babur was driven out of Central Asia to Kabul by the Uzbeks, where he seized Southern Afghanistan from the Arghuns. The accounts of the Arghun invasion and their settlement in Sindh are also offered by the succeeding sources like the *Tarikh-i-Sindh* alias *Tarikh-i Masumi* (*c.* 1600 CE) of Mir Muhammad Masum, *Tarikh-i-Tahiri* (*c.* 1621 CE) of Syed Tahir Muhammad Nisyani, *Beglar Nama* (*c.* 1625 CE) of Idraki Beglari, and the *Tarkhan Nama* (*c.* 1654 CE) of Syed Mir Muhammad bin Jamal bin Jalal al-Din Hussaini Shirazi. All of these accounts are quite authentic and reliable, owing to eyewitness evidences but conversely seem to be 'deficient in commemorating the valorous deeds' of the Arghuns and the Tarkhans.[76]

The *Nusrat Nama-i-Tarkhan* serves as a model in tracing the compilation of authentic historical accounts by the Mughals. It covers the period of these Mughal tribes' rule in Sindh, up till 1560 CE, specifically including the civil war between Isa Tarkhan and his son, Mirza Baqi Tarkhan.[77]

The *Habib al-Siyar* (Beloved of Virtues), is a prominent three-volume book on the general history of Persia and India, which also covers this period and was compiled in 1521 CE, by Ghiyas al-Din Muhammad Khwand Mir (d. 1534/37 CE), who served the emperors Babur and Humayun and is considered to be a renowned historian of Persian origin. The *Nusrat Nama-i-Tarkhan* validates this book regarding the date of Babur capturing Qandahar; the overthrow of the Arghuns; their migration to Sindh, and the seizure of Thatta by the Arghuns in 1522 CE. On the other hand, the accounts of Mir Masum contradict this information.[78] The author of the *Nusrat Nama-i-Tarkhan* substantively mentions that the first Arghun attempt to capture Thatta was made in 1520 CE. He quotes this date in three different places:

...در سال نهصد و بیست و شش رای عالی وی بران قرار یافت که ...
بحکومت قندهار گذاشت ... بموکب همایون به نیت فتح بلاد سند روان گشت.[79]

Translation: In 926 AH (1520 CE), he decided to appoint his nephew Mirza Muhammad Isa ... to rule over Qandahar ... and he himself, along with his fortunate cavalcade, proceeded forward to conquer the Sindh.

واین فتح بلند و نصرت ارجمند (تته) در سال نهصد و بست و شش واقع شده بود.[80]

Translation: And this eminent and esteemed victory took place in 926 AH (1520 CE).

The author also describes the date of Mirza Isa Tarkhan I's victory over Miyan Muhammad son of Darya Khan in the same year, in a self-composed chronogram:

سال تاریخ از خرد جستم   گفت یک فتح میرزا عیسیٰ [81]
926 AH (1520 CE)

Translation: I explored the year by my wisdom. It said: a victory of Mirza Isa.

He also eliminates controversy associated with Shah Beg's death, which according to him took place in 1522 CE/ 928 AH, as he writes:

در شہر شعبان کہ ... این تاریخ گفتہ:

چون اندر شہر شعبان رحلتش بود   شدہ تاریخ رحلت 'شہر شعبان'
928 AH (1522 CE)

و بعد از ان در سال نہصد و سی سہ بہ طرف مکہ معظمہ فرستادند ...[82]

Translation: In the month of Shaban ... which on the whole indicating: As his death took place in the month of Shaban, the date of his demise is '*Shehr-i-Shaban*' (the month of Shaban). Afterwards, in the year 933 AH, they sent towards the Holy Makkah.

However, the author offers a good amount of eyewitness accounts of the period of Mirza Isa Tarkhan I and all his close associates and nobles, including Amir Alikah Arghun. Some chapters on the Tarkhan dynasty were authenticated by Mirza Isa Tarkhan himself. Even though the author was a contemporary of Mir Masum (d. 1606 CE), he does not mention anything about Shaykh Abu Sa'id Purani in his book. This indicates that there was no significant link between the two eminent historians or their families.

The author discusses the reasons of Shah Beg Arghun for withdrawing from Qandahar to Kabul in detail, of which there are no other records, including the *Tuzuk-i-Baburi*, the autobiography of the Mughal Emperor Babur. Mir Masum merely mentions that according to Babur, Shah Beg came to Qandahar to learn the rules of governance from him.[83] However, both the *Nusrat Nama-i-Tarkhan* and *Tuzuk-i-Baburi* contradict each other in fixing the date of Shah Beg's departure from Qandahar.[84]

The author of the *Nusrat Nama-i-Tarkhan* describes two major reasons behind this significant historical event. One was that Shah Beg Arghun was displaced due to the impolite behaviour of his father towards Babur and thus he left Qandahar for Kabul. Another reason given by him was that one of Babur's devoted nobles, Amin Dost Nasir Beg, had tried to win Shah Beg over to serve Babur. Therefore, Shah Beg had come and stayed at Babur's court for two years and then returned. In contrast to his punctilious attitude to the Arghuns, Syed Mir Mohammad Bayazid Purani deliberately gives a scant account of Humayun's exile and his wandering in Sindh for three years. On the other hand, Mir Masum gives detailed accounts on the subject.⁸⁵

The author also deliberates on the cordial relations and esteemed devotion that developed between Shaykh Jalal al-Din Abu Yazid Purani and his brother, Abu Sa'id, with Shah Beg Arghun. The relations between the Purani's and Shah Beg were so close that once Abu Sa'id Purani fell ill at Mashur. Shah Beg refused to leave Mashur because of this, though there was the threat that Babur would attack him. When Abu Sa'id Purani could not recover and died of his illness, then Shah Beg, Mirza Ka'i Khusro, Zinak Tarkhan, and Amir Baba Beg buried him in Mashur and constructed a mausoleum despite objections by the townsfolk.⁸⁶

Apparently, the author of the *Nusrat Nama-i-Tarkhan* was very well acquainted with contemporary learning and scholarly trends. His analytical approach is evident from his critical remarks on classical Persian literature. He comments on the hyperbolic exaggerations of Firdausi in *Shah Nama*. He remarks that Firdausi had begun to repent of his irrationality and confessed his absurd rendition of the story of Hazrat Yousuf (AS).⁸⁷ The author quotes some verses from the *mathnawi* entitled *Yousuf Zulaykha* erroneously attributing them to Firdausi.⁸⁸ These are given below:

بگفتم در ان بر چہ خود خواستم   ز ہر گونہ نظم آراستم
بسی کاشتم تخم و بیخ بزہ   اگر چہد لم بود ازان نامزہ
زبان را و دل را گرہ بر زدم   ازان تخم کشتن پشیمان شدم
دو صد زان نیر زد بیک مشت خاک   کہ آن داستانہا در غیست پاک
شب و روز ز اندیشہ پرداختہ ⁸⁹   چہ باشد سخنائ برخاستہ

The date of the author's demise mentioned on the flap of the book is given as 1564–1565 CE, whereas at the end it is mentioned as 1562–1563 CE. This contradiction confuses the reader.

The *Nusrat Nama-i-Tarkhan* is also very useful as the most authentic source for the history of the author's Purani Syed family of Sindh for which, as mentioned before, there is no other adequate source available. The only and the rarest manuscript of this book conserved in the library of Aligarh Muslim University fortuitously was retrieved by the German scholar Professor Anne Marie Schimmel. She handed its copy over to Syed Hussamuddin Rashidi, who subsequently assigned Dr Ansar Zahid Khan the valuable task of editing and publishing it who ably edited this book and wrote a thorough and illuminating introduction of sixty-four pages including annotations. The preface is written by Dr Riazul Islam, who dedicated it to Syed Hussamuddin Rashidi. This book is an asset to the literature on the history of Sindh. Dr Muhammad Saleem Akhtar[90] and Dr Mazhar Mahmud Shirani[91] wrote comprehensive critical appraisals on the *Nusrat Nama-i-Tarkhan*, which mainly deals with the inaccuracies committed in the text during its editing. However, these articles refer largely to its linguistic assessment, which does not encompass the criteria of its historical significance and evaluation.

After an all-inclusive analysis of the above-mentioned works, one may conclude that political historical literature during the early medieval period concentrated primarily on political history. The historians paid no attention to providing accounts of contemporary scholars, saints, poets, artists, etc. If any general reference is made, it is casual and in the context of the rulers. Then later in this period a significant breakthrough took place. A copious body of historical literature began to be compiled that was non-political. Scholars, poets, Sufis, and other celebrities found a place in historical narratives. Thus, besides political histories, some accounts of non-political literature of historical significance were also produced that not only substantiate the political accounts but also provides an extensive amount of information on the era's socio-cultural, religious, and economic conditions.

Genres of Non-Political Historical Literature: *Tadhkiras*, *Malfuzat*, and *Insha*

The Arghuns and Tarkhans not only radically changed the political scenario but also contributed to bringing about progress in the societal and economic set-up of Sindh. Their passion for literature and knowledge is evident from the works that were composed during this period. Like the political chronicles, another new genre of literary merit developed: story-writing. The Arghuns brought this literary practice from Persia. Mirza Jani Beg and Ghazi Beg Tarkhan termed it *qissa-khwani* (story-telling).[92] Muqim, one of the nobles of Mirza's court, and Mulla Murshid and Mulla Asad, companions of Ghazi Beg, were some renowned *qissa-khwans* (story-tellers) of the period.

Also, during the reign of the Mughal Emperor Shah Jahan (r. 1628–1658 CE), Khawaja Aman Sayfi, a famous Persian poet of the Mughal court, composed seven stories titled the *Haft Akhtar* (Seven Stars) in prose and seven stories in poetry, entitled *Bahman Nama* (History of the Bahman Kingdom, that was situated in South India).[93] Further, Abu al-Fath Qabil Khan, a famous Mughal official of Emperor Aurangzeb, composed his famous story entitled the *Qissa-i-Kamrup* (The Story of Kamrup), a territory situated in northeast India, near Bengal and Assam.[94]

Another important historiographical tradition that began emerging in Sindh and other regions of India during the medieval period, was *insha* (epistolography). A considerable amount of *insha* literature was compiled in India as well as in Sindh. The earliest *insha* collection from Sindh is the *Munshat-i-Mahru* or *Insha-i-Mahru*, a collection of letters that were collated towards the end of the fourteenth century, by Ain al-Mulk Mahru, a noble of Muhammad bin Tughluq's (r. 1325–1351 CE) and afterwards of Feroz Shah Tughluq's (r. 1351–1388 CE). The collection contains documents and letters sent to leading officials and individuals of consequence. They contain interesting details about the workings of the Tughluq administration.[95]

The *tadhkira* literature (biographical directories of poets, scholars, Sufis, and other literary celebrities) was another genre that proved a great asset to non-political historical literature. *Tadhkira* literature is full of anecdotes and interesting bits of information that aid in envisaging a picture of social life during this period of transition. The *Tadhkira Lubab al-Albab* of Muhammad Awfi[96] is regarded as the first work of its type compiled in India and includes almost 300 references to poets. It was written in 1221–1222 CE and was dedicated to Qabacha's minister, Ain al-Mulk Fakhr al-Din Husain bin Abi Bakar al-Ash'ari of Uch. Sometimes the *tadhkira* of any individual personality transformed into *malfuz* literature.

The literal meaning of *malfuz* is 'words spoken'. It is generally used for informal utterances of Sufi saints, or the proceedings of the periodic religious meetings, assemblies, and casual gatherings that they had with their disciples and admirers.[97] For the proper understanding of human life and the behaviour of a region in its true historical perspective, it is essential to search for, examine, assess, study, and utilise such varied, though scattered source material. The working of mystic thoughts and ideas may be traced from these compilations. They provide information about the character and spirit of the people of that time, or whatever period the *malfuz* literature may have been written in, and the various factors that weave the multi-faceted fabric of society, including the social, cultural, and religious psyche of the period.

Around the start of the fourteenth century, there was a fresh surge of Sufi saints and mystical proselytising in the subcontinent. This flowering reached its zenith by the mid-fifteenth century. Sufi saints were people who fulfilled the demand of the time and social circumstances for spiritual guidance and alleviating the miseries and sufferings of the common people. Their *khanqahs* (monasteries) were open to all. People of all strata and walks of life came to these seers. These places were used as centres of learning for students and disciples and there were lessons and discussions on theology, mysticism, scholastic philosophy, ethics, morality, etc., which the saint led. The utterances of the saint were punctiliously noted by devoted followers with his express or tacit approval.[98] It is believed that Hasan Sijzi[99] introduced this unique genre of religious literature called *malfuz* in India. He compiled the discourses of his *murshid* (saintly religious leader) Nizam al-Din Awliya, titled the *Fawa'id al-Fuad* in 1308 CE.[100]

In this manner, a considerable number of such works were composed. In its nature, *malfuz* literature constitutes a significant non-political history source material and is considered one of the most important literary achievements of medieval India, which began to be cultivated systematically and methodically, as a branch of hagiological literature. Besides serving as a book of guidance for people generally and a manual of spiritual instructions and elucidations of mystical concepts to disciples, the main theme of these compilations revolves round the personality and spiritual achievements of the saint and his status in society. Thus, this literature embraced almost every aspect of social life at all levels and in all matters, temporal and spiritual. Thus, literature served as a source of information for the socio-cultural, religious, and literary movements of the period. It also sheds light on the life and difficulties of ordinary people. No other genre of medieval literature depicts such a vivid image of contemporary society as *malfuzat*.

Some contemporary scholars viewed this literature as unreliable. They fabricated authoritative statements to try to denigrate its significance and value. In this regard, Dr Shaykh Muhammad Ikram opined that most of the available *malfuz* literature concerned weird and supernatural elements.[101] However, the legends and miraculous anecdotes it contains are identifiable and may be treated with circumspection or ignored. On the other hand, numerous *malfuzat* that deal with the lives of eminent scholars, poets, ascetics and saints, with particular reference to their personal lives and may even provide large or small selections from their works and thoughts.

The *Siraj al-Hidaya* (The Light of Guidance) is considered to be the first compilation in this regard in Sindh, though it is no longer extant. It is a collection of conversations of a famous Sufi saint of Uch Sharif Syed Jalal al-Din Bukhari Makhdum Jahaniyan (1308–1384 CE), transliterated by one of his close disciples, Maulana Ahmad Moin Siahposh, in Uch.[102] This work contains substantial knowledge of historical significance regarding the prevailing political and cultural conditions. It was composed at the time when the saint visited Delhi and provides notable accounts about the Thatta campaigns of Sultan Feroz Shah Tughluq.

The *malfuzat* compiled in India can broadly be categorised into two groups: first, those where the narrative is formed mostly on anecdotes and secondly, those where the discussion is mainly thematic and only interspersed with anecdotes. The best examples of the first group are the *malfuzat* of Shaykh Nizam al-Din Awliya (d. 1425 CE); while that of the second group are the *Siraj al-Hidaya*, mentioned above and the *Ma'dan al-Ma'ani* (The Spiritual Mine), the discourses of Shaykh Sharaf Al-Din Maneri (d. 1371) who was a famous Sufi saint of the Firdawsiyya order in Bihar. The narratives in these *malfuzat* are relatively more objective and doctrinaire.[103]

Sindh as a whole is known as the land of Sufi saints and sages who fostered the message of love, amity, and brotherhood in Asia and beyond. These Sufi mystics have large followings in all faiths and in every stratum of society. A massive amount of the *tadhkira* work also supplements tales of miracles, *malfuzat* and *maktubat* (epistles) related to these saints.

Almost all *malfuzat* were compiled in Persian, but a few of them were composed in Arabic. The *Tadhkirat al-Murad* of Hafiz Haji Muhammad Hussain Safa'i alias Shaykh Hussain Safa'i Thattawi, is one such. It is an impressive and spectacular work that was compiled almost five hundred years ago. It is regarded as the earliest extant work of the genre of *tadhkira* cum *malfuz* literature compiled in Sindh.

Tadhkirat al-Murad: The First Hagiographic Account (Biography Including *Malfuz* Literature) Compiled in Sindh

The *Tadhkirat al-Murad*[104] is a biography of Syed Muhammad Hussain, alias Shah Murad Shirazi (d. 1487 CE), a renowned Sufi saint of Makli and Thatta. The author is Muhammad Hussain Safa'i Thattawi, who was a disciple of the saint. The work is all about Shah Murad's life. The prominent twentieth century religious scholar and historian Ijazul Haque Quddusi (d. 1406 AH) erroneously considers Syed Ali II (d. 1573 CE) descendent of Shah Murad from his brother and disciple Syed Ali Shirazi Kalan as the author of the *Tadhkirat al-Murad*[105] which is not accurate. Syed Ali II compiled *Adab al-Muridin* (which is a guideline for the disciples of Shah Murad Shirazi).[106] Regarding his antecedents, the author, Muhammad Hussain Safa'i Thattawi, states that his ancestors left their homeland Shiraz due to the disruptions of the Rafidis, a famous dogmatic cult. They settled in Sindh.[107] His mother was a domestic servant of Shah Murad Shirazi. Once, during his childhood, his mother requested Shah Murad to pray for his progress in piety and righteousness. Shah Murad blessed him with virtuous deeds.[108] Unfortunately, we find no reference to his early education and tutors though, in the preface of his book, he refers to himself as a *hafiz* (a person who has memorized the Holy Quran) and *haji* (a Muslim who has made the pilgrimage to Makkah).[109] He devoted his whole life to the service of his *murshid*, renouncing all worldly desires and aspirations. Under the patronage of his mentor, he was soon elevated to the status of a *wali* (religious guide or saint).[110] Shah Murad appointed him as one of his *khalifas* (apostles). Syed Mir Ali, Shaykh Albu and Miyan Ahmad were the other apostles of the holy man. Shaykh Safa'i died in 1525 CE and was buried next to the grave of his *murshid*.

The author was a great scholar of Arabic—a fact amply evinced in his book. He is highly regarded in Sindh for his Sufism. Other works also provide references about his life and work. Qani, however, did not mention him in his book, *Tuhfat al-Kiram* (The Gift of the Noble), though in episodes regarding Shah Murad Shirazi, Qani gives references that are clearly about Shaykh Hussain Safa'i and his book *Tadhkirat al-Murad*.[111] The author of *Tadhkirat Awliya-i-Sindh* (The biographical directory of the Sufi saints of Sindh) states that Shaykh Hussain Safa'i belonged to the Samma period. The author of *Tuhfat al-Tahirin* (The Gift of Virtuous People), which is a book about the various saints buried in Thatta and in the Makli hills, writes that Shaykh Hussain Safa'i was elevated to the highest rank of spiritual succession and was famous for his virtue and charity; for aiding the poor.[112] This elevation was according to an old, dogmatic faith that gave Sufi Shaykhs spiritual authorisation. As Shaykh Ahmad Sirhindi (1564–1624 CE), an Indian Islamic scholar from Punjab, a Hanafi jurist, and a prominent member of the Naqshbandi Sufi order, in his book entitled the *Risala-i-Tahlilha* (The Book in Praise of God), writes:

> The Sufis get their authority directly from God and the Prophet [PBUH]. It is they who sustained the universe; and it is they who gave rain and food to the people.[113]

However, Shaykh Hussain Safa'i does not provide the date of the compilation of his work, but in the text, all the accounts of his *murshid* are mentioned as being in the past, so we can assume the book was written after his demise. As we know, Shah Murad Shirazi died in 1488 CE and Shaykh Hussain Safa'i died in 1525 CE, so it can be inferred that the book must have been written during the thirty-seven-year period, i.e. from 1488 to 1525 CE.[114] According to the author himself, he compiled the biographical memoirs, narratives of miracles, and religious discourses of his Shaykh, Shah Murad Shirazi, because he felt deeply indebted to him. He recorded this work for his spiritual happiness and blessing. In this regard, he writes:

قال الفقير الحقير الضعيف الحافظ الحاجى المريد لحضره السيد الحسين المقلب باسم السيد المراد قدس الله تعالى سربو عليه الرحمة الى يوم الجزاء ان مرشدى و صاحبى افضل من الاولياء.[115]

Translation: Hafiz Haji, an inferior disciple of Syed Hussain alias Syed Murad said that my mentor and friend is superior among all Sufi saints.

The author displays his eloquence and excellent command of Arabic. He begins the book with a brief *muqaddima* (preface). After this comes the traditional, Muslim ascription to God and paying reverence to the Holy Prophet (PBUH) and also the *Awliyas*. Then he explains the purpose of his compilation. The author also records the proceedings of his Shaykh's *majalis* (spiritual gatherings). A deficiency in the book is that he does not bother much about dates.

This book is comprised of twelve chapters and a brief preface. It includes accounts about Shah Murad Shirazi's birth, lineage, childhood, education, miracles, attributes, virtues, generosity, and death. It also describes his spiritual succession to his four deputies (*khalifas*) mentioned earlier, Syed Mir Ali, Shaykh Albu, Miyan Ahmad, and the author himself.[116] In medieval India, it was a common practice for a Shaykh to divide his spiritual succession into different parts and award the parts to his close disciples so they could take care of the affairs of his mission. First, he would bestow a robe on each disciple and nominate him as his *khalifa*.

There were three methods to appoint a *khalifa*. The first involved the Shaykh receiving a sign indicating the Divine will to appoint a person as deputy, or *khalifa*; in the second, the Shaykh himself might choose one of his devotees on the basis of his virtue and piety; and the third was that a *khalifa* might be appointed on recommendation. Shaykh Baha al-Din

Zakariya of Multan (d. 1266 CE), of the Suhrawardiyya order,[117] was the first to nominate his own son as his successor and thus set an example of maintaining the succession within the family. Later on, this tradition was adopted by some other mystic orders too. The Shaykh was at times conferred with gracious titles by his disciples and followers, such as Sultan al-Awliya (king of saints), Ghauth/Ghaus al-Azam (great helper), Mahbub-i-Subhani (beloved of God), etc.

The author of the book mentions innumerable biographical narratives and anecdotes regarding Shah Murad Shirazi. He writes about the precognitive accounts of his *murshid*'s auspicious birth[118] and relates stories of his spiritual career in a manner peculiar to Islamic hagiography. He states that Shah Murad Shirazi displayed signs of virtues and spiritual command from his childhood. He further tells that at the age of forty, his *murshid* started to follow the mystic rule of life (*tariqat*) fully and took an oath of fealty (*bai't*) to receive spiritual blessing. He stressed upon his followers and successors to offer Friday prayers at the Qadeem Kabir Jami Mosque, because he said it was superior to other mosques and people who worshipped there received greater blessings.[119]

Though the contents of the *Tadhkirat al-Murad* mostly comprise oral testimonies and anecdotes, the author provides ample evidence from various written sources, including the *Hazar Masnad* (A Thousand Thrones); *Tawarikh* (The Histories); *Hisab al-Ahtisab* (The Account of Accountability); *Al-Ikhlasah* (Sincerity or Devotion); *Al-Dastur* (The Rules and Regulations); *Sirat al-Gadhruni*; *Shijrah al-Sada't al-Tayyabin al-Tahirin* (The Genealogy of the Syeds, Virtuous, and Chaste People); *Qazi Bedawi*; *Mawahib al-Dunya* (The Gifts of the World), etc.[120] The author also quotes Quranic verses as references[121] following the traditional writing style of Islamic mysticism. This was the time when the study of mysticism was passing through a phase of exponential growth in Sindh. The author particularly focuses on the life and notably the miracles and virtues of his Shaykh. He creates religious suppositions and maintains that his Shaykh was imbued with sacred powers.

The anecdotes are a very important part of the Sufi literature of *malfuzat*, *tadhkiras*, and treatises on the principles of Sufism, and also in other related works. These anecdotes are termed *latifas*.[122] The significance of Sufi anecdotes can hardly be exaggerated. It requires a different methodology, which has not received the attention it deserves.

The *Tadhkirat al-Murad* also abounds in anecdotes that trace the people who originally witnessed these events and confirm their authenticity.[123] There are some other works of this type like the *al-Risala al-Qushayriyya* (The Treatise of al-Qushayri), and the *Akhbar al-Akhyar* (Conduct of the

Pious). The *Tadhkirat al-Murad* mentions the story of the *shir-o-gulab* (milk and rose), which the author of the *Tuhfat al-Tahirin* (c. 1789 CE), Shaykh Muhammad Azam Thattawi also reproduces in his book.[124]

Briefly, the story runs as follows: Syed Muhammad Hussain, known as Pir Murad, on attaining the age of forty, established his circle of adherents at Thatta. On coming to know of it Shaykh Sadr al-Din, *nabira* (grandson) of Syed Baha al-Din Zakariya of Multan, sent an emissary with a cup of milk filled to the brim, to summon the Syed with the message that the entire realm of Sindh was under his spiritual jurisdiction and like the cup of milk, there was no place for another saint. Miraculously, the milk remained fresh all the way from Multan to Thatta and not a single drop spilt from the glass. The Syed sent back a reply to the effect that the Multan saint was a descendant of Hazrat Abu Bakar (RA) while he himself was a descendant of the Holy Prophet (PBUH), therefore it was the Shaykh's duty to visit the Syed. Then he placed a few roses in the glass of milk and miraculously the roses remained fresh all the way from Thatta to Multan. Accordingly, the Shaykh went to Thatta to visit the Syed.[125] This story, however, seems doubtful. The identity of Shaykh Sadr Al-Din of Multan, who is identified as the *nabira* (grandson) of Syed Baha Al-Din Zakariya of Multan is uncertain.[126]

The numerous anecdotes quoted in the *Tadhkirat al-Murad* reveal that the *murshid* would hold the sessions of his table talks at any time when he was free. They were generally informal. The *murshid* would sit surrounded by his *khalifas* (deputies), select *murids*, and any visitors who might be present. Any subject could crop up during the course of the conversation, or someone present might pose a question. The *murshid*'s answer could be short or long. The answers were rarely if ever premeditated. They would reveal the range and depth of the saint's knowledge and no matter how serious the discourse, the gathering seldom lost its informal mood.[127] Consequently, the answers were rarely if ever a premeditated discourse. It was this informality that gave these anecdotes their peculiar charm and flavour and ensured their popularity. Thus, both the *latifas* and *malfuzat* suited each other. The *latifas* had indeed no small role in the popularity of the *malfuz* literature.

The *Tadhkirat al-Murad* also provides incidental remarks about the other contemporary Sufi saints such as Shaykh Isa (Langoti), Shaykh Sadr al-Din of Multan, the *khalifa* of Shaykh Makhdum Baha al-Din Zakariya of Multan, Haji Baha al-Din, Shaykh Talha, Shahid Buzurg Syed, Pir Albo, and Shaykh Nathar. It tells us that Shah Murad Shirazi lived during the days of Jam Nizam al-Din Nanda (d. 1509 CE), the Samma ruler who was impressed by the generosity, miracles and virtuous nature of Shah

Murad and used to send gifts to him. The author regarded Jam Nanda as a just, pious, and generous ruler.[128] One of Nanda's nephews, Jam Murk became a devotee of Shah Murad. He was soon elevated to the rank of *khalifa* due to his dedicated service and devotion. Later, he assumed the title of Pir Albo (the *pir* who is not greedy in any way).[129]

The author furnishes evidence regarding his *murshid*'s generosity, marvels, and greatness. He tries to prove various similarities between the life of the Holy Prophet (PBUH) and that of Shah Murad Shirazi.[130] Providing a genealogy, the author traces his *murshid*'s connection to the family of the Holy Prophet (PBUH) through Hazrat Imam Hussain (RA).[131] The author points out that in his mystic discourses Shah Murad Shirazi preached against falsehood, backbiting, slander, and crying during *tazia*[132] processions. He also prohibited drumbeating without any reason. Shows of meditation and dancing during *sama* (a musical session to recite mystical poetry) were strictly forbidden as well.[133] Shah Murad Shirazi proved his arguments from tenets in the Holy Quran, *sunnah*, and *hadith*. He counselled his disciples to follow these rules strictly. He made observance of *sama* conditional.

Undoubtedly, Sufism remained popular in Sindh for a long period. This mystic preaching had a deep influence on religion and it affected the dogma to different degrees. The induction of Sufism in Islam changed its orthodox outlook in many ways, which ultimately brought about a change in the spirit of Muslim society. Sufism was more humane, more liberal in forgiving human weaknesses, and more tolerant of other beliefs. Thus, the author's *murshid* emphasised ethics so much that it seemed that *tasawwuf* (mysticism) was nothing but *akhlaq* (morals). Ethics is a major theme in this work and left its impact on society. By its nature, Sufism had a deep connection with poetry and (with some exceptions and qualifications) mystical music.

The author mentions a number of narratives in the introduction of the book, about his own solitary and reclusive way of living.[134] He remained absorbed in prayer and meditation day and night in an isolated place in some old ruins. This place still exists and is known as Takht Shaykh Hussain near Thatta.[135] After the death of Shah Murad, the author became an anchorite and Shah Hasan Arghun twice sought his permission to visit him, but Shaykh Hussain Safa'i did not see him.[136]

This evidence also indicates that the Shaykh was the undisputed authority and enjoyed the respect and honour of his disciples and regarded himself as superior to the worldly ruler. It was generally believed by the people that political authority was subordinate to the spiritual powers of the Sufi saints and that the affairs of the state were run according to their guidelines; that every Sultan got political power because of the blessings of some Sufis and no worldly ruler could be successful without the blessings of the Sufi saints. From the time of the Sultanate period, this belief was propagated among the people through mythical tales. Although the authenticity of these stories is doubtful, the disciples and the followers of the Sufis saints popularised them.

During the Mughal period, the role and influence of the Sufis in state affairs declined considerably as the Mughals were absolute and forceful monarchs who conquered the land by their own hands.[137] With the emergence of provincial Muslim dynasties in the fourteenth and fifteenth centuries, one also emerged in Sindh that followed the above mentioned polity of Sufi saints. Furthermore, Sufi orders spread throughout the subcontinent: in Gujarat, Sindh, Bengal, Deccan, Kashmir, etc. Often, if they received grants of lands in the countryside, or if they found no patronage in the cities, the Sufis would settle in the rural areas where they influenced the peasantry and converted them into being their followers.

As far as the matter of fulfilling the needs of their livelihood is concerned, we find that the Sufis living singly or in the *khanqah* (their monastery) had three options: either they could accept *futuh* (unsolicited charity), or under certain circumstances and conditions they could earn a living (*kasb*), or, again under certain circumstances, they could beg.[138] It is evident that Syed Murad was so venerated that he did not accept any state money or charity. In the later period, the majority of Sufis disapproved of *kasb*; that is precisely why the option of *futuh* and begging came into prominence.

It has been seen in history that traditions are invented on the basis of belief, faith, and superstitions that are widely and popularly accepted without challenge. Like other Indian regions, mystic traditions in Sindh were also invented from time to time by individuals, groups, parties, and even the state to fulfil their interests or to further the community's cause. These traditions relate to mystic personalities, cults, festivals, ceremonies, and rituals. They are promoted in such a way that once the roots of these traditions become strong, they help other and different groups and their interests to accept their legitimacy as well. Usually history is used to help promote these traditions. The older a tradition; the more widely is its legitimacy accepted. This is the reason why we find numerous mythical accounts in mystic literature and thus it is necessary to trace these with caution. The study of invented traditions enables us to understand the mind, motives, and designs of the individuals and parties who supported and strengthened them in order to further their own interests.

Nonetheless, different from the above-mentioned work, the first noted *tadhkira* (biographical directory) of the poets compiled in Sindh was titled *Rawzat al-Salatin* by Fakhri Harawi. This hagiography comprises of the biographical records of many poets and poetesses, including some royal grandees such as Shah Beg and Shah Hassan, the Arghun rulers of Sindh.[139]

Tadhkira Rawzat al-Salatin: The Earliest Biographical Account (*tadhkira*) of the Poets Compiled in Sindh

Rawzat al-Salatin includes special references to the life and career of Shah Hasan (r. 1524–1556 CE), the Arghun ruler of Sindh. Its author, Fakhri Harawi, cultivated a refined taste for Persian poetry and literature. He also compiled a book on history, which comprised of ethics, legends, and anecdotes. His celebrated works include the *Haft Kishwar* (*c.* 1521 CE), *Lata'if Nama* (*c.* 1522 CE), the *Bustan al-Khayal*, *Tuhfat al-Habib* (*c.* 1523 CE), *Sana'i-al Hasan* (*c.* 1551 CE), and the *Jawahir al-Aja'ib*, which is also known as the *Tadhkirat al-Nisa Sana'i wa Bada'i*, the *Arudh wa Qawafi*, and some *mathnawis*[140] and *ruba'iyats*[141] but unfortunately a number of these works has gotten lost.[142] E. Blochet refers to the *Rawzat al-Salatin* in his directory of Persian manuscripts but erroneously mentions Bengal as its place of compilation, which was actually the dominion of the person the book is dedicated to, Abu Al-Fath Hussain Shah Ghazi, the Sultan of Bengal and Gor (Lakhnauti).[143] There was a surge of Persian poetry and literature as well as mystical writing in Bengal during this period, encouraged and patronised by the Hussain Shahi Sultans. Fakhri Harawi wrote this book at the instance of this Sultan.[144]

The real name of the author was Maulana Sultan Muhammad, while Fakhri Harawi was his pen name. Some sources, like the *Lata'if Nama* (in the British Museum) erroneously mention his name as Fakhri bin Sultan Muhammad Amiri.[145] The author introduces himself as Fakhri bin Muhammad Amir al-Harawi in the book. Fakhri's father was Muhammad Amir, who was also a poet and a learned man and who used the pen-name Amiri. Some scholars, especially those of the early period, like Taqi, Kashi, Mir Imad al-Din Muhammad Hussaini, and Springer, et al, incorrectly considered Fakhri as being the same as Amiri, but this misapprehension got removed very soon.[146]

Fakhri's father composed a *diwan* (a collection of poems by a poet). His family was domiciled in Herat from the time of his grandfather, although this was not their native land. Fakhri was born in Herat in 1497 CE.

His family was prominent in Khurasan and other parts of Persia. Fakhri composed verses paying tribute to his patron Shah Ismail, the Safavid king of Persia (d. 1524 CE). He also dedicated one of his compilations entitled *Haft Kishwar* (The Seven Countries) to him. Likewise, his *Lata'if Nama* (A collection of anecdotes), which was a Persian version of the *Majalis al-Nafa'is* (Assemblies of Precious Things) written in Turkic by Mir Ali Sher Nawa'i (d. 1501 CE), who is regarded as the foremost poet of the Turkic language hailing from Central Asia,[147] Fakhri also included some couplets in praise of Shah Ismail Safavid.[148] Fakhri supplemented a chapter at the end of the book, comprising of a biographical directory of the poets and scholars beginning from the period of the Timurid prince Shah Rukh Mirza (d. 1447 CE) till Shah Ismail Safavid.

Fakhri Harawi in his book states that he left Persia in the days of Shah Tahmasp Hussain (r. 1523–1576 CE) with the intention of performing a pilgrimage to Makkah. He came to Thatta, the then capital of Sindh in 1540 CE during the reign of Shah Hasan Arghun (d. 1555 CE). Harawi was also an eyewitness of the days of Humayun's wandering in Sindh.[149] Shah Hasan Arghun's name is apparently similar to Abu al-Fath Shah Hussain Ghazi, the dedicatee of the *Rawzat al-Salatin*; to whom Fakhri Harawi also dedicated his *Sana'i-al Hasan* (aka *Sana'i-al Husn*), which is a biographical directory of the contemporary poets.[150]

The *Tarikh-i-Masumi*, which contains the earliest mention of *Rawzat al-Salatin*, refers to Fakhri Harawi as a contemporary of Mirza Shah Hasan Arghun. On the other hand, Mir Masum erroneously considers Shah Hussain Takdari as the author of this work.[151] It appears from the text that Mir Masum never met Fakhri Harawi, nor had he seen his book *Rawzat al-Salatin*. However, Masumi writes about Fakhri:

مولانا فخری هروی مردمی خوش طبع و اکابر بوده و شعر نیز
میگفته بعضی تصنیفات دارد در صنایع و بدایع و عروض و قوافی.[152]

Translation: Maulana Fakhri Harawi was a cordial human being and reckoned to be a religious leader. He was also a poet. He authored some books on the art of figures of speech, prosody, and rimes.

The author of the *Ma'athir-i-Rahimi* also quotes Masumi's statement, further adding that Fakhri was an elegant calligrapher too.[153] Walih Daghistani (d. 1756 CE), a famous Persian poet of the Mughal court who migrated from Isfahan, in his *Tadhkira Riyad al-Shuara* (The Garden of the Poets) compiled in 1748 CE, writes that Fakhri was one of the most pious and virtuous persons of his times who possessed a commendable understanding of mysticism. He was a contemporary of Shah Tahmasp of Persia and served him as his official poet.[154]

There seem to be as many different views and opinions about the date of its compilation. According to Qazi Akhtar, *Rawzat al-Salatin* was compiled in 1553–1554 CE, while Dr Khayyam Pur opines that it was written between 1551 and 1555 CE and Agha Abdul Hayee Habibi considers 1553 CE as the year of its compilation. Syed Hussamuddin Rashidi finally infers after a thorough discussion and analysing a number of internal evidences regarding some important and documented events that the *Rawzat al-Salatin* was written between the years 1549 CE and 1551 CE.[155]

At the time, when Fakhri arrived in Sindh, it had become a place where Persian immigrant scholars assembled. The scholars had to leave their native lands due to the political aims of the Safavids against the Ottoman Empire, and the Safavids' propagation of the Shi'ite doctrine. During the sixteenth and seventeenth centuries, leading members of the orthodox Sunni intelligentsia were frequently executed, or deprived of their posts. On the other hand, in Mughal Sindh, there was an emphasis on Divine learning, regardless of sect. Due to the unfavourable religious environment in Safavid Persia, a large number of nobles and men of learning migrated to Sindh and settled in. Lack of proper patronage towards the literati was another important cause of these migrations of scholars seeking better economic prospect in Mughal Sindh. These Persian poets and scholars obtained patronage and support from the Arghun and Tarkhan rulers and later from Mughal governors in Sindh.[156]

Fakhri Harawi was one such immigrant from Herat. When he arrived, the intellectual environment of Sindh was favourable for promoting cultural activities. Shah Hasan Arghun's court was a place of assembly for the poets and scholars of Herat. Fakhri Harawi remained attached to this court for about fifteen years, from 1540 to 1555 CE. It is evident that this was the time when Shah Hasan Arghun had received a *diwan* of poems by the Timurid ruler of Khurasan, Shah Hussain Ba'iqara. Shah Hasan's praises for this *diwan* inspired Fakhri to compile the *Rawzat al-Salatin*.

The *Rawzat al-Salatin* is extensive in its scope. It contains information about the rulers and poets of Persia, Central Asia, Iraq, and India, which amount to a total of seventy-four. The book begins with the customary ascription to God as the Beneficent and Merciful. Thereafter, a foreword, or preface is provided, in which the author gives an outline of the book. The preface, which starts in the name of God and praises the Holy Prophet (PBUH), is interspersed with a number of gracious couplets and stanzas (*nazams* and *ruba'i*). The author also elucidates the reason for writing this book. He illustrates the usefulness and significance of his compilation on this topic. The preface also describes a brief description of each chapter.

The book is subsequently divided into seven *abwab* (chapters). The first chapter is about Bahram Kor, Sultan Sanjar, and Tughral Beg Seljuk, the famous Central Asian poets and also provides an account of the origin of Persian poetry. The second chapter gives details about the Mughal and Uzbek luminaries and poet kings and contains specimens of their works. The third chapter is about the Chagatai kings, the Timurids, and the accounts of their poetical compilations. In the fourth chapter, the author gives accounts of the literary and poetical works of the rulers of Iraq. The fifth chapter is about the poetry of some of the Mamluk kings of India, while the sixth deals with noblemen and amirs who composed poetic works. The final chapter focuses on the author's patron, Shah Hasan Arghun, including samples of his poems such as *mathnawis*, *bay't*, *ghazal*, *matla'a*, *qasida*, *nazam*, and *ruba'i*, etc.

It appears from the text that at the time of compilation of the *Rawzat al-Salatin*, Fakhri consulted other works of similar genre, such as the *Tadhkira al-Shuara* of Daulat Shah; *Silsilat al-Dhuhab* of Maulana Jami; *Zafar Nama* of Sharf al-Din Ali Yadhdi; *Habib al-Siyar*; and *Majalis al-Nafa'is* of Mir Ali Sher Nawa'i. The author also used his *Lata'if Nama* as a source and borrowed some verses and descriptions verbatim, particularly for its supplemented ninth *majlis* (chapter) and *majlis* seventh and eighth.[157]

The language of the book is simple and it is written in a straightforward manner, in which Arabic words and verses are frequently used. Qazi Akhtar opines that Fakhri wrote in a simple style, however, in places he tried to embellish the text with ornate words but could not fulfil the requirement of the text in this manner. Be that as it may, the book does not present the rhetorical and ornate style of classical Persian (termed as *insha pardazi*), which makes it different to contemporary *tadhkiras* and histories.[158]

Both of Fakhri Harawi's compilations are graded as fourth and fifth respectively, amongst the foremost compilations of this category of *tadhkira* literature. These books are specimens of the rich literary heritage of Sindh. It may be stated that apparently Indian *tadhkira* literature was first produced in Sindh, as the first two works of this genre originated here. This directory also includes interesting material, with dozens of Turkish verses composed by immigrant rulers of Turkic origin.

The *Rawzat al-Salatin* is not only significant for the reason that it is the foremost compilation of its subject but also in terms of its historical significance. It is the most laudable and momentous effort. It includes unique and rare narratives about different rulers and aristocrats that may not be found anywhere else. For instance, it is the first and only source, which describes Sultan Feroz Shah as a poet and provides six specimens of his poetry (*ghazals* and other elegies).[159] The author also gives details about the compositions of Abu al-Hasan Langah,[160] Malik Shams al-Din Poz Khan,[161] Malik Fakhr al-Din,[162] and Malik Hussam al-Din. These were all eminent officials of Sindh.

The *Rawzat al-Salatin* reveals some interesting and unique facts, particularly regarding the history of Sindh, such as the details of Shah Hasan's literary gatherings;[163] the contribution of the literary heritage from Khurasan; the standing ovation by Shah Hasan in Shah Hussain Ba'iqara's honour when the latter's *diwan* was presented in his court. The *Rawzat al-Salatin* is rightly considered as the earliest source that divulges that Shah Beg Arghun was a poet who used the pen-name of Nafasi. The author gives some of the specimens of his poetry as a token. Besides his literary accomplishments, the author also provides some very rare and authentic supplementary accounts about Shah Hasan's life and career, calling him Amir Shah Shuja, his title during his lifetime.[164]

The author gives information about the literary contribution of Shah Beg in a book titled the *Mutakhid al-Ajala* on *ilm-i-nahaw* (syntax).[165] Apparently, this book described many events in the life of Shah Hasan Arghun and provides specimens of his poetry that have come to light for the first time.[166]

On the other hand, Mir Muhammad Masum, in his famous book, *Tarikh-i-Sindh* (The History of Sindh), has also provided a comprehensive account of Shah Hasan, describing the latter's literary taste and talent with his pen-name, *sipahi*.[167] Qani also quotes Masumi verbatim in his *Tuhfat al-Kiram*[168] and reproduces five couplets of Shah Hasan in his *Maqalat al-Shuara*. However, Fakhri's work is unique as he replicates five *ghazals* and three *ruba'iyats* of Shah Hasan, which may not be found in any other source. At the end of the book, Fakhri includes a lengthy eulogy in praise of his patron, to solicit a generous reward. At the end, the author contributes a eulogy in praise of Shah Hasan. The opening couplet of this eulogy is given below as a specimen:

دلم سرمست جام عشق و عقل کل زبان دانش   نگوید نشنو دهر دو جزاز توحید یزدانش[169]

The *Rawzat al-Salatin* is brief in its narrations but includes scores of important historical accounts. Fakhri describes the events of Humayun's flight from India to Persia via Sindh and gives interesting bits of information. He writes in detail about the rebellion of Kamran and Askari against Humayun and later, their defeat at the hands of Humayun; the imprisonment of Askari and Yadgar Nasir Mirza and their execution at the time of Humayun's invasion of Badakhshan in 1546 CE.[170] He also provides some details about Hindal Mirza's life before his execution. The author gives accounts of Bahram Mirza, son of Shah Ismail Safavid, and Abdul Aziz Khan, the son of Obaidullah Khan Uzbek.

Rawzat al-Salatin may be an authentic and valuable source, but its text has some discrepancies when it comes to dates. The author briefly describes some events in the lives of various personalities. Mostly, he overlooks details and provides inadequate information about the origin of these personages and the compilations of their works. Selections from their poetry are also insufficient. Though the author borrowed accounts from *Tadhkira Daulat Shah, Majalis al-Nafa'is*, etc., but he also includes some rare and unique bits of information from his personal knowledge. As mentioned before, he transcribed five *ghazals* of Feroz Shah Tughluq, which are found anywhere else.[171]

The two oldest manuscripts of *Rawzat al-Salatin* are conserved in the Bibliotheca National Paris (Nos. 320 and 321). The others are in Berlin, Leningrad, and Istanbul. The writing script of these manuscripts is *Nast'aliq* (one of the main calligraphic hands used in writing the Perso-Arabic script). Because these manuscripts are not free from errors, they are deficient in authenticity and historical value. The painstaking task of editing its Persian text was carried out by one of Pakistan's foremost authorities on Sindh, Syed Hussamuddin Rashidi, who edited the *Rawzat al-Salatin*, the *Jawahir al-Aja'ib* (The Wonderful Jewels), and the *diwan* of Fakhri Harawi, collectively in a single volume, along with a comprehensive introduction of seventy-seven pages in Urdu that highlights the significance of its original text.

Syed Hussamuddin Rashidi provided extensive details about the life and times of the author and his family, in addition to a complete account of events. He used the most authentic and oldest manuscripts from Paris, Berlin and Leningrad, to corroborate the text. Rashidi elucidated details about the manuscripts of these three works. He provided comprehensive marginal notes with original Persian text in order to make it more authentic and valuable. This outstanding work was published by the Institute of Sindhology, University of Sindh, Jamshoro, in 1968.

Jawahir al-Aja'ib (The Wonderful Jewels): The First *Tadhkira* of the Poetesses Compiled in Sindh

The author of *Rawzat al-Salatin*, Fakhri Harawi, also composed another *tadhkira* which was unique. It was a compilation of the biographies of thirty-one poetesses. It was titled the *Jawahir al-Aja'ib* and is believed to be the first biographical directory of female versifiers.[172] The author dedicated and presented it to Haji Mah Begum, the talented queen of Shah Hasan. Fakhri later joined the court of Akbar at Agra, where he made further improvements in the *Jawahir al-Aja'ib* and re-dedicated it to Akbar's foster mother Maham Begum.[173] This *tadhkira* could not achieve much fame by its original name, instead it came to be known as the *Tadhkirat al-Nisa*.[174]

After the death of Shah Hasan Arghun, in January 1555 CE, conditions of internal chaos and disorder prevailed in Sindh because Shah Hasan Arghun left no heir behind. One of his nobles, Mirza Isa Tarkhan took the control of lower Sindh, while Sultan Mahmud Bhakkari grabbed power in upper Sindh, with its capital in Bhakkar. Fakhri Harawi joined the court of Mirza Isa Tarkhan due to his association with Mah Begum, the widow of Shah Hasan Arghun, whom Mirza Isa Tarkhan married in order to secure the support of the Arghun clan. Mah Begum, like the other Mughal ladies, was a woman of great talent, who possessed a refined taste for literature and poetry. The *Jawahir al-Aja'ib* is the third and the last directory of Fakhri Harawi compiled in Sindh.

It is firmly believed that Fakhri had already completed this female biographical directory by the year 1554 or 1555 CE. In the meanwhile, he received the news of Akbar's accession to the throne, so he decided to leave Sindh and start his journey towards the Mughal capital in search of a new place to settle. After his arrival at the Mughal court, Fakhri changed the dedicatee's name in the preface and altered some of the verses as well. He included a *qasida* in praise of Maham Anga (aka Mah Anga) and as mentioned above dedicated the book to her. Fakhri also praised Akbar's queen, Salima Sultan Begum and secured her patronage. He stayed at the capital till 1562 CE.

According to Springer, the year of compilation of the *Jawahir al-Aja'ib* is 1540 CE, which he erroneously deciphered from a couplet in the preface.[175] Springer wrongly stated that this book was dedicated by Fakhri to Muhammad Isa Tarkhan, the then ruler of Sindh, hence his mistake.[176] Dr Shamsullah Qadri suggests that it was compiled between the years 1556 and 1562 CE. Syed Hussamuddin Rashidi firmly believes that this book had been compiled by June 1555 CE and Fakhri dedicated it to Haji Mah Begum at the time when she was getting married to Mirza Isa Tarkhan after observing her *iddah* (mandatory period of waiting observed by a Muslim widow before she can remarry). Later, the author migrated to Delhi during the reign of Akbar, who had ascended the throne in June 1556 CE.[177] Dr Syed Ali Raza Naqvi also agreed on the date designated by Syed Hussamuddin.[178]

In the brief preface of this book, the author highlights the purpose of compilation. He states that for a long time he had wished to dedicate one of his works in honour of Emperor Akbar. One night, while he was reading the *Tuhfat al-Habib*, he came on the *ghazal* of Mehri of which the opening verse is as follows:

حل هر نکته که بر پیر خرد مشکل بود   آزمودیم بیک جرعه می حاصل بود[179]

This suggested a new possibility to the author. He changed the preface of his book and wrote the following verse:

کا هی بملازمت بلقیس زمان رفیع مکان و همای دوران ...
حاجی بیگم اید الله تعالی عمره و دولته میر سیدم.[180]

Translation: Sometimes I was honoured by the company of... Haji Begum. One day on my return I was so pleased and excited that I decided to dedicate this book to her.

Thus, after much deliberation, he decided to dedicate *Jawahir al-Aja'ib* to Haji Mah Begum (Daughter of Muhammad Muqeem Arghun),[181] altered the preface with the above verse, and changed the name to *Tadhkirat al-Nisa*. Fakhri also included some eulogising couplets (*qasidas*) for Akbar on the celebrated occasion of his coronation, in order to present the book at Akbar's court.[182] The author further added a panegyric to Haji Mah Begum at the end and mentions her name in another elegy in the book as well.

Fakhri had previously also made similar alterations in the couplets of one of his books and rededicated it; this was his work *Lata'if Nama*, which he had originally dedicated to Darmish Khan and later assigned it to Shah Hasan in the *Rawzat al-Salatin*.[183] In this book, there were also two couplets in praise of Shah Ismail Safavid, in which he revised and pledged to Shah Tahmasp in *Jawahir al-Aja'ib* when the latter ascended the throne after the death of his father Shah Ismail.[184]

In the new preface of *Jawahir al-Aja'ib*, Fakhri narrates the accounts of his arrival and stay in Sindh, but he did not mention anything about his service of sixteen years to Shah Hasan.

This work also begins in the name of God, followed by a preface. The book has no index, and no chapters. However, the text subsequently follows headings as titles or names of poetesses. The accounts of the poetesses are rather brief. Dates are rarely mentioned. The text contains examples of verses composed by these poetesses, starting from Dil Aaram to Nisa'i. The author includes two poetesses of the Turkic language as well.

Fakhri writes Persian prose in a florid style, which was the style of all cultured people not only in India, but in Persia too. He frequently uses ornate and elaborate words, and expressions following the contemporary trend.

However, the information in *Jawahir al-Aja'ib* is brief like that of *Rawzat al-Salatin*, but its originality and value are unsurpassed. It is distinct in its genre because of the uniqueness of its subject. Although other writers had also compiled works of poetesses, such as Awfi, who discussed a famous poetess named Rabia Khuzdari and Daulat Shah, who give accounts of two poetesses named Mahasti and Jahan Khatoon in their works, Fakhri is regarded as the pioneer as he deals with thirty-one poetesses in his unprecedented work and tries to make a more or less comprehensive directory on the subject. He opened new vistas for forthcoming *tadhkira* writers. The example he set was followed by his successors like Radhi, Taqi Kashi, Taqi Awhadi, Wala Daghistani, Sher Khan Lodhi, and Lutf Ali A'azar. Among these compilers A'azar and Sher Khan thereafter reserved a chapter for poetesses at the end of their books. A'azar gives accounts of eight poetesses, while Sher Khan discusses fifteen.

There is a controversy in Islam regarding poetry. Some orthodox schools maintain poetry is forbidden. Fakhri Harawi justifies composing verses in Islam. Awfi and Daulat Shah Samarqandi have also upheld that poetry is permissible. Fakhri states that once the Holy Prophet (PBUH) made corrections in a verse composed by Hazrat Ayesha (RA). He quotes the *Bostan* of Abu al-Layth Faqir as his reference, he writes:

> ...And Abu al-Layth Faqir, who was also dubbed Abu Hanifa the second, wrote in his book, titled, Bostan... One day, the relatives of Hazrat Aisha [RA] requested her to be their guest. She obtained permission from the Holy Prophet [PBUH] to be their guest. Upon receiving the permission, she became their guest and graced the occasion. On the event, she recited a couplet.[185]

Here, Fakhri mentions the couplets composed by Hazrat Zulaykha (RA), Hazrat Ayesha (RA), and Hazrat Fatima al-Zehra (RA) respectively, while he justifies legitimacy of composing poetry in Islam. Some of such couplets are given below for instance:

اتینا کم اتینا کم فحیونا نحییکم   فلو لا العجوۃ السوداء ما کنا بوادیکم
فلو لا طاعۃ الرحمن ما کنا بوادیکم[186]
صبت علی مصائب لوانها   صبت علی الایام صرن لیالیا[187]

The *Jawahir al-Aja'ib* provides sufficient record for the upcoming literature of its kind. Taqi Kashi and Taqi Awhadi utilized this valuable source to a great extent, especially the latter, who extracted a huge amount of substance from this book.[188] These authors mention *Jawahir al-Aja'ib* by the title *Tadhkirat al-Nisa* as it had become famous by this name.

Each manuscript of *Jawahir al-Aja'ib* provides accounts of a different number of poetesses. The manuscript that is in the Royal Library of Oudh gives accounts of twenty lady poets; the text, which was published by Shaykh Abu al-Qasim Mautashim, tells of twenty-three ladies, while Syed Shamsullah Qadri's print deals with twenty-seven poetesses. The manuscript used by Syed Hussamuddin Rashidi has narratives about the maximum number of poetesses, which is thirty-one.

It also includes accounts of Hazrat Zulaykha (AS), Dil Aaram the beloved of King Behram Kor, Badshah Khatoon, Jahan Khatoon Shirazi, Khanum-i-Haram Muhammad Khan Shibani, Ismati Khawafi, Arzu-i-Samarqandi, Hayat Harawi, and Nisa'i, etc. On the other hand, the author doesn't give much significant biographical data about these poetesses. He neither mentions the dates of their births and deaths, nor any details of other famous contemporary personalities and rulers. For this reason, it is difficult to ascertain the periods these ladies lived in.

However, like the *Rawzat al-Salatin*, the *Jawahir al-Aja'ib* does contain several concise biographical accounts and some are such rare anecdotes of the poetesses that this makes this compilation a valuable source of historical information. It shows us that Muslim ladies were very talented and competent. He praises the beauty and charm of Jahan Khatoon as well as her elegance, humour, and perception, which is illustrated by her repartees and jests with Obaid Zakani and the great Persian poet, Hafiz Sherazi (1350–1390 CE).[189] The author also indicates the excellent and perfect command Mehti Ganjwi and Badshah Begum had over composing rhymes.[190] He admires some chaste and pious women for their virtuous conduct, such as Ismati Bibi and Syed Begum.[191]

At places, Fakhri refers to the poetry of some other poets to make a comparative analysis of the meaning, rhyme, and diction; he cites, for instance, verses of Nihani Shirazi and Nisa'i Fakhar al-Nisa.[192] It appears from the narratives in this book that most of the poetesses were insightful, eloquent, jocular, and witty. He especially admires Khanzada Turbati and Purtawi Tibrizi for these qualities.[193]

In praising Khanzadah, he writes that her cordiality was proverbial.[194] For Bicha Munjama, he acclaims that she was noble, good-humoured, and a lady of rare breeding. She was unmatched as far as the knowledge of astrology is concerned.[195] Some poetesses, meanwhile, he praised for their skill and proficiency in composing fine poetry like Afaq Begum Jalayar, Ismati, Syed Begum, Hayati, Nihani, etc. He also points out that some ladies, such as Nisa'i and Nihani Shirazi composed *ghazals* identical to other famous contemporary compositions. The author tells us about the friendly and sociable contacts of these ladies with their contemporary male poets and highlights the congenial literary environment of the era.

It can be said that the author did not select the finest poetry of some of the poetesses. Often, he quoted trite and banal verses that were according to the hackneyed contemporary trend of the time, for example, in the pieces he selects of Mehri, Bicha, Dha'ifi, and others. Even though the author apparently had a good collection of the works of these poetesses to choose from, most of the poetry he cites doesn't reflect feminine sweetness and elegance. However, the author praises his own selection exceedingly and calls it a peerless work.[196]

Thus, the *Jawahir al-Aja'ib* was the last compilation of Fakhri Harawi in Sindh. After spending sixteen or seventeen years in Sindh he migrated to Delhi. He left because of the condition of chaos in Sindh owing to the rivalry and struggle for power between Mirza Isa and Mahmud Bhakkari after the death of Shah Hasan.

In the recent past, the first prints of the *Jawahir al-Aja'ib* were published by Naulakshwar, Lucknow, India. Syed Shamullah Qadri also published its text in an Urdu magazine. With the help of these two, and one other manuscript, Syed Hussamuddin Rashidi edited the *Jawahir al-Aja'ib*. He made corrections, wrote explanatory notes in the text and margins, and it was published by the Institute of Sindhology, University of Sindh, Jamshoro in 1968, in a collective volume. Syed Hussamuddin Rashidi furnished both of the prefaces separately in this book in order to explain the circumstance in which Fakhri changed the title and dedicated it to another personality.

However, after the fall of the Tarkhan dynasty, Sindh became a part of the Mughal Empire in 1591–1592 CE in Akbar's reign. During the Mughal period, Sindh gained political and administrative stability and organisation, and it blossomed in the field of literary pursuits. Akbar was a great patron of learning, art, and literature. He provided economic support to scholars, *ulema*, Syeds, etc. His successors also bestowed stipends on scholars and learned people. Some scholars from Sindh visited the Mughal court during the reign of Shah Jahan and Aurangzeb. For instance, Makhdum Rahmat was invited by Aurangzeb and he was rewarded and appointed *sadr* of Thatta because of his erudition and command over the *mathnawi* of Maulana Rum (a marvellous classic Persian book by Jalal al-Din Rumi, a thirteenth-century Muslim Sufi mystic poet, jurist, and theologian).[197] Subsequently, the links between Sindh and the Imperial court gradually grew closer and more cordial, and a large amount of political and non-political literature on the history of Sindh was thus produced.

CHAPTER 3

Political Literature/Chronicles

The sources of the history of Sindh compiled during the Mughal era were mainly of a political nature. Copious in quantity, the multifarious genres of literature and methods of historiographical research were regarded as a literature with a great potential. With the increase of Mughal power and influence, the production of this literature became more prolific. Mughal interest concentrated on fostering literary and scholarly activities, thus the development of the art of writing history grew rapidly. During the seventeenth and eighteenth centuries, the subcontinent benefited in this regard from this environment. Though the literature produced during this era was deprived of the natural, forceful flow it would have had if it were indigenous to the land, Persian nevertheless began to be widely accepted in Sindh. Sada Rangani writes in this regard:

> The Sindhis rapidly acquired complete grasp over the language and Persian became a meritorious vehicle of expression…Almost all the histories of Sindh e.g. *Tarikh-i-Masumi*, *Beglar Nama*, *Tarikh-i-Tahiri*, etc., were written in Persian and a few *diwans* of *ghazals* were also produced.[1]

In order to secure royal patronage, intellectual and literary activities started to flourish in all parts of Sindh. Despite the departure of some native scholars to other parts of India, the standard of literary activities bequeathed to Sindh by the Turkic conquerors was maintained and in fact contributed to raising the bar. The interchange of poets and scholars with Persia and Central Asia certainly continued for a time, but this finally became dormant. Contacts of Sindh with Persia and Central Asia resulted in the use of Persian as the language of the court and literature, except for occasional local peculiarities. Even though Turkic was the language spoken by the Mughals in their homes, Persian did not lose its importance. The Persian language also gained ground in the field of religious studies that earlier had been exclusively in Arabic for centuries.

An extremely large number of general histories appeared during this era in India, only two of them however, are noteworthy. The first is the *Tarikh-i*

Ilchi-i-Nizamshahi (The History of the Ambassador of Nizamshahi), written by Khawr Shah during the second half of the sixteenth century, and the other is the *Tarikh-i-Alfi* (The History of the Millennium), compiled at the instance of Emperor Akbar on the millennium celebration of the birth of Holy Prophet (PBUH). It was a collective work done by more than ten eminent scholars, among whom Mulla Ahmad Thattawi (d. 1588 CE) was a major contributor and Asaf Khan Jafar Beg and Abdul Qadir Badayuni's participation was significant as well.[2]

The *Tarikh-i-Alfi* was written by a native of Sindh, Mulla Ahmad Nasrullah Thattawi. However, it is not considered a part of the literary assets of the age. The major portion of the *Tarikh-i-Alfi* comprises of a general history of the Muslim rulers from the death of the Prophet Muhammad (PBUH), down to the year 1589 CE. The author with the other members of the panel was unable to complete the book in the required time.[3] Dr A. Haleem highlights the rudimentary nature of this account as he states:

> The method of treatment in the *Tarikh-i-Alfi* is crude and primitive. Like the ancient Greek and early Arab histories, events are compiled serially for each year and the histories of all Muhammadan countries are discussed without a break with only a remark and other events of the same year. It is in fact a descriptive chronological chart in which important events are omitted occasionally.[4]

Imperial patronage encouraged history writing, which was said to have enjoyed a degree of popularity right from the beginning of Mughal rule. The Mughal period in Sindh is significant for its richness in historical literature in the form of contemporaneous political histories. The literary contribution of Sindh comprises several outstanding historical compilations, which are no less significant than work compiled in other parts of the Mughal Empire. This extensive list of historical chronicles includes numerous illustrious histories, such as the *Tarikh-i-Sindh* alias *Tarikh-i-Masumi*, *Beglar Nama*, *Tarikh-i-Tahiri*, *Tarkhan Nama*, *Tarikh Mazhar-i-Shahjahani*, and *Intikhab-i-Muntakhib* (*Intikhab Nama*). From this historical literature of political nature, much valuable information can be gleaned.

Tarikh-i-Sindh alias *Tarikh-i-Masumi*

The *Tarikh-i-Sindh* (The History of Sindh), commonly known as the *Tarikh-i-Masumi* (History by Mir Masum), is considered one of the earliest and most valuable general histories written in Sindh. It is regarded as one of the most significant works on regional history in medieval India. This book was written by Mir Muhammad Masum Shah Bhakkari, also known as Syed Nizamuddin Mir Muhammad Masum, during the reign of Akbar.[5] Other notable works contemporary to the *Tarikh-i-Sindh* and compiled in other parts of India, are *Tabaqat-i-Akbari*, a history of India from the early Muslim invasions to the thirty-eighth year of the reign of Akbar (*c*. 1593–1594 CE); *Akbar Nama* (Book of Akbar, *c*. 1596 CE); *Zubdat at-Tawarikh* (The Best of all Histories, *c*. 1605 CE); *Tarikh-i-Firishta* (History by Firishta,[6] *c*. 1609–1610 CE, which is about the rise of Muslim power in India till the year 1610 CE); *Ma'athir-i-Rahimi* (*c*. 1616 CE, Rahimi was a contemporary biographer); and *Muntakhab at-Tawarikh* (The Selection of Chronicles, *c*. 1646–1647 CE).

It may be noted that another book with the same title as the *Tarikh-i-Masumi* was written in Bengal by a historian named Muhammad Masum bin Hasan bin Salih in 1660 CE, on the history of Bengal. This book includes biographical accounts of Shah Shuja, elucidating the events of the war of succession in which Shuja marched against his brothers.[7]

Regarding the famous book on the history of Sindh, *Tarikh-i-Masumi* by Mir Masumi, the author mentions his name in the preface and credits himself for undertaking this compilation:

اما راقم این صحیفه محمد معصوم المتخلص به 'نامی' بن سید صفائ الحسینی الترمذی...، را مدتسیت که در خاطر فاتر این معنی خطور میکرده که شمه ای از وقائع فتح و احوال حکام سند در قید کتابت در آورد۔[8]

Translation: The author of this book, Muhammad Masum alias 'Nami' son of Syed Safa'i al-Hussaini al-Tirmizi…, a brief account of the rulers of Sindh and their conquests has been compiled in this book.

Some other contemporary inscriptions, such as the *Chahal Zeena* (Forty Steps), named after a flight of stairs carved in the side of a mountain to the north-west of Qandahar, by order of the Mughal Emperor Babur, also mentions the name of Mir Masum:

در زمانی که اعلی حضرت خاقانی حکومت قندهار را به نواب نامدار شاه بیگ خان کابلی مفوض فرموده بودند، بندۀ درگاه محمد معصوم ... در سلک امراء نامدار بکومک قندهار آمد۔[9]

Translation: At the time when His majesty entrusted the command of Qandahar to the renowned Nawab Shah Beg Khan Kabuli; Muhammad Masum, a renowned commander came to Qandahar to help him out.

Mir Masum's father, Syed Safa'i al-Hussaini al-Tirmizi al-Bhakkari, was a descendent of Baba Hasan Abdal Sabzwari from his mother's side, whose family stayed in Qandahar.[10] S.H. Hodiwala refers to an inscription engraved under the author's supervision on the Buland Darwaza at Fatehpur Sikri, which also reveals that Mir Masum was a descendant of Baba Hasan Abdal. Thus, he was obviously proud of his ancestry.[11] Mir Masum's family basically belonged to Tirmiz, from where his father migrated to Qandahar. Later on, his father Syed Safa'i came to Bhakkar and joined the services of Sultan Mahmud Khan (d. 1574 CE). There he married in the family of Syeds of Khabrut (near Sewistan) and had three sons; the youngest one, born on 7 February 1538 CE, was Mir Muhammad Masum.[12] After the death of Shah Qutub al-Din Harawi (d. 1563 CE), the *Shaykh al-Islam*[13] of Bhakkar, Sultan Mahmud appointed Syed Safa'i in that position until his death in 1583 CE.

Mir Masum sought to supplement and complete the 'Great Qandahar Inscription' that was engraved under the direction of his father, commemorating the conquest of Qandahar. Qandahar was the only part of Babur's dominion that was mentioned in the original epigraph and the primary object of inscribing it had been to record and commemorate the conquest of the great stronghold. Subsequently, Qandahar was again lost by Humayun and won back by Akbar and this time Masum's son, the author, thought it to be appropriate to have another inscription engraved in the citadel, in which the names of all the other prominent cities, towns, and districts that comprised the Mughal Empire, from Orissa and Gaur-Bangala in the East, to Bandar Lahri and Thatta in the West, were carved.[14]

Conversely, the accounts of Masum's early life and education are not available. Badayuni states that he was a meticulous student who possessed a refined taste for Persian poetry, under the pen name of 'Nami'.[15] He remained busy in acquiring knowledge of theology after the death of his father. He secured an early education from the eminent scholars of his time, such as Mulla Muhammad of Kangri, Qazi Datta of Sewistan, and Shaykh Hameed of Darbela.[16] Besides other literary activities, he was very fond of hunting. He was first associated with the court of Sultan Mahmud Khan of Bhakkar (d. 1508 CE), a subsidiary of the Arghun and Tarkhan rulers of Sindh.

After the death of his father, Mir Masum migrated to Gujarat, where he developed friendly relations with Khawaja Nizam al-Din Ahmad, the author of *Tabaqat-i-Akbari*, then joined the Mughal services as *diwan* (the finance minister) of Gujarat. He was first elevated to the *mansab* (rank) of *yak hazari*[17] (one thousand) in 1584 CE and afterwards promoted to the *mansab* of *panj hazari* (five thousand).[18] A *jagir* (land grant) was also assigned to him at Bhakkar, including the *parganas*[19] of Darbela, Kakari, and Chanduka.[20] He participated in many battles with Akbar and Abdul Rahim Khan-i-Khanan, where he showed bravery and chivalry. Akbar also sent him to the court of the Safavids of Persia as his ambassador. At the time, he was conferred the imperial title and elevated to the post of *Amin al-Mulk*[21] by Akbar.[22] In 1598, he was appointed the governor of Sindh and Sibi by Akbar. After the death of Akbar, Jahangir appointed him as *Amin al-Mulk* of Bhakkar.[23] He retired from the imperial services in 1606 CE, left the post to his son, and went to Qandahar, where he died in 1610 CE.

Mir Masum was an eminent historian, poet, traveller, physician, soldier, diplomat, and epistolographer of his era. He has shown his excellence in every field. He composed a *qasida* (eulogy) on the occasion of Emperor Jahangir's enthronement. He also wrote two *diwans* of *ghazals* comprising five thousand verses, a *Diwan-i-Ruba'iyat*, the *Saqi Nama*, and a *khamsa* containing twelve thousand verses, a collection of five *mathnawis* having titles of *Husn wa Naz*, *Madan al-Afkar*, *Pari Surat*, *Akbar Nama*, and *Haft Naqsh* for which he took inspiration from Shaykh Nizami Ganjawi. These works are regarded as great literary assets of Sindh. Masumi used the pen name of '*Nami*' as a poet, which he also mentioned in the preface of his book, the *Tarikh-i-Sindh*.[24]

This *nom de plume* is also written on many epitaphs at different places in Sindh, such as the mosque of *Eidgah*[25] of Bayana and epigraphs inscribed by the author's son, Mir Buzurg.[26] Besides the *Tarikh-i-Masumi*, the author compiled some other prose works on different subjects such as the *Tib Nami* (A Book on Medicine by Nami) and *Mufrad'at Nami* (The Affluences of Nami). He was an excellent calligrapher as well. During different military expeditions, he compiled historical narrations at the royal behest, some of which still exist. Ishwari Prasad appraises him as, 'Being a man of versatile genius, he wrote on a number of subjects. He gives the history of the Arghun dynasty and a detailed account of Humayun's wanderings in Sindh.'[27]

Since Mir Masum joined the imperial services after the fall of Bhakkar to the Mughals, it seems that he compiled *Tarikh-i-Masumi* in order to provide an authentic record of the conquest of Sindh by his new patrons in 1593 CE, as well as to record the exploits of the previous rulers, such as the Arghuns, Tarkhans, and Sultan Mahmud Khan.[28] As the author himself participated in the final operation against Jani Beg (r. 1585–1593 CE) at Thatta, it was supposed to be a part of his service to record the final story of passing the country of Sindh to the Mughals.

The *Tarikh-i-Masumi* of Mir Masum is regarded as the third historical work compiled in Sindh; the others being the *Chach Nama* and the *Nusrat Nama-i-Tarkhan*. The *Tarikh-i-Masumi* enjoys its status as the foremost account of the history of the Mughal conquest of Sindh. The author allowed his contemporaries, such as the authors of *Beglar Nama*, *Tarikh-i-Tahiri*, and *Tarkhan Nama*, to reproduce narratives from his work.

Nizam al-Din Ahmad (d. 1621 CE) acknowledges *Tarikh-i-Sindh* as one of his sources of information in the preface of his book titled the *Tabaqat-i-Akbari*, a general history of India for the first thirty-eight years of Akbar's reign (till 1593 CE).[29]

With limited source material, Masumi undertook the task of writing a comprehensive history of Sindh so earnestly that no other source on the history of this province is styled with this epithet, i.e. *Tarikh-i-Sindh*. Besides, some other Arabic works written outside India, the *Chach Nama* was the only available source that could provide a record to Masumi of the history before the Arab period. The *Tarikh-i-Sindh* was written in *c.* 1600 and the *Tabaqat-i-Akbari*, in *c.* 1593–1594. It may be noted that certain chapters of the *Tarikh-i-Sindh* and the *Tabaqat-i-Akbari*, particularly relating to the early history of Sindh are, to a great extent, identical, as if one is a verbatim reproduction of the other.[30] This proves that certain parts of Masumi's *Tarikh-i-Sindh* that had probably been compiled earlier than 1593–1594 CE, must have been incorporated by Nizam al-Din in his *Tabaqat-i-Akbari*.

Masumi himself mentions only three books as his sources: the *Tarikh Mir'at al-Jinan* (The Mirrors of Paradise), *Tarikh-i-Guzida* (The Select History), and the *Chach Nama*.[31] But a thorough study of the book reveals that the author also benefited from other authentic Persian and Arabic sources, such as *Futuh al-Buldan* (The Book of the Conquests of the Lands) *Tarikh-i-Yaqubi* (The History by Yaqubi), *Tabaqat-i-Nasiri*, *Tarikh-i-Ferozshahi* (The History of Sultan Feroz Shah), *Tarikh Tabaqat-i-Bahadurshahi* (The Categories of the Bahadurshahis), *Tarikh-i-Mubarakshahi* (The History of the Mubarakshahis), *Tabaqat-i-Akbari*, etc.[32] It also appears from the text that the author borrowed information from the *Chach Nama* for the history of the Arab and pre-Arab periods of Sindh, and the *Rawzat al-Safa* (Garden of Purity) and *Habib al-Siyar* (The Friend of Biographies) for the history of the Arghuns.[33] Masumi's work has been extensively used by many successive historians like Badayuni, Ali Sher Qani, and the authors of the *Ma'athir al-Umara* (The Biographies of the Mughal Officers), *Mir'at-i-Dawlat-i-Abbasia* (Mirror of the Abbasid Rule), and *Bagh-Mani* (Garden of Manes), in fact, it served as their main source and these authors largely benefitted from this work. This ample use and utility of the *Tarikh-i-Masumi* as a source by later historians substantiates its value as an authentic and reliable source.

Mir Masum does not mention the date of compilation of the book, but at places, the text plausibly led later historians to fix the date of its composition to around 1600–1601 CE.[34] Though Masumi's *Tarikh-i-Sindh* was completed after Nizam al-Din's *Tabaqat*, Abu al-Fazl's *Akbar Nama* and Badayuni's *Muntakhib al-Tawarikh* and all other contemporary works, are subsequent to Masumi's *Tarikh*. The chronology appears to be self-evident and the dates of composition of these works and their sequence should not, therefore, have been open to question, or doubt.[35]

The author mentions in the preface that he compiled his *Tarikh-i-Sindh* for the benefit and guidance of his son, Mir Buzurg. The author wanted him to learn from the wisdom of his ancestors; to distinguish right from wrong and what is useful from useless.[36] However, this statement does not seem genuine as the book is not of a didactic nature. Rather, it is an account of political history; a narrative of facts and events written with a literary flourish, as was the fashion amongst the medieval literati of the era. The knowledge of the author about contemporary events is reliable and mostly based on first-hand accounts.

The book is divided into four chapters. The first is about the pre-Muslim history of Sindh and its conquest by the Muslims; the part that covers the rule of Arab governors, all the way up to Haroon al-Rashid's period, is very sketchy and based completely on the *Chach Nama*. The second chapter is related to the history of Sindh during the Sultanate of Delhi, most of the information is derived from earlier sources, such as the *Tarikh-i-Mubarakshahi*, *Tabaqat-i-Nasiri*, and *Tarikh-i-Ferozshahi*, consequently, it is not of much historical worth.[37] Some parts of the second chapter about the history of the Soomras and the Sammas are drawn from the *Tarikh Tabaqat-i-Bahadurshahi* of Hussam Khan that most probably is the first work on this topic. Nizam al-Din and Firishta also benefited from this work for the early history of Sindh (Thatta) and Multan and acknowledge their gratitude to it as their source.

On the other hand, Mir Masum, who borrowed accounts from the *Tarikh Tabaqat-i-Bahadurshahi*, for the history of the Soomras and the Sammas, neither mentions it as a source nor refers to its author's name. The information on this period may not be considered as being very authentic and is contradictory to the original sources. The third chapter deals with the history of the Arghuns and the Tarkhans and a detailed account of Humayun's stay in Sindh. The fourth chapter is devoted to Akbar's conquest of Sindh in 1592 CE. This chapter is the core subject of the book, which may rightly be regarded as the author's main contribution based on his eyewitness and authentic accounts and valuable records.[38]

The *Tarikh-i-Masumi* furnishes a diverse account of the causes of the Arab invasion of Sindh, one that is significantly different from other sources. According to this book, the Umayyad Caliph Walid bin Abdul Malik employed some Syrians to purchase Indian slave girls and Indian products. These Arabs were assaulted and kidnapped by sea-pirates from Debal, the major seaport of Sindh. Walid sent an expedition to recover these people. Masumi writes:

> In the days of Abdul Malik, the caliph appointed assistants in Sindh for buying Indian slave-girls and other goods; accompanying some Syrian traders they entered Sindh, and the slave-girls and goods which they needed were brought and they sailed through the sea. When they reached at the port of Debal, which is now known as the port of Thatta and Lahri, a band of sea-pirates attacked and killed most of them. The rest of the people became hostage...and the caliph sent an army to take revenge on the accused clan.[39]

This account is contrary to the *Chach Nama* and the other Arab sources, such as the *Futuh al-Buldan* of Baladhuri, which state that the reason for the invasion was that ships carrying orphans and widows of some Arab traders sailing from Ceylon were attacked and plundered near the coast of Debal. Since Raja Dahir, the Brahman ruler of Sindh refused the demand of Hajjaj bin Yousuf, the then Umayyad viceroy of Iraq, regarding compensation and reparation of the women, the latter decided to send an expedition against him.[40] One may also find some divergence in the text, with the records of some other sources, particularly the *Chach Nama*, about the accession of Raja Dahir[41] and the definite advance of Muhammad bin Qasim's expedition in Sindh.[42] The *Tarikh-i-Masumi* also mentions the myth that was considered a fact at that time, about the execution of Muhammad bin Qasim by Caliph Suleiman, due to a fake charge made by the daughters of Raja Dahir.[43]

The dynastic list of the Samma rulers given by Masum is very similar to that given in the *Tabaqat-i-Akbari*, the *Tarikh-i-Firishta*,[44] and the *A'in-i-Akbari*, but the names and regal periods are not identical and all of them are derived from the *Tarikh-i-Bahadurshahi* of Hussain Khan Gujrati, similar to that recorded in the *Tabaqat-i-Akbari*, which the author admits truthfully.[45] The initial date is not stated anywhere and the discrepancies make it difficult to construct anything with exact chronology. But a fairly correct list can be drawn on the basis of three and four fixed dates, such as the dates of accession of Jam Unar (1335–1336 CE), Fath Khan (1398–1399 CE), and Jam Nanda (1461–1462 CE) and his death (1508 CE). Jam Nanda's ascension and death are two points about which the provincial and imperial history agree and are certainly determined.[46]

Masum also removes a pitfall, as Muhammad Tahir and others also did, about the name of Jam Babaniya to have been the name of not only the father of Jam Unar, the founder of the Samma dynasty but also of that of its most renowned member, Jam Nizam al-Din Nanda.[47] Masum erroneously indicates that Sikandar, Karan, and Fath Khan were the sons of Jam Tamachi, while it is stated in Dowson's version that Fath Khan was Sikandar's son and not Tamachi's.[48]

The date of the succession of Jam Nizam al-Din Nanda after the death of Jam Sanjar, mentioned by Masum, is 1461–1462 CE/866 AH. Qani also corroborates Jam Nanda's tenure of forty-eight years, starting from 1461, to 1508 CE (866 to 914 AH). On the other hand, Nizam al-Din Ahmad and Firishta assert that he reigned for sixty-two years. However, that may not be correct, as it would leave no time for the reign of Jam Feroz, which lasted from 914 to 928 AH. In the inscription on Jam Nanda's tomb at Thatta, it is stated that the foundation stone was laid in 1509 CE/915 AH. The year of death is not stated, but clearly that event had taken place sometimes before, most probably in 1508 CE/914 AH.[49]

Mir Masum's account substantially corroborates that of Ibn Battuta (who visited Sindh in 1333 CE during the Samma rule) on many instances, including the suppression of a tribal rebellion that was centred around Sehwan.[50] The revolt rose due to the undeserved nomination of a Hindu accountant named Ratan as castellan of Sehwan by Sultan Muhammad bin Tughluq. Consequently, the Samma chief, Unar, and a nobleman named Qaisar, joined hands and attacked Ratan at night and killed him. Subsequently, Unar took refuge with his tribe, while Qaisar was executed by imperial forces. The Sultan soon re-established his authority through his military chief, Imad al-Mulk.[51] The author also sheds light on cordial diplomatic relations between Mahmud Khan of Bhakkar and Shah Tahmasp Safavid of Persia (the former conferred the latter with the title of Khan-i-Khanan).[52]

The accounts in this book about the campaign of Shah Hasan Arghun against the Langah rulers of Multan and their struggle is unique and worth mentioning.[53] The detailed description of the Mughal campaign against Sultan Mahmud Khan of Bhakkar and its subsequent administration by imperial functionaries offers rare insight into the matter.[54] The narratives about the Mughal commander and Mir Gesu Khan, Governor of Bhakkar, are worthy of acclaim. The author calls him مرد تند مزاج و بدخوئ (an ill-tempered and malicious person).[55] Gesu Khan muddled things up and was unable to extirpate the rebels in Bhakkar. He was hated by the Mughals and the Sindhis alike, due to his atrocities and misconduct. His failure infuriated Akbar, who replaced him with Tarsun Muhammad Khan as the *Fawjdar*[56] of Bhakkar, in April 1575 CE. This quality of portraying a considerably realistic picture of the Mughal administration distinguishes *Tarikh-i-Masumi* from all other contemporary sources.

The *Tarikh-i-Masumi* possesses a substantial quantity of historical information as compared to other regional histories, yet it has its shortcomings. The author doesn't acknowledge some of the sources he utilized (for instance, *Habib al-Siyar*) and he does not appear to have consulted any Arabic sources for the conquest of Sindh. Apart from this, he does not properly reproduce the information previously given by the *Tabaqat-i-Akbari* and *Ma'athir-i-Rahimi*. For instance, the story of Jam Khayr al-Din, narrated by Masum is incorrect. Rather, it seems identical to the story of Kabak or Kapak, the son of Dawa, Khan of the race of Chughtai, who was the son of Genghis, in an old history of the Mongols, titled the *Shajrat al-Atrak*.[57]

Furthermore, in the closing segment of his, book there are several lapses in dates. One that is very noteworthy is on the last page, where the author does not mention the date of Mirza Jani Beg's arrival at the imperial court of Akbar. Mirza Jani Beg's defeat and surrender was in 1593 CE. Masum is said to have completed his book in 1601 CE, so he was very much present at the time. He ends his book with the observation: 'And taking Jani Beg with him, he set out for attack and on ... they met his Highness'.[58]

From the last few lines that cover the period 1593 to 1601 CE, we may assume that this portion has been written by some other person. Another, though a less likely possibility, is that it was a lapse on the part of the author himself, because he did not give this part much attention, since he was otherwise occupied, having been called upon by the emperor to go on a diplomatic mission to Shah Abbas Safavid of Persia in 1601–1602 CE.[59] The first rationale for this assumption is that this period of eight years has been dealt with in a manner that does not match the nature and style of the rest of the book. The second is the important date relating to the death of Mirza Jani Beg is also not mentioned. Surely, an author like Masum would not have made such an oversight.

In fact, the whole text of *Tarikh-i-Sindh* is not chronologically arranged in some places and some chapters lack cohesion, particularly those regarding the history of the Delhi Sultanate.[60] Furthermore, some major accounts, like the war between Jani Beg and Abdul Rahim Khan-i-Khanan are missing, while certain events have been repeated in the chapters that follow. Sometimes, the dates of the same event do not correspond to each other and at places the author's simple and smooth language and style becomes ornate and complex. All these factors lead us to infer that the author had composed different parts and chapters of his book at different times and possibly at different places, and under different circumstances. The last few sentences describing the end of Mirza Jani Beg's exciting career in 1601 CE, seem to be a piece of scribbling that might have been added to the original text. As mentioned above, the author does not mention the year of his death and only writes, 'On the 25 Rajab, Mirza Jani Beg died of brain fever'.[61] On the other hand, Abu al-Fazl mentions the exact date as 25 Rajab 1009 AH/30 January 1601 CE.[62] The date given by Masum is identical to the date given by Abu al-Fazl. In actuality, the Tarkhan died of excessive drinking which brought on paralysis and delirium tremens.[63] There is no truth in the report that Akbar had Jani Beg poisoned on account of his having made an indiscreet remark in connection with the capture of Asirgarh.[64]

Along with political information, Masumi's account offers a good deal of information about the fauna and flora of Sindh. It describes the beasts, buildings, crops, and rites and rituals of Sindh. For instance, it tells us that the horses found in Arakan (situated between Siwi, Bhakkar, and Sitapur) were not inferior in any way to Arab steeds.[65] The author also states that, near Siwi, the cotton plants were as tall as berry trees. People had to climb over them to pluck the cotton and snakes abounded in this area.[66]

Furthermore, he describes the engagement of Sultan Mahmud with Taj Khanum, the daughter of Tardi Beg in 1557 CE, which was celebrated with great jubilation like a festival. The buildings, bazaars and streets were illuminated with lights and festooned with decorations. A lavish dowry was given to the bride.[67] The author gives descriptions of the renowned contemporary personalities with special reference to the *ulema*, scholars, poets, saints, *qazis*, Syeds, and Shaykh, famous places, architecture, festivals, and rituals of Sindh.[68] He expresses the profound devotion and deep love the Sufi mystics and *ulema* had for the common people. In this regard, he writes about the virtuous deeds of Shaykh Hammad Qureshi and Shaykh Roohullah, the famous Sufi saints of Sindh: 'Shaykh Roohullah son of Shaykh Hammad Qureshi, was one of the greatest saints and his inspirational tomb has been a place of circumambulation for devotees'.[96]

Such historical accounts about religious, literary, and scholarly life cannot be found in any other source. The author tells us about the Syeds and *ulema* of Bhakkar, who were contemporary to Sultan Mahmud Khan, such as Shah Qutub al-Din Muhammad, Mir Syed Safa'i, Shaykh Mir Ghaurmani, Maulana Abdullah Mufti, Qazi Dawood, Mir Muhammad Purani, Mir Abu Mukarim, Makhdum Qazi Usman, and Maulana Qasim Diwan, etc.[70] Here, he quotes some self-composed verses which he composed on the demise of his father Mir Syed Safa'i. These odes highlight his poetic excellence, revealing his eternal devotion and love for him:

شاه قریشی سید صفائ   کافراخت فلک لو ای نورش
ناگاه ازین جهان فانی   افتاد بآن جهان عبورش
تاریخ چو جستمش ز نامی   گفتا "بر نور باد گورش"[71]

1191 AH (1777 CE)

> Translation: Shah Qureshi, the pure Syed; the sky raised high his flag of light. All of a sudden he passed away from this world to enter the eternal world. As I look beyond the date (of his demise) for his name, a voice cries: May his grave be filled with light.

The *Tarikh-i-Masumi* is unique as it also provides description of the geography and topography of different regions of Sindh. It includes ethnic descriptions of the Baloch and other native tribes of the province, like the Samijas, Jarijas, Darijas, Korai, Lohana, Sehta, Machi, Koricha, Haler, Jats, Khokhars, and Channas that helps us learn about several historical places that do not exist any longer.[72]

The book's narrative is largely straightforward and concise in style, but in places it becomes ornate and complex. However, overall, he does not indulge in unnecessary details and gives a great deal of interesting and relevant information that makes the book an authentic and valuable source. Dr M.H. Siddiqui pays tribute to *Tarikh-i-Masumi*, stating:

> Mir Masum was unrivalled in his knowledge of history and his *Tarikh-i-Masumi* is an everlasting monument of his talents in this field.[73]

Dr Saleem Akhtar, commenting on the information given by the author, writes:

> Mir Masum's writings suffer from insufficient care about dates and consistency, an inadequate acknowledgement of sourced and, largely

as a result of an attempt to encapsulate history, a lack of perspective...
his description of events is not as adequate as that of *Ma'athir-i-Rahimi*
and *Akbar Nama*, or even the comparatively brief treatment of the
Tabaqat-i-Akbari...even with all these defects, the value of *Tarikh-i-Sindh*, as the earliest history of the Arghuns and Tarkhans, can hardly be
overemphasized.[74]

Despite some lacunas, the value and authenticity of *Tarikh-i-Masumi*
cannot be denied, as it covers over a millennium of Sindh's history. It
starts from the Rai dynasty (*c.* 484 CE) and goes all the way to the Mughal
conquest of Sindh in 1591 CE.

Beglar Nama (The Book of Beglar)

Within a decade after the completion of the *Tarikh-i-Sindh*, also known as
Tarikh-i-Masumi of Mir Muhammad Masum of Bhakkar, another scholar
from Sindh, Idraki Beglari, undertook the task of writing a biography
of his patron, Amir Khan-i-Zaman Shah Qasim (1540–1610 CE), under
the title of *Beglar Nama*.[75] The author wrote this book at the instance of
Khan-i-Zaman Shah Qasim Beglar.[76] After the death of his benefactor, he
completed the book around 1623 CE with the constant encouragement and
patronage of Khan-i-Zaman's sons and successors, Amir Abu al-Qasim
Beglar Sultan and Shah Muqim Sultan.

Unfortunately, we don't have enough information about the life and
career of the author. Almost all the information about his life is based upon
assumptions. Though most of the earlier scholars accredited the authorship
to Idraki,[77] a few mistakenly stated it was Abu al-Qasim Khan-i-Zaman
Arghun who was the benefactor of the author.[78] However, besides this
major work, Idraki Beglari also composed numerous poetic works with
the pen name 'Idraki'. Mir Ali Sher Qani quotes one of his couplets in
his *Maqalat al-Shuara*:

چو ادراکی غلام درگه اوست   مطیع لطف و بیگه اوست
همیشه از خدا خواهد حیاتش   بود از جان غلام التفاتش[79]

His date of birth is not known, but he was born in Thatta and belonged
to the Beglar clan of the Arghuns, a Turkish tribe of Samarqand.[80] Qani
mentions that 'Idraki Beglari was from the Turkic Arghun tribe.'[81]

The author acquired knowledge of the Quran, hadith, fiqh, Arabic
and Persian grammar and composition, and mastered all these subjects

in addition to other academic disciplines of the time. It is evident that he had a close association with Amir Shah Qasim and later joined his services. Here, he decided to compile the biographical account of his patron. In addition, he composed a *mathnawi* with the title of *Chanesar Nama* (c. 1601–1602 CE). This *mathnawi* is based on a romantic folklore of Sindh. The author also dedicated this book to his master, Amir Abu al-Qasim Beglar, son of Shah Qasim. The date of its compilation is 1601 CE, which is mentioned in a couplet.[82] Although the date of the author's death is not confirmed, it is believed to be 1625 CE, because the author mentions the date of his patron, Abu al-Qasim Beglar's demise, in his book, which is 1623 CE and it is an acknowledged fact that he was alive when it happened.[83] He is most likely buried in Nasarpur, where he spent almost all of his life and which was the *jagir* and centre of the Beglars in Sindh.[84]

The exact year of the compilation of the *Beglar Nama* is not known, but it seems that it was started before 1608 CE and completed around 1623 CE. It appears from the text that the book was written in two parts: the first part, up until chapter 31, was compiled in 1608 CE (1017 AH), as the author mentions in the text:

اکنون بتاریخ یک هزار و هفده سال عمر شریف حضرت که روز افزون و از شمار بیرون باد بهفتاد سال رسید بر مسند دولت تکیه فرموده بر بستر استراحت اسوده۔[85]

> Translation: At present in 1017 AH, the age of Hazrat, may he live long, is seventy years and he sits on the throne, relaxing on the bed of tranquillity.

In chapter 32, which is the last chapter of the book, dealing mainly with the virtues and merits of the successors of Amir Qasim Shah Beglar, the author mentions 1624 CE/1033 AH as the year when Amir Abu al-Qasim Sultan died and he was still engaged in the process of making additions and improvements to his compilation.[86] This infers that the author began writing the main thirty-one chapters of this book before 1608 CE and completed them by 1608 CE when the Sultan was alive. The last chapter, meanwhile, was completed in the year 1624 CE, or soon after. Syed Hussamuddin Rashidi also substantiates this fact in the preface of the *Mathnawi Chanesar Nama*.[87] Dr N.A. Baloch and Syed Hussamuddin Rashidi both infer that the *Beglar Nama* was written in 1608 CE, prior to the *Tarikh-i-Tahiri*.[88]

The book was written with two main purposes in mind. The author wrote it on the orders of Shah Qasim, son of Amir Syed Qasim Beglar, who wanted to preserve the saga of valour and gallantry of his ancestors and the Tarkhan rulers of Sindh. The document is an account of the historical facts and deeds of the Tarkhans and also those of Amir Shah Qasim Beglar and his successors, particularly Abu al-Qasim Sultan.[89] Idraki Beglari, highlighting the purpose of its compilation in his preface, writes: 'With this intention, he decided to elaborate all the marshal exploits and affliction of His Majesty (Mirza Jani Beg) from his childhood to old age...and most of the events of Sindh, which have taken place from olden times till date in such a way that the text is free from metaphors and flowery language and is comprehensively written.'[09]

The author further mentions the purpose of this book and its title in the preface: 'As this book consists of events and...memorable deeds of "Beglar", therefore the title is given in his name.'[19]

As mentioned above, the book contains thirty-two chapters, along with a preface and a concise preliminary note. It provides a detailed account of the life and times of the Arghun and the Tarkhan rulers and their *amirs*, especially Shah Qasim Beglar. It also throws light on the socio-cultural life of the people of Sindh.

As the *Beglar Nama* is a biography of Shah Qasim, it provides accounts of his life and times, revealing that his complete name was Amir Shah Qasim, son of Abuk Beg, son of Chuchak Beg Lar. He was conferred with the title, Khan-i-Zaman. He belonged to the Beglar tribe, hailing from Samarkand.[92] He was a descendant of Hazrat Ali (RA). His ancestors left their native place and migrated to Tirmiz, from where they further migrated to Samarkand due to the vicissitudes of their fate and upheavals of the era. Malik al-Shuara Suzini composed an ode for them:

سمرقند یثرب شد و مکه ترمذ   ز مکه بیثرب خرامید سید[93]

Translation: Samarqand, Yathrab (Madina), Makkah, and Tirmiz; The Syed gracefully walked from Makkah to Yathrab.

During their stay in Central Asia, they intermingled with the native Turks and established matrimonial links with the Beglars of the Arghuns, who were the descendants of Genghis Khan.[94] After the assassination of Tagha Timur Sultan, Khurasan came under the control of the Mughals; consequently, Amir Qasim Beglar migrated to Sindh during the reign of Mirza Shah Hussain Arghun. Amir Qasim Beglar owed all the prevailing skills and talents. He was an outstanding military commander, horseman, expert at archery, and was famous for his bravery and courage. When he entered the services of Shah Hussain Arghun, he settled in Sindh and married the daughter of the Bhatti Raja of Jaisalmer. Amir Shah Qasim

Beglar was born at Umarkot in Sindh, in the year 1540 CE/947 AH. Soon, his father Amir Qasim Beglar died in 1547 CE/954 AH.

After the death of his father, Amir Shah Qasim's mother raised him and provided him with an education in the arts. He was as talented as his father in equitation, fencing and archery. He had no equal in valour and gallantry. Mirza Shah Hasan Arghun was so impressed by him that he took him under his guardianship. At the age of sixteen, or seventeen, he went to Bhakkar to join the services of Mirza Isa Tarkhan.[95] In the same year, he fought in several battles with his master and showed zeal and courage. For his heroism, he was awarded a high accolade by the rulers of Sindh. Idraki Beglari, not only devoted the first chapter of his book to Amir Shah Qasim, but in almost all the chapters, he praises his patron for his fine qualities and noble virtues, such as generosity, audacious courage, prudence, statesmanship, enlightened mind, etc. He praises him in the following words:

عالی ہمت، پروقار، حلیم پر از مہر و محبت، منبع جود و کرم، باریک بین، روشن رای، قدرشناس، مربی فضلای زمان، شہسوار و تیر انداز ماہر و غیرہم۔

Translation: [He was] highly courageous, full of greatness, forbearing, a fountain of generosity and magnanimity, insightful, broad-minded, appreciative, patron of learned scholars, an expert rider, and archer.

Amir Shah Qasim secured different important positions such as the governorship of different regions. During the reign of Mirza Muhammad Baqi, he held authority over Nasarpur.[96] Subsequently, after the conciliation between Mirza Jani Beg and the Khan-i-Khanan, he visited the court of Emperor Akbar and precious gifts were bestowed on him. He returned in 1592 CE.[97]

Beglar Nama does not mention anywhere the year of Amir Shah Qasim's demise. However, the editor of the book and other sources allege that he died in 1610 CE. He was buried in Tando Allah Yar. Khan-i-Zaman Shah Qasim served under a number of Mughal rulers, such as Mirza Shah Hussain, Mirza Isa Tarkhan, Mirza Muhammad Salih Tarkhan, Mirza Jan Baba Tarkhan, Mirza Muhammad Baqi Tarkhan, Mirza Jani Beg Tarkhan, Emperor Akbar, and Mirza Ghazi Beg. Through *Beglar Nama*, we find out that he had three wives and seven sons: Amir Abu al-Qasim Sultan; Mirza Qasim Sultan; Mir Shah Muqim Sultan; Mir Fath Beg Sultan; Mir Yaran Beg; Mir Salim Khan; and Mir Murad Khan.[98] The most famous amongst all is Amir Abu al-Qasim Sultan, who possessed a refined taste and talent for poetry and logic. He had an outstanding capability of genius and intelligence and went under the pen name, 'Beglar'. He was famous for his bravery, equitation, and swordsmanship, and died in 1624 CE (1033 AH).[99] The author gives a brief background on all his sons, including some details about Mir Shah Muqim Sultan.

While the author does not mention any sources, it is apparent that he mostly relied on what his patron told him while compiling the work. However, his position as an official certainly must have helped him in the collection of evidence and data.

The book is a specimen of an ornate, complex, and over-elaborate writing style. The author frequently uses homophones. He writes:

چون سپاه ظلام با اعلام سیاه فام، بصفت 'واللیل از ادبر'،
پشت داد و خسرو کشور خاور بالطیفہ 'والصبح ازا سفر'،
ظاهر گشت، ورایات ضیا بر صفحہَ غبر انداخت.[100]

In places Arabic expressions and phrases have also been used, which proves the influence of Muslim culture on the author. In his explanations the author presents arguments and evidences from the Quranic verses and the *hadith*. These are couched in elegant Persian prose, interspersed with verses and Arabic maxims. *Beglar Nama* is a durable monument of the skill and proficiency of its author. The enormous use of poetic expressions is deliberate and serves to accentuate the statement and grab the reader's attention. For instance, while elaborating the attributes of Mirza Ghazi Beg, the author recognises his non-proficiency in the language and embellishes the statement with a self-composed stanza:

برون است اوصاف شاه از حساب   نگنجد درین تنگ میدان کتاب
گر این جملہ را سعدی املاکند   مگر دفتر دیگر انشا کند[101]

Translation: The qualities of a king are uncountable, which cannot be mentioned in a book.
If Saadi expresses them in one sentence, he might need another register.

The protagonist of the book is Shah Qasim Khan Beglar, an *amir* of Sindh, around whom the author weaves contemporary history and describes wars and the administrative set-up. This work is not considered an important historical document. It provides a brief history of Sindh till the Tarkhan period. It is mainly significant for having a detailed account of the life and times of Shah Qasim Khan Beglar. It follows the style of the *Shah*

Nama of Firdausi since the author describes the deeds of valour and chivalry of his patron.[102] He also praises him for his generosity, hospitality, justice, and good morals. However, it is more historically genuine and less dramatic and hyperbolic than epics.

Beglar Nama is apparently contemporary to the *Tarikh-i-Masumi* and was written some years prior to the *Tarikh-i-Tahiri*. However, this book is not comparable with *Tarikh-i-Masumi* in its value and historical significance. Rather, it is considered a comprehensive biographical account of Amir Shah Qasim, a Tarkhan nobleman. The *Beglar Nama* also narrates the battles that Shah Qasim fought with Muhammad Salih Tarkhan, Jan Baba, Abdul Baqi Tarkhan, Mahmud Khan (the governor of Bhakkar), and the Khan-i-Khanan, giving complete descriptions and details.[103] It also provides a history of Sindh and a of review of contemporary developments. It is regarded as an important and authentic historical source in understanding the war strategies and military stratagem of the era. At the same time, it provides a reliable and detailed account of the struggle for supremacy between different political powers in Sindh, including the force sent by Akbar under the Khan-i-Khanan to occupy the province.[104] For this reason, the *Beglar Nama* holds an important position among the primary historical sources on Sindh.

Although it is primarily a biographical memoir, it also furnishes information about the internal political struggle and tussle for power of contemporary Tarkhan rulers. Shah Qasim played a vital role in a number of these developments. Besides the political history, the *Beglar Nama* provides an interesting picture of the socio-cultural life of the people of Sindh and details about the native tribes inhabiting different parts of the province, as well as their rituals and customs. In this regard, it is second only to the *Mazhar-i-Shahjahani* (which will be discussed later) in its scope and its attempt to shed light on regional culture.[105] It also describes the geography and topography of Sindh with information about different places, rivulets, and the flora and fauna.[106]

It is evident that the people of Sindh were well acquainted with Persian classical literature. They were fond of reading the poetry of Saadi, Nizami, Ganjwi, including the *mathnawis* and *Shah Nama*. The author himself is influenced to a large extent by the style of *Shah Nama*. For this reason, he uses the names of Persian kings and legendary heroes for similes, such as describing Purzal as Behram Gaur and Khan-i-Zaman as Rustam-i-Dastan. He writes:

> When Purzal rode on the mountain on his horse, he had all the courage and firmness of Bahram who made his horse run in the fields.[107]

At another place, he writes:

> The chivalry, courage, and boldness shown by Khan-i-Zaman, the leader of the brave and valiant of the era in an event that had occurred at that time, was like a story which cannot be found even in the Rustam-i-Dastan and when warriors and brave soldiers hear about it, they are amazed.[108]

Yet despite its biographical value, the *Beglar Nama* suffers from some deficiencies. For instance, it neither gives any information about the origin of the Beglars, nor their migration to Sindh. The author does not mention anything about important events like the demise of Khan-i-Zaman in 1610 CE, or the blinding of Abu al-Qasim Sultan at the instance of Mirza Ghazi Beg. Further, the book does not mention anything about the differences between Mir Abu al-Qasim Sultan and Mirza Ghazi Beg, although the narratives the author writes about Mirza Baqi and Jan Baba are thorough and complete.

Apart from this, the author erroneously cites the name of the ruler of Jaisalmer as Rai Dhar Raj,[109] whereas his actual name was Rawal Har Raj. Abu al-Fazl states that Rawal Har Raj's daughter was married to Akbar in 1569 CE. She gave birth to a daughter named Mahi Begum, who died in the twenty-second year of his reign 1577 CE).[110] Idraki also refers to some places by names that are absolutely corrupted and hence some of them were difficult to identify, such as Nirohi must be Sirohi; Bahalmir must be Bahadmir, also known as Barmer, Balmer, or Badmer in Jodhpur; Kutchh-Nakti is Kutchh-Nagan; Ramdinpur must be Radhanpur near Ahmadabad; and Kotare is Kotra, a town in Jaisalmer.[111]

On the positive side, the *Beglar Nama* presents new and unique information on the battles fought between Mirza Jani Beg Tarkhan and Abdul Rahim Khan-i-Khanan. Also, as mentioned before, the book provides a picture of the geographical structure of the province and the socio-political background of the times. The author was, however, conscious of his mistakes and wrote an addendum to the book. His remarks in the book indicate that in 1608–1609 CE, he was still busy writing this work and afterwards the process of improvement and additions continued up to 1624 CE.

Dr N.A. Baloch states:

> The only other work comparable to *Tarikh-i-Tahiri* is *Beglar Nama* written by Idraki Beglari which also pertains to the Arghun and the Tarkhan period, but it is essentially a biographical work centring on the part played by the author's patron Shah Qasim Khan Arghun (d. 1610 CE) during the Tarkhan

period. In some respects, *Beglar Nama* throws some side-lights and gives details of several internal events, particularly during Mirza Muhammad Baqi's reign, which are not found in *Tarikh-i-Tahiri*.[112]

The historical graveyard of Amir Syed Qasim Khan Beglar was discovered in 1953 CE, in Tando Allah Yar. Photographs of some historical graves and tombs boosted its historical value, the discovery drawing the attention of several historians. Dr Baloch decided to conduct a study of the *Beglar Nama* in detail. Elliot had already reviewed it in the nineteenth century and translated extracts from it. Copies of its manuscript were in Paris, India, and London and were thus out of reach. The only copy that was preserved here was in the royal library of the Talpur Amirs of Sindh, at Tando Muhammad Khan. The Sindhi Adabi Board entrusted the duty of preparing an authentic text of it to Dr Baloch, because the previous manuscripts were not properly rendered and thus required corrections and improvement. Dr Baloch managed to acquire the copy from Paris and edit the text. He wrote a brief note in English and provided an index listing the names of important tribes and personalities. Furthermore, Muhammad Siddique Memon translated its Sindhi version in 1948 CE, which was published by the Sindhi Adabi Board.

Tarikh-i-Baldah-i-Thatta alias *Tarikh-i-Tahiri*

Alongside the *Beglar Nama*, another notable work on the history of Sindh was compiled during the second quarter of the seventeenth century, titled the *Tarikh-i-Baldah-i-Thatta*, but also referred to as the *Tarikh-i-Tahiri*, by the eminent scholar Mir Tahir Muhammad Nisyani, also known as Syed Tahir Muhammad. The author's name is mistakenly recorded as 'Lasyani' in the *Tuhfat al-Kiram*.[113] This work occupies a unique place among all historical accounts of Sindh, because the author was a personal eyewitness to most of the events he has narrated in the book. Thus, the work is a testament to the historical approach of the author.

The author provides several references about his life and family background. Apart from the *Tarikh-i-Tahiri*, there are some other sources, such as the *Tuhfat al-Kiram* and the *Maqalat al-Shuara* of Mir Ali Sher Qani Thattawi, which also provide us with details of the author's life. The latter mentions his name as 'Tahir' and that his major works are *Tarikh-i-Tahiri*; *Naz-o-Niyaz*; and *Abiyat* (poems).[114]

In *Maqalat al-Shuara*, Qani also mentions a chronogram-cum-elegy composed by the author, on the sad demise of his patron, Mirza Ghazi Beg

Tarkhan.¹¹⁵ Qani regarded Tahir as a learned man and a talented poet of his times. Qani's acknowledgement highlights the author's deep interest in literary activities and his preeminent status in contemporary literary circles.

Mir Tahir Muhammad states that his ancestors migrated from Astrabad, Iran, to Sindh, after the occupation of Sindh by Shah Beg Arghun. They settled in Thatta, in the Quarter of Bhai Khan and were associated with Mirza Muhammad Baqi Tarkhan, Mirza Muhammad Pa'inda Tarkhan and Mirza Jani Beg Tarkhan (1544–1585 CE).⁶¹¹ Since his family served the Arghuns and the Tarkhans for three generations, his family members were well-acquainted with the details of all the important events that occurred during the rule of these foreign dynasties in Sindh.¹¹⁷ He belonged to a branch of a Syed family commonly known as the 'Baghai Sahrai Syeds' of Thatta.¹¹⁸

One of the author's family members, Abdul Qadir, joined the services of the Arghun and the Tarkhan rulers and served under Mirza Shah Hasan Arghun (d. 1555 CE) and Mirza Isa Tarkhan (d. 1565 CE).¹¹⁹ His maternal grandfather, Jam Umarshah, was the headman of the local Sahta community, who held valuable property in the district of Darbela. Jam Umarshah and his sons remained in the service of Humayun, while he stayed in northern Sindh during his flight to Persia.¹²⁰ Syed Hasan, the author's father was a 'man of excellent merit', who entered the military service of Mirza Muhammad Baqi Tarkhan (d. 1585 CE) and later continued his services under Mirza Jani Beg. He rose to the rank of commander. He also fought in the battle between Mirza Jani Beg and the Khan-i-Khanan, in 1591–1592 CE, for the Mughal conquest of Sindh.

The author was born in 1582 CE, in Thatta.¹²¹ He grew up under the guardianship of his father, whom he refers to by several names, such as Syed Hasan, Miyan Hasan, and Hasan.¹²² His father imbued religious devotion in him and a love for learning. During the author's childhood, his father Syed Hasan was accused of the murder of Mirza Baqi Tarkhan in 1585 CE but was soon exonerated of this charge with the help of Mirza's faithful servant.

Soon, Syed Hasan became one of the distinguished nobles of Mirza Jani Beg Tarkhan's court. At the time of the Mughal occupation of Sindh, in 1591–1592 CE, Syed Hasan was forty years old and was considered to be one of the most capable commanders stationed at Thatta. Depressed by the defeat of Mirza Jani Beg, Syed Hasan retired from his career.¹²³ After the retirement of his father, Mir Tahir Muhammad entered the services of Mirza Ghazi Beg Tarkhan, in 1601 CE. He accompanied Mirza Ghazi Beg during his visit to the imperial court of Akbar in 1604 CE, where he stayed for some time.[124] He mentions the date of Emperor Akbar's demise in a chronogram composed on the occasion:

در سنه هزار و چهارده که وفاتحضرت خاقان زمان، عرش
آشیانی بود، تاریخ وفاتش در وقت 'فوت اکبر شه' یافته.[125]

1014 AH (1605 CE)

Translation: The demise of His majesty Khan-i-Zaman, whose abode is heaven, took place in 1014 AH (1605 CE). His death took place at the time of Emperor Akbar's demise.

After Jahangir's ascension to the throne in 1605 CE, the author returned to Thatta with the permission of Mirza Ghazi Beg, while the latter was preparing for his journey to Qandahar, where he was appointed as the Mughal governor. At this time, the author discontinued all other activities and devoted himself fully to his studies. Within a very short period, he secured a very good command over Persian poetry and prose. He learned from the most knowledgeable personalities of the time, like Akhund Ishaq Bhakkari, who was a Sufi and very well-versed in the Persian classical works of Hafiz, Saadi, Rumi, and Jami. Subsequently, Mir Tahir Muhammad cultivated his poetic talents under the guidance of his mentor. He also studied the *qasidas*[126] of Khaqani and Anwari under the mentorship of Mir Zahir al-Din, son of Shakrullah Shirazi, and within a year, started to compose verses with the pen name of 'Nisyani'.[127] However, Mir Tahir Muhammad showed more interest in prose than poetry. He again joined the service of the Mughals and provided Mirza Ghazi Beg's campaign in Qandahar with some reinforcement in March 1607 CE.[128]

It is alleged that Mir Tahir Muhammad was then granted leave and allowed to return to Thatta in 1609 CE, when Mirza Ghazi Beg proceeded towards Lahore from Bhakkar on Jahangir's orders, to attend the royal court that was being held there.

Mirza Ghazi Beg died in Qandahar, in 1612 CE. This left a shocking impact on Mir Tahir Muhammad, as he lost his patron and guardian during a precarious political period. The author migrated to Darbela, the home town of his maternal grandfather, Chief Umarshah, where he lived a quiet life for the next six, or seven years. During this period, he pursued his interests in reading and writing. He also compiled the story of Leela/Lilan-Chanesar in Persian prose and successfully collected some source material for his compilation while he searched for a patron.[129] In order to find a patron to sponsor his task of compiling a history of the Arghuns and the Tarkhans, the author attached himself to the entourage of Nawab Shah Beg, alias Khan-i-Dauran, the governor of Qandahar, who belonged to the Arghun family.[130] He writes that it was a contemporary trend for every author to find a benefactor to sponsor their work.[131]

Due to his involvement in other political activities, the author could not find sufficient time to achieve his literary task. Meanwhile, Nawab Shah Beg died in 1621 CE [132] and his son Shah Muhammad Beg succeeded him, after which the author became a devotee of Shah Muhammad Beg. He refers to him as, 'An accomplished and learned man of his times.' Shah Muhammad, who was granted a *mansab* of one thousand six hundred and the governorship of Thatta, was also awarded the title of Adil Khan, by Emperor Jahangir, in 1619–1620 CE.

In his brief career, Adil Khan only attained the post of One Thousand *Hazaria*. In the author's own words:

> I attached myself to my patron just for the sake of writing this history...I left the service of my patron and retired to this unrewarding corner, leading a quiet lonely life, praying for the long life of the Emperor and my patron, and hoping that God might raise him to such a high position with the Emperor that I might not be in need to turn to anyone else.[133]

At the instance of Shah Muhammad Beg, Adil Khan, Mir Tahir Muhammad started the compilation of *Tarikh-i-Baldah-i-Thatta* (History of the Capital City of Thatta), also known as *Tarikh-i-Tahiri* and finally presented the first part of its introduction (*Khutba*) to his patron in 1621 CE. Some people, who were present at the occasion, may have been envious and passed resentful remarks. Mirza Shah Muhammad Beg Adil Khan recommended him to incorporate some improvements in the work.

It can be inferred from the text that after the preliminary introduction, most of the work was completed by the author in draft form, in Multan, where his patron was appointed sometime in 1621 CE.[134] Consequently, the author transcribed a fair copy, but these were merely drafts of the various sections and chapters, or they were separately written accounts of various events. The book had not yet been edited and compiled. Unfortunately, Tahir's patron died unexpectedly soon after this. Consequently, the author lost his support and could not compile and edit his final draft[135] and retired.[136] However, after a few years, he returned to Thatta around 1627–1628 CE, perhaps when Mirza Isa Tarkhan II, son of Jan Baba, was the governor there. The author might have died at the age of sixty-one, in 1641 CE, in Thatta and was buried in his family graveyard of Baghai Syeds in the Makli Hills.[137]

The picture one gets of Mir Tahir Muhammad's personality as reflected in his writings, is of an unpretentious, humble, truthful and religious man. He was straightforward and sincere, and never lavished false praises on important people. He appreciated merit and criticised indecent manners, irrespective of the persons and situations involved. He even criticised his patron, Mirza Ghazi Beg, for his wrong deeds.[138] He was a man of great courage and resilience, dedicated to his work even in unfavourable conditions. He was recognised as a literary man of outstanding repute as well as an able military man and civil servant.

Syed states that his reason for compiling this book was that no one in the past had written the history of the Soomras and Sammas. He further states that no one had yet made any attempt to compile a history of Sindh that focused on the Arghuns and Tarkhans in particular;[139] in other words, a book from which, 'one could extract [the] required information and benefit from it'.

The fact is that several authors had compiled works on the Soomras and Sammas in Hindi, in which the author was not well conversant. Apart from this, there are Mir Masum's *Tarikh-i-Sindh* and Idraki's *Beglar Nama*. However, the significance of *Beglar Nama* is mainly as a biographical account and not a general history. Mir Tahir makes no mention of this book, but does cite a few references to Mir Masum's *mathnawi*, titled *Husn wa Naz* and had known Mir Buzurg, the son of Mir Masum, personally. However, we find no similarity between Mir Tahir's book and Masum's *Tarikh-i-Sindh*. Therefore, we can certainly assert that though Tahir Nisyani knew about this work of his deceased contemporary, he was neither not familiar with it, nor did he use it as source.

Mir Tahir's father and grandfather had served the Arghun and Tarkhan rulers and he himself was attached to the entourage of Mirza Ghazi Beg, so he felt indebted to pay his gratitude to his late patron by composing this work.[140] The sponsorship and support of Nawab Shah Beg (Khan-i-Dauran) and his son, Mirza Shah Muhammad Beg Adil Khan, encouraged him to carry out such an important task and personally check its progress.

Similar to the *Tarikh-i-Masumi* and *Beglar Nama*, the *Tarikh-i-Tahiri* is essentially regional in its scope. It concentrates on the history of the Arghun and the Tarkhan rule in Sindh and deals only generally with the Soomras and Sammas. The document is of the utmost value for the study of the war expeditions and the detailed accounts of the lives and times of Mirza Shah Hassan, Mirza Isa Tarkhan, and Mirza Ghazi Beg Tarkhan.

The *Tarikh-i-Tahiri* comprises an introduction (*deebacha*) and five chapters or, literally, 'stages' (*tabaqats*). The following five sections are titled and enumerated as *tabaqats*: Tabaqa First – The Soomras; Tabaqa Second – The Sammas; Tabaqa Third – Mirza Shah Hassan; Tabaqa Fourth – Mirza Isa Tarkhan; Tabaqa Fifth – Mirza Ghazi Beg Tarkhan. Between *tabaqa* four and five, there is a section titled 'Mirza Painda Muhammad Khan, son of late Mirza Muhammad Baqi'. However, this section or chapter is not mentioned in the list of contents, which implies that the author might have intended to give titles to this and other sections in his manuscript as *tabaqats*, but did not improve or revise his work to make a final draft, probably because he had lost heart and lacked motivation after the short-lived career and death of his patron. Thus, he left the previous titles as they were.[141]

When Mir Tahir Muhammad began the compilation of this book in Multan, he included a number of drafts describing different events in his patron Mirza Shah Muhammad Beg Adil Khan's life. He rewrote and rearranged these after incorporating the improvements that were suggested by his patron. Apparently, he admits that he finished this work hastily and might have thought of revising it and giving it its final form at a later date. This indicates that Mir Tahir Muhammad did not complete his work as he intended to and suddenly stopped at the events that took place in Thatta after the sad demise of Mirza Ghazi Beg, in 1612 CE. He did, however, provide some additions to the text by 1620 CE as he had planned to do, and may even have included one more chapter recounting the events from 1612–1621 CE. According to Dr N.A. Baloch, who edited the book, this might have been his tenth *tabaqa*. Even in its present form, the work could have been more appropriately divided into ten chapters, or *tabaqats*,[142] as follows:

Tabaqa First – The Soomras;
Tabaqa Second – The Sammas;
Tabaqa Third – Arrival of Mirza Beg Arghun and his conquest of Sindh;
Tabaqa Fourth – Mirza Shah Hassan Arghun;
Tabaqa Fifth – Transfer of power from the Arghuns to the Tarkhans;
Tabaqa Sixth – Mirza Isa Tarkhan;
Tabaqa Seventh – Mirza Baqi Beg Tarkhan;
Tabaqa Eighth – Mirza Painda Muhammad Tarkhan;
Tabaqa Ninth – Mirza Jani Beg Tarkhan;
Tabaqa Tenth – Mirza Ghazi Beg Tarkhan and the end of the Tarkhan rule.

The book begins as most did at the time, in the name of God, the Beneficent and Merciful. There follows a preface-cum-introduction of thirty-two pages that includes praises for Allah Almighty and the Holy Prophet (PBUH). Subsequently, the author provides some biographical references about himself for which we found no other source. The text also occasionally includes the author's self-composed couplets in order to embellish and enhance the meaning of the text, for instance:

ندارد پشیمانی آن گاه سود   چوشد کار از دست بی خرد
کہ در کار غافل نباید غنود143   منم پنبہ در گوش، بیدار باش

کہ از کلک بخشد بمردہ روان   زبان سخنور دم عیسوی است
نر اندی کسی نام شان بر زبان144   بہ محمود، فردوسی ار جان نداد

The first two chapters are related to the Soomra and the Samma periods of Sindh and end with an account of Jam Feroz's defeat at the hands of Shah Beg Arghun, based on oral testimony, or hearsay. The next two chapters provide an exhaustive account of the Arghun and the Tarkhan rule in Sindh, mostly taken from eyewitness reports of the relatives, friends, and contemporaries of the author. The fifth chapter, which is an extension of the previous chapters, is a summary of the author's personal observations and impressions regarding the life and career of the author's patron, Mirza Ghazi Beg Tarkhan, which extended over almost two decades of Sindh's history.

The major portion of the book comprises the history of the Arghuns and Tarkhans in Sindh. The author recounts the events of Mirza Ghazi Beg's rule at Thatta in detail. He provides descriptions of his court, referring to it as a place where distinguished scholars, particularly poets such as Mulla Rashidi and Mulla Murshid Brujurdi, gathered. He also narrates a detailed account of the rebellion of Abu al-Qasim Sultan, citing firm evidence derived from eyewitness sources.[145]

He provides a detailed account of his experience in Mirza Ghazi Beg's Qandahar campaign of 1607 CE and describes the dreadful conditions of a famine that spread in the area at the time of the siege of Qandahar by his patron, whereby they suffered a great deal of hardship.[146] He also records the events that took place in Sindh during the period of Khusro Khan Jarkas (1601–1612 CE), a chief of Thatta, who misappropriated the revenues besides monopolising the key administrative post for his family members and favourites during the absence of Mirza Ghazi Beg. This spread discontent all over the province.[147] He reports the news of

Mirza Ghazi Beg's death at Qandahar in 1612 CE, which he received from those who were present at the time.[148]

The author wrote his book based on eyewitnesses, or information he collected from his father and other family members. He neither quotes any source, nor does he attempt to probe the cause and effect of any incident. He does not specifically refer to the sources he had at hand. However, his position as a Mughal official helped him out in the collection of evidence. As Mir Tahir Muhammad found no source material on the subject, he benefitted from the oral traditions such as folklore, hearsays report from *bhats* and *charans*, and some eyewitness accounts.

When it comes to the rule of the Soomras and the Sammas in Sindh, the author completely depends upon the oral testimonies from different sources that he did not substantiate,[149] as is implied in the text of the book.

However, several works on the history of the Sindh had already been compiled, such as the *Chach Nama*, *Nusrat Nama-i-Tarkhan*, *Tarikh-i-Sindh* alias *Tarikh-i–Masumi*, and *Beglar Nama*. These compositions constitute comprehensive accounts of the Rai and Brahman dynasties of the pre-Muslim era and the Arab conquest of Sindh, with geographical descriptions of important places, besides the detailed accounts of the Arghuns and the Tarkhan dynasties. But apparently the author did not take these into account.

Supplementary facts appear to indicate that he might have known about two of the later works, the *Tarikh-i-Masumi* and *Beglar Nama*, since Mir Tahir refers to the story of Sassui-Punnu, versified by Mir Masum, under the title *Husn-o-Naz* in his work, which implies that he was aware of Mir Masum's literary contribution. His respectful and admiring comments on the late Mir Masum also suggest that he had known him personally.[150] He also mentions Masum's son, Mir Buzurg.[151]

Regarding *Beglar Nama*, he refers to the *Chanesar Nama*, the romantic folklore versified by Idraki Beglari.[152] For these reasons, it is hard to believe that these works were not accessible to the author. It is possible that they might not have been known publicly for quite some time after their compilation and hence Mir Tahir Muhammad may not have been properly acquainted with them—consequently, he does not make use of any of these works.

Nonetheless, Tahir's book is a specimen of fine Persian writing. In terms of language and presentation, it surpasses some of its other contemporary works, despite the fact that it heaps undue praise on various public figures. The descriptions Mir Tahir Muhammad provides in his book are picturesque and rich in detail.[153] Despite the occasional lengthy paragraph and complex sentence, it displays a combination of a simple yet graceful, albeit somewhat intricate, or ornate style. Persian odes are used at times to adorn the text, but their use is not as abundant as it was in previous works like the *Chach Nama* and *Nusrat Nama-i-Tarkhan*, etc.

The author also uses Arabic words and phrases that show the influence of the prevailing Arab-Persian culture on the author. In the text, the author uses numerous synonyms, such as:

فلاکت و ہلاکت (calamity)، فہم و فراست (wisdom)،
بی رحمی و ستم کاری (cruelty)، ناموس و ننگ و
حشمت و جلالت (modesty or splendor) وغیرہ۔

He also incorporates well-known dictum for embellishing the text, for instance:

از قبیل بزرگی بہ عقل است نہ بسال، تا پیر شوی بیاموزی وغیرہ۔

Translation: Greatness is by virtue of wisdom not by oldness, keep learning till you get old, etc.

He also uses idiomatic expressions in order to make the text elegant, such as:

روی را سیاہ ساختن، پا از گلیم بیرون نہادن، نان کسی در روغن افتادن، از مرکب زندگانی پیادہ گشتن و پیوست کاسۂ سرکسی بدر آوردن۔

Though, the language of the text is Persian, it would be of immense interest to look for indigenous words commonly employed by a writer of Persian origin. For instance, کهت is used instead of رختخواب to mean 'bedding'; جری بوتی is used instead of بیخ ونبات to mean 'roots and plants'; گھری is used in place of ساعت for 'time'; گہات in place of ساحل for 'river bank', and so forth.

Furthermore, excessive use of ornate and complex text is another characteristic of the writing-style. Two examples of such expressions are as follows:

ہنوز از مقراض سحر گیوان عنبر آگین رنگین شب نبریدہ، و
مو کب صبح کاذب کہ فریب بخش بیدار دلان شب زندہ دار
است، نتاختہ و صندل سفید روز ید بیضای آفتاب بر صدق افق
نہ نشاندہ بود کہ سواری از ہر دو جانب بہر آرایش جنگ
آواز داد۔[154]

Translation: It was still dark and the sunshine had not yet been successful in replacing the darkness of the night and the early morning light was not yet enough to spread clear day-light on the horizon so as to herald a rider from either side to get ready for the fight.

الغرض آدم شناسی کار کلی و هنر عظیم است، این صاحب دولت و اهل سخن از این قسم مردم شناسی بود، در اندک عمر صاحب سخن و ذو فنون در هر فن چنان گردیده که علم و حلم و داد و دهش و صورت و سیرت و نظم و نثر ثانی نداشت.[155]

Translation: Anyhow, recognizing humans is a great ability and magnificent art. This rich and eloquent person was living among great people who possessed the talent of recognizing the worth in humans. Very soon, he became an expert in all those skills in which there was no one other than him, such as knowledge, patience, generosity, appearance, conduct, and composing poetry and prose.

As mentioned earlier, Mir Tahir Muhammad refers to the folk tradition as a source for the periods of the Soomras and Sammas, but evidently, he did not exploit them. He only documented such accounts that were already common knowledge without any assessment or examination. For this reason, his folklore accounts about the Soomra and the Samma periods are semi-historical and may not be considered as being quite authentic. Yet the accounts related to these periods are significant as they are the earliest written records about Dalurai and Saint Chutto Umrani. The author provides valuable annotations on popular folktales like Badi al-Jamal, Umar-Marui, Sassui-Pannu, Leela-Chanesar, and the well-known epic of Dodo Soomro and Sultan Ala al-Din Khilji. In this semi-historical reference, one may incidentally discern some historical truth, such as the rivalry between the Soomras and the Sammas for supremacy, the subsequent downfall of the Soomras, and the rise of Samma power in Sindh.[156]

In the *Tarikh-i-Tahiri*, it is stated that the labouring classes and landholders of the Samma were Hindus. However, Elliot mentions that they were strange followers of their faith, because they never drank wine without partaking of a young buffalo calf.[157] According to H.T. Sorley, during the days of the last Samma ruler, Jam Nizam al-Din Nanda (1460–1508 CE), Islam spread widely over Sindh and a large section of the population converted to the religion.[158] It also reveals from the text that the author committed errors in pronouncing the names of some of the Soomra and the Samma rulers. For example, he incorrectly mentions the name of Jam Tughluq as Jam Taghrur. On the other hand, the accounts of Jam Nizam al-Din Nanda are devoid of substantial historical information. Some of the information is unique in its nature; for instance, 'his references about Darya Khan are much significant which neither be matched up favourably to the historical accounts about the same person given by Mir Masum in his *Tarikh-i-Sindh* alias *Tarikh-i-Masumi* and by Idraki Beglari in *Beglar Nama*, nor with the rich folklore accounts which are current about him up [Darya Khan] to this day.'[159]

Similar to his treatment of the history of the Soomra and Samma periods, Mir Tahir also depends on oral testimonies for the history of the Arghun and Tarkhan rulers more willingly than written records. According to his statement, he met the criteria for checking the authenticity of these reports through verification by more than one reliable eyewitness source. As he writes, 'It is certain that neither Nisyani receives repeated stories, nor does he accept them. Whatever he has narrated in his book is authentic and corroborated by reliable sources. For any lapse of events and exaggerations, all the responsibility goes to the chain narrators.'[160]

In the same way that the author is an authentic source for the events of Mirza Ghazi Beg's period but not for the Soomra and Samma periods, similarly, his narrations might be true only for the Tarkhan but not for the Arghun era, which he derived mostly from popular hearsay. In fact, some of the information about the contacts of his maternal grandfather and uncles (Chief Umarshah of Darbela and his sons) with Emperor Humayun may be considered reliable and authentic since they are derived from the family record, particularly the narrations about the promissory grant issued by the Emperor in favour of Chief Umarshah.[161]

The author's accounts about the reign of Mirza Muhammad Baqi's reign are based on information from eyewitnesses and he mentions his sources by name. His father, Syed Hasan had personal knowledge of most of the accounts of the periods of Mirza Painda Muhammad and his son Mirza Jani Beg; he states, 'I quote it from my father, Miyan Hasan'.[162]

Thus, the *Tarikh-i-Tahiri* occupies an important position among all the histories of Sindh. It may rightly be regarded as the only source that provides a detailed and to some extent reliable account of the Arghun and the Tarkhan periods (1520–1592 CE).[163] However, most of its accounts are more or less identical to those mentioned in the *Tarikh-i-Masumi*, till the period of Mirza Jani Beg. Tahir's main contribution comes after the year 1592 CE, whereas Mir Masum's work ends after the demise of Mirza Ghazi Beg in 1612 CE. The *Tarikh-i-Tahiri* is particularly significant as it is the earliest literary source in which couplets composed by Mirza Ghazi Beg Tarkhan under the pen name of Waqari are mentioned. For instance:

بزم عشق ست 'وقارى' بادب باید بود که در آن جز بلب زخم تکلم کفر است[164]

On the other hand, according to Mir Tahir Muhammad's own statement, mentioned previously, he ended the work rather hurriedly and could not revise it. For this reason, the sequence of some events lacks structure in a proper chronological order. The author was aware of this defect and admits his shortcoming. For example, he writes about Mirza Shah Hassan Arghun's campaign of Kutch earlier and his occupation of Multan afterwards, even though the two events occurred the other way round. He describes the siege of Thatta by the Portuguese as the last event of Shah Hasan's period, whereas in actual fact it occurred in the first year of Mirza Isa's reign (1556 CE).[165]

Some factual errors are also found in the dates of some events and the time periods of dynasties. For instance, the periods mentioning the rule of the Soomras, Sammas, Arghuns, and Tarkhans are not correct and even the time periods mentioning the reign of Jam Nizam al-Din Nanda and Mirza Shah Hassan are not accurate. Dr N.B. Baloch points out that inaccuracy in dates can be found in almost all the manuscripts of *Tarikh-i-Tahiri*. This may be due to haste or errors by the author himself that afterwards could not be corrected, as the draft was not revised finally. Some of the dates mentioned are off by as many as ten years, despite the fact that they took place not too long prior to the authors birth and the facts of which should have been familiar too him since these were important developments.

The work includes major mistakes, like Mirza Jan Baba's meeting with Mirza Muhammad Baqi, which in fact took place in 1568 CE and not 1578 CE as mentioned by the author; and Khan-i-Khanan's invasion of Sindh, which happened in 1600–1601 CE and 1591 CE.[166] Regarding the sacking and burning of Thatta by Mirza Isa Tarkhan, the author cites the dates 1565–1566 CE, but the *Tarkhan Nama* states the correct year, which was 1556 CE.[167] The accounts of the Portuguese also corroborate the year mentioned by the latter source, as the raid began in November 1555 and ended in November 1556 CE.[168] The author mentions 1576 CE as the last year of Mirza Isa Tarkhan's reign, which again is incorrect. The *Tarikh-i-Masumi* and *Tarkhan Nama* cites 1566 CE as the year of his death. Abu al-Fazl validates it, stating that Muhammad Baqi Tarkhan sent an embassy to Akbar's court, informing him about his father's and professing his own allegiance.[169]

Such errors are apparent in the introduction, where the author mentions ten *tabaqats* (chapters) but in the text there are only five segments, out of which only four are specifically designated as *tabaqats*. The author gives an abrupt conclusion. He gives a brief account of events that took place in Thatta after the death of Mirza Ghazi Beg in 1612 CE and then apparently stopped writing. This too indicates that the author hadn't completed his work in its final form.[170] It is possible that the author might have included one more chapter to the final draft afterwards in which he describes the events that occurred from 1612–1621 CE.

Apart from the political history, the author elucidates the socio-cultural aspect of contemporary society. He tells us about many strange customs of the Soomras, including the strong branding the stamp of slavery upon the shoulders of the weak.[171] The author of the *Mirat-i-Sikandari* (The History of the Independent Sultans of Gujarat) also mentions that Sultan Mahmud bin Latif (1537–1554 CE) actually revived this custom and enforced it in the turbulent parts of his kingdom:

> With a view to putting down the turbulence, he ordered all those who remained in his territories and worked at the plough to be branded on the right arm, and if any Rajput or Koli was found without the brand mark, he was killed.[172]

The author of the *Tuhfat al-Kiram* also states that the nails of such people were extracted by the roots.[173]

However, the most important aspect of this society was to maintain the prestige and pride of the social hierarchy. Folklore relating to the Soomra period also offers a great deal of information about the social life of the times. The norms and sensibility of the people can be gleaned from them. Also, these tales are particularly significant in depicting attitudes towards women. They show that women were respected for positive qualities: honesty, integrity, piety, and loyalty. They glorified women for being courageously willing to sacrifice their lives for the sake of love. The purity of a woman is exalted in the stories of Umar-Marui, Moomal-Rano, Ganga-Umar, Leela-Chanesar, Dallu Rai-Badi al-Jamal, and Chattu Amrani-Fatima. All these characters epitomise socio-cultural and moral values, as well as the psyche of the people of that era. Qani reproduces all these stories in his *Tuhfat al-Kiram*.[174]

In *Tarikh-i-Tahiri*, the author relates these tales as well. In the story of Umar-Marui, he narrates how the heroine, Marui, is tempted by lavish luxuries, riches, and high status as a queen, but she spurns all these and follows the path of chastity, steadfastness, and loyalty to her family.[175]

The story of Moomal-Rano shows that even in the fifteenth century, a woman from the upper classes had the right to choose the most intelligent and handsome husband for herself.[176] In the story of *Ganga Umar*, the author mentions that this was one of the several causes for the defeat of the Soomras by Sultan Ala al-Din Khilji. The author states,

> it was heard from the villagers of that region that the Soomra king had taken away Umar Tameem's beautiful wife Ganga by deceit. The oppressed husband visited King Ala al-Din Khilji and submitted his petition. The just king sent a *nishan* (royal order) to the tyrant to appear before him. If he comes to the court and satisfies the oppressed husband he would remain unharmed, otherwise he would find his country destroyed by the king's mighty army and his family would be made captive by the forces. As soon as the messenger reached the tyrant, he came to pay homage to the king. He offered him numerous gifts and attained the honour of kissing the royal threshold. But the king was not taken in by the tyrant's blandishments. When the claimant and the defendant came face to face the tyrant was thrown into prison for the offences he had committed. The wrath of the king towards the tyrant was so great that he announced that he would remain in prison till he died in order to set an example for other evildoers.[177]

In another narrative, the author asserts that the towns of Alor and Brahmanabad were destroyed due to the curse of two oppressed ladies named Badi al-Jamal and Fatimah, because the ruler Dallu Rai had assaulted their grace and honour.[178] The story of Moomal tells the tale of the Hindu custom of burning a widow on her husband's pyre.[179] It states that during the early days of the Soomra rule, women preferred suicide to avoid the disgraceful and dishonourable life of a widow.

From a thorough analysis of all these stories, we can conclude that women enjoyed a privileged position in society and commanded immense respect. This historical record highlights the patriotism of Marui; the self-esteem of Leela; the wisdom and courage of Moomal; the consistency of Kaunro; the steadfastness and bravery of Sassui; the chastity of Ganga; and the love and sacrifice of Bhagul Bai. These stories show that there was a trend of polygamy among the men of the aristocratic ruling class[180] and that they were often involved in extra-marital affairs. Even a married woman was not secure from the advances of a man. On the other hand, in many instances a woman from the upper class could choose her own husband and even send a marriage proposal to the man she preferred.

The society in Sindh by the end of the fourteenth century may have been polygamous, but generally only the nobility and royalty indulged in this custom. Historical evidence proves that there was social discrimination between men and women. Since men from the upper classes were allowed more than one wife, they could choose at least one spouse of their own choice even from outside their clan. As a rule, women had neither the right to select their life-partners nor to marry outside the family, however, there were exceptions among females of the upper classes. Marriage was usually for life, although divorce was theoretically possible but very rarely resorted to.

In such a class-based society, historians depicted women of the poor classes in the guise of Marui, Sassui, Ganga, and Noori, as virtuous ladies, while the women of the upper classes, like Leela, Moomal, and Kaunro, were portrayed as being arrogant and self-centred and who would turn a blind eye to their duties and veer away from the path of virtue. The women of the lower classes, despite being suppressed, played a vital role in society. By participating actively, she retained an equal share in the economy. She had to prove the importance of her existence through hard work and struggle.

The book also highlights the practice of Sufism across Sindh. When Sufism became the common religious practice, it was associated with the rise of various orders of dervishes and mendicants. In the *Tarikh-i-Tahiri*, it is stated that:

> Besides the shrine of the 'Shaykh of Shaykhs', Shaykh Patta, there were some ten or twelve other places in Thatta where devotees went to worship. Dervishes would perform their dance at these shrines. These excitable men often work themselves into a catatonic state of holy ecstasy. It is said that in this state some of them would cast themselves off the mountain of Makli onto the rocks but because of the blessing of their *murshid* they were not harmed at all. Though this custom of dancing is considered against the tenets of Islam by many sects, it has been passed down from generation to generation and all attempt of the *ulema* and the authorities to stop it has not succeeded.[181]

In fact, popular Sufism degenerated into a form that was considered irreligious by the orthodox *ulema*.

The successive works like the *Tarkhan Nama* and *Tuhfat al-Kiram* borrowed verbatim accounts from *Tarikh-i-Tahiri*, for the periods of the Arghuns and Tarkhans. The prime contribution of *Tarikh-i-Tahiri* is that it elucidates various aspects of the contemporary socio-economic and political history of Sindh, which is important in understanding the tenor of that age.

Mazhar-i-Shahjahani (The Manifestation of the Emperor Shah Jahan): The First Manual on Mughal Administration in Sindh

Mazhar-i-Shahjahani was written by Yousuf Mirak, son of Mir Abu al-Qasim Namakin of Bhakkar, in 1634 CE. During the era of the great Mughals there were a number of official and unofficial writers who endeavoured to compile an account providing a more or less comprehensive picture of the Mughal administration. These narrations have been limited by the quality and scope of the information available to the authors. The *Mazhar-i-Shahjahani* is a unique work of this kind, written from a perspective of what the author saw of the Mughal administration in Sindh.

Studies of the Mughal administration in Sindh always rely on this notable work and are supplemented by some other indigenous historical sources. It is evident that the author intended to send his compilation to Emperor Shah Jahan to apprise him of the maladministration, tyranny, and corruption of Mughal governors in Sindh, but it did not reach him and was most likely intercepted. The *Mazhar-i-Shahjahani* is also regarded as a 'mirror for princes',[182] which is the term that was commonly used for those ethno-political tracts primarily 'designated to present princes with a picture of the ideal ruler and his officials'.[183]

The *Siyasat Nama* (The Book on Politics) of Nizam al-Mulk Tusi (c. 1018–1092 CE) is considered the foremost among all the post-Muslim Persian works produced on this topic. Later on, there is the *Akhlaq-i-Humayun* (The Virtues of Emperor Humayun), written by Qadi Ikhtiyar al-Din Harawi in 1506–1507 CE. Babur regarded this book as the leading compilation of its kind in Mughal India.[184]

The *Mazhar-i-Shahjahani* was discovered providentially in 1955. Though no accounts of the life of the author, Yousaf Mirak, can be found in any chronicles of that time or later, we are able to glean from intermittent evidence and supplementary references available in the text of the book itself, substantial information on him. According to one source, Mulla Mir Sabzwari, the progenitor of Yousaf's family, was a man of scholarly background hailing from Bayjaq, a village situated in the suburbs of Sabzwar in Herat, the capital of Khurasan. He was a Hussaini Syed and the custodian of the shrine of the eighth Shi'ite Imam, Ali al-Rida at Mashhad. During the period of turmoil and bloodshed in 1500–1501 CE caused by the conflict between the rising power of Shibani Khan Uzbek in Central Asia and the Safavids of Persia, Mulla Mir Sabzwari and his dependents migrated towards the southeast. They reached Qandahar and were granted refuge by the Timurids, where Mulla passed away.[185]

Mir Abu al-Qasim, also known as Namakin, was one of Mulla Mir's sons and the father of the author of *Mazhar-i-Shahjahani*. Namakin was also an author in his own right who wrote a notable book on epistolography, titled *Munshat-i-Namakin and* dedicated to Emperor Akbar (this compilation is further dealt with in the chapter on *insha* writing).

According to Hussamuddin Rashidi, Namakin at some stage Namakin travelled to Kabul and entered the service of the ruler of Kabul, Mirza Hakim, son of the Mughal Emperor Humayun. Later, Mir Abu al-Qasim Namakin proceeded to Lahore, where he joined the court of Emperor Akbar, who conferred upon him the *jagirs* of Bhera and Khaushab. He soon established his position in the service of the Mughals. After the Mughal occupation of Sindh, Mir Abu al-Qasim was entrusted with some important assignments in Sindh and was assigned the *sarkar* of Bhakkar, excluding the *parganas* of Darbela, Kakari, and Chanduka.[186]

His family soon became prominent among the other imperial *mansabdars* and was associated with a number of Mughal *jagirdars*. The eldest son of Mir Abu al-Qasim Namakin, Abu al-Baqa Amir Khan, followed his father's career after his death. His family was known as the Amir Khani Syeds. Another branch of the family stayed at Bhakkar. They were known as the Qasim Khanis. Yousuf was a younger brother of Mir Abu al-Baqa Amir Khan and belonged to the Bhakkar branch. However, he joined his elder brother in Sehwan, when he was made the *jagirdar*. Some of them stayed at Sehwan, as the author himself spent most of his life there.

Unfortunately, we have very little information about Yousuf Mirak's early years of life. The very first reference to the author in his book goes back to 1607 CE, when Abu al-Qasim Namakin was assigned a *jagir* in Sehwan. He sent Yousuf ahead to take care of affairs in Sehwan until his arrival.[187]

The author had earlier accompanied his father during his service in Bhakkar, Gujarat, Sehwan, and Jalalabad. After the death of his father in 1609 CE, he lived with his elder brother Mir Abu al-Baqa Amir Khan, who had been given possession of the Sehwan *jagir* jointly, with Shamshir Beg Uzbek, by Emperor Jahangir. Mir Abu al-Baqa went to Agra with his family in order to record his discontent about having to share the *jagir*. Yousuf Mirak decided to remain in Sehwan permanently,[188] showing his independent judgement on the issues. The author was conferred a *mansab* as well, but he soon resigned from it and lived a contented life supported by a modest allowance, free from the arduous obligations and responsibilities of service to the Mughal emperor. He remained at Sehwan from 1607 to 1628 CE.

There was a streak of audacity and determination in Yousuf Mirak's character and he was independent in his views. He had deep insight into the affairs of administration in Sindh, so the Mughal administrators in the region frequently sought his advice and guidance, particularly Shamshir Khan. Despite a degree of rivalry with his brother, he seldom took any decision without consulting Yousuf Mirak. The author contributed a lot to the literary and cultural heritage of Sindh. This outstanding composition of his proved his skill and talent as an erudite and knowledgeable scholar of Arabic and Persian, with a command of prose and poetry.

When Shah Jahan ascended the Mughal throne in 1628 CE, he immediately appointed Ahmad Beg Khan as the governor of Sehwan. Ahmad Beg was the nephew of Asaf Khan, father-in-law to Shah Jahan. Asaf Khan was appointed as the governor of Multan but did not go there. Yousuf Mirak's brother, Mir Abu al-Baqa, was sent to Multan to act as proxy governor to Nawab Asaf Khan.

Ahmad Beg was a debauch and spent most of his time in the *harem*. He showed very little interest in statecraft and entrusted all his responsibilities to his brother, Mirza Yousuf. He was the *de facto jagirdar* of Sehwan and a cruel and vicious man, who drew sadistic pleasure from imposing physical and mental torture on the public.[189] He endeavoured to maximise his own wealth by unethical and unscrupulous means. Mirza Yousuf's employed criminals, who openly robbed people on the streets and forcibly exacted excessive and unjustified taxes from the traders and peasants.[190] Mir Yousuf Mirak calls him Hajjaj bin Yousuf II.[191] Because of the unduly oppressive rule of Mirza Yousuf, some native tribes rose in rebellion. This was the grave situation in which Yousuf Mirak left Sehwan and reached Multan to join his brother. At this time, Yousuf Mirak planned to undertake a visit to Agra to inform the Emperor of the miserable conditions to which Ahmad Beg and his wicked brother had reduced the people of Sehwan.[192]

Around this time, Mir Abu al-Baqa received orders for a new assignment as governor of Thatta and Ahmad Beg was sent to Multan. Abu al-Baqa took Yousuf Mirak with him to Thatta. The elder brother of the author was an expert in diplomatic affairs and court etiquette. He knew Mirak's naïve intention of reporting Ahmed Beg's tyranny to the emperor would probably get him in trouble, so he did not allow him to go. Shortly after his arrival at Thatta, Yousuf Mirak fell ill. His illness as well as the appointment of such an incompetent person like Ahmad Beg as the governor of Multan, which was a far more important and fertile region than Sehwan, demoralised Yousuf Mirak. Furthermore, there was the danger he would be intercepted while passing through Multan to reach Agra. His doubts lowered his zeal. Subsequently, he decided to write a book about the matter and present it to the emperor.[193]

Thus, the author started writing the book first under the title of the *Mazhar al-Tadbir*, which the author mentions in the text.[194] Later on, he styled it as the *Mazhar-i-Shahjahani*, since he intended to dedicate it to Shah Jahan. While it is evident that the author intended to complete this book by the end of 1628 CE, it in fact took much longer. The exact year of its compilation could not be ascertained, but there were some incidental remarks in the text mentioning 1634 CE as the year of its completion.[195] Most probably, the author started the compilation of this book earlier than 1629 CE and took almost six years to do this painstaking task. At the time of its completion in 1634 CE, the author included some more significant events in the text.[196]

During this period, Yousuf had lived in Thatta as long as his brother remained the governor, but in May 1632 CE, he returned to Sehwan when his brother was transferred to Junagadh.[197] In Sehwan, he rose to a high status due to the support of the new Mughal *jagirdar*, Dindar Khan. The author liked him because of his 'leniency, piety and humanitarian attitude, but he still lashed out at his weak rule and the misconduct of his officials.'[198]

Mir Abu al-Baqa was at the time serving as the viceroy of Junagadh. It seemed that the author would never get the honour of presenting his book to the emperor.

The book consists of two major segments; part one contains four chapters (*abwabs*). Except for chapter two, the *abwabs* are further divided into a number of sections, as *fasls*. Part one presents a code of behaviour for ruling a kingdom; the politics of the country; managing the administration of the government according to the current political trends that were elaborated by the author. The author devoted this first part as a 'mirror for princes', to show them an ideal ruler to emulate. It relates interesting anecdotes regarding the kings, ministers and functionaries from preceding dynasties such as Sultan Mahmud Ghaznavi, Sultan Samir, and Malik Shah. There is a thorough discussion in the book about the discipline and training of *mansabdars* that may be regarded as a useful guideline for upcoming rulers. The author draws attention towards the evils and hardships faced by governors, *qazis* (judges), *muftis* (jurists), *sadrs* (heads of the religious department of the state and provinces), *muhtasibs* (officials responsible to keep a check on public morals), scholars, Sufi saints and common citizens. The author provides references from the Quran and the classical poetry of Firdausi, Hatfi, Saadi, Nizami, and so forth, to support his recommendations. He also borrowed extracts from *Ikhlaq-i-Mohsini* (Etiquette of Benefactors) regarding the qualities of chivalry, courage and endeavour that are necessary for a ruler.

Part two, which is this book's area of focus, provides historical accounts of the Mughal period in Sindh. It is also divided into four chapters (*abwabs*) and chapter four is sub-divided into five sections, or *fasls*.[199] Part two describes the contemporary political, economic, geographical, religious and social conditions besides giving particular reference to the administration of four different regions (*sarkars*) of Sindh: Bhakkar, Siwi, Thatta, and Sehwan which were under the rule of Mughal governors.

The book begins in the name of God, in the traditional Islamic way of starting work. There is no preface or introduction. The account is a running narrative of lengthy paragraphs. The author ends with an epilogue (*khatima*). In the process of writing, he makes use of numerous technical administrative terms and phrases.

The first chapter of part one, provides an account of the affairs of the region of Bhakkar, including the details of all its eight *parganas*[200] such as Matilah, Alor, Ladah, Kakan, Kakari, Darbela, Jatoi, Chanduka, and Takar. The author discusses the discrepancies that have crept into the administrative setup, particularly the economic hindrances and also suggests remedies. The descriptions of different towns and villages, the topography, along with the various chiefs and *jagirdars* who were the masters of the land, have all been mentioned.[201] The second chapter provides information about the land, history and the people inhabiting the region of Siwi. This chapter is comparatively brief and deals mainly with affairs of revenue and military administration.[202]

The third chapter narrates accounts of the affairs of the region of Thatta. It deals with its geography and demographic description and literary contribution. This chapter is further divided into three main segments related to events that occurred during the governorships of Shamshir Khan Uzbek, Muzaffar Khan Mamuri, and Syed Bayazid Bukhari. It provides a brief description of the four *sarkars* of Thatta, namely Thatta, Chachkan, Nasrpur, and Chakar Hala. The author also offers some suggestions for the administrative and economic development of this region.[203]

In the fourth chapter, the author is about the region of Sehwan. This chapter is the most expansive and is divided into five sections. The first provides a brief topographical and demographical description of the region and its eleven *parganas* such as Baghbanan, Patar, Nayrun Qalah, Kahan, Bubakan, Haweli Sehwan, Nayrun, Sann, Junejah, Khittah, and Lakut.[204] The second section deals with the seditious and criminal elements in this region and how their mischief led to the collapse of law and order in Sehwan. It tells of the impact this had on the neighbouring regions of Bhakkar, Thatta, and Jaisalmer.[205]

Section three gives an exhaustive description of the causes of the ruination of the peasants of Sehwan and the strengthening of insurgent elements,[206] while section four comprises a brief account of suggestions to improve the region and contains information about the seasonal crops and the different taxes and duties levied by the state.[207] The last section provides suggestions on how to quell the insurgency that had broken out in the region and advises that the army is needed for the purpose.[208]

The author ends with an epilogue on 'treading the path of virtue for kings, *wazirs* and *amirs*; [which is more difficult for them] because of their preoccupation with the world and the easy way for them to follow this path is to obtain the virtues that are mentioned in section one of chapter one of part one of his book and the way to avoid the pitfalls that threaten them is described in section two of chapter one.'[209]

Yousuf Mirak does not specifically refer to the sources he utilised, but obviously he must have been in possession of some native Persian chronicles and other books had already been written on the subject. For the first part of the book, the author implies that he consulted some earlier compilations on this subject, for instance, the *Siyasat Nama* of Nizam al-Mulk Tusi[210] and the *Fatawa-i-Jahandari* (The Rulings on Temporal Government)[211] of Ziya al-Din Barani, etc.[212]

The second part of the book deals only with contemporary and eyewitness accounts of events and references and the author did not need to consult any source for this part. However, the text suggests some references from the *Tarikh-i-Sindh* of Mir Muhammad Masum for the chapters relating to Bhakkar and Sehwan.

The language of the *Mazhar-i-Shahjahani* is simple and it is written in a straightforward manner. The author maintains the flow of the language throughout the book. The style varies according to the need of the narration. The author uses numerous well-known as well as unfamiliar technical administrative terms, words and phrases in the text, which are difficult to understand for an ordinary reader. The language of the text is occasionally blended with the Arabic words for instance: ‑الحمدلله والمنته، والى یومنا، خلق الله.[213] In one place, he quotes an Arabic couplet with its Persian translation which shows the dominating influence of Persian language in the literary circles:

شعر:

يا اكرم الخلق مالى من الوذ بہ
سواک عند حلول الحادث العم

ترجمہ:

اي گرامي تر ز خلقان من ندارم ملتجا
جز تو چون آيد قيامت يا بود مرگ تنم²¹⁴

He occasionally adorns the text with poetic expressions for accentuating the statement. Revealing the oppressed conditions in Sehwan, he writes:

چو خواهد کہ ويران کند عالمے نہد ملک در پنجۂ ظالمے ²¹⁵

Translation: When He (Allah) wants to destroy mankind, the country is given into the hands of a cruel ruler.

The native author of foreign origin also occasionally uses some words and terms of indigenous Sindhi language, for instance:

'چبوتر، 'دکہ خور (دھکہ)، 'جير (چھپر)'

The *Mazhar-i-Shahjahani* is notable because it introduces a new concept into the art of political literature, which was at the time still in its formative stage. This was the era when the study of history dealt merely with the history of the rulers and the aristocrat class. Idraki Beglari had already compiled such a work, in which he provided references about different features of the Beglar potentates and their bureaucrats.²¹⁶ In this era, Yousaf Mirak compiled a record of the administrative progress of the period, which in its own way was also a manual for administrators. This work covered the socio-economic condition of the people. It is a unique source of the history of Sindh that gives a different perspective regarding the land and its people during the first half of the seventeenth century. It is a seminal composition in its category and a masterpiece of historical significance.

Besides the political history, it also contains a very great amount of information about the geo-topographic conditions of Sindh during the Mughal era. It describes a number of provinces and *parganas* and the habits and characteristics of the people and races that inhabited the region. The book apprises us about the craftsmen here. It also tells about the forts and citadels situated in Sindh. It deals with different aspects of the Mughal administration in the regions of Bhakkar, Siwi, Thatta, and Sewistan. This had never been recorded earlier. Besides the accounts of the Mughal government, the book also offers incidental remarks about the Arghun and

Tarkhan administrations.[217] For this purpose, the author frequently quotes the *Tarikh-i-Sindh* for elaborating his accounts.

The *Mazhar-i-Shahjahani* is a significant source, particularly for eyewitness accounts of the period after the conquest of Sindh by the Mughals in 1591–1592 CE. It reveals that Akbar only seized the *sarkars* of Bhakkar and Sewistan, including Lahiri Bandar, while the rest of the territory was entrusted to Mirza Jani Beg as a *jagir*. It particularly offers substantial information about the affairs of the region of Sewistan for which we find no other source. It gives details about the unruly and turbulent tribes inhabiting the nearby regions.[218] The book is also useful because the author provides personal analyses of the benefits and harm caused by successive Mughal administrations and what they contributed to the development of the region.[219]

The author suggests some administrative measures for the improvement of governance, such as the division of duties and responsibilities among different functionaries like the *bakhshi* (military pay-master and intelligence officer) and the *waqa'i nawis* (secret news-writer).[220] He recommends that judicial and religious matters should be freed from the influence of the civil authorities.[221] The book explicitly traces the origin of different native tribes and clans and this makes this chronicle unrivalled for source material among all other books of that time.

Besides analysing the working of the Mughal administrative machinery in Sindh, Yousuf Mirak also gives eyewitness accounts about the atrocities, dereliction of duty and misrule by Mughal aristocrats, for instance Mirza Rustam, Mirza Muzaffar, Ahmad Beg Khan and his brother, Mirza Yousuf. The latter was appointed the *jagirdar* of Sehwan by Shah Jahan.[222] The book maintains that the Mughal emperors failed in controlling the tyrannous tendencies of some of their nobles. In this regard, the author also discusses the corruption that crept into the system of land grants due to the administrative malfeasance of these Mughal nobles. Likewise, Mirak provides strong evidence of the authority and dominating powers of Noor Jahan and her family over the state affairs during the last phase of Jahangir's weak rule.

The sectarian conflict between the Sunni and the Shi'as, which increased remarkably during the sixteenth and seventeenth centuries has also been dealt with by the author. Though there is no direct evidence, but some other contemporary sources also report the extreme sectarian tension between these two major sects of Muslims during this period.[223] Thus, we can appreciate that there was a serious situation and it needs to be examined critically without any biases or prejudices.[224] This volatile situation resulted many times in armed conflicts between the two sects.

In one such incident that occurred in 1642 CE, the author's nephew, Abdul Razzaq, lost his life.[225] As far as the issue of conversion in Sindh is concerned, the *Mazhar-i-Shahjahani* is the earliest work that clearly mentions the reason. The author states that the majority of people who converted belonged to the Muslim peasant class. They changed their sect/religion due to their deplorable economic conditions.[226] In this regard, the author sheds light on religious deterioration in Sindh, which was caused by social and economic decline.

As pointed out, this work is mainly based on the author's personal observations. For this reason, it may rightly be regarded as the most important first-hand source for the Mughal history of Sindh. Dr M. Saleem Akhtar highlighting its historical significance rightly states:

> This work is a most valuable source of information on the history of the imperial *jagirdars* in Sindh, its administrative setup, revenue system and classification of lands, the ethnic composition of its population, its trade and commerce, weights and measures, geography and topography, and the rites and customs of the local people...no writer on the socio-economic of Sindh during the sixteenth and seventeenth centuries can afford to overlook this book.[227]

It is a matchless encyclopaedia on the working of the Mughal administration in Sindh up to the reign of Jahangir. In the *Mazhar-i-Shahjahani*, the pursuit of truth has transcended all other considerations. The author made every effort to uncover the facts.

The *Mazhar-i-Shahjahani* is an exceptional work on history, which presents a simple narrative. While it mainly deals with the administrative measures and exploits of the Mughal functionaries in different regions of Sindh, it also describes the social, cultural, and economic conditions of the era. At a time when political history was practically the sole consideration of the historian, a narration of such nature opened new vistas and widened the conspectus of historical literature in Sindh.

Backed by only brief political information, the importance of the work lies in the author's efforts in outlining the geographical and topographical features of Sindh; tracing the tribes and describing its financial resources, society and custom. In short, the work is significant in regard to the social, economic and political history of Sindh during the sixteenth and seventeenth centuries. The author not only describes the events, but also tries to analyse its cause and effects. He gives his opinion and suggests measures to rectify the administrative and social problems.

The author pursues his interest in dealing with each *sarkar* and *pargana* separately,[228] particularly in regard to the yield of revenue. Individual personalities, generally relating to the ruling aristocracy, have not been treated as vividly as in other contemporary historical works. As the ruling aristocracy mainly comprised outsiders of Persian and Turanian origin, they showed little sympathy and consideration for the local populace of their *jagirs*. In this regard, the author states that rent-farming and extortionist demands of *amils* (revenue collectors) and *arbabs*[229] were two more customs that caused a great deal of hardship to the peasants, which harmed the country.[230]

Mir Masum and Mir Abu al-Qasim Namakin were generously praised by Mirak for their concern for the welfare of the peasantry, but other historians, such as Shaykh Farid Bhakkari, have levelled allegations against them of being immoderate.[231] Mirak gives eyewitness accounts of the dreadful socio-economic conditions of Sehwan during the tenure of Ahmad Beg; how people were robbed openly in the streets, the traders hard-pressed by excessive taxes and the people bound to pay taxes at whatever rate the official dictated. No one could travel around without the *dastak* (written permission) of Mirza Yousuf, for which they had to pay a fee. The life and honour of the native people was overtly disregarded under his tyrannical rule.[232]

In one way or another, the author earnestly displays feelings of patriotism.[233] He realises the genuine problems of the era. He draws upon his deep feelings for Sindh and his acquaintance with every part of the region to propose realistic solutions for them. He argues that due to Ahmed Beg Khan's (*jagirdar* of Sewistan) oppressive measures, some Sindhi scholars deserted their homes and settled in other parts of India.

Regarding the violations of law and order by some turbulent tribes, Mirak recommends that they should be quashed by the force of arms. In support of his stand, the author gives examples from past and existing circumstances in Sindh. He also generously quotes from aphorisms, legends and anecdotes of ancient rulers, so that future generations may benefit from them.

However, there is another side of the picture regarding the insurrections of turbulent local tribes in Sindh during this era. Mirak and the other contemporary historians are members of an alien aristocracy hailing from Central Asia, ruling over a conquered populace. Thus, he condemned native tribes that revolted whereas the local people considered these seditious activities as a struggle for liberty. He also used abusive and unseemly remarks for some native tribes of Sindh, such as the Shoros, Samijahs and Baloch and called them malefactors.[234] On the other hand, he praised the Palijas, Korijas, Linjars and Narijas for their obedient and submissive manner towards their feudal lords. He writes:

> ...the Palijas, Korijas, Linjars, Narijas; all these four tribes have always been submissive to feudal-lords. This government was prosperous and thriving during the days of the Tarkhans. But control of the Tarkhans was weak over the three above mentioned tribes up until the enraged people executed Rustam, the eldest son of Khusro Beg—the ruler of Thatta. He gathered an army against the stubborn and turbulent masses.[235]

The author displays extraordinary skill in tracing the origins of different native tribes of Sindh, along with their subsequent branches. In this regard, no other contemporary surpasses it. The book substantially expands and complements the information already provided by Abu al-Fazl in his *A'in-i-Akbari*.[236] During the reign of Shah Jahan, a very large number of such works were compiled, including the *Tarjumat al-Ahadith al-Arba'in fi Nasihat al-Muluk wa'i Salatin* (The Translation of the Arabic Narrations in the Book of Counsel for Kings) of Shaykh Abdul Haque Muhaddith Delhvi, for the guidance of the Emperor, but they were wide-ranging and in nature. The *Mazhar-i-Shahjahani* is significant for not including ethical counsels but giving solutions to specific problems. The author surpassed all his predecessors in India, including the much-celebrated author of the *Fatawa-i Jahandari*, Barani.[237] Dr Zahuruddin Ahmad opines that 'After the *A'in-i-Akbari*, *Mazhar-i-Shahjahani* is the foremost history of its type, which truly depicts the contemporary social, political and economic life'.[238]

Like his early years, very little is known about his old age and demise. Sources of the time indicate that he most likely died in Sehwan and was buried there. On the other hand, Syed Hussamuddin Rashidi argues that while the author did die in Sehwan, he was buried in the historical necropolis of Makli, since his brother, Mir Abu al-Baqa, was appointed the governor of Thatta till 1647 CE. The graves at Makli are in such a derelict state and there are no epitaphs; hence it is impossible to identify them.[239] The original manuscript of this book was with the author till 1638–1639 CE, when he finally handed it over to Mir Diya al-Din Yousuf, the son of his elder brother, Abu al-Baqa Amir Khan, for safekeeping.[240] Luckily, it was recovered from oblivion after more than three-and-a-quarter centuries and acquired for its author a hard-earned place among the eminent historians of Sindh during the Medieval-Muslim era.

Syed Hussamuddin Rashidi found an original manuscript in 1955 and edited its Persian text with detailed marginal notes, corrections, and traced the lineages of the author and Mughal Empress Nur Jahan. He has also given a 76-page introduction in Urdu that includes details about the life of the author, his family background and some essential and important information about the book. An addendum has been provided in order to correct the mistakes found in the manuscript.

Rashidi gives references from other authentic historical sources in the marginal notes. The book was published by the Sindhi Adabi Board, in 1962. Its Sindhi translation, rendered by Niyaz Humayun, was also published in 1979, by the Sindhi Adabi Board and includes a foreword and explanation about the administrative units (such as *sarkars* and *parganas*) of Sindh, along with notes on its geography during the seventeenth century. Dr M. Saleem Akhtar translated the *Mazhar-i-Shahjahani* into English, with an introduction and commentary. This provided helpful assistance to Rashidi in his painstaking task. The meticulous efforts of these scholars have made the source more valuable as a chronicle of the history of Sindh.

Tarkhan Nama, or *Tarikh-i Sind Dar Zamana-i Arghun Wa Tarkhan* (The History of Sindh During the Reign of the Arghuns and Tarkhans)

The tradition of preserving books that provided an authentic record of their ancestors had become a trend among the Sindhi Mughals. One such work is titled the *Tarkhan Nama*. The author, Syed Muhammad dedicated this book to his patron, Mirza Muhammad Salih Tarkhan (d. 1061 AH), son of Mirza Isa Tarkhan II. The latter had heard that there was a book on the history of the Arghun and Tarkhans titled the *Arghun Nama*. Having a desire to know the virtues and real worth of his ancestors, he requested his friend, Syed Mir Muhammad, to search for and send this book to him. Apparently, this book was no longer extant and Syed Mir Muhammad's utmost efforts to find it proved in vain. Finally, Mir Muhammad decided to write a new book on the subject, under the same title.[241] For this reason, the *Tarkhan Nama* is also known as the *Arghun Nama*, as mentioned by C.A. Storey and many other scholars.[242] This is the only book compiled by the author. Zahuruddin Ahmad and Nabi Hadi erroneously mention Syed Jamal Hussaini Shirazi as the author of the book under a double title, as the *Tarkhan Nama/Arghun Nama* compiled in 1651 CE.[243]

Nevertheless, the information about the author and his ancestors collected from different available accounts, including the *Tarkhan Nama* itself, is inadequate. From the scattered information, it transpires that the author Syed Mir Muhammad belonged to a reputed Inju Syed family, hailing from Shiraz, Iran. The author's ancestor, Syed Muhammad,[244] alias Miran Muhammad, migrated from Shiraz due to the turmoil and havoc created by the Mongol invasion there, and settled in Sindh[245] during the reign of the Samma ruler, Jam Salah al-Din (1388–1399 CE). After some time, one of the sons of Miran Muhammad, Syed Ahmad (d. 1441 CE) moved to Thatta, where he settled permanently. His family established close ties with a reputable Abbasid family of Thatta through marriage.[246]

Because of their virtues, both Syed Muhammad's grandfather, Syed Ali II and his father, Syed Jalal II, rose to high positions in the courts of the successive rulers of Sindh. They consequently secured the patronage and support of the Arghuns, Tarkhans and the Mughal rulers. Syed Ali II was given the prestigious position of *Shaykh al-Islam* during the Arghun and the Tarkhan periods. Syed Ali II was sent as the emissary of Shah Hassan Arghun, to the court of Humayun, after he regained the throne. Another reference made by the author shows that even the Mughals had high regard for Syed Ali. Akbar was born (1542 CE) during Syed Ali's visit to Umarkot and the author tells how the new-born baby was first draped in a piece of cloth taken from the Syed's attire.[247] Furthermore, after the death of Shah Hassan Arghun in 1555 CE, Syed Ali accompanied his body along with his wife, Mah Begum, to Makkah for his funeral.[248]

After the death of Syed Ali II in 1574 CE /1061 AH, his son Syed Jalal, the author's father assumed the post of *Shaykh al-Islam*. Syed Jalal developed a close association with the Tarkhan rulers of Sindh when he married the daughter of Mirza Muhammad Salih Tarkhan, son of Mirza Isa Tarkhan, in 1585 CE. When Mirza Baqi Tarkhan went on a pilgrimage to the shrine of Shaykh Farid at Pakpattan, he sent Syed Jalal as his emissary along with his daughter, Sindhi Begum, to Emperor Akbar, who was holding court in Multan. Mirza Baqi was anxious because he feared that Akbar might attack Sindh, so he was offering his daughter in marriage.[249] However, Akbar refused the proposal,[250] but delayed his campaign of Sindh at that time.

After the death of Mirza Baqi, his successor, Mirza Jani Beg Tarkhan, also sent Syed Jalal to the court of Akbar, in 1585 CE. At the time, Sadiq Muhammad Khan was marching on Sindh on Akbar's orders.[251] On Syed Jalal's request, Akbar ordered Sadiq Muhammad Khan to withdraw and the emperor bestowed an elephant and other gifts on Syed Jalal.

The author was most likely born around 1586–1587 CE and was his parents' first child.[252] We find no information about his early life, nor his academic and political career; it is only known that the author was closely associated with Mirza Muhammad Salih Tarkhan, who was one of the important rulers of the Tarkhan dynasty. Shah Jahan appointed him *fawjdar* of Thatta and Sorath (Junagadh) and later promoted him as governor of Thatta.[253] Sources reveal that Mir Muhammad had two sons, namely Syed Mir Buzurg and Syed Abdullah, but no biographical details of them are available. We also come to know from the *Tarkhan Nama* that Syed Mir Buzurg had a son named Mir Zain al-Abidin, commonly known as Syed Lutfullah, who became a prominent Persian poet under the pen-name Qani. He compiled a book titled the *Hirz al-Bashar*.[254]

However, the date of compilation of *Tarkhan Nama* has not been cited specifically by the author, but in the genealogical table at the opening of the book, he mentions the year 1654 CE, when referring to his work. This facilitates us in finding out the date of its compilation. Furthermore, other evidence in the book also suggests that the author started writing it around this time. He states in the preface that Mirza Muhammad Salih Tarkhan, the *fawjdar* of Sorath (Junagadh), expressed a desire to know the past record and family history of his ancestors in the year 1651 CE.[255] We also found evidence from other sources, such as the *Mir'at-i-Ahmadi* of Ali Muhammad Khan and *Badshah Nama* of Abdul Hamid Lahori, that Mirza Muhammad Salih Tarkhan was the *fawjdar* of Sorath during the period 1652 to 1654 CE, when Sindh was under the overlordship of Emperor Shah Jahan.[256] Therefore, it seems highly likely that 1654 CE is the date of its compilation.

The document is purely a narration of facts and particulars about the Arghun and Tarkhan dynasties in Sindh. In the preface, the author explains that his benefactor, Mirza Muhammad Salih Tarkhan, son of Mirza Isa II, assigned him the task of searching out an old work written on the Tarkhans, titled the *Tarkhan Nama*. Syed Mir Muhammad also belonged to the Tarkhan family and as such, would be preserving information about his ancestors as well. However, despite his best efforts, he could not trace this book.[257] Therefore, Syed Mir Muhammad decided to write a book on the topic with the same title, the *Tarkhan Nama*, in order to satisfy his patron.[852]

As the main objective of Syed Mir Muhammad was to highlight and maintain a history of the ancestors of Mirza Muhammad Salih Tarkhan, the author provides more attention to the old ancestors and delves deep into the past and in regard to his contemporaries, the Tarkhans, he restrains himself to brief accounts.

The book begins with the customary ascription to God and tribute to the Holy Prophet (PBUH).[259] This is followed by the preface, in which the author eulogises his patron, Mirza Muhammad Salih Tarkhan, with Arabic phrases, Quranic verses and a few Persian couplets.[260] The book has been divided into eight parts dealing with the origin and biographical accounts of different Arghuns and the Tarkhan rulers from Shah Beg Arghun, to Mirza Isa Tarkhan II respectively.

The author wrote two treatises after the preface. The first part begins from the time of the first Arghun ruler in Central Asia in 1469 CE, along with a comprehensive genealogical table starting from Hazrat Nuh (AS) right down to Nawab Mirza Isa Tarkhan in 1651–1652 CE, including Mirza Salih and thus covering about 200 years of Arghun Tarkhan history.

The second part comprises a brief history, mainly genealogical, of Hazrat Nuh, till Amir Iltutmish bin Aieko Timur, a descendent of Genghis Khan and the Tarkhan's claim descent from Aieko's eldest son. This part is divided into two chapters, or *fadals*. The first *fadal* deals with the accounts of the expulsion of Genghis Khan from Mongolia and the settlement of his successors' rule in Persia and Central Asia and the second provides accounts of a descendent of Genghis Khan, Sultan Islam Ghazan Khan bin Arghun Khan bin Abaqa Khan bin Halagu Khan. The editor eliminated this section from the printed text, as it is not relevant to Sindh's history.

The printed text of the *Tarkhan Nama* begins with the preface that leads to the accounts of the successors of Arghun Khan, son of Abaqa Khan, who laid the foundation of the Arghun dynasty in Qandahar and Sindh, consecutively. As mentioned above, the layout of the book is divided into eight parts, each describing the accounts of Amir Shah Beg Arghun, Mirza Shah Hasan Arghun, Mirza Isa Tarkhan, Mirza Muhammad Baqi Tarkhan, and Mirza Painda Beg Tarkhan, along with Mirza Jani Beg Tarkhan, Mirza Ghazi Beg Tarkhan, and Mirza Isa Tarkhan II, separately and successively.

As far as the source material is concerned, it appears from the text that the author had consulted a number of important works relating to the history of Sindh, for instance, the *Tarikh-i-Tabari*; *Tarikh-i-Guzidah*; *Mujma' al-Ansab*; *Zafar Nama*; *Rawzat al-Safa*; *Nigaristan*; *Tarikh-i-Humayuni*; *Akbar Nama*; *Tarikh-i-Tahiri*; and *Muntakhib-ut-Tawarikh*.[261] These contemporary, or near contemporary sources furnish very authentic and valuable records on the history of Sindh during that era. Two notable omissions are *Tarikh-i-Sindh*, or the *Tarikh-i-Masumi* of Mir Muhammad Masum and the *Beglar Nama* of Idraki Beglari, which had already been compiled in 1600 CE and 1608 CE, respectively. It is probable that either these books were not available to the author, or the information furnished by these sources might have been provided by other contemporary sources.

As the *Beglar Nama* is nearly contemporaneous with *Tarikh-i-Tahiri*, the author might have selected the latter, the *Tarikh-i-Tahiri*, as his source and overlooked the former.[262] Regarding *Tarikh-i-Masumi*, while Syed Mir Muhammad does not refer to it as his source, a thorough comparison of these two books reveals that the author of the *Tarkhan Nama* borrowed extensively from *Tarikh-i-Masumi*, particularly for the history of the rule of the Arghuns and Tarkhans.[263]

Interestingly, the language of the text is simple; it is written in a straightforward manner, which is somewhat unique and ahead of the literary trend of the time. The author has maintained a fine flowing style throughout the book. Moreover, it is free from the customary exaggeration, overstatement and flowery language of other existing works. Distinct from his precursors, Syed Mir Muhammad adopts an approach unusual to the times, of writing simply and concisely narration and circumventing irrelevant and unnecessary descriptions of events. For this reason, the core subject in his accounts does not waver and remains constant and to the point, unlike the narrative in earlier books. Although, the author follows the customary style of embellishing the text with the odes, and Quranic verses,[264] even these are sporadic and more or less restricted to the preface. In the text, the author mentions an elegy composed by Mirza Ghazi Tarkhan, referring to the incident of the recapture of Qandahar from the insurgent Qizilbash:

آنان کہ دعویٰ لمن الملک داشتند   چون یافتم ز لطف تو بر قندھار دست
از ہول جان گریزان گشتند آنچنان   بر اسپ شان نیافت تو گوئ غبار دست [265]

Translation: Others claimed the throne; I secured control of Qandahar due to your kindness. Due to the fear of death, they ran away so fast that nobody could restrain their horses.

Dr Arshad Islam, while highlighting the historical significance of the *Tarkhan Nama*, writes:

> The main importance of *Tarkhan Nama* lies in the fact that it is the only complete book about the Tarkhan dynasty giving details about the history of the Arghuns and the Tarkhans of Sindh, their origin, migration from Central Asia and their settlement in Sindh.[266]

The *Tarkhan Nama* may surely be regarded as the sole authority over all other sources for the period of the Arghun and Tarkhan rule in Sindh, a span of 200 years. It provides supplementary information that cannot be gleaned from any other contemporary source. For instance, the details the author gives about Mirza Muhammad Baqi Tarkhan's (1566–1585 CE) accession to the throne of Thatta, and the manner in which he routed out and crushed the uprising of the seditious Arghun nobility, are worth mentioning.²⁶⁷

This work presents an unbiased description of the murder of Bega-Begi Agha, daughter of Mirza Isa Tarkhan, and her two children, at the instance of Mirza Baqi Tarkhan.²⁶⁸ The succession of Mirza Jani Beg and his marriage with Mirza Baqi's aunt,²⁶⁹ Shah Jahan's orders to Mirza Isa Tarkhan to imprison *Sharir al-Mulk* and Mirza Isa's successful journey to the imperial court where he was conferred the status of *Sahib-i-Naubat* and given a reward of one lakh rupees and his *mansab* increased by one thousand,²⁷⁰ are some of the accounts of historical significance in this work that are not found in any other. The *Tarkhan Nama* is the only book that records the date of birth of Mirza Shah Hasan Arghun and his relations with the Shaykhs, Syeds, and scholars of the times, including his *murshid*, Shaykh Dhulmanan, Shaykh Mirak Purani, Mirza Qasim Tagha'i, and Syed Ali Sherazi.²⁷¹

Interestingly, though the *Tarkhan Nama* was compiled at the instance of Mirza Muhammad Salih Tarkhan, it doesn't provide adequate information about him or his son. It gives no information about the socio-cultural and economic history of Sindh. While its aim was to be a specified history of the Arghuns and the Tarkhans, it is still silent on the literary and scholarly activities of Mirza Shah Hasan Arghun, Mirza Jani Beg Tarkhan and Mirza Ghazi Beg Tarkhan.

Later works, such as the *Dhakhirat al-Khawanin* of Shaykh Farid Bhakkari and *Tuhfat al-Kiram* of Ali Sher Qani Thattawi, mention these, referring to their poetry under the *noms de plume* of Sipahi, Halimi, and Waqari, respectively.²⁷² The reason for failing to provide information about the geographical, social, cultural, and economic life of the people of Sindh may be attributed to the fact that the main aim of the author was to compile a political history of the Tarkhan dynasty. For this reason, he concentrated mainly on political events, with special reference to the military campaigns of the Arghuns and the Tarkhans.

The book is an excellent arrangement of facts about the early Tarkhans. The most genuine and significant part of the book is its factual outlook on the Tarkhans, who were his contemporaries. This information has a great deal of authenticity, because it is based on either the author's personal observation, or information collected based on eyewitness accounts at that time. However, the section about the origin of the Tarkhans highlights a new perspective on this dynasty. In the beginning, the author, citing the etymology of the word 'Tarkhan', writes: 'The word "Tarkhan" is a title whose literal meaning is "shedding blood" and idiomatically, it stands for an "autocrat". [He does] whatever he wants to and is exempted from discharging any service and his sins will be pardoned till his ninth generation.'[372] He further mentions: 'A lofty title was bestowed on a group of people by the great and fortunate king, Amir Timur Gurjan. Among them, is the tribe of Amir Aeiku Timur Arghun Khan, son of Hulagu Khan, son of Tuli Khan, son of Genghis Khan…the Tarkhans, who ruled over Sindh and Qandahar are descendants of Amir Aeiko Timur.'[472]

Regardless of its authenticity and reliability as a valuable source of the history of Sindh, the *Tarkhan Nama* is characterised by some deficiencies and shortcomings. Frequently, the work shows discrepancies in dates when compared to other contemporary histories and established facts. The *Tarkhan Nama* mentions that Mirza Abdul Ali Tarkhan died in 1630 CE/1039 AH,[275] while the epitaph on his grave reads 9 Rajab 1040 AH/11 February 1631 CE). Syed Mir Muhammad committed such a glaring error despite the fact that he wrote this book in Thatta, where Mirza Abdul Ali Tarkhan was buried. Another discrepancy appears in the date of death of Nawab Mirza Isa Tarkhan, which Mir Muhammad recorded on 13 Muharram 1061 AH/6 January 1651 CE,[276] while other contemporary sources, like the *Badshah Nama* and *Amal-i-Salih* mention his death on 13 Muharram 1062 AH/26 December 1651 CE.

Another contradiction seems to have occurred in the year of Mirza Ghazi Beg's death. Syed Mir Muhammad states it was on 11 Safar 1020 AH/25 April 1611 CE,[277] while other reliable sources, like *Dhakhirat al-Khawanin* and *Tarikh-i-Tahiri* mention this event on 11 Safar 1021 AH/13 April 1612 CE. The date mentioned in the later sources is evidently correct as their authors were contemporaries of Mirza Ghazi Beg and the same date is also inscribed on the chronogram.[278] Syed Mir Muhammad puts Mirza Jani Beg's death in Rajab 1011 AH/December 1602 CE,[279] while the epitaph on his tomb indicates that he died on 23 Rajab 1009 AH/2 February 1601 CE.

At one point, Syed Mir Muhammad states that Mirza Jan Baba Tarkhan, son of Mirza Isa Tarkhan, was assassinated by Mirza Baqi Tarkhan in 979 AH/1571–1572 CE,[280] but the epitaph on his grave mentions that this tragic event took place in 978 AH/1570 CE. Furthermore, Mirza Isa Tarkhan died in 973 AH/1565 CE, as testified by his epitaph, while the author of *Tarkhan Nama* alleges 974 AH/1566–1567 CE as the year of his death.[281] Another discrepancy seems to be regarding the date of arrival of Humayun in Sindh, which, according to other contemporary sources, is 974 AH/1540 CE, while Syed Mir Muhammad puts this event in 949 AH/1542–1543 CE.[282] And lastly, Mirza Shah Hassan died on 12 Rabi al-Awwal 962 AH/4 February 1555 CE according to Masumi, Firishta, and Nizam al-Din Ahmad, but Syed Mir Muhammad states that it was on the 12 Rabi al-Awwal 961 AH/15 February 1554 CE.

In another place, Mir Syed cites the date of the death of Muhammad Khan Shibani erroneously as 1509 CE. Apparently, the author borrowed this account of Babur's invasion and siege of Qandahar from *Tarikh-i-Masumi*. Masum gives the date as 1511 CE.[283] But unfortunately, he too is wrong, and the correct date stated in the *Babur Nama* is 2 December 1510 CE.[284]

On the other hand, the date of Shah Beg Arghun's death is controversial. The *Tarkhan Nama* states that it was 1520 CE *Tarikh-i-Masumi* mentions it as 1522 CE; the *Tarikh-i-Tahiri* gives it as 1518 CE and Firishta and Nizam al-Din Ahmad state 1524 CE. Modern historians are also divided in opinion in this regard. Some follow Masum, while others say Nizam al-Din Ahmad et al. are correct.[285]

Besides these errors in the dates of such important events, another grave deficiency of *Tarkhan Nama* is that certain important events that should be described in detail are dealt with quite superficially. For instance, the *Tarkhan Nama* provides rather inadequate details about the historic event of the defeat and exclusion of Mirza Shah Beg Arghun from Qandahar in 1507 CE; on the other hand, *Tarikh-i-Masumi* provides a detailed and comprehensive account of this important event.[286] Similarly, whereas *Tarikh-i-Masumi* and *Ma'athir-i-Rahimi* narrate a thorough account of Mirza Shah Beg taking refuge with Shah Ismail Safavid in 1510 CE and his loss of support in this court, which resulted in his imprisonment and finally his flight;[287] all these significant events are treated in quite an inconsequential manner in *Tarkhan Nama*.

In regard to another episode, the Turkish traveller, Syed Ali Reis (1553–1555 CE), gives a much more comprehensive account of the events of Mirza Shah Hasan Arghun's period. Further, Syedi Ali Ra'is, who was an eyewitness to the events he describes, reports that Isa Tarkhan, one of Mirza Salih Hasan Arghun's nobility, declared his independence in 1553 CE and assumed the title of Humayun Shah in the Nasirabad fort,[288] whereas Mir Syed does not provide these details.

The war of succession, fought between Mirza Jani Beg Tarkhan and his uncle, Mirza Muzaffar Tarkhan, in 1584 CE, is undoubtedly an important incident and is described in great detail in the *Tarikh-i-Tahiri* and *Beglar Nama*, but the author of *Tarkhan Nama* does not so much as even mention it.[289] Likewise, the *Tarkhan Nama* does not provide any account regarding a major historical event, i.e. Mirza Jani Beg Tarkhan's daughter's marriage with Mirza Iraj Beg, son of Abdul Rahim Khan-i-Khanan, in 1591 CE, when the Khan-i-Khanan defeated the Tarkhan ruler and subjugated Sindh in the name of Emperor Akbar.[290]

Furthermore, it seems the author of *Tarkhan Nama* is confused about a place called Talti, which is situated six, or seven miles north of Sehwan and appears to have been on the left bank of the river Kalri. In one place, he calls it Thatta and at another, Talahti.[291]

This work seems to be very rare and only six manuscripts are available—five in the British Museum and one in the India Office Library. Syed Hussamuddin Rashidi prepared a Persian text of the *Tarkhan Nama*, with the help of two original manuscripts that he tried to make as authentic as possible. He also included an exhaustive introduction. This work was published by the Sindhi Adabi Board, Hyderabad, in 1965. However, the manuscripts were not very authentic and contain many flaws. Rashidi points this out in the preface. The Sindhi translation of this work was rendered by Mirza Abbas Ali Beg, and published by the Sindhi Adabi Board, Hyderabad, in 1994.

Intikhab-i-Muntakhib, or *Intikhab-i-Muntakhib al-Tawarikh* (*Intikhab Nama*)

The *Intikhab-i-Muntakhib al-Tawarikh* (The Selections from Discerning Histories), commonly known as the *Intikhab Nama* (The Book of Selections)[292] is generally considered as world history. It was written and compiled by Abdul Shakoor, a native of Thatta. This work is actually a selection from, or a summary of, the *Muntakhib-ut-Tawarikh*, written by Muhammad Yousuf Ataki (of Atak) in 1646 CE, during the reign of Shah Jahan.[293] By the way, there are at least twelve other books with the same title as *Muntakhib-ut-Tawarikh*, compiled by different authors from India and Persia.[294] Some of the extracts of Muhammad Yousuf Ataki's book are also translated by Elliot and Dowson for their well-known work on the history of India.[295] Muhammad Yousuf Ataki followed the pattern of general histories and compiled an exhaustive survey of events during the reign of Shah Jahan, to whom he dedicated his book.[296]

The author of *Muntakhib-ut-Tawarikh* mentions in the preface of his book that the *Tarikh-i-Masumi* and *Hadiqat al-Awliya* were in his hand at the time of compilation. In addition, he had some other sources related to Sindh. He was very well aware of the historical significance and individuality of Sindh. At the very outset, it appears that the author also used plenty of other sources such as the *Tarikh-i-Tabari*; *Tarikh-i-M'ajam*; *Tarikh-i-Guzida*; *Majma al-Insab*; *Tarikh-i-Banakti*; *Rawzat al-Ahbab*; *Milad al-Nabi*; *Rawzat us-Safa*; *Habib al-Siyar*; *Nigaristan*; *Tarikh-i-Jalal al-Din Sayuti*; *Mirat al-Jinan*; *Tarikh-i-Humayuni*; *Tarikh-i-Sindh*; *Akbar Nama*; *Tarikh-i-Nizami*; *Tarikh-i-Ba'it al-Mamur*; *Tarikh al-Hukama*; *Tadhkira al-Attar*; *Nafhat al-Ans*; *Hadiqat al-Awliya*; *Aja'ib al-Balda*; *Aja'ib al-Dunya*, etc.[297]

It apparently seems that Yousuf made no attempt to enquire, improve or correct what he borrowed from previous works. Instead, he just incorporated and summarised them. For this reason, this work has not achieved much consideration and has remained obscure. Moreover, it has not been published yet, but its manuscripts are present in many libraries. The *Muntakhib-ut-Tawarikh* runs into one *muqaddima* (preface) and five *qisms* (chapters) and a *khatima* (conclusion). The fourth chapter is further divided into two sections, and its second part is about Persia, India, and Sindh. This section is divided into six *fasls*. The fourth *fasl* deals with the history of the rulers of Sindh, starting from the Brahmans and up to the Tarkhans.[298]

When the *Muntakhib-ut-Tawarikh* was completed, its copies also reached Sindh, which is apparent because the author of the *Tarkhan Nama*, Syed Mir Muhammad mentions that he used it as a source. That was only ten years after its completion. He refers to it with the title of the *Muntakhib be Badal Yousufi*.[299] However, Mir Ali Sher Qani found this book titled the *Muntakhib-ut-Tawarikh* after a century. Qani utilised it as a source for his book, titled *Tuhfat al-Kiram*, particularly for the history of the Soomra period. Qani also evaluated and examined it from a critical perspective. The *Muntakhib-ut-Tawarikh* is so important and well-known among scholars of the history of Sindh that not only historians of yesteryear, but modern-day professors of Sindhi history use it as source material as well, such as Dr Daudpota and Syed Hussamuddin Rashidi, who consulted it when they edited the *Tarikh-i-Masumi* and *Tuhfat al-Kiram*, respectively.

In the seventeenth century, Shaykh Abdul Shakoor Thattawi chose this massive work and collected material from it to compile his work titled *Intikhab-i-Muntakhib*.[300] But unfortunately, this work could not be much known to scholars and researchers, including Mir Ali Sher Qani.[301]

The *Muntakhib-ut-Tawarikh*, written by Muhammad Yousuf Ataki, includes authentic and comprehensive accounts of the period of Shah Jahan, from the time of his accession. Shaykh Abdul Shakoor Thattawi, during the period of Aurangzeb Alamgir, prepared an abridged version of this work, under the title, *Intikhab-i-Muntakhib*, alias *Intikhab Nama*, possibly at the emperor's implied consent, in order to expose his father's conduct and prejudice during the war of succession.[302] It is apparent that the book was completed in 1673–1674 CE/1084 AH.³⁰³ This date is derived from the following chronogram:

الحمد کہ انتخاب والا   از دیدۀ عقل انتخاب است

تاریخ تمام آنخرد گفت   باغایت <u>فضل</u> + <u>انتخاب</u> است ³⁰⁴

1054 + 30 = 1084 AH/1673–1674 CE

Only some minor traces can be found regarding the life of the author of the *Intikhab-i-Muntakhib*. He writes in the preface of the book that he belonged to the Qureshi family and his ancestors came to Sindh during the time of Muhammad bin Qasim's invasion and settled in Bhakkar. They were teachers and traders by profession. His grandfather, Abu al-Qasim, was a great scholar and tutor of Mirza Jani Beg, the ruler of Thatta who appointed him as the *sadr* of Thatta after his accession and fixed twelve thousand as his annual allowance. He accompanied Jani Beg on his journey to Agra for meeting Emperor Akbar. The author's father Abdul Wasay, one of the best calligraphers of the times, served under the Tarkhan Amirs of Sindh.³⁰⁵ Mir Ali Sher Qani, the author of the *Tuhfat al-Kiram* states:

> ...he (Abdul Wasay) was one of the best calligraphers in *nastaliq* script during his times. In the service of Emperor Shah Jahan, he was appointed as a *munshi* to inscribe *farmans* (decrees) and *nishans* (orders). Shah Jahan assigned him land grants to fulfil his livelihood requirements. So, he left his job and settled in his *jagir*. Abdul Wasay had seven sons named Shaykh Abdul Sami, Shaykh Abdul Shakoor, Shaykh Abdul Ghafoor, and Shaykh Muhammad Moin, Shaykh Abdul Haque, Shaykh Muhammad Sharif and Shaykh Abdul Rauf. Each of them was greatly proficient in the art of calligraphy like their father, and were elevated to their father's place.³⁰⁶

However, Qani neither provides further details about this family, nor does he deliberate on their scholarly, or literary contributions. At the conclusion of *Tuhfat al-Kiram*, he mentions Abdul Shakoor in the list of the people whom he excluded from another book by him, the *Maqalat al-Shuara*, which was a famous biographical directory of the poets of Sindh. Though he refers to him as, 'A great personality, famous for having command over composing fine odes,'³⁰⁷ he was not certain whether this was the same person who compiled *Intikhab-i-Muntakhib*. One of Abdul Wasay's sons, Shaykh Abdul Ghafoor, was a famous chirographer whose masterwork, the inscriptions on the Shahjahani mosque of Thatta, are still extant. He completed this assignment in 1657 CE.³⁰⁸

Abdul Shakoor was born in 1634 CE, in Thatta. He acquired knowledge of the contemporary arts and had a keen interest in history.[309] After completing his studies, he joined the royal services as a *munshi*. During those times, the development and progress of Persian literature was at its zenith. *Diwans, kulliyats, tadhkiras,* histories and *inshas*, were thriving. The author was a talented and erudite person who had command over writing regional history and epistolography, or *insha nawisi*, which was a famous contemporary art. Besides the *Intikhab-i-Muntakhib*, there are some other books authored by him, for instance, the *Muntakhib Kalam*, of which we have no information. The only manuscript is conserved in the library of Aligarh University.

Another book of his is the *Mufid Mawarikhin*, written in 1659–1660 CE. It comprises biographical accounts of well-known historians.[310] His work, the *Tarikh Do az Dah Imam* (The History of the Twelve Imams), consists of twelve chapters, one on each of the Imams. Abdul Shakoor also compiled a book called *Zikr al-Hussain* (*c.* 1668 CE),[311] which was written with the help of evidence extracted from the *Rawzat us-Shu'hada* and other reliable sources. As the title of the book states, it is about the life of Hazrat Imam Hussain (RA), from his birth till martyrdom. The manuscripts of these works are present in the Shirani Collection in the library of Punjab University.[312]

The *Intikhab-i-Muntakhib* was intended as a book on general history, but it has come to be considered a valuable source for the history of Sindh. It begins with an introduction of the author and his family. This introduction itself is a worthy addition to the literary legacy of Sindh. The author himself explains the compilation of his book as follows:

> Among the low-grade learners of *insha* writing (epistolography)…he (Abdul Shakoor, writing in third person) through his determination… when he was above forty, then always pursuing his favourite activity… insomuch as this broken pen [of his] started to unveil hidden meanings from metaphors of the passages and counsels [he studied]…and he adopted this pursuit as his profession.
>
> (Reverting to first person) By coincidence, one day while attending a large gathering, I came across a famous and illustrious book entitled *Muntakhib-ut-Tawarikh*…. In the beginning, I was only intent on reading it but after a short period, when its author passed away…I started thoroughly analysing the book whenever I found free time and it continued to hold my interest—and later from its text…I selected some extracts and prepared a brief anthology out of it.[313]

This book deals with the history of the world from creation to the period of the Mughal Emperor Shah Jahan. Following the pattern of the *Muntakhib-ut-Tawarikh*, the *Intikhab-i-Muntakhib* also comprises of a preface followed by chapters or *qisms* (five in *Intikhab-i-Muntakhib*) and a conclusion, or *khatima*. In the first chapter, the lives and activities of the apostles of Islam are recounted. It begins with Hazrat Adam (AS) and ends with Hazrat Isa (AS). The second chapter deals with the history of the world; the famous kings and emperors before the times of the Holy Prophet Muhammad (PBUH). The third chapter gives information about the life and times of the Holy Prophet (PBUH) and the four Rightly Guided Pious Caliphs. The fourth chapter records the history of Muslim dynasties from all over the world and the final chapter deals with the history of the Muslim rulers of India.

The language of the *Intikhab-i-Muntakhib* is simple and straightforward. The author has maintained a smooth flow throughout the book.[314] The style bends and moulds according to the need of the narration.

The *Intikhab-i-Muntakhib* provides an authentic, valuable and reliable account of the history of Sindh during the time of the Brahmans, Arghuns, Tarkhans, and the Mughals such as Akbar, Jahangir, and Shah Jahan. It contains very important and worthy historical information, particularly regarding the Mughals. Since the author, his father and grandfather all served in the royal courts, they had easy access to official documents. Although it purports to be selections from *Muntakhib-ut-Tawarikh*, there are several accounts of substantial size in it that are original and are not taken from the primary compilation. These accounts are particularly about the Soomra dynasty of Sindh, the *Intikhab-i-Muntakhib* tells us about the more or less seventeen Soomra chiefs, who ruled over lower Sindh, mentioning their reigning periods. It not only corroborates *Tarikh-i-Masumi* in this regard, but also gives some additional information about the Soomra rulers, among whom some appear with Muslim names.[315]

At the end of the book, the author provides detailed accounts of Mirza Isa Tarkhan, Mirza Baqi and Mirza Jani Beg. As the Tarkhans were the protectors of the author and his family, their downfall broke his heart. He writes: 'Alas! The rule of the Arghuns and Tarkhans came to an end.'[613]

The author calls Chach bin Selaij 'جوانى خوش منظر' (a handsome young man), and praises his charismatic eloquence, his command over mathematics, the Sindhi and Hindi languages and being a fine scribe.[317] Describing the attributes of Jam Feroz, the author writes that when Jam Feroz ascended the throne, he spent most of his time in the female quarters. Whenever he came outside, he used to engage in dissolute activities with musicians and pranksters. The masses were prey to the excesses of his officials and when his deputy, Darya Khan, tried to restrain them from such offensive acts, they belittled him.[318]

The author also provides references about the migration of the *ulema* from Herat after its occupation by Shah Ismail Safavid, in 1512 CE and his persecution of Sunni scholars. One such scholar was Makhdum Abdul Aziz Abhari Muhaddis, who came and settled in the district of Kahan, in Sindh, with his sons Maulana Athir al-Din and Maulana Muhammad. Maulana was proficient in all contemporary Muslim theology. He had compiled numerous books, such as the *Sharah-i-Mushkwat*.[319] The author borrowed these accounts from the *Tarikh-i-Masumi*.

It is apparent in the text that the districts of Sindh, including Kahan and Baghan were so fertile and rich that when Babur came here in 1514 CE, he devastated these regions and his soldiers took one thousand camels with them that the farmers had been using to turn the wells for irrigation.[320] This description clearly depicts the prosperity of the region. The author describes the destruction of Thatta at the time of Shah Beg Arghun's invasion of Sindh, in 1520 CE. A great number of people were taken captive. Finally, Qazi Qadan, the renowned scholar of Thatta, managed to pacify the furious king who then announced an amnesty for the lives and property of the rest of the people.[321] After the conquest of Sindh, Shah Beg visited Bhakkar and ordered a fort to be built.[322]

The author informs us about a unique Sindhi custom before a battle. He states that when the forces of Shah Hasan Arghun confronted the army of Jam Feroz outside Thatta, the latter got off their horses and took off their turbans. Thereafter, they fought bareheaded. This was a traditional way of showing that they would fight to their death.[323] Highlighting the bravery and courage of Mirza Salih Tarkhan, the author writes, 'He was a great warrior of his times who achieved marvellous victories. In 1571 CE, he was assassinated by a Baloch named Murid, whose father had been beheaded by him.'[324]

This stupendous work is very rare and has not been printed yet. Only a few copies of its manuscripts are available at the India Office Library, Aligarh University Library, Kitab Khana-i-Majlis, Tehran, and in the Shirani Collection of the Punjab University Library, Lahore.[325]

CHAPTER 4

Tadhkira and *Malfuz* Literature

Distinctive from political chronicles, there are other genres of medieval Indian historical literature of non-political nature. This source material includes *tadhkiras*, *malfuzat*, *insha*, poetic works, etc. These non-political sources are fundamental for analysing history. They are considered original material, which provide authentic, unbiased, and reliable accounts which can corroborate the events narrated in political chronicles. These alternative sources of history have a fascination of their own, as they deal with real people who have left their mark in time and have a humanising effect on the subject. From these sources, we may touch the lives of the common people about whom history was generally not written. These accounts reveal human emotions, interactions, values, and attitudes of the past. These human expressions provide history with colour and excitement and link us directly to the people involved.

With the advent of Islam, Islamic mysticism spread in Sindh as well as in other parts of India. Sindh had always been the land of Sufi saints. There are numerous Sufi shrines of different mystic orders, such as the Suhrawardiyya, Qadri, etc. As Islamic mysticism flourished in the region, various scholars began to compile works on the lives of Sufi saints and this trend soon achieved a degree of popularity. Muslim Sufism was a very powerful agency that unveiled many aspects of the glorious culture and history of Sindh. As mentioned above, this religious movement engendered a rich repository of non-political historical literature, such as the *tadhkiras* and *malfuzats*, which existed separately from political and official chronicles. These include biographical works of the Sufi saints, hagiography, and the utterances and discourses of Sufi saints. This literature is regarded as a rudimentary source for scholars of history—one that gave a new shape to the Indo-Mughal historiography of the medieval period. It deploys a different method from the one applied to political chronicles to sift out historical information. This genre must be studied keeping in mind its type and the attitudes, objectives, and motivations of the author.

The writers of such literature had a vision and perspective of history that was very different to that of the official court historians. However, studying these writings can uncover socio-religious, cultural, political, and economic aspects of the lives of common people. There is a need to focus on the repetitive quality of such historical literature, which is recognised as an adverse trait inherent to Muslim literary traditions. This tends to give modern day historiographers a sceptical attitude to such source material. Current scientific methods in historiography not only reject the role that past societies played in the conception of the above-mentioned genre, but sometimes they also fail to perceive the distinctive features of each medieval work.

Biographical literature, where a number of biographies of eminent personalities were compiled in Arabic (*al-rijal*), held a significant status in early Muslim historical literature. However, *tadhkira*, which is a more intellectual-oriented compilation of biographical directories of poets, scholars, literati and artists, as well as eminent personalities, is distinct from *al-rijal*, and goes beyond classical hagiography (memoirs of the saints) and of normal lexicons and encyclopaedias. Following the same pattern as *rijal*, *tadhkira* literature emerged as an important genre of local history in the fourteenth century[1] and soon became popular among the intelligentsia of Sindh as well as in other parts of India. In the sixteenth and seventeenth centuries, when *tadhkira* as a genre became progressively more trendy, admired, and traditionally familiar in literary circles, it was expected that every talented author or poet should compile such a work in a common courtly language such as Persian.[2] In collective biographies of generally eminent personalities, which were comparatively rarer than more cerebral biographical anthologies, statesmen seem to feature less than theologians, saints, poets, and men of learning.

By and large, *tadhkira* literature comprises two major types: one, the general ones, dealing with the life and the works of the eminent men of learning, or saints, up to the lifetime of the author; two, the specialised ones, which refer to that only of a specific period, or type. This work may also be categorised with reference to its arrangement—either chronologically, or geographically, according to the native country, family, type of work, and so on.[3] Jan Rypka represents a rather contradictory outlook of his vision in this regard:

> [This form of literature is] compiled from the feudal and religious viewpoint of the ruling classes which lead to an empty torrent of words at the expense of actual biographical data, to unreliability and incompleteness. Characteristic traits are at best too far generalized, as a rule they convey

nothing and it is hardly possible to glean from them anything of fundamental value.

But he nevertheless states: 'Despite all their defects they are nevertheless extremely important and, in many cases, the only source.'[4]

However, the tradition of compiling *tadhkira* literature of celebrated people traces its origin from the growth and development of the discipline, technically known as the *asm'a al-rijal*. This science of *asm'a al-rijal*[5] became the basis of biographical works and several voluminous works, including the biographies of the people who were quoted as authorities on the *hadith*, or *sirah* narrations that were compiled.

The earliest compilation in this regard was the *Kitab Tabaqat al-Kubra* of Ibn Sa'ad (d. 845 CE) in eight volumes, a compendium of biographical information about famous Muslim personalities like the Holy Prophet (PBUH), his companions, and followers (the *Taba'in*), while the *Vafayat al-A'yan* of Ibn Khallikan (d. 1282 CE) follows a general character. Some of these works are devoted to the celebrated figures of particular sections of society, like the *Mu'jam al-Udaba* of Yaqut and *Tarikh al-Hukama* of Qifti, which deal with scholars and intellectuals in particular fields.

Tadhkira literature was also produced in regions other than India, such as Herat and Central Asia. One was titled the *Tadhkirat al-Awliya* (Memoirs of the Saints) by the renowned poet, Farid al-Din Attar (d. 1230 CE) that included a copious collection of biographies of about seventy holy personages of the first three centuries of Islam (from the seventh to the ninth centuries CE), including their famous sayings. The *Athar al-Wuzura* of Haji Saif al-Din Nizam al-Fazl and the *Nafahat al-Uns* of Jami are also well-known *tadhkiras*.

The oldest available work of this kind composed in India is Awfi's *Lubab al-Albab* (The Quintessence of the Hearts), written in 1221–1222 CE at Uch and was dedicated to Ain al-Mulk Fakhr al-Din al-Ash'ari, minister to Nasir al-Din Qabacha (r. Multan, 1203–1228 CE). It includes certain bits of information which are of immense importance regarding the history of Sindh and Multan. In this book, the author narrates the lives and critically analyses the works of the Persian poets up to his contemporaries.[6] Awfi himself substantiates his work as the earliest one among all of such kind. Sindh may truly feel proud that the first such monumental work was on its terrain. This compilation is important because it provides traces of the inception and development of Persian literary activities in the region of the sub-continent.

During the early period, most of the *tadhkira* works were compiled in Arabic, but one work, titled the *Wafayat al-A'yan* (The Death of Prominent

Men) by Ibn Khallikan (d. 1282 CE) was also translated into Persian.[7] With the development of Persian as the official and court language, most people started compiling their works in Persian. In the late fifteenth century, Daulat Shah Samarqandi (d. 1494–1495 CE) composed his *Tadhkirat al-Shuara*, or *Tadhkira Daulat Shah* in 1487 CE, though this work is not considered very reliable due to discrepancies in dates and data. The author doesn't seem to know about the book, *Lubab al-Albab*, since apparently, he has not consulted it, otherwise, he would have not had committed such mistakes. Another book, the *Majalis al-Nafa'is*, was composed by Mir Ali Sher Nawa'i, in 1490 CE. The *Rawzat us-Salatin* and *Jawahir al-Aja'ib tadhkiras* were compiled by Fakhri Harawi in 1546 and 1554 CE, respectively. The *Nafa'is al-Ma'asir* of Ala al-Dawla Qizwini is another important *tadhkira*, which was compiled in 1565–1566 CE. It contains succinct accounts of Babur, Humayun, and Akbar, including biographical notes on contemporary Persian poets.[8] Hasan Nisari Bukhari composed a biographical directory of contemporary celebrities entitled the *Madhkar al-Ahbab* in 1576 CE.

In 1591 CE, Ali bin Mahmud al-Hussaini compiled another *tadhkira*, under the title of *Bazm A'ara'i* alias *Tadhkira al-Shuara* and dedicated it to Abdul Rahim Khan-i-Khanan, the Mughal commander and a great patron of art and literature during the reign of Emperor Akbar. The author of the *Bazm A'ara'i* took frequent verbatim references from Awfi's *Lubab al-Albab*. Likewise, Amin bin Ahmad Radi composed a copious *tadhkira* of many general biographies titled *Haft Aqlim* (Seven Regions) in 1593 CE, in which he mentions the *Lubab al-Albab* as his source and quotes several references from it. It was arranged geographically and contains about 1,560 biographies.[9]

Similar to *tadhkira* literature, the compilation of *malfuzats* was another very famous historiographical tradition pioneered in Sindh during the Mughal period. This genre of historical literature, which has a spiritual aspect, a literary idiom of its own, and a definite methodology behind it, is unique from all other types. These narrations are written in a succinct style, with a thoroughness of thought. They are completely free from the influence of ruling authorities and so from any political biases and prejudices. The information gathered from mystic records presents a very different perspective to the notions formed and perpetuated by the political chronicles. For this reason, *malfuz* literature has great value in understanding important fragments of medieval Indian society.

This genre of non-political historical literature quickly grabbed the interest of the people, and the trend of compiling *tadhkira* cum *malfuz* literature soon became a necessary activity in all mystic orders in Sindh.

It was the contemporary custom for disciples to record the discourses of the Shaykh. The purpose of these works is to spread the mystical thoughts and glory of the respective saint. This literature provides accounts of mystic gatherings and thereby descriptions of the daily life of Sufi saints. However, the method and technique used in the compilation of this literature may vary from person to person. It thus needs to be analysed with a systematic and careful approach, particularly in order to find glimpses into the everyday lives of the people of the era.

Among the various *tadhkiras*-cum-*malfuzats* written on the lives of the Sufis in India, the *Siyar al-Awliya* of Mir Khurd (compiled between 1351–1382 CE); the *Akhbar al-Akhyar* of Shaykh Abdul Haque Muhaddis Delhvi (compiled after 1587 CE); the *Thamarat al-Quds* of Lal Beg; the *Ma'athir al-Kiram* of Ghulam Ali Azad Bilgrami (*c.* 1737 CE); the *Ma'arij al-Wilayat* of Shaykh Ghulam Moin-al-Din; and the *Khazinat al-A'asfiyah* of Ghulam Sarwar, are a few that provide valuable historical information of the times.[10] Thus this literature offers historians many insights into the socio-religious conditions of the times and such information is seldom found in official chronicles.[11]

The tradition of *tadhkira* literature in Sindh was introduced by Qazi Mahmud Thattawi, who wrote the biographical accounts of the Sufi saints of Sindh, titled the *Tadhkirat al-Awliya*, in 1572 CE. Unfortunately, this book is not traceable yet, though we find references to it in succeeding works. Qazi Mahmud belonged to the Abbasid family of Thatta, where he had been appointed as the *mufti*. He was also a reputed poet and a contemporary of Mirza Isa (r. 1554–1567 CE) and Mirza Baqi Tarkhan (r. 1567–1585 CE).[12] Another book with the same title was later written by Mufti Ghulam Sarwar Lahori (d. 1890 CE) and is an authenticated biographical memoir of the great Sufis of the Punjab. It became well known in many parts of India.[13] The *Hadiqat al-Awliya* is one of such works compiled in Sindh during the Mughal period.

Hadiqat al-Awliya-i-Sindh: The First Biographical Directory of the Sufi Saints of Sindh

This *chef d'oeuvre*, describing the lives of the saints of Sindh is titled the *Hadiqat al-Awliya-i-Sindh* (The Garden of the Sufi Saints of Sindh).[14] The *Hadiqat al-Awliya-i-Sindh* provides biographical accounts of forty-one *mashaykhs* and dervishes of Sindh, particularly highlighting their attainments and miracles such as Shaykh Baha al-Din Zakariya of Multan; Sadr al-Din Qatal of Multan; Rukn al-Din (Shah Rukn-i-Alam) of Multan;

Uthman Shahbaz Marwandi (Lal Shahbaz Qalandar); Pir Puttho; Hammad Jamali Thattawi; Shah Murad Shirazi; Shaykh Nuh Bhakkari; Qazi Datta of Sehwan, etc. The author Syed Abdul Qadir bin Syed Hashim Thattawi, a Hussaini Syed, was a renowned Sufi saint of Sindh,[15] though not much is known about the author's progenitors. The only reference that the author provides about himself in the book is as follows:

اما بعد، می گوید عبد حقیر و بندۀ پر تقصیر، اضعف عباد الله الغنی القوی، عبدالقادر بن هاشم بن محمد الحسینی غفر الله لہ و احسن الیہما و الیہ بغفرانہ اللائقہ جناب فضلہ والناشی من محض فضلہ و کرمہ ... الخ [16]

Translation: May God rest in peace the soul of Abdul Qadir bin Hashim bin Muhammad al-Hussaini and bestow His blessings on the departed soul.

About the author's ancestors, Mir Ali Sher Qani Thattawi writes in his *Tuhfat al-Kiram*:

...undoubtedly, they were prominent people of their times. The place of their origin is not known; though, the author's father Syed Muhammad Hashim was a contemporary of Mirza Jani Beg Tarkhan (r. 1585–1599 CE), who composed a *qasida* (eulogy) in his praise. The *Siyar us-Salatin* is one of the finest compilations of Muhammad Hashim dedicated to his patron, Mirza Jani Beg that still survives. Like his father, the author himself was a renowned and eminent pious personality of his times, who compiled a masterpiece under the title of the *Hadiqat al-Awliya*.[17]

Qani in another tadhkira compilation on the biographies of the poets of Sindh, titled the *Maqalat al-Shuara* (A Biographical Directory of the Poets of Sindh), states that Syed Abdul Qadir bin Syed Muhammad Hashim was among the contemporaries of Amir Khusro Khan, who composed some couplets in praise of the famous poet.[18] Syed Hussamuddin Rashidi, the internationally acclaimed scholar of history and literature of Sindh, who eruditely edited the *Hadiqat al-Awliya-i-Sindh*, regarded him as a native of Thatta. However, like Qani, he was not certain about his native place.[19] Finally, Dr Hamid Ali Khana'i resolved this question and proved in the light of *Shajrah-i-Tayyaba Sada't-i-Nasarpur* (Genealogy of the Syeds of Nasarpur), that Syed Abdul Qadir was a native of Nasarpur and not Thatta.

This genealogy reveals that the author's father, Syed Hashim, was a highly esteemed, pious, and virtuous personality. Many people were enlightened by his intellectual and academic excellence and came under his patronage. He had two sons, Abdul Khaliq Shah and Syed Abdul Qadir, both of whom were famous reverent personalities of their times.[20]

Abdul Qadir's grandfather, Syed Muhammad al-Hussaini's father, was Syed Mubarak. He was an ancestor of the Rizwi Syeds of Nasarpur and was an eminent scholar, dervish, and saint of his times. Muhammad Hashim was the author of numerous books and compiler of a *diwan* (collection of poetry). He ran a *madrasa* (educational institution) in Nasarpur.[21] Syed Abdul Qadir was a man who was an admirable and greatly revered person; a poet and scholar of unique taste and talent. He was well-versed in the *hadith*, *fiqh*, and *tafsir*[22] and compiled numerous books on them.[23]

The couplets composed by the author are mentioned in the preface of his book, the *Hadiqat al-Awliya*. Rashidi sahib selects two out of them as the finest example of his poetry:

جمال صورت معنی، کمال دین و دول   نهال دولت و جاه و گل حدیقهٔ جان [24]
از فیض نشاء کرم او جهانیان   بمایهٔ نشاط و طرب، همدم و ندیم [25]

Some of the author's odes are incorporated in the biographical memoirs of Hazrat Lal Shahbaz Qalandar, Pir Puttho, Shaykh Jiono, Pir Murad, and Syed Ali Shirazi. He also composed a eulogy in praise of Shah Jamil Garnari.[26] Though the author does not furnish sufficient information about his life and career, internal evidence in his book implies that he was very devout about attending mystic gatherings. He provides references to his meetings with contemporary Shaykhs and mystics, such as Dervish Rukn al-Din,[27] Shaykh Para'i Weerdas,[28] and Makhdum Nuh Halai.[29] The date of the author's death is not known.

The author expounds that he spent a whole year collecting information from reliable contemporary scholars, saints, and through other authentic sources. Thereafter, he critically examined the data he had gathered and completed his assignment by 1607–1608 CE /1016 AH.[30] He mentions the year of its completion at the end of the book:

رسید این نامہ درحد تناهی   ز هجرت بود الف و شانزده سال [31]

Translation: Now this book came to its end, in the one thousand and sixteenth year of *Hijra*.

Syed Abdul Qadir dedicated his book to Khusro Khan Chakras, who was the president of the regency council that had been set up by Mirza Jani Beg to rule on behalf of his minor son, Mirza Ghazi Beg. The author of the *Dhakhirat al-Khawanin*, Shaykh Farid Bhakkari, also expresses his admiration for Khusro Chakras and writes that he was a righteous man and was held in high esteem as a pious Muslim. He was generous and kept himself close to the poor, never ignoring a man in need.²³ It may be said that Khusro Khan Chakras was indeed worthy of this dedication as he was the most capable and sincere person of the time. He is credited with building 360 public works, including mosques and monuments during his tenure of office.³³ Qani also praises him. He writes that Syed Abdul Qadir dedicated his *Hadiqat al-Awliya* to Khusro Khan, who merited the dedication. Qani also composed verses in his praise.⁴³

As was the custom, the book begins with the customary ascription to God. The author frequently uses Persian and Arabic couplets to embellish the text and eruditely describes the attributes of the 'Creator of the World' and hymns the praises of Almighty Allah in a very sophisticated manner, and he also praises the Holy Prophet (PBUH), revealing his deep devotion for him.

The book runs into forty-one chapters, each of which is devoted to a Sufi saint. There is also a preface and an appendix in which he gives the biography of Syed Jamil Shah Garnari, the *murshid* of the author. In the preface, he mentions the purpose of compiling this directory. He states that his desire to preserve a record of the biographical data and discourses of prominent religious scholars and Sufi saints persuaded him to compile this work. It took almost a whole year to carry out this painstaking task.⁵³

Although, the author mainly based his work on reliable oral testimonies and evidences, he referred to some written sources as well, such as the *Nafhat al-Anas* of Maulana Jami, particularly for a brief account of Shaykh Baha al-Din Zakariya of Multan; another written source he used is the *Kinz al-Ramuz* of Amir Sadat Hussaini for the memoirs of Shaykh Sadr al-Din Qattal (d. 1285 CE).³⁶

The third source that he utilised, according to him, is the *Tarikh-i-Humayun* or *Tarikh-i-Humayuni*, from which he gleans the events of Sultan Muhammad bin Tughluq's life and times. However, it seems the author was mistaken. Syed Hussamuddin Rashidi infers that the author mistakenly considered Barani's *Tarikh-i-Ferozshahi* as the *Tarikh-i-Humayuni*, which contains the accounts of several saints, such as Makhdum Nuh Hala'i, Dervish Wahaio, Dervish Raju, and Setya Dal, etc.³⁷

It is evident that the author had no other source of the *tadhkira* genre at hand at the time of his compilation and was unaware of the *Tadhkirat al-Awliya* of Qazi Mahmud Thattawi, which was the only other *tadhkira* on the lives and times of Sufi saints of Sindh that had been compiled so far.[38] For this reason, he had to rely on conventional oral versions and eyewitness accounts.

This book is in the nature of a literary flourish, so common among the medieval literati. Despite the simple and straightforward style of other contemporary sources, such as the *Tarikh-i-Sindh* alias *Tarikh-i-Masumi*, *Tarikh-i-Tahiri*, and *Beglar Nama*, the author of the *Hadiqat al-Awliya* indulges in a complex and elaborate mode of writing. This evidently indicates that he preferred a classical hagiographic style in spite of the contemporary prevailing literary traditions. The text is blended with Arabic and other unfamiliar words and phrases that make it difficult to read. For instance, he uses terms like:

مطرز، حقده آن و آليق، مطيه، استنمامتى، صحارى، طريق برارى، [39]
محط، اتساع، بلب تجبيل، تقبيل، وثاق، تنفير، مجبول، تمساع، اقتناص،
اصياد، حجرات [40]

The author is a noted scholar of Islamic hagiography and he copiously interjects Quranic verses in the text. In this manner, he tries to impress the reader with his eloquence and verbosity. He makes hyperbolic exaggerations when he relates the marvels and miracles of the saints, accentuating idolisation over factuality.

The *Hadiqat al-Awliya* is regarded as an authentic and valuable historical source which, besides the other hagiographies of the mystics of Sindh, also includes 'scattered lines of mystical poetry'.[41] It provides plenty of information about the sixteenth century. After 1530 CE, during the reign of the Arghun King Shah Hussain, political havoc spread in Sindh, during which a group of Sindhi mystics migrated to Burhanpur in Central India. They used to recite Sindhi odes during the *sama'* gatherings, when the music was playing and dancers were whirling in full ecstasy (*wajd*).[42]

It is apparent that there is no authentic source and reference for ancient Sindhi poets and their poetry. Among the books and *tadhkiras* which provide scattered bits of information, the *Hadiqat al-Awliya* can rightly be regarded as the earliest and one of the most valuable and reliable sources for the history of Sindhi literature. A substantial number of references are available in it and from which much of the history of Sindhi poetry can be traced. For instance, it reveals a Sindhi couplet that Shaykh Hammad Jamali composed in paying tribute to Jam Tamachi:

جوٹون، مت اوٹو، جام تماچى آء   سباجھى باجھ پئى، توسين تتوراء [43]

Dervish Nuh Kibra'i composed the following verse at the time of an argument between Jam Salah al-Din and Jam Tamachi:

جوٹون وجيين جهوری ماريو   جام تماچی شهرين چاڑ هيو ⁴⁴

The author also provides references to the Sindhi poetry of Ishaq Aahingar, which he heard from Para'i Veerdas.⁴⁵

Syed Abdul Qadir elaborates on the mystic gatherings of saints and thereby describes the religious activities. The accounts of these venerated Sufi saints also include details of their celebrations, like *urs* and *fatiha* and this sheds light on the socio-religious and cultural life of the people of Sindh. The philosophy of Persian poets such as Attar, Hafiz, and Jami, deeply influenced Sindhi mystic thoughts and poetry.⁴⁶ The author is rightly commended for compiling such a masterpiece of historical significance. It is a unique source for the political and cultural history of Sindh at a time when there were books only about the activities of the rulers and the aristocratic class. The author enthusiastically displays his feelings of scrupulous devotion to the dervishes and Shaykhs. The *Hadiqat al-Awliya* is a significant source of mystic thought, ideas, and preaching in medieval Sindh. He divides the Sufi saints of Sindh into three major categories according to their grades and orders, such as:

صاحب سلوک و شريعت، کامل مجذوب، فنا فی الله⁴⁷

This refers to the first type of saint who strictly follows orthodoxy. The second type he terms *majzoob*. They are those whose religion immerses them in ecstasy. A *majzoob* is a person lost in religious fervour and divorced from the outside world. The third type of Sufi saint, called *fana fillah*, are those who remember nothing but Allah Almighty. *Fana fillah* is the first stage of self-annihilation on the way to becoming one with Allah.

Among all the saints mentioned by Abdul Qadir, Makhdum Nuh Hala'i is of particular significance. According to the author, Makhdum Nuh frequently visited Thatta to meet his friends and disciples. The author deciphers the date of his demise as: ھ 899.بود نوح بنی شيخی -

He also mentions numerous references to Makhdum's life and activities. In one place, the author writes:

> I have heard from Makhdum Nuh that the people of his spiritual world say a religious personality can learn a lot from Hazrat Khizar (AS).⁴⁸ By the grace of God, he would ask me to lead the congregational prayers so he could offer prayers behind me. I responded to him to go ahead as per the advice.⁴⁹

The book basically seems to be an anthology of Sufi writing that deals with the revelations and miracles of the Sufi saints of Sindh. The author states that on a Friday, Makhdum Sabir Kalahari went to Jami Masjid (The main mosque) to offer his Friday prayers and deliver the Friday sermon and he stood not behind but beside the Imam's prayer mat. When other people came, they said the place was for the Qazi and he must leave it. The Makhdum said, 'I am the Qutub (the person who delivers the sermon) and the Qutub is senior to the Qazi.' The people mocked him and removed him from the place forcibly. When the congregation stood up to say their prayer there was no room for him. He addressed the mosque, 'O, mosque! People prostrate themselves, why don't you?' With these words, the mosque, along with the roof, and walls, collapsed and all the people died under the debris.[50]

The stories of miracles and marvels of the saints are elaborated with hyperbolic imagery and myths and therefore one must tread with caution when examining them. This assimilation of Islamic hagiographic anecdotes and legends by the author adds colour to the narrative. For this reason, Syed Hussamuddin Rashidi, in his introduction to the *Hadiqat al-Awliya*, writes that through the depiction of wonderful miracles the author has tried hard to prove that each one of the personages is so powerful that they exist in a higher spiritual realm of the extra-human ideals and actions.[51] For example, in the biography of Dervish Ibrahim, he writes, 'Once he wondered why the Dervish sometimes needed to go the toilet whereas he was free from the necessity of eating… When the Dervish left the toilet…a servant saw two little eggs were there which were very fragrant. He picked them up and folded them in his handkerchief.'[52]

Besides describing the miracles of the saints, the author also offers interesting bits of information about the religious and socio-cultural aspects of the life of common people, for which we find no other source.

Tadhkira Mashayikh-i-Sewistan: The Biographical Directory of the Sufi Saints of Sewistan

The *Tadhkira Mashayikh-i-Sewistan* is one of the several compilations of a non-political nature. It belongs to the genre of classical hagiography (memoirs of the saints) of South Asian medieval saints. It is a biographical directory of fourteen Sufi saints who are buried in Sewistan, today known as Sehwan, such as Uthman Marwandi, or Lal Shahbaz Qalandar (d. 1274–1275 CE) and his contemporary and subsequent saints, i.e. the fourteen Sufis who are buried in Sewistan. After Lal Shahbaz Qalandar, Sehwan became a centre of Sufism.

Sehwan is regarded as one of the oldest towns in Sindh. It has existed since the times of Alexander the Great's invasion, in 325–326 BC and one of its oldest forts is said to have been built by him. At the time of the Muslim invasion in 712 CE, it was one of the four major provinces of Sindh called Sewistan. The Muslims named it Sehwan.[53] It came under the Mughals in 1612 CE, with the appointment of a Mughal governor. During the Muslim period, Sindh became the centre of mystic activities. Many mystic orders and shrines flourished here. In this manner, writing on mysticism took root rapidly. The greatest Sufis of Sindh, Shah Abdul Latif Bhittai (1689–1752 CE) and Sachal Sarmast (1739–1829 CE), also belong to this blessed land.

Unfortunately, no accounts are extant about the life and career of the author of the *Tadhkira Mashayikh-i-Sewistan*. The author only mentions his name as Abdul Ghafoor bin Hyder at the beginning of the text.[54] He compiled this account of biographical memoirs of the Sufis and *mashayikhs* of Sewistan around 1629–1633 CE, when Deendar Khan was the Mughal governor of Sewistan.[55] According to Dr Zahuruddin Ahmad, the book was completed in 1632 CE/1043 AH.[56]

Syed Muhammad Bhawah, alias Nawab Deendar Khan, was devoted to Sufism and the saints. The author mentions that the governor visited various shrines and showed a keen desire to know much about the saints entombed there. Then Deendar Khan ordered the author to collate the biographical memoirs of the native mystic saints in order to glorify their name. Thus, the author collected information by interviewing knowledgeable persons and seeking available sources. He finally compiled this analogy and submitted a copy to the custodians of the tomb of Lal Shahbaz Qalandar, so that people would know all about the life and marvels of that saint in the future.[57]

This *tadhkira* is compiled in a very succinct genre and is a booklet of twenty-one pages. Each page contains sixteen lines. It includes a commentary on the lives of fourteen Sufis, *viz.* first and foremost, Makhdum Uthman Qalandar, Lal Shahbaz, Shaykh Channa Imran, Qazi Burhan al-Din, Shaykh Nakhrij, Syed Mohib Afghani, Haji Sadr Lakha, Shaykh Dodha, Qazi Dittah, Qazi Idrees, Shaykh Topin, Makhdum Iskandaria, Syed Salaar Ghadhi, Shaykh Ahmad Sanda'i, and Syed Miyan Jalal. The style of the document is simple and straightforward, forgoing the customary flowery language of medieval times. The author embellishes the text with a number of chronograms, mentioning dates of important events. Occasionally, he quotes Quranic verses in order to highlight the significance of the matter.

There is a brief preface, followed by the accounts of the Shaykh and Sufi saints of Sehwan. There is no division of content into chapters. The author gives a great deal of attention to the life of Lal Shahbaz Qalandar, for which he refers to the *Tadhkira Mashayikh-i-Sindh* and also the *Tarikh-i-Ferozi* (*Tarikh-i-Ferozshahi*).[58] The book is significant as it is comprehensive, authentic, and details the earliest accounts of Lal Shahbaz Qalandar's life (d. 1361 CE). It may rightly be regarded as the leading source in this regard. For the other *awliyas*, he collected information through his personal efforts.

The *Tarikh-i-Ferozi* is the foremost source of information about the venerated saint, which mentions his arrival in Multan and his wholehearted welcome by the ruler of the city, Prince Sultan Khan, son of Ghayas al-Din Balban. The prince offered him to stay in Multan but Lal Shahbaz Qalandar refused his offer.[59]

The book also gives descriptions of the epigraphs inscribed in the mausoleum of Lal Shahbaz Qalandar, the adjacent mosque, and other edifices in Sehwan. These include three of the oldest epigraphs in Sindh. The oldest and most momentous among these was inscribed at the time of the construction of a tomb that was built for Sultan Muhammad bin Tughluq. The sultan died in Thatta, during a campaign in Sindh and was first buried here. Later, his body was exhumed and buried in Tughluqabad (New Delhi).[60] This epigraph exhibits a chronogram mentioning the date of demise of the sultan, which is 1353 CE.

This work is unsurpassed by any other compilation of its kind for the reason of the distinctive style of the text. The author deserves praise for his outstanding effort to preserve the records of the fourteen notable and almost legendary religious personalities of Sindh.

Unfortunately, this book got lost some time after its compilation. However, some references were made to it during the last century. In 1959, Khan Bahadur Khudadad Khan referred to it in the last segment of his *Lubb-i Tarikh i-Sindh*.[61] Hakim Fath Muhammad of Sehwan in his compilation *Qalandar Namo* (Sindhi) used it as a source, while Maulana Din Muhammad Wafa'i also used it for his *Tadhkira Mashayikh-i-Sindh* in 1989. Dr N.A. Baloch wrote an article on it, which was subsequently published in the *Quarterly Mehran* in English, in 1970 and later in Urdu, in 1972.[62]

Syed Hussamuddin Rashidi first mentioned the *Tadhkira Mashayikh-i-Sewistan* in his introduction to the *Hadiqat al-Awliya* in 1967, but it was limited only to mentioning the name. Later, Rashidi received this manuscript from his friend, Simon Dig, who got it from the library of the Royal Asiatic Society, London. He published this text in the *Quarterly Mehran* (3–4, 1979), and after five years, Niyaz Humayuni translated it into Sindhi in the same journal. Rashidi sahib intended to publish it after conducting erudite research on it as he had done for the *Makli Nama*, with corrections and marginal notes, but unfortunately, he passed away in 1982 and could not do this task.

Professor Dr Ghulam Muhammad Lakho, a distinguished scholar and an expert on the history of Sindh, initiated the process of publishing its edited Persian text, along with its Sindhi translation in a booklet form, on the celebration of 758th death anniversary of Hazrat Lal Shahbaz Qalandar in 2010. It was published by the Committee Jashn-i-Lal Shahbaz, district government, Jamshoro-Sindh, leading to the subsequent rediscovery of the book. Dr Lakho regards it as the foremost source on the history of Sehwan. And while there are some flaws in it, the work has preserved valuable traces of Sindh's history that cannot be found in any other source. It is a milestone in the history of the mystics of Sindh.[63]

Since the author's benefactor, Deendar Khan, was devoted to the Sufi saints, the author compiled this hagiography according to his taste and expectations. Following the traditional Islamic hagiographic style, the author glorified the stories of miracles and marvels of the *awliyas*. These accounts are beyond any logic and reason and are quite unbelievable. An anonymous person wrote this note on the title page of the manuscript:

رسالهء هذا، عبدالغفور ابن حیدر برای پیشکش و نذر نواب سید بهوه بهوه مقلب به دیندار خان در سنه یکهزار و سینه هجری بمقام تالیف کرده موسوم به ... تذکرۀ مشایخ سیوستان ... گردانید. در حقیقت حکایش خالی از هذیان مجانین ق مبهوتین نیست و کاتب 25 صفر سنه یکهزار یکصد و نود و شش هجری بخط خواندنی باتمام رسانید.[64]

Translation: Abdul Ghafoor bin Hyder, wrote this book in 1039 AH titled the *Tadhkira Mashayikh-i-Sewistan* for presenting it to Syed Bhawa alias Deendar Khan... Actually, its accounts are not free from mistakes and myths and this scribe transcribed it on 25 Safar 1196 AH.

In this mode, the author tries to highlight the exalted spiritual status of these mystic saints. Even so, heightened religious zeal is no excuse for spreading an exaggerated, necessarily fictitious image of the saints. In pursuing such idealism, medieval hagiographers seem to be influenced by Persian literature. Jan Rypka expresses in this regard that:

> It must be borne in mind that Persian lyrical poetry began in a sphere of vigorous reality, yet soon became involved in a mysticism which is frequently quite incompatible with Islam, and, whilst professing mystic love, becomes to such an extent obsessed by eroticism that is not always possible to draw a reliable dividing line between real and super-mundane love.[65]

The anecdotes and accounts of miracles that abound in the book help us in understanding the spirit of the time and the social and cultural milieu of the period. Through these anecdotes, moral lessons were taught to the people, such as the anecdote about the destruction of a place of sin when Lal Shahbaz arrived in Sehwan.[66] There is a story about an attempt made by Dallu Rai to seduce Fatima, the wife of his brother Makhdum Chattu Amrani.[67] Through these anecdotes, the author tries to highlight the significance of chastity in Muslim society. It is interesting to note that in some other previous sources, such as the *Tarikh-i-Tahiri*, it was mentioned that the towns of Alor and Brahmanabad were destroyed due to the curse of two oppressed ladies, named Badi al-Jamal and Fatima, because the ruler Dallu Rai made an assault on their grace and honour.[68]

In Abdul Ghafoor's book, there is another story of the rebirth of Shaykh Nakhraj that also seems fictitious. The author writes:

> On the Eid day, when the chief of the fort came out of the city accompanied by a huge gathering to go to Eidgah with his protocol...a man wearing a shroud stepped out from a ruined grave and asked the passers-by what was happening? The people replied that today is Eid day and the chief was making an appearance at the place where Eid prayers would be offered. On hearing all this, the man went back down into the grave and said: I did not have this in my mind. People of understanding interpreted the event that the man appeared from his grave thinking it might be doomsday or God knows better. Later on, this grave was reckoned to be that of Shaykh Nakhraj and became very popular among people.[69]

Regardless of these unrealistic anecdotes, the *Tadhkira Mashayikh-i-Sewistan* is regarded as a valuable source for a chronicle of the development of the Sufi mystic order and the biographical accounts of the famous Sufi saints during the eleventh century. It gives their correct names, lineage, and place of burial. Most of them are untraceable now. It also mentions some important epigraphs placed at different tombs of Sehwan that unveil some historical information and dates. The chronogram related to the construction of Lal Shahbaz's shrine reveals that it was constructed in 1356 CE, by Malik Ikhtiyar al-Din, the governor of Sindh and Multan, during the rule of Sultan Feroz Shah Tughluq:

ـ بعہد دولت فیروز شہ، سلطان دین پرور   کہ خاک در گمش سازند، شاہان جہان افسر

Translation: During the reign of Sultan Feroz Shah, who is preserver of the religion; all the rulers of the world are devoted to him.

عمارت شد مقام شیخ عثمان مروندی، کو   ولی اللہ باز اسفید میر بحر بود و بر

Translation: The shrine of Shaykh Uthman Marwandi was built ... the saint of Allah is the lord of sea and land.

بروز ہفتم از ماہ رجب مبنی شد این روضہ   بسال ہفصد و پنجاہ و ہفت، ہجرت مہتر [70]

Translation: On seventh of the month of Rajab, the shrine was built...in the year 757 after hijra.

The book also suggests that Malik Ikhtiyar al-Din constructed the tomb of Lal Shahbaz Qalandar's *khalifa*, Syed Ali, in 1357 CE.[71] The date of renovation and reconstruction of Qalandar's shrine and a mosque within its premises by the Mughal governor Deendar Khan, in 1629–1630 CE, is also mentioned in another chronogram.[72] The author provides some other chronograms relating to the erection of the Jami Mosque and other mosques and monasteries located in Sehwan. He provides references about the location of the grave in which Sultan Muhammad bin Tughluq was first buried, after his death in Thatta.

During the Mughal period, an original work in this category of a collection of historical biographies, was compiled by Muhammad Sadiq Hamadani, under the title, *Tabaqat-i-Shahjahani* (The Classes of Shah Jahan). It included the biographies of 871 eminent personalities who lived in Persia and India under the rule of the Timurids, from the reign of Timur, up to that of Shah Jahan (from 1370 to 1636 CE). A little earlier, Syed Noor al-Allah bin Syed Sharif Shushtari composed the biographical memoirs of eminent Shi'ite saints and rulers from 1585 to 1602 CE, in Lahore, titled the *Majlis al-Muminin* (The Meeting of the Faithful).[73]

Collections of biographies compiled by scholars are extremely rare in early Indo-Muslim literature, the foremost work of this kind is the *Khulasat al-Hayat* (The Quintessence of Life), written by Ahmad Thattawi in the sixteenth century.[74] An important branch of biographical literature in India is the compilation of biographical directories of Mughal noblemen, such as *Ma'athir al-Umara* of Samsam al-Dawla Shahnawaz Khan.

During the Mughal rule in Sindh, *tadhkira* literature came to be shaped in abundance and appeared as a valuable source of information for the social, cultural, and literary history of the epoch. Besides, it includes some accounts of a political nature that can be used to corroborate political history. In the process of reconstruction of the social and cultural activities of the literati, nobility, scholars, and Sufi saints, the significance and value of *tadhkira* literature cannot be denied.

The *Dhakhirat al-Khawanin* of Shaykh Farid Bhakkari is regarded as the earliest of its type and provides a great deal of information about the Mughal nobility in Sindh.

Dhakhirat al-Khawanin: The Earliest Biographical Directory of the Mughal Nobility

The *Dhakhirat al-Khawanin* is an exceedingly useful and authentic historical account of the history of the Mughals. As the title of the book indicates, this is a biographical directory of the Mughal nobility, ulema, Sufis, and literary celebrities from the time of Akbar, till 1650 CE. This gigantic work is a great contribution to the historical literature of Sindh. The author dedicated it to Nawab Shaista Khan, an eminent Mughal nobleman.[75] Dr Zahuruddin Ahmad refers to it under a different title, the *Tadhkirat al-Umara*,[76] one that has not been used by anyone else. There is another such directory also called the *Tadhkirat al-Umara*, which was compiled by Kewal Ram, during the reign of Aurangzeb. Subsequently, the contents of the *Dhakhirat al-Khawanin* were later extracted by another scholar, Shahnawaz Khan, for his stupendous work on a biographical directory of the Mughal nobles, titled the *Ma'athir al-Umara*.[77]

The author of the *Dhakhirat al-Khawanin*, Shaykh Farid Bhakkari, was an eminent scholar, historian, and biographer of his time and had been employed in the service of the Mughals in Sindh and other places for a substantial period of time. During his appointment in the Deccan, he started the compilation of this work in 1649 CE and completed it in 1650–1651 CE, as is mentioned in the text.[78]

Other books have been compiled on the lives of the statesmen, officers, and nobles of the state, but as far as it is known, none before that of Shaykh Farid Bhakkari. He is rightly justified in referring to this fact in his introductory remarks. He states that historians had produced volumes on the lives and works of the kings, but nobody had cared to write an account of the nobles; for this reason, he undertook the task of compiling this work. Besides the *Dhakhirat al-Khawanin*, the author states that he wrote some other books and mentions the titles of two of them: *Tarikh-i-Shahjahani* and *Tuhfa-i-Sarandazkhani*. But unfortunately, we neither have any information nor any copy of these works.[79]

The author, Shaykh Farid Bhakkari, was the son of Shaykh Maruf, a native Sindhi scholar. He claims to be a descendant of a Faruqi Shaykh family and also of the family of the *sajjada nasheens* (custodians) of the shrine of Hazrat Shaykh Baha al-Din Zakariya of Multan.[80] His father, Shaykh Maruf, first joined the services of Mirza Isa Beg Tarkhan at Thatta, but attained a more exalted position, fame, and honour when he joined the Mughal forces during the reign of Akbar. He accompanied the Mughal forces during the siege of Bhakkar in 1570 CE. After the occupation of Bhakkar by the Mughals, he gained the trust of the Mughal governor, Nawab Murtaza and was appointed as the *sadr* of Bhakkar with full authority.[81]

Shaykh Farid was born at Bhakkar, as his name indicates, but the date of his birth and death are neither mentioned in his own work, nor by any other contemporary source.[82] The *Danish Nama-i Adab-i Farsi* (International Bibliotheca of Persian Literature) mentions 1651 CE/1061 AH as the year of his birth, but this statement is incorrect.[83] Dr Moin al-Haque, who edited *Dhakhira*, states that, 'It would be reasonable to put it in the last decade of the tenth century of Hijra [last decade of the sixteenth century CE].'[84]

Though not much is known about the author, we know he belonged to a noble and esteemed family of Bhakkar and many of his relatives were well-known in elite and literary circles. For instance, one of his maternal uncles, Muhammad Ishaq Bhakkari, was a reputed scholar of the era. Muhammad Ishaq was also a classmate and one of the closest friends of Mir Muhammad Masum Bhakkari, a distinguished Sindhi historian of the Mughal period.[85] Muhammad Ishaq Bhakkari was at one time appointed the tutor of Mirza Ghazi Beg, the son of Mirza Jani Beg.[86] He was the one, who introduced Mir Masum to Nizam al-Din during his posting in Gujarat, where Muhammad Ishaq himself was appointed as *wakil*[87] and *diwan* (finance minister). He also remained successful in acquiring a prestigious *mansab* for Mir Masum.[88]

We find meagre information in the *Dhakhirat al-Khawanin* regarding the author's early life and academic career. The author mentions the name of Mulla Mustafa Allami Jaunpuri as one of his teachers from whom he acquired the knowledge of *ilm al-aruz* (the laws of poetry), calligraphy, and inscription.[89] He also tells us about Mulla Mustafa Allami Jaunpuri's famous scholarly discourses with Mulla Thattawi, which continued for almost seven days. He also refers to Mir Abu al-Qasim Namakin as his teacher.[90] He attained the knowledge of *ilm al-kalam*[91] from Mulla Ahmad Thattawi. He was well-versed in Persian, Arabic, Pashtu, and Hindi, besides Sindhi, which was his mother tongue.

There was a generous *amir* during the reign of Jahangir, Syed Murtaza Bhakkari, who had a *jagir* in Bhakkar. In the early part of his professional career, Shaykh Farid was appointed the caretaker of Murtaza's *jagir*.[92] According to the author himself, he first joined Mughal services as a *wakil* of Abu al-Fath Deccani when the latter defected to the Mughals and joined the Khan-i-Khanan, the Mughal governor of the Deccan. In 1606 CE, the author was appointed the *fawjdar* of Lucknow.[93]

After the campaign of Udaipur, Shaykh Farid was conferred a *mansab* of sixty-five *sawar* (horsemen). He was not content with this, so he returned to his native place. After two years, he was installed as *amin* of the *suba* (province) of Berar, where he lived for nearly eight years, with elevation of his *mansab* to five thousand.[94] He participated in Khan Jahan Lodhi's campaign of Deccan in 1610 CE and became *diwan* of Jahangir's wife, Nur Jahan (1577–1645 CE) in 1615 CE.[95] He was again appointed as *bakhshi-i-kul*[96] of the *sarkar* of Khan Jahan in 1628 CE, where he was entrusted with some important duties.

When Khan Jahan Lodhi (d. 1631) the popular Afghan Mughal governor of Deccan rebelled against Shah Jahan, early in his reign, Shaykh Farid remained loyal to the Mughal emperor. However, despite this, when he went back to Bhakkar the Mughal noblemen regarded him with suspicion and he found that he was in serious trouble. Fortunately, another Mughal nobleman, Mirza Muhammad Hussaini, took him under his wing and he was able to re-establish his reputation.[97]

From a number of incidents quoted in the pages of his work, the personality of Shaykh Farid emerges as a man of learning, mature wisdom, loving habits, balanced disposition, compassion and someone helpful. The most striking aspect of his character is that he seems to be a man of great objectivity, free from personal biases and rancour and who worked with almost all the leading Mughal nobles.

He also worked under Mahabat Khan (d. 1634 CE)[98] for a long period, starting from 1630 CE.[99] Later, he held the position of *Wakil-i-Mutlaq al-Inan* (regent of Mughal affairs) of the *sarkar* of Dalmau, near Lucknow, in 1632 CE. In this capacity, Shaykh Farid made untiring efforts for the improvement of the financial conditions of this region. Later, he became *amin* (land surveyor/assessor) and *waqa'i nawis* (news writer/royal reporter) of almost a dozen fortresses in Deccan in 1650 CE. He had a lengthy and variegated career, extending over a period of almost half a century under the Mughals which provided him opportunities for establishing personal contacts with the distinguished nobles about whom he wrote first-hand information in his book.

The author mentions that he initiated the compilation of the book at the instance of Khan-i-Khanan Nawab Shaista Khan, a notable courtier of Shah Jahan.[100]

The first volume of the book deals with Akbar's reign and gives biographical accounts of 184 nobles of his court; the second deals with 226 nobles of Jahangir's period; and the third with the nobles of Shah Jahan's reign. It gives details about the activities of the Mughal nobles appointed to different *sarkars* of the Mughal Empire. The author also describes many events in Sindh, particularly detailed accounts of Mirza Jani Beg, Ghazi Beg, and Isa Tarkhan II.[101] He gives a description of the conquest of Sindh by the Khan-i-Azam. The author also gives biographies of the famous scientists, poets, literary men, artists, and writers of Sindh.

The events are authentic as they were gathered by the author himself, either from personal experience and knowledge or from consulting his contemporaries, and some he must have collected from hearsay evidence; also, no doubt he must have sought information from his father who was familiar with the Mughal court as well. For the most part, the author narrates brief accounts in his book, but in some instances, he provides a detailed rendition.

It was not possible to compile such an extensive work without carefully studying the authentic material he had. Apart from collating information personally, he also refers to books; for instance, he quotes the *Tarikh-i-Nizami*[102] about Bairam Khan; he refers to the *Tabaqat-i-Akbari*,[103] which he calls the *Tarikh-i-Nizami* of Nizam al-Din Ahmad, to describe the story of the submission of Dawood Khan, the king of Bengal; similarly, he also cites the *Tuzuk-i-Jahangiri* and other contemporary works, mostly while recounting current political events and affairs.

As far as the language of the text is concerned, it is simple and straight forward. Since the author was a native of Sindh, he employs numerous Hindi and Sindhi words and expressions in his text which are usually not found in other Indo-Persian works. For instance: گھڑی (moment), پلنگ (bed), کوری (coin), چودھری (headman of a village), چوڈول (a children's ride), چوکی (check post), کڑھ (piton), چوپربازی (an indoor game people used to play with a dice), بھٹیارہ (cook), پوت (son), ٹانکہ (stitch), etc.[104] In several places he quotes maxims in local dialects. For instance, he writes:

آگ لگنتی جھونپڑہ جو نکلے لابھ

ترجمہ یعنی از خانہ آتش گرفتہ ہر چہ آید نفعے است.[105]

Translation: Whatever comes out (is rescued) from the house on fire, are gains.

In addition, the author uses Arabic proverbs and dictums. As he was fond of composing chronograms, he occasionally quotes these chronograms in order to mention the dates of the death of significant personalities. Moreover, he mentions the date of the conquest of the Fort of Daulatabad, as he himself was present on the occasion:

'قلعہ مفتوح شد'،
'دولت آباد فتح نمودند'
و 'دیوگیر فتح شد'،
'سروپای نظام الملک
شکستہ'. 106

As mentioned earlier, the *Dhakhirat al-Khawanin* is regarded as the foremost compilation of its kind that comprises a directory of the Mughal nobility. Prior to it, there was a tradition of compiling hagiographical accounts (biographies of saints and poets). However, some historical accounts did reserve some pages for the accounts of the Mughal aristocrats, such as the *A'in-i-Akbari*, *Tabaqat-i-Akbari*, *Padshah Nama*, and *Amal-i-Salih*, etc.

Abu al-Fazl, the author of *A'in-i-Akbari*, provides a list of Mughal courtiers, but he only mentions their names and titles without any other details. Explaining the reason for this, Abu al-Fazl stated that nobody else except the emperor was 'praiseworthy', so he did not elaborate on the achievements of anybody other than the emperor.[107]

The *Ma'athir al-Umara* of Shahnawaz Khan and the *Tadhkirat al-Umara* of Kewal Ram are two other notable compilations of biographical directories of the Mughal officials and grandees. They were written more than a hundred years after the *Dhakhirat al-Khawanin*.[108] It is apparent that the authors of both of the above-mentioned works took motivation from the work of Shaykh Farid Bhakkari.

Another important feature of the book is that it is a highly interesting and useful work that also provides rare information about the elite class. It was so highly regarded by other contemporary scholars that the author of the *Ma'athir al-Umara*, Samsam al-Dawla Shahnawaz Khan, mentions it as his source in almost six places. Samsam al-Dawla freely, rather almost wholly, borrowed Shaykh Farid's statements. His book is also valuable because of the details he gives about the habits, behaviour, and interesting facts about the personal lives of many noblemen during the reigns of Akbar, Jahangir, and Shah Jahan.

Shahnawaz Khan, who himself uses *Dhakhirat al-Khawanin* as his source, tries to diminish its value by declaring it to be unauthentic and claims it is based on hearsay. However, it is clear that Shaykh Farid was meticulous about the authenticity of the accounts. He took great care in determining the facts before recording them. He was so concerned about the accuracy of dates that he uses chronograms describing important events and these help the reader determine the correct dates of the events.

The frequent use of appropriate chronograms also substantiates the author's refined taste for poetry. Dr Moin al-Haque, who edited and wrote an exhaustive introduction of the *Dhakhirat al-Khawanin*, considers Shaykh Farid to be a talented poet, as he claims he composed couplets that he quotes at two different places in his book. The poems from which the couplets are quoted are titled *Sipah Sal'ar Rafty* (Commander Left) and *Rukh-i-mard* (Face of a Man)[109] in praise of Muhammad Khan Niyazi[110] and Nawab Rashid Khan[111] respectively, who were the two distinguished Mughal noblemen.[112] However, this statement does not seem correct as the author himself states that he was humming the verse in praise of Niyazi, which would seem to indicate that they are from a eulogy written by some other poet. The other stanza apparently is also not written by him and actually by a famous Persian poet Anwari. The author states that he included the said verses by the famous poet in a letter of sympathy he wrote to Rashid Khan, after the latter broke his leg from falling off a horse.[113]

The author's perceptive nature is evident in various accounts recorded by him in the book. For instance, when he accompanied the army of Khan Jahan Lodhi during his campaign to Burhanpur in 1610 CE, he keenly observed all of the latter's strategies and activities, whom he regarded as his 'great benefactor'.[114] For this reason, we find authentic (eyewitness) accounts of Khan Jahan's career and activities, particularly the details of his rebellion against Shah Jahan, which are not found in any other source.

A discourse of Shaykh Farid with Mahabat Khan on the merits of Khan Jahan evidently proves that he was very much impressed by the latter's virtues and generosity.[115] Under the command of Mahabat Khan, Shaykh Farid witnessed many events of historical significance in person, such as Mahabat Khan's farewell ceremony in *Bagh Dehrah* (a garden) in 1632 CE.[116] This was a memorable occasion, which was recorded by the author with minute details.

Furthermore, the events of Mahabat Khan's victories over the Deccani states and his exploits provide brilliant eyewitness accounts of Mughal warfare in the South, which are extremely authentic and of utmost historical significance. The Maratha uprising in terms of Shahji

Bhonsla's activities; his exploitation of his treaty with the Mughals; the assistance given by Deccani states to the Marathas; Fath Khan's appeal to Mahabat Khan for providing help against the Marathas; and then his treacherous conduct towards the Mughals and conquest of Daulatabad in 1633 CE, are some of the important topics for which the book proves to be an authentic source.[117] Shaykh Farid also gives evidence about the rebellion of Jagat Singh, son of Raja Basu in 1642 CE, for suppression of which the emperor sent an expedition known as the Battle of Mau, in which the author also participated.[118]

Describing a number of events, the author refers to his own participation, or his presence at the event; for instance, on the occasion of Jahangir's marriage with Nur Jahan, in which the author corroborates the denial of any scandalous story of Jahangir's love affair with Mihr-un-Nissa (Nur Jahan) even before she married her first husband Sher Afghan (d. 1607 CE), and it was in the sixth year of his coronation that Jahangir sent the marriage proposal to Nur Jahan (1611 CE).[119] The author further praises Nur Jahan's talent for her innovations in different fields like perfumes, cloth, dresses, etc. He also highlights her concern for impoverished women and her various charitable actions to help them. The author also states the well-known incident of Abu al-Fazl's repentance from apostasy at the time when the former was in Deccan.[120]

The *Dhakhirat al-Khawanin* furnishes information about many minor incidents that were not much known among the Mughal officials and are not found in any other source like the *Ma'athir al-Umara*. Furthermore, it mentions and provides details about numerous Hindu officials; *diwans*, *wakils*, *pishdast*, *amils*, *karoris*,[121] etc., who served in imperial posts. Some such eminent Hindu *amirs* and *mansabdars* are Rai Durga Das, Rai Goverdhan, Rai Bihari Das Khanna Khatri, Rai Chaturbhuj, and Gokal Das, etc., to whom the author pays ungrudging tribute, though he highlights their deficiencies such as accepting illegal gratification, indulging in intrigues, etc., on the other hand, he also describes their virtues, the good they did, their helpful attitude towards people and their fellow townsmen, and the pains they took to benefit them. In this way, the author provides an idea about harmony between the Hindus and the Muslims.[122]

The book divulges some interesting facts about some distinguished personalities, such as Mirza Isa Khan Tarkhan, who apart from being a ruler, was also a gifted poet and a talented musician with a deep love for Sindhi and Hindi music.[123] Gardening and cultivation of fruit-bearing trees were hobbies of Mir Abu al-Qasim Namakin.[124] The book also speaks about Mir Muhammad Masum Bhakkari's zeal for farming and agriculture. It tells us that Mir Muhammad Masum Nami, the author of *Tarikh-i-Sindh*, was a skilful scribe, great poet, and renowned historian of his time.[125] It highlights the generosity of Jaswant Rai and the honesty and loyalty of Raja Birbal and Khawas Khan, who were famous Mughal noblemen of Akbar's period.

The book dilates on the deeds of some noblemen Shah Jahan's period. The most detailed account found in the *Dhakhirat al-Khawanin* is that of Mahabat Khan. This narration occupies 156 pages in the printed book. Other *mansabdars* are discussed in brief. The book also contains interesting bits of information about the contemporaries of the author, which are not found anywhere else. For instance, Abu al-Fazl, Abdul Qadir Badayuni, Akhwand Darwiza (the author of the *Dabistan al-Mazahib*) mention Bayazid Ansari, alias Pir Roshan (d. 1585 CE), as being an infidel and heretic, but contrary to this Shaykh Farid declares that he was a monotheist who had observed *shari'a* law throughout his life. The author refers to Pir Roshan's book compiled in Pashto entitled the *Khayr al-Bayan* to prove his statement:

آن کتاب مدل بر اثبات وحدت وجود است، دلایل و حجت ساطع و برہان قاطع از روی نص ق احادیث و اقاویل بزرگان سلف آوردہ۔ [126]

Translation: That book is an authentic source that proves the concept of *wahdat al-wujood*.[127] It provides knowledge duly corroborated by the holy Quran, *hadith*, and utterances of religious scholars.

As Shaykh Farid was greatly devoted to the eminent Sufi saints and their preaching, he himself was a disciple of Mir Abdullah Mishkin Qalam.[128] In Ajmer, he enjoyed the company of famous *awliyas*, such as Khawaja Haji Muhammad, Qazi Muhammad Sharif Jaunpuri, Shaykh Muhammad Mohi al-Din, Raja Abdul Qadir Manikpuri, Hakim Ata'i, etc. He was particularly, a great admirer of Shaykh Baha al-Din Zakariya[129] and Miyan Shaykh Junaid of Gujarat and he mentions them with great regard in his book.[130]

Shaykh Farid describes a number of events related to the lives and preaching of the Sufi saints. He furnishes accounts of other distinguished Sufi saints with admiration and respect thereby showing his ardent love for mystic orders. His accounts about mystic celebrations like *urs*[131] and reciting of *fatiha* for the deceased, shed light on the socio-religious and cultural life of the people of Sindh. He mentions the tombs and mausoleums of different Sufi saints and tells of the extensions and repairs of these monuments. The description of the art and architecture of such places not only refers to the culture but indicates the economic conditions of the region too.

The author quotes many incidents about the miracles and virtues of these Sufi saints. He highlights their loving attitude towards people, even their enemies. One such saint was Shaykh Junaid, the *murshid* of Shaykh Farid Ganj-i-Shakr of Pattan.[132] From these incidents, a structure of Sindhi society can be gleaned that can enable scholars to understand the deep devotion and love of the people for Sufi saints[133] and there are numerous relevant rituals and rites which are still popular and prevail in society today. These events also throw light on some of the beliefs of these Sufis, which the orthodox *ulema* and imperial noblemen objected to. The author also points out some contemporary socio-religious activities such as the Roshaniya movement, which were condemned by Mughal historians as being heretical.

The Roshaniya was a mystical movement in the time of Humayun and Akbar, named after its founder, Bayazid Ansari, alias Pir Roshan (d. 1585). The theories were very pantheistic and were condemned by the orthodox *ulema* and jurists. Yet this mystical movement seems to have survived beneath the surface of religious life during the seventeenth century.[134] Shaykh Farid mentions this movement in a positive light, which, according to him, evoked deep devotion and utmost sincerity in its followers.

Further, the *Dhakhirat al-Khawanin* mentions the development of literary and cultural life in Sindh during Mughal rule. The author also gives detailed accounts of the famous poets, scholars, and *ulema* besides the Mughal nobility. It appears from the text that most of the Mughal officials were great patrons of learning and literature and promoted scholarly activities. Shaykh Farid provides details about Sarandon Khan Alma, the *fawjdar* of Dalmau, who allocated generous amounts for granting allowances and gifts to *ulema* and dervishes so much so that he failed to pay full dues to his soldiers.[135] Some accounts reveal tales of cruelty and oppression of some of the Mughal officials on the locals and also their associates who were weaker. The author also tells us about the foreign policy and diplomatic relations of the Mughals, particularly the Safavids of Persia.

It is evident from the text that the author was quite independent of any influence on his views and never hesitates in criticising and sometimes even condemning the vices of the powerful men about whom he writes. For example, he informs us that Mirza Abdul Rahim Khan-i-Khanan was an irascible hypocrite, but he had very strong principles. He tells us about the pleasure-loving, debauched, and merciless temperament of

Nawab Murtaza Khan; the spiteful nature of Mir Masum Bhakkari, who loved to be flattered,[136] and the cruelty, frankness, inconsistency in his religious thoughts, and disregard of religious practices of Mahabat Khan. This information about the personal character traits of such renowned personalities is very rare and valuable.

Apart from all this, the book is a great source of information on art, architecture, and fine arts, like music, painting, etc., under the Mughals. It is indispensable because it gives detailed information about matters that Shahnawaz Khan in *Ma'athir al-Umara* usually only summarises. There are interesting bits of information about events, occurrences, lives, customs, buildings, etc., which throw light on the personal as well as professional lives of some of the great noblemen of the time. The book contains substantial information about the literary as well as architectural activities of the period. It provides quite a good deal of information about the modes of transportation, dress, food, perfumes, customs, sports, games, music, learning, and weapons as well as the different methods of punishment that were particularly invented by some *amirs*. Highlighting its historical significance, Dr Ziauddin A. Desai states:

> This pioneer biographical directory of Mughal noblemen, despite its somewhat confused, complicated and at times not quite clear diction, lack of some dates of events, at times not correct statements, and other such shortcomings, based as it is on personal and first hand witness accounts, comprises a very important source-material, particularly for the non-official—though it does provide some new information on the [official] field too—and social life of the time of Akbar, Jahangir, and Shah Jahan.[137]

Despite the authenticity and undoubted historical worth of the book, it displays some deficiencies. The author commits discrepancies in the dates of many important events about the lives and times of the nobles. Further, he does not facilitate the reader with descriptions of the important places mentioned by him. Sometimes, he indulges in digressions, and incorporates irrelevant details running into more than one page, which affects the sequence of the narration. He does not follow any order or sequence or uniformity of approach as does Samsam al-Dawla in his *Ma'athir al-Umara*.

At times, the author omits the titles and designations of the nobles or uses them in anticipation or irrespective of the time they were held.[138] These shortcomings have been compensated by the editor Moin al-Haque, to some extent by writing marginal notes, which facilitate using the book as a historical source.

Only two manuscripts of the *Dhakhirat al-Khawanin* are available; one in the library of the Pakistan Historical Society and the other in that of the Anjuman Taraqqi Urdu, Karachi.[139] With the help of both of these manuscripts, the Pakistan Historical Society published the text edited by Dr Moin al-Haque in three volumes. However, Ahmad Munzawi informs us about another manuscript in the *Fehrist Mushtarik Nuskha'i Khatti Farsi Pakistan* (Directory of Persian Manuscripts in Pakistan).[140] Its translation in English is rendered by Ziauddin A. Desai and published by the Idara Adbiyat-i-Dilli, in 1993.

Apart from these three major works in the *tadhkira* category, *viz. Hadiqat al-Awliya*; *Tadhkira Mashayikh-i-Sewistan*; and *Dhakhirat al-Khawanin*, there are some other shorter compilations. The only available source that mentions these other *tadhkiras* is the *Hadiqat al-Awliya*. Dr Zahuruddin Ahmad reproduced these accounts from the *Hadiqat al-Awliya* word-for-word in his book, the *Pakistan mein Farsi Adab ki Tarikh* (*ahd-i-Jahangir se ahd-i-Alamgir tak*). These accounts are given below.

The *Risala-i Fat'hiya* (The Book of the Songs of Victory): This compilation was written in 1610 CE. The author, Makhdum Fath Muhammad, was a grandson of Makhdum Nuh Halai (d. 1592 CE), a leading mystic saint of the Suhrawardiyya order in Hala, Sindh. The author also composed verses with the pen name of 'faqir'. This account is consequently divided into three major parts. The first 658 pages are devoted to the topic of mysticism. Then the author provides the biographical accounts of Makhdum Nuh. The manuscript of this book is rare and is present only in the personal collection of Makhdum Muhammad Zaman I (1640–1704 CE) who was a renowned scholar, poet, and leader of his time. He was the seventeenth *Sajjada Nasheen* of Ghous al-Haque Makhdum Sarwar Nuh's shrine in Hala and a forefather of the late Makhdum Amin Fahim.[141]

The *Bayan al-A'arifin* (The Speeches of Sufis): This book was written by Muhammad Rada bin Abdul Wasay, alias Mir Darya'i in 1628 CE. It consists of seven chapters with a preface and conclusion. Each chapter is subsequently divided into eleven parts, known as *fadl* (sections). This book gives the complete biographical accounts, the *malfuzat*, and *a'urad* (Quranic supplications) of Shah Abdul Karim Bulri[142] and his contemporaries.[143]

The *Yamin al-Barakat* (The Sources of Blessings): The author of this compilation, Mehta Mol Chand, was a Hindu yogi of Sehwan (Sewistan). He collected the biographical accounts of Lal Shahbaz Qalandar and compiled them in 1661 CE. However, the contents of the book are considered to be neither very authentic nor accurate. The author traces the genealogical tree of his own family and highlights his association with the shrine of this venerated Sufi saint of Sindh. At the very beginning, the book includes some odes of different poets praising the saint, which includes the *qasida* of the Hindu poet, Karpal.[144]

The *Dalil al-Dhakirin* (The Arguments of the Narrators): The author of the *Dalil al-Dhakirin*, Haji Panhwar, completed this book in 1694 CE. It was written in the seventeenth century, during the period of Makhdum Muhammad Zaman I of Hala (who is mentioned above as well). This book is historically valuable because it relates some unique accounts regarding the contemporary socio-political conditions. The author describes the mutual relationships and affection of the contemporary saints and religious personalities for each other. He also gives valuable information about the historical mosques of Sindh. The book is divided into four chapters. The first comprises the biographical accounts of Makhdum Nuh's ancestors. The later three chapters include the biographies of Makhdum Nuh and other contemporary mystics.[145]

The *tadhkira* literature produced in Sindh, despite some shortcomings, is a significant source of information on various aspects of life and society during a period when the Mughal rule was at its peak. *Tadhkiras* are an indispensable source of historical information and deserve the attention of, and proper utilisation by scholars and researchers of Mughal history.

CHAPTER 5

Insha Literature (Epistolography)

Letter-writing and the art of writing epistles is commonly called *insha*.[1] *Insha nawisi*, also known as *insha pardazi*, or epistolography, was another prevailing expression of literary activity in Mughal Sindh. *Insha* literature does not refer only to private and social correspondence, but all letters of public, political, and diplomatic matters. During the medieval period, it was the most pertinent expression of men of learning to show their erudition and literary abilities. Excellence in drafting letters and documents, the art of officials, lay in a highly elaborated and forceful style.[2]

This literature mainly falls into two categories: 'epistolographic manuals', written to guide people in the art of letter-writing, and the *insha*, collections of letters and documents that were actually dispatched. The latter facilitates in determining historical facts and often provided information that was not available from other sources.[3]

Zinat al-Kuttab (The Art of Secretaries), or *Rutbatal-Kuttab*, written by Abu al-Fazl Bayhaqi (d. 1077 CE) is regarded as the earliest work in Asian history in *insha* literature. As its title suggests, it is a manual of instructions on secretarial practices and the formal style to write letters.[4] It was indeed a handbook of the times for officials and chancery practices. The author himself calls it 'unique in its treatment of that art (*funn*)'.[5] This book provides an early history of the functions of a *dabir* (secretary) as an official of the Arab, Persian, or Turkic dynasties in Persia.

In India, *al-Tawassul-ila't-Tarassul* of Baha al-Din Baghdadi, seems to be a model of this art, which included showing some official documents dating from 1182 CE.

However, Amir Khusro's work, *Aijaz i-Khusrawi* (*c.* 1319 CE), is considered a pioneer of sorts and one that traces the origins and introduces the art of *insha* writing in India. It provides a great deal of information on the socio-cultural and literary history of medieval India. These literary essays of Khusro show literary power and he presents actual drafts of letters written by poets.

Insha-i-Mahru of Ain al-Mulk Mahru is another important work in this category. It includes examples of 134 letters and documents of different types, like *manshurs* (manifestos), *misals* (examples of correspondences), *ahd namas* (official treaties), *ard-dashts* (petitions), personal letters, proclamations, etc. These letters were dispatched officially to different authorities, scholars, and public workers and thereby provide interesting bits of information about the functioning of the Tughluq administration (r. 1321–1398 CE).[6]

Further regarding regions in India, two compilations; one by Mahmud Gawan, the *Riyaz ul-Insha* and the *Insha-i-Shah Tahir*, or *Insha-i-Tahir Wahid* (*c.* 1545 CE), which is the collection of letters of Shah Tahir Hussaini to Burhan Nizam Shah of Ahmadnagar, appear to be very important sources for the cultural and political history of the Deccan (the south). These compilations also shed light on the diplomatic relations of the Deccani states with the foreign world, particularly Persia.[7]

Similarly, other Indo-Muslim literature, particularly that of the period of the great Mughals, is full of several copious *insha* collections. The earliest in this period is the compilation of *Baday'i al-Insha* or *Insha-i-Yousufi* of Maulana Hakim Yousufi of Herat (*c.* 1533 CE) during the period of Humayun.

A significant compilation near the end of this era is *Nigar Nama-i-Munshi* (*c.* 1683 CE), written by an anonymous author, who used the pen-names Munshi and Malik Zadah. It is a valuable collection of documents of Aurangzeb's reign. The *Nigar Nama-i-Munshi* comprises two major *daftars*, or sections, which follow an introduction largely devoted to the subject of *insha nawisi* (draftsmanship and epistolography). The book includes letters of appointments, *diwans* (registers containing records of revenue collection), and orders.[8] At the court of Akbar was his famous biographer and poet, Abu al-Fazl (d. 1602). He was also a consummate letter writer. His nephew, Abdul Samad, compiled and published a collection of official letters and *farmans* (decrees) in 1606 CE, titled the *Insha-i-Abu al-Fazl*, also known as the *Maktubat-i-Allami* (The Epistles of Allami), which is considered a masterwork and an authentic and useful source in understanding the author's own ideas with reference to some of the cultural and religious developments and trends of the epoch.[9]

Ruqqat-i-Abu al-Fazl (The Letters of Abu al-Fazl) is another collection of Abu al-Fazl's letters, which is equally interesting. It comprises private letters written by Abu al-Fazl to his friends and contemporaries, collected by his nephew, Noor Muhammad. Abu al-Fazl 'was something more than a mere conventional official historian.'[10] Abu al-Fazl's elder brother, Faizi (d. 1595 CE) was one of the 'nine gems' of Akbar. He also left behind a collection of *insha*, which was also collected and edited by Noor Muhammad and titled the *Latifa-i-Faizi*. This is another valuable source regarding the Mughal period from which contemporary socio-cultural, religious, and literary trends can be gleaned. These letters throw light on the diplomatic relations of the Mughals with the Deccani states and the socio-cultural conditions of other regions that the author visited.[11]

During the reign of Jahangir, Har Karan, son of Mathurdas Kanboh of Multan, was a celebrated name in the field of *insha* literature. He composed a work titled the *Insha-i-Har Karan*, between 1624 and 1630 CE. It contains official letters of appointments that throw light on the functioning of Mughal officials and various Mughal administrative practices. It also includes letters of authority exempting specific traders from the payment of *baaj* (tribute) and *zakat* (tax to be given to the poor). Information about the economic conditions can be gathered from it as well.[12]

Emperor Aurangzeb Alamgir in particular took a keen interest in promoting the art of letter writing. There were three eminent *insha pardazans* in the court of Aurangzeb who held the office of *mir munshi* (chief secretary): Abu al-Fath Qabil Khan Wala Jahi, his brother and successor Muhammad Sharif Qabil Khan, and the next successor Mulla Uthman Fazil Khan, who came from Sindh.

Aurangzeb himself possessed command over this art and produced numerous masterpieces. Collections of Aurangzeb's letters, or *Ruqqats*, such as the *Raqa'im-i-Kara'im* (The Collection of the Epistles of Emperor Aurangzeb); *Kalamat-i-Tayyabat* (The Pure Words); *Ramz wa Ishara ha'i Alamgiri* (The Signs and Codes of Aurangzeb); and *Dastur al-Amal-i-Aagahi* (Code of Conduct or Rule of Law), are of immense historical importance.

Apart from the above-mentioned compilations, there is a great deal of other *insha* literature composed under the aegis of the Mughals. For instance, the *Chahar Bagh* of Hakim Abu al-Fath of Gilan (d. 1581 CE); *Munshat-i-Namakin* (*c.* 1598 CE) by Mir Abu al-Qasim Namakin; *Zubdat al-Insha* (Compendium of Letters) by an anonymous writer compiled during the reign of Jahangir; *Insha-i-Munir* (Letters of Munir; *c.* 1644 CE) by Munir Lodhi; *Gulshan-i-Balaghat* (Garden of Balaghat in the Deccan; date unknown) of Abdul Wahab Fana'i; *Bahar-i-Sukhan* (Blossoms of Speeches) by Muhammad Salih Kanboh (d. 1674 CE); *Munshat-i-Brahman* (Epistles of Brahman; *c.* 1657 CE) by Chandra Bhan; *Insha-i-Amani*, or *Insha-i-Khanazad Khan* (*c.* 1637 CE) of Amanullah Khanazad Khan; and *Insha-i-Baqir Khan* (*c.* 1637 CE) of Baqir Khan Najm-i-Sani, are some of the famous works on *insha*.[13] Besides their literary value, these works are of great historical significance too. These compilations provide glimpses into the literary, cultural, and religious life of people, in addition to the prevailing ideas and thoughts of the period.

The period of the Great Timurids also witnessed the development of historical literature in Sindh. By far the largest part, or almost all of this literature was in Persian which, by the way, was not the mother tongue of the Mughals. *Insha nawisi*, or letter writing, emerged as a highly esteemed talent that involved having immense control and command over the language. A considerable amount of *insha* literature was produced in Sindh as well. The earliest collection compiled in Sindh is the *Munshat-i-Mahru* (The Epistles of Mahru) of Ain al-Mulk Mahru, which contained interesting information about the working of the Tughluq administration.[14]

Sindh produced a number of *insha pardazans* (epistolographers) who were experts in the art. Maulana Yar Muhammad Yari (d. 1570 CE) of Herat is one well-known name attached to the court of Sultan Nasir al-Din Mahmud of Bhakkar (d. 1574 CE). Since he was also a distinguished poet, Sultan Mahmud, the ruler of upper Sindh, sent him to the court of Akbar as his representative.

The *insha* literature produced during the Mughal period in Sindh comprises three major works: *Munshat-i-Namakin*, *Aadab-i-Alamgiri*, and *Raqa'im-i-Kara'im*.[15]

Munshat-i-Namakin (The Epistles of Namakin)

Munshat-i-Namakin was compiled in 1598 CE, towards the end of Akbar's reign. It is regarded as a masterpiece among the compilation of manuals dedicated to the emperor.[16] Unique in its contents, which include a curious and extensive depository of authentic documents of great historical interest, *Munshat-i-Namakin* is a book for the instruction of epistolography. It comprises sample letters and documents, which were designed to serve as models and standards for *munshis* and *dabirs* for use on different occasions. It was written by Abu al-Qasim Khan Namakin, a Hussaini Syed hailing from Herat, who was said to be a 'seasoned soldier, shrewd commander, astute administrator, prolific writer, and an enlightened builder.'[17]

Abu al-Qasim first served Mirza Muhammad Hakim, son of Emperor Humayun. Later, he proceeded to Lahore, where he joined the court of Emperor Akbar, who bestowed upon him the *jagirs* of Bhera and Khaushab. Soon, he won Akbar's confidence by the virtue of his loyalty and talent. This *jagir* was in the proximity of the salt ranges in the Sindh Sagar Doab.

Ma'athir al-Umara mentions that Mir Abu al-Qasim presented Akbar a cup and a plate[18] and some other utensils[19] made of salt, as a token of his loyalty to his 'salt'. Akbar appreciated the pleasing manner of Abu al-Qasim and conferred upon him the nickname of '*Namakin*' (*namak* means salt). Henceforth, this sobriquet became an inseparable part of his name. Syed Hussamuddin Rashidi considered this epithet as having connotations with '*namak halal*' which means 'loyal' or 'grateful'.[20] On the other hand, Hermann Ethé, the compiler of the *Catalogue of Persian Manuscripts in the Library of the India Office* interprets this title 'Namakin' as 'the witty' which is also substantiated by Dr Saleem Akhtar.[21]

Mir Abu al-Qasim Namakin secured distinguished positions and ranks under the Mughals. He participated in several battles with the Mughal forces, including the campaign of Gujarat (1573 CE), Orissa (1574 CE), Bihar (1574 CE), and Bengal (1576 CE), where he showed his superior military capabilities.[22] As a reward for his outstanding performance, Akbar gave him an elevated status and subsequently appointed him to Bhakkar in 1596 CE[23] after the subjugation of Sindh in 1591–1592 CE.

The author was entrusted with some important assignments in Sindh. He was assigned the *Sarkar* of Bhakkar excluding the *parganas* of Darbela, Kakari, and Chanduka, which belonged to the *jagir* of Mir Masum Bhakkari.[24] Namakin rapidly got promoted by the virtue of his meritorious services, elevated as the governor of Bhakkar, in 1598 CE. At imperial orders, Mir Abu al-Qasim Namakin accompanied Mirza Ghazi Beg Tarkhan, the successor of Jani Beg and new ruler of Thatta to visit the Mughal capital in October 1606 CE, a few days before the demise of Akbar.

During the reign of Jahangir, Mir Abu al-Qasim Namakin was elevated to a *mansab* of 1,500. He was later sent to Jalalabad to lead a campaign. When he was on the way to Jalalabad, in May 1606 CE, he was ordered to block the western bank of River Chenab to intercept the rebel Prince Khusro, who was trying to cross it. Jahangir rewarded Mir Abu al-Qasim for his contribution to the arrest of Khusro by promoting him to a *mansab* of 3,000.[25] Subsequently, Namakin proceeded to Qandahar with Mirza Ghazi Beg Tarkhan, with a strong contingent of his loyal Mughal soldiers.[26]

Unfortunately, he could not come back to Sindh and died a year later, while travelling towards Sehwan. His body was carried to Bhakkar for burial.[27] The date of his death is revealed from the following chronogram as 1018 AH (1609 CE), which is inscribed on the epigraph on his grave:

چونکہ تاریخ سال فوت نوشت
گفت ملہم مرا بگوش ضمیر
سال فوتش کہ 'بادجاش بہشت'[28]

1018 AH (1609 CE)

Many of Mir Abu al-Qasim Namakin's sons and grandsons occupied influential and prestigious positions under the Mughals, dating from the period of Akbar, till Aurangzeb, such as Amir Abu al-Baqa Amir Khan; Amir Abdul Karim Amir Khan; Yousuf Mirak (author of the *Mazhar-i-Shahjahani*); Mir Abu al-Makarim Shahud (composer of *Mathnawi Pari Khanah*); Suleiman Syed Ashraf (compiler of *Raqa'im-i-Kara'im*); and Amin al-Din Khan Hussain (compiler of *Malumat al-Aafaq* and *Rushhat al-Fanun*). Furthermore, other members of this family, such as Zia al-Din Yousuf, Mir Razi al-Din Khan Fida'i, Mir Hyder al-Din Abu Turab Kamil, Mir Muhammad Ata, and Mir Abu al-Wafa, were also renowned personalities of their time. There are many architectural remains, including mosques and monuments, that are a testament to the prominence of this family, such as the Safa-i-Safa in Bhakkar and the Safa-i-Wafa in Sehwan, constructed in commemoration of Mir Abu al-Qasim Namakin.[29]

Mir Abu al-Qasim was well-known for his valour and literary talent. He possessed a refined taste in poetry. He used to arrange gatherings of poets and scholars at his place. And while none of his poetic works is extant, we have come to know of another work of his that has been lost, titled the *Jawami al-Jawahir*, on the philosophy of Islam.[30] The author dedicated it to his patron, Mirza Ghazi Beg Tarkhan (d. 1612–1613 CE).[31] Dr Momin Mohiuddin is of the opinion that both of these works were probably compiled during the author's stay in Bhakkar. However, Hussamuddin Rashidi, in a reference to the *Biyad* of Miyan Ghulam Ali Madah, mentions some of Namakin's verses in it.[32]

Munshat-i-Namakin is probably the only collection that comprises an exhaustive documented record of the early period of Akbar's reign. It also corroborates and adds to the information furnished by other contemporary existing chronicles. This book may rightly be regarded as the first treatise of the Mughal period that includes the legal contracts and deeds signed during the period.

It contains a vast number of authentic documents, most of which are of great historical significance. The author was able to gain access to these because of his personal association with the *sadr* (head of the religious department) of Bhakkar, Shaykh Maruf, Qadi Jafar Mufti, and Maulana Ismail.

The author served under Jahangir for only a few years. At this time, he did not make any attempt to update his compilation after its final revision in 1599 CE. Consequently, the book does not contain any document on Jahangir's period. The only document that does not belong to Akbar's reign is the copy of *farman* of Ulugh Beg, addressed to the last Syed Sultan of Delhi, Ala al-Din Alam Shah (1445–1478 CE).[33] This document has been added to the text of the modern published version of the book, as an appendix due to its great significance in understanding the nature of Syed's rule in India.

The *Munshat* was completed in 1598 CE, during the forty-fourth regal year of Akbar, to whom Namakin dedicated this masterpiece.[34] In the preface, the author states that he compiled this work at the instance of his friends.[35] He further elaborates that the documents included in this book fall into three different categories: first, the compositions of the compiler himself, then the letters and communications received by him, and finally, a selection of the writings of other masters of the style.[36] Most of the documents fall into the last two categories.

Namakin, was a distinguished man of learning and wrote in a florid and ornate manner, which was the only accepted style in *insha* writing at that time. He often used Arabic idioms and Quranic verses. The book includes specimens of all the branches of *insha* writing, including the *tawqi'at* (pronouncements) and the *mahawarat* (dictions and idioms).

Namakin uses *munshats* (epistles) of the masters, mandates, and state papers as his source. He further adds some letters addressed to him by his friends and contemporaries. It is also evident that the author took copious references from the previous authentic works on the subject, avoiding mentioning their names, for instance, the *Tarikh* of Hafiz Abru (d. 1431 CE); Kamal al-Din Hussain Yazdi, the *Nama-i-Nami* of Khwand Mir (d. 1535 CE); the *Tarikh-i Humayun* of Bayazid Bayat (*c.* 1591–1592 CE), the *Sharaf Nama* of Marwarid, and the *Akbar Nama* of Abu al-Fazl (*c.* 1596 CE).[37]

The book comprises a brief preface, eight chapters, and a rather long *khatima* (conclusion). Each chapter further runs into several *fasls* (sections). The first chapter describes the origin and development of the art of epistolary, its style, and modes of writing; the second deals with the drafting of royal decrees and diplomas; the third comprises of specimens of different salutations, complimentary epithets, verses, and correspondence between the members of elite classes; the fourth chapter includes letters addressed to the superiors by the inferiors; the fifth deals with the model letters exchanged between the various categories of people like spiritual preceptors, teachers, pupils, and family members;

the sixth presents different kinds of epistles and explains the significance of correspondence, including letters of condolence and congratulations; the seventh chapter gives examples of letters pertaining to civil contracts and legal deeds, instruments and documents; and the eighth includes short letters (*ruqa'at*) on various topics.

All these sections contain a copious number of documents. Sometimes, scores of specimen and model documents have been provided under one head. This aspect of the book gives an idea about the richness, variety, and volume of its material. The epilogue, which is quite different in scope than other similar works, is devoted to religious topics and abounds in various types of prayers, e.g. one of these supplications is recommended for recovery, or prevention from different diseases. This part of the book also includes profound sermons (*khutbat*) that are worth consideration.

Munshat-i-Namakin also includes the letters of Akbar's period, particularly in relation to Sindh.[38] These letters throw light on some aspects of contemporary arts and learning, such as calligraphy, etc. This material may be used as a valuable source for revealing different aspects of the history and culture of Sindh during the Mughal era. Hermann Ethé signifies this attribute of the *Munshat* writing:

> [It is] a large *insha* or detailed work on letter writing in all its private and official forms, together with an elaborate treatise on the proper composition of prayers and invocations for all emergencies, illustrated throughout by numerous specimens.[39]

Munshat-i-Namakin is unique and the most useful among all other contemporary works of its kind, such as the *Insha-i-Abu al-Fazl*, *Latifa-i-Faizi*, and the *Ruqq'at-i-Hakim Abu al-Fath Gilani*. Each of these comprises correspondence of one individual, while the *Munshat* includes an immense collection of letters of numerous dignitaries.

The first decree copied in this book is the famous order of Shah Tahmasp, the ruler of Persia, to Muhammad Khan Sharaf al-Din, the governor of Khurasan, informing him about Humayun's impending visit to Persia in 1544 CE and ordering him to arrange a grand welcome for him and make arrangements for his journey to the capital.[40] This *farman* (decree) is also cited in many other such collections of letters and historical accounts such as *Akbar Nama* and the *Ma'athir-i-Rahimi*. Both of these works borrowed their accounts from the Ottoman Prince Bayazid's (1525–1561 CE) memoirs of his refuge with Shah Tahmasp, after being dismissed from the governorship of Konya by his father, Sultan Suleiman I.

The *manshurs* (manifestos/guidelines) given in the third *fasl* seem to be closely modelled on the manifestos and decrees drafted by Abu al-Fazl in the *Maktubat-i-Allami*.[41] These documents are about the activities of Akbar's nobles and other contemporary events. For instance one of these is a letter addressed to the Khan-i-Khanan by Akbar, after his return from Kashmir.[42] Likewise, the fourth *fasl* includes samples of the *fathnamas* (letters of victory), mainly about Akbar's conquest of Chittor in 1568 CE and the Fort of Mankot and Shergarh.[43] The letters-patent addressed to the author are copies of Akbar's orders, granting him *jagirs* in the *Sarkar* of Bhakkar, with the authority of having administrative control over it.[44]

The author also includes numerous *ard-dashts* (petitions) of unique nature. One such petition is addressed to Akbar by the Khan-i-Khanan in reply to the emperor's order for his appointment to be the tutor of Prince Salim; which was in the twentieth year of his reign.[45] A considerable amount of the material is borrowed from the Timurid chancelleries of Central Asia and Khurasan, since the author himself belonged to a distinguished family of Khurasan under the Timurids. These documents contain a lot of information on how the Timurid institutions evolved under the Mughals.

These model letters reflect the general norms and rules of the Mughal administration and provide an insightful review of the intellectual and social dynamics of the period, which can help us understand the discourse in literary circles at the time. The documents of legal nature shed light on the contemporary legal processes and procedures and enable us to get an idea about the kind of legal problems faced by the people, which compelled them to approach the courts. The appointment orders provide worthy information about the duties and functions of the state officials at various levels, from the *wakil-i-mutlaq* (regent of Mughal affairs), to *qaush begi* (the person who looked after the aviaries that housed pigeons, hawks, falcons, and other birds), and from the *sadr* (head of the religious department), to the *mutawalli* (caretaker) of a *dargah* (shrine).[46]

The *Munshat-i-Namakin* offers interesting information on the diplomatic relations of the Mughals. As the author had access to state documents, preserved in the central *Diwan-i-Risalat* in Agra and the private collections, at the end of the book he adds the letters addressed to Emperor Akbar by Shah Abbas Safavid I (1587–1629 CE) of Persia. Most of these are identical to those in other such collections, like the *Majma al-Insha* (Collection of Epistles; *c.* 1733–1734 CE) by Qasim Aiwaugli Hyder.

The copies of correspondence of diplomatic nature, such as Akbar's letter to Shah Tahmasp and letters of Shah Tahmasp and Abdullah Khan

Uzbek to Akbar, are of significant historical value. Shah Tahmasp's letter to Akbar was written to make amends for having made an odd request in an earlier letter that the title of *khan-i-khanan* (the chief noble) and *sipah salar* (military commander) be conferred upon Sultan Mahmud Bhakkari.

The letter of Shah Tahmasp addressed to Akbar's mother, Hamida Bano Begum also known as Mariam Makani (1507–1604 CE) and Akbar's letter to Shah Tahmasp, are unique historical documents, which are not found in any other book, not even in the *Akbar Nama* and *A'in-i-Akbari*.[47] Dr Riazul Islam presents Shah Tahmasp's letter to Akbar in the form of a summary in his book titled *A Calendar of Documents on Indo-Persian Relations (1500–1750)*,[48] but its full text has not been published yet.

Shah Tahmasp's letter to Hamida Bano Begum is significant because it is the only known document of its nature from the early Mughal period. One does not come across any other instance of a Mughal lady receiving a letter from a ruler of another country. This letter seems to be an attempt to enlist her support for the restoration of friendly ties between the two courts. Other contemporary sources also corroborate that Shah Tahmasp's embassy to the Mughal court in 1562 CE was aimed at reinstating congenial relations that had broken off after the Persian occupation of Qandahar in 1558 CE.[49]

It may be noted that by the time Shah Tahmasp's letter reached India, Hamida Bano Begum did not enjoy the considerable political power as before, because Akbar (b. 1542 CE; r. 1556–1605 CE) had successfully reduced the harem's influence in state affairs by 1562 CE.[50]

The *Munshat-i-Namakin* includes a number of *fateh namas* (letters of victory) issued by Akbar. It was a longstanding tradition among Muslim rulers to convey news of a victory by issuing a letter.[51] For this purpose, accomplished experts and eminent writers were assigned to compose *fateh namas* under the sultans of Delhi as well.[52] These *fateh namas* could serve as an important source of information for getting detailed accounts of significant battles. For instance, the *Fath Nama-i-Chittor* is very useful as a reliable source of a precise history of the siege and subsequent conquest of the fort. It reveals that the entire garrison of Chittor was put to the sword by the Mughals when the fort fell. The *Fath Nama* clearly mentions this dreadful fact in detail.[53]

The *Munshat-i-Namakin* is undoubtedly a great source of information for the socio-economic, religious, political, and administrative aspects of the history of India in general and of Sindh in particular. It reveals very interesting facts about the prevailing norms of high society and suggests that the people of that era used to copy and preserve their personal letters and state documents with great care and circumspection. *Insha* works like the *Munshat* were admired in the literary circles and copied by *munshis*, who were assigned to keep a record of them.

The orders for the appointment of Shaykh Kabir as the *sajjada nasheen* (hereditary administrator) of the *dargah* (shrine) of Shaykh Baha al-Din Zakariya of Multan and Shaykh Rukn al-Din of Multan,[54] suggest the extent of imperial influence over the affairs of such socio-religious institutions that were previously considered to be outside the domain of state power. Prior to this, the post was hereditary, but this licence virtually reduced it from being one having great monastical authority to only a profession. All the disputes concerning it came within the purview of the Qazi's court.

However, the emperor had regard for merit and the hereditary rights of the appointees as well. In the *Munshat*, an appointment order to the post of *Shaykh al-Islam* (the chief jurist-consult of a city or realm) is also reproduced.[55] This significant post was supposed to be synonymous with that of *sadr us sudur* (head of the religious department) whose function was the implementation of *shari'a* and to look after the needs of the religious classes under the sultans of Delhi.[56] However, the documents in the *Munshat* regarding the duties of the *sadr* clearly indicate that under the Mughals the post of *Shaykh al-Islam* was not synonymous with that of the *sadr* and their duties and responsibilities did not match each other.[57]

In the first chapter of the *Munshat-i-Namakin* that deals with the origin of the art of epistolography, the author took the *Nama-i Nami* of Khwand Mir as one of the main sources and reproduced it almost verbatim. Khwand Mir refers to the *Tarikh* of Hafiz Abru and Kamal Al-Din Hussain Yazdi as authority for the description of the origins of writing, which was the use of the pen by the Prophet Idris (AS) and the introduction of sacramental superscriptions by Bahaman bin Isfandyar Kayani[58] for the first time.[59] The author however makes frequent alterations by using synonyms to lessen the impression of plagiarism, but in places he shows his complete dependence on the way Khwand Mir has expressed himself. For example, he copies the *Nama-i Nami* almost verbatim for mentioning a post of vizierate:

فهرست فرامین کامکاری و عنوان مناشیر نامداری حمد و ثناء مالک الملکی است کہ در دیوان سخن قسمنا---[60]
فهرست فرامین کامکاری و عنوان مناشیر نامداری سپاس و ستائش بادشاهی را سزاوار است کہ در دیوان کثیر الفیضان سخن قسمنا---

At another place:

انشاء فرامین سرکار سلطنت و جهانبانی بمعتمدی تعلق نماید که
خامه مشکین شمامه اش بتحریر کلمات بلاغت آیات رقم نسخ بر
توقیع خوشنویسان اقطار جهان کشیده باشد و--- چون مولانا غیاث
الدین---

انشاء فرامین سرکار بادشاهی و املا مناشیر روزگار شهنشاهی--- که
خامه مشکین شمامه اش بتحریر کلمات بلاغت آیات رقم نسخ بر
توقیع خوشنویسان--- و چون فصیح الرین---

There are numerous examples that confirm that Namakin plagiarised the *Nama-i Nami* directly and indirectly at length.[61] The text also reveals that the author utilised all the famous works compiled during the Mughal period on *insha* as source material, such as the *Sharaf Nama* (*c.* 1597 CE) the famous book of Sharaf al-Din Bitlisi (a medieval Kurdish historian and poet) (1543–1599 CE) and the *Sahifa-i-Shahi* of Mulla Wa'iz Hussain Kashifi. The contents in the third *fasl* confirm this fact. For instance, the collection of prayers, admirable adjectives, and the verses he uses are all borrowed from the *Sahifa-i-Shahi*. The following couplet is copied verbatim by Namakin:

ای عبارت تو توضیحات منهاج دوا   و ز اشارات تو ککلیات قانون شفا [62]

Translation: The phrases spoken by you are the explanation of the path of remedy and your signs are the keys for getting cured.

The fifth, sixth, and eighth *fasls*, which are on epistles, condolence and congratulatory letters, and official correspondence, respectively, are based on the *Bada'i al-Insha* (a famous book on *insha* during the Mughal period). In fact, they are almost exact copies of it.[63] Since in the text the author largely incorporates previous works on epistolography, his own contribution to the compilation of this work is making it so thorough and exhaustive, in which he assembled innumerable, scattered and important documents, thereby preserving their contents. He also collected relevant extracts from such other works which do not seem to be extant any longer. Similarly, the seventh *fasl* presents important legal documents and *qabalat* (title-deeds and contracts) that were prominent among experts of this type of literature during this extended period in history. Probably the *Nama-i Nami*, among other things, was the foremost treatise on *insha*, which deals with civil contracts. Dr Momin Mohiuddin, commenting on this aspect of the *Munshat-i-Namakin* states that, 'our author, who knows the tricks of epistolary compositions, offers old wine in new bottles.'[64]

Despite the above-mentioned similarities with previous works, the *Munshat-i-Namakin* is unique from other traditional works on epistolography in many ways. Some of its contents include such subject matters and items which would not qualify as a part of an *insha* collection. For instance, the entire discussion in the concluding part of the book deals with religious matters of daily life, and remedies for some common diseases, subjects which conventionally did not fall in the purview of *insha*.[65] The supporting documents in this regard include legal and contractual ones, including those related to purchasing important items; other records and letters pertaining to normal activities of daily life, or important documents such as *nikah nama* (marriage contract). These throw light not only on legal procedures but the conditions prevalent in contemporary society.

It appears that Muslim women had rights and powers in marriage during the early Mughal period, to an extent that women of the twenty-first century don't possess.[66] The reason for including the documents related to religious matters is to show the author's religiosity as well as his knowledge of jurisprudence. This provides significant insight into the religious practices, beliefs, and even superstitions prevalent in society.

The book also highlights the nature of stresses, strains, and tensions that were more or less common among people and how they sought to ward them off with the help of invocations and charms. There is also some material on humour. The author prefaces this section with the general remarks that humour and wit are well-received by the people as they serve as means of refreshing the soul and providing entertainment to the mind; though, excessive indulgence in humour and hilarity leads to forgetfulness, negligence, and causes dullness of heart. The author balances his judgement with a precept stating that constant seriousness saddens the heart while too much joviality and jesting affects religious sensibility.[67]

The *Munshat-i-Namakin* mentions some unusual posts such as *mansab-i-wizarat-i-kul sarkar-i Humayun*.[68] No reference to such a designation is found in any other source. A comparison of functions and powers of this post proves that it is the same as the *wizarat-i-diwan-i kul* (prime minister) on which Muzaffar Khan was appointed in August 1563 CE, as mentioned in the *Akbar Nama*.[69] Abu al-Fazl gives a summary of this order while reporting Muzaffar Khan's elevation to this unique post. The *Munshat* also includes an appointment order for the post of *mir-i bahr* (lord of the sea or fleet, i.e. an admiral) for keeping watch on rivers and fords besides maintaining boats and sailors, etc., and those who guarded fords and the river crossings.

I.H. Qureshi argues that the Mughals did not have a sea-faring navy worth the name but did have a department for the purpose. There is a controversy between Dr Parmatma Saran, a renowned scholar of medieval Indian history and Qureshi about the functions of the *mir-i-bahr*. Saran states that this post concerned a sea-fearing navy;[70] Qureshi did not agree with his viewpoint.[71] The *Munshat* supports the conclusion drawn by Qureshi and is absolutely silent about Saran's assertions regarding this issue.[72]

A grave drawback of this work, and one that may diminish its worth as an authentic historical source, is that in most of its documents, the names and dates have been omitted. This might have been done due to the author's assumption of the purpose of this book being simply concerned with the art of *insha*-writing and he had no idea that in future his comments and collection of documents would have historical significance. Even so, some of the documents do contain dates such as the *Fath Nama-i-Chittor*[73] and many more mention names of persons and places or some other details, which indicate the date and protagonists. Subsequently, it is quite possible in many other documents to establish the identity of persons involved and dates too by comparing their contents with facts included in other contemporary sources. Despite these shortcomings, the *Munshat-i-Namakin* is, in fact, one of the largest *insha* collections of the Mughal period, comprising a wide range of documents. This gives it unique significance not only as a source of history, but as a book of great literary interest as well, providing the only available specimens of a number of types of documents.

Only three manuscripts of the *Munshat-i-Namakin* have been found: one is in the India Office Library, London; the second in Maulana Azad Library, AMU, Aligarh; and the third in Salarjung Museum, Hyderabad, India. The selected text of the *Munshat-i-Namakin* is edited by Ishtiaq Ahmad Zilli, who did his PhD research on it; his thesis is titled, 'The Mughal State and Culture: Selected Letters and Documents from the Munshat-i-Namakin'; this book was published by the Manohar Publishing House from New Delhi in 2007.

Aadab-i-Alamgiri/Munshat-i-Alamgiri (The Letters of Aurangzeb)

The *Aadab-i-Alamgiri* is mainly an assemblage of letters by Aurangzeb (letters dated from 1650 to 1658 CE) transcribed by his *mir munshi* (first secretary) Abu al-Fath Qabil Khan (d. 1662 CE), along with some of

Abu al-Fath's own letters. Also, in this collection are letters written by Muhammad Sadiq Muttalibi Khan of Ambala (dated from *c.* 1675 to 1680 CE) on behalf of Prince Muhammad Akbar (1657–1706 CE), one of Aurangzeb's sons. Muttalibi was a scribe of Prince Akbar. The book also includes a description of the war of succession. This book was compiled in 1704 CE, by Muhammad Sadiq Muttalibi Khan.[74]

The manuscripts of the *Aadab-i-Alamgiri* are available in the collections of Rieu, Ethé, Ivanow, and Brown and are also found in the Asafiya Library, Rampur and Bankipur.[75] The edited text by Abdul Ghafur Chaudhry has been published by the Research Society of Pakistan, University of the Punjab, Lahore, in 1971.

Aurangzeb's scribe, Abu al-Fath, alias Qabil Khan, was a scion of a noble family of Lahiri Bandar. Thatta was his native town. At the age of fourteen, the author joined the Mughal services as a petty officer.[76] He was sent to Lahiri Bandar, a *jagir* of Aurangzeb's and then to Multan to transfer the revenue record, in 1649 CE.[77] This was the time when Aurangzeb was entrusted the governorship of Multan, with the additional charge of Sindh.[78]

Abu al-Fath was only twenty-eight years old at that time. After a satisfactory examination of the records by Aurangzeb, al-Fath wrote a letter in Persian requesting Aurangzeb to provide expenses for his return journey to Lahiri Bandar. Aurangzeb was so impressed by the way the petty officer expressed his appreciation for his (Aurangzeb's) auspices and his exquisite writing style, that he decided to include young Abu al-Fath in his board of *munshis*.[79]

In this position, Abu al-Fath served Aurangzeb for almost twelve years and accompanied him to different places as a member of his personal staff. At the time of Aurangzeb's accession to the throne in 1659 CE, he was entrusted the post of *mir munshi*, or *munshi al-Mumalik* (chief secretary) and bestowed upon with the title of Qabil Khan. By this time, he become almost blind and was suffering from severe arthritis.[80]

Near the end of his career, Abu al-Fath humbly requested the emperor to reinstall him on the previous post but did not receive a positive response. It seems from his letters that he had probably lost the emperor's confidence during the war of succession and was demoted from his post.[81] At the age of forty, Qabil Khan ultimately succeeded in securing retirement from the service after his repeated representations to the emperor and through the intercession of some influential nobles.[82] According to his statement, another reason for his premature retirement was his wish to live a humble and secluded life like a dervish, a characteristic he inherited from his ancestors.[83] The scribe was granted an annual allowance of Rs 5,000[84] but it could not support his financial needs adequately. He wished to settle in Burhanpur after his retirement but soon changed his plan and made Lahore his destination, where he led a secluded life. Then, the emperor summoned him once again to Delhi, where he died in 1661–1662 CE.[85]

Qabil Khan enjoyed the confidence of the emperor throughout his career, except for a brief interregnum towards the end of his service. He drafted all types of highly confidential correspondence. Sometimes he was entrusted with other important diplomatic duties, which included mediation between various nobles and explaining the outcome, along with his personal observations, to the emperor.[86]

He is also credited with the compilation of the *Dastur-i-Danish* and the *Qissa-i-Kamrup* in prose.[87] The latter is based on the romantic tale of 'Kamrup and Kamlata' (a prince and princess of Ayodhya), which the author dedicated to Aurangzeb. This work was later versified by Mir Ali Sher Qani.[88] However, his major work is considered to be embodied in the *Aadab-i-Alamgiri*; upon which rests his fame. Abu al-Fath's two younger brothers Muhammad Sharif and Muhammad Shafi were also talented *munshis* of the Mughals. Muhammad Shafi was employed by Prince Muhammad Sultan, the eldest son of Aurangzeb.[89] He too caught the attention of Aurangzeb and was subsequently promoted to a relatively high position.[90] Abu al-Fath's maternal uncle Muhammad Shafi was also a *munshi*.

The date this compilation was completed, i.e. 1703–1704 CE, was mentioned by Sadiq Muttalibi of Ambala, in a chronogram in the preface:

"گل از باغ جان" شد چو تاریخ او   بباغ ارم دل نـ بندد کسے[91]

1115 AH/1703–1704 CE

Sadiq Muttalibi compiled this work for the benefit and guidance of his son, Muhammad Zaman, and calls it:

'دستورالعمل کاردانی و عمل دستور فرزانگی۔'[92]
(The code of conduct and rules of wisdom). [93]

Since, the main purpose of the compiler was to guide his son in formal letter writing, he did not pay much attention to the chronological order of these epistles. Sadiq writes in the preface merely that he collected specimens of different types of epistles from numerous sources and compiled them. He left the task of arranging them in chronological order to the need and will of those who would read his book for guidance.[94]

Aadab-i-Alamgiri comprises three major parts. The first part includes 536 epistles of Aurangzeb, all of them written before his accession. These letters are a very good source of information about the early career of Aurangzeb. His entrance into the affairs of state mainly started during his governorship of Multan, in 1647 CE. The second part contains the description of the war of succession among the sons of Shah Jahan, while the third consists of 146 letters of Prince Akbar. The letters cover the period before his rebellion against his father, in 1680 CE. There are also some letters written by Prince Muhammad Sultan in this collection.

According to the etiquettes of the Mughal court, the princes and the nobles were required to be able to compose letters to the emperor in their own hand, which were formally known as the *arad-dasht* (petitions).[95] This duty necessitated these personages to acquire a certain level of erudition and literary accomplishment. Aurangzeb is exalted at a higher degree of merit in the art of *insha* writing. The letters he addressed to his father, Emperor Shah Jahan, included in the *Aadab-i-Alamgiri*, are almost invariably his own work. Otherwise, he would verbally instruct Abu al-Fath to transcribe his verbal orders and comments into letters and then dispatch them to the addressees. The work also comprises some personal letters of Abu al-Fath, covering the period from 1650, to 1661 CE.[96]

Aurangzeb's epistles are addressed to his father, Emperor Shah Jahan, family members, ministers, and nobles. A review of the salutations of the extensive list of letters enables us to learn about the wide array of members of the contemporary Mughal aristocracy.

Apart from the emperor, there are different categories even in the royal family. Aurangzeb uses different titles, addressing styles, and contents for each of them according to their rank and status. The epistles are of a diplomatic nature, in which the emperor addressed rulers of different kingdoms, such as the king of Balkh and Bukhara, Adil Shah of Bijapur, and Qutub Shah of Golkonda, are more distinguished than the other letters. Besides this, there are letters to *ulema* and *mashaykhs*; these too are addressed more respectfully.

The letters addressed to Sa'adullah Khan and Mir Jumla, etc., express the feeling of harmony that existed between the devoted and sincere officials and Aurangzeb. Most of the letters are somewhat judgemental in nature, commenting on and relating matters to manifestations of human behaviour and psychology.

The letters to military commanders and the jurists, however, evince a unique approach. These letters unveil information about different military campaigns; the submission of turbulent tribes; fiscal and monetary issues; geographical conditions; fauna and flora; climate of different regions and war threats and sieges of forts, all narrated in a fairly straightforward manner. An entire chapter is devoted to the art of using proper titles for public figures, which is a very significant feature of epistolary. The compiler also provides a list of appropriate titles.[97] No other epistolographic compilation of the Mughal period was written on such an elaborate scale as the *Aadab-i-Alamgiri*.

As a *mir munshi*, Abu al-Fath had access to all the overt and secret state records, as well as the emperor's personal and domestic documents, which probably imbued his work more in the style of the times. The contemporary style of court circles was ornate and turgid. All state correspondence and most private letters also followed the same school of prose. The tendency of reducing poetic expressions to word-play and verbal trickery and prose to crossword puzzles, introduced by the Indian-born writers, reached its peak during the reign of Aurangzeb and this is particularly noticeable in the letters drafted by Abu al-Fath in this compilation.[98]

Often, the author uses Persian words and phrases for the sake of rhyming, to make the diction ornate. On the other hand, the style of Aurangzeb is simple and straightforward. He was an expert in elaborating the text with appropriate poetic expressions. In the same manner, he refers to the Quranic verses to emphasise this statement.

The *Aadab-i-Alamgiri* may rightly be regarded as an authentic and valuable source of information about a vast number of historical events that had either been overlooked by authors of other chronicles at the time or were treated rather cursorily in their works.

Sadiq Muttalibi increased the worth of his compilation by adding some of his own letters drafted on behalf of Prince Akbar during his campaign against Marwar, which sheds light on the significant contemporary events in that region.[99] He also appended an account of the War of Succession, and the hostilities between Aurangzeb and his brothers.[100] However, most of the accounts narrated by Muttalibi are borrowed from other sources, which are still extant in their original forms.[101] For this reason, Sadiq's input in this regard hardly merits any worthy consideration.

The text of the *Aadab-i-Alamgiri* reveals that the art of writing official letters had gained a degree of significance during the period of internal and external turmoil under Aurangzeb, when the letters started to be composed in secret codes and cryptic form. The emperor was quite vigilant and suspicious about the loyalty and sincerity of his officers. He frequently altered the duties of his officers in order to maintain security.

This compilation comprises a variety of information on the socio-cultural, political, religious, judicial, civil, military, and economic progress of the Mughal Empire. A letter addressed to Shah Jahan by Aurangzeb, describes some cultural aspects of Thatta such as the famous chintz cloth produced there, which Aurangzeb sent to the emperor who was fond of it.[201]

We learn from the letters that Aurangzeb took the initiative of constructing a ship harbour on the coast of Thatta during his viceroyalty, which ultimately increased the trade and commerce of the region. Aurangzeb informs Emperor Shah Jahan about the rich and fertile land near the River Indus. He writes that the places where the Baloch resided were very fertile and extensively cultivated. Many places are well known for their green pastures.[301] He also mentions the pleasant climate of Naushehro in Sindh, writing that a view from the upper story of the building seems to be fascinating due to its refreshing air and green grass pastures.[401] This type of information may not be gathered from any other source.

The information about the preparation and the strategy for the Qandahar campaign and the proposed routes for reaching Qandahar is also unique in its nature; it also tells us about the planning that was being done in this regard by both sides.[105]

It is evident from some letters, that Qabil Khan was one of the most trusted *munshis* of Aurangzeb. The strict and to some extent bitter instructions that Aurangzeb sometimes dictated to Prince Sultan, were usually drafted by the *munshi*. He was occasionally delegated such duties which could only be assigned to the most reliable subordinate. For instance, at the critical junction, when Shah Jahan, under the influence of Dara Shikoh, ordered Aurangzeb to immediately curtail his campaign of Bijapur in 1657 CE, it was Abu al-Fath who was sent by Aurangzeb to Mir Jumla in order to secure his support. His letter contains a thorough record of his meeting with Mir Jumla, giving details of his conduct and an analysis of all aspects of the case.[106] He also informs Aurangzeb about the changing political scenario and conspiracies in the court of Agra, which he received from his personal resources.[107]

Abu al-Fath's letters mention that he accompanied Aurangzeb during all of his military campaigns, particularly the siege of Bidar, Bijapur, and Golkonda. Some of the petitions addressed to Aurangzeb throw light on the links between Sindh and the Deccan, particularly the province of Khandesh.[108] During that time, some of the *ulema* migrated from Sindh and settled in Burhanpur. The author also requested his master to grant him permission to reside permanently in Burhanpur, or Aurangabad.[109] Later, after retirement, he wrote a request to Aurangzeb to assign him lands in Lahore[110] and he mentions that he did not wish to return to his home town, Thatta, for permanent residence due to the city's deplorable conditions. According to the author, by that time Thatta had been completely destroyed. But subsequently it seems from his epistles that he went there after the accession of Emperor Aurangzeb to the throne.[111]

A thorough analysis of the details of Qabil Khan's sudden retirement reveals a very good picture of Mughal rule and regulations regarding civil machinery. It tells us that the *jagirs* of the *mansabdars* were confiscated after their resignation or death. Nonetheless, retired officers were usually granted a fixed cash pension, or in some cases, another compensation was arranged.

The salary scales for officials of the court were fixed, according to the *A'in-i-Akbari*. Payment orders (*dastak*) were issued by the provincial *bakhshis* (chief paymaster, the official who kept the army records and paid the troops). Shah Jahan personally wrote most of his letters addressed to Aurangzeb. This fact is revealed by the letters of Aurangzeb in reply to the emperor's orders. He usually writes:

'بقلم خاص زینت نگارش یافته'
(embellished with the special pen) or
'بخط قدسی خاص مبارک'
(with special sanctified hand-writing).

However, Aurangzeb complains that during the last years of Shah Jahan's reign, some of the decrees were not written personally by the emperor, but rather according to the guidelines of Dara Shikoh.

The letters that are added to the book by Muhammad Sadiq, the *mir munshi* of Prince Akbar, addressed to Emperor Aurangzeb and other officials, provide authentic and useful information about the campaigns of Mewar and Marwar. They reveal that although Aurangzeb was far away from the battlefield, he was still vigilant and aware of the situation.

The book is a very good source for understanding the art of writing *insha* of that time, including technical terms and attitudes adopted by Mughal officials. It is one of the most widely studied works on *insha*. It has found a place in every public and private collection of books on the Mughal history of India.

Raqa'im-i-Kara'im (The Notations of Greatness)

Aurangzeb's reign (1657–1707 CE) is the richest in terms of compilations of official orders, correspondence, and the private letters of the emperor and others. This massive body of work includes the *Ruqqat-i-Alamgiri* (The Epistles of Aurangzeb); *Kalimat-i-Tayyibat* (The Fine Odes); *Kalimat-i-Aurangzeb* (The Words spoken by Aurangzeb); *Ahkam-i-Alamgiri* (The Decrees of Aurangzeb); *Shujat-i-Alamgiri* (The Gallantry of Aurangzeb); *Dastur al-Amal A'agahi* (The Code of Conduct), etc. The *Raqa'im-i-Kara'im* is a unique collection with only a few cases of repetition of letters that are already given in other collections.

The full text of the *Raqa'im-i-Kara'im*, with its English translation and an introduction by Syed Muhammad Azizuddin Hussaini, was published by the Idara Adbiyat-i-Dilli, New Delhi, in 1990. Its manuscripts are available at the British Museum; Bodleian Library; Maulana Azad Library, Aligarh Muslim University; National Archives of India; Khuda Bakhsh Library, Patna; National Museum, New Delhi; and the India Office Library.

The author of the *Raqa'im-i-Kara'im*, Syed Ashraf Khan Hussaini, was the son of Amir Abdul Karim Amirkhani Sindhi. The author named the compilation *Raqa'im-i-Kara'im*, because of his love and respect for his father, Amir Abdul Karim.[112] The author provides no reference to his life and career in the preface of his book. He was the grandson of Amir Abu al-Baqa Amir Khan, an influential and prominent Mughal governor of Multan, Thatta, and Sehwan and a great-grandson of Mir Abu al-Qasim Namakin, the author of the *Munshat-i-Namakin*. Because the author's ancestors had been in Sindh for a long time and had adopted it as their dwelling place, his father was given the epithet of Sindhi.[113]

However, his family had been employed in the Mughal services for generations and many of his family members had enjoyed successful and influential careers under the Mughals, as mentioned in detail in the preceding pages. His father joined the Mughal services during the reign of Aurangzeb, in 1683 CE, when the latter was staying at Aurangabad.

First, he was appointed as *darogha* of *Ja-i-Namaz* (guardian of the emperor's prayer mat), a position very close to the emperor. He rose rapidly in his career due to his devoted services to the emperor. He was delegated to Deccan accompanying Khan Jahan, with the Mughal envoy after its successful occupation by Aurangzeb's son, Prince Shah Alam, also known as Muhammad Mu'azzam, who later ascended the throne as Bahadur Shah I (b. 1642; r. 1717–1712 CE). He was also entrusted with the duty of revenue collection after the fall of Golkonda and was bestowed the title of Multafat Khan in return for his faithful services.

Soon, he secured the important post of *darogha-i-khawasan* (superintendent of personal attendants) and was conferred the prestigious title of Amir Khan, in 1706 CE.[114] The author of *Ma'athir al-Umara* compliments him in the following words:

INSHA LITERATURE (EPISTOLOGRAPHY)

خان مذکور بجودت فہم و ادراک و شگرفنحیثیت و بلندئ استعداد
(کہ ازان بہ قابلیت تعبیر رود) ممتاز بود۔[115]

Translation: The 'Khan', who was mentioned, held a distinguished position due to his understanding, grip on affairs, dignity, and talent, which can be interpreted as his capability.

The author was a talented poet. Qani mentions his name in his *Maqalat al-Shuara*, under the pen name of 'Multafat'.[116] The author of the *Raqa'im-i-Kara'im* compiled the collection of epistles of the Mughal Emperor Aurangzeb in 1718–1719 CE, after his death.[117] He provides a brief preface at the beginning of the book. The work mainly comprises letters which were written by the emperor to Nawab Amir Khan, the author's father and a reputed Mughal nobleman of Sindh, though some letters addressed to other people are also included in it.

The *Raqa'im-i-Kara'im* is written in elegant Persian prose, resplendent with metaphors and quotations. The work sheds light on various events of historical significance, including Aurangzeb's theory of kingship, his administrative policies, rule and regulations, agrarian and fiscal reforms and their implementation, his religious views, etc. Some of the epistles highlight the nature of the relationship of Aurangzeb with his sons, nobles and contemporary scholars, religious men and saints.

The *Raqa'im-i-Kara'im* is important because it mentions the sort of details that are omitted from other works of Alamgir's era (1658–1707 CE), such as the *Ahkam-i-Alamgiri* (Decrees of Aurangzeb). For instance, there is the case of Muhammad Amin Khan, the Mughal nobleman. The *Ahkam-i-Alamgiri* states he requested the emperor to assign him the post of *mir bakhshi*, because he was *Sunni*. Both of the posts of the *mir bakhshi* were held by the followers of the *Shiite* sect at the time. Aurangzeb replied that the posts were assigned by the virtue of merit and not sects. But contrary to this, in a letter in the *Raqa'im-i-Kara'im* addressed to Muhammad Amin Khan, he displays sympathetic feelings towards him. He promises him that if an opportunity arose, his name would also be considered for the post of *amir al-umara* (head of the *amirs*).[118] In fact, the son of Muhammad Amin Khan was appointed *sarpaich-i-yamini* (jewelled crescent for the right hand) at a minor age and on a lower grade, against Mughal rules and regulations.[119]

The text of the *Raqa'im-i-Kara'im* also highlights different official posts and their functions and significance in the state machinery. For instance, it suggests that the post of *waqa'i nawis* (secret agent) was an important one, as it was responsible for giving intelligence reports to the emperor. If a situation got out of hand and the *waqa'i nawis* had failed to give prior information to the emperor, the official was castigated severely. It is also evident that there was no institution like the *bait al-mal* (public treasury) under the Mughal administration. Instead, there was a royal treasury, which was the personal property of the emperor. In Aurangzeb's letters, one may find unnecessary repetition of the term *bait al-mal*, which in fact never existed.[120] It is highly likely that this term was used by Aurangzeb to give the Mughal Empire the outward appearance of an Islamic state.

The *Raqa'im-i-Kara'im* also sheds light on the diplomatic relations of the Mughals with countries such as Persia, Central Asia, Arabia, etc. The book also asserts that the economic condition of the Mughal Empire was sound. The Sharif of Makkah knew that Hindustan was a prosperous country. For his own interest, he used to send an envoy every year to India. He would collect money for the needy people of India but would use it for his own welfare. This issue was brought to the notice of the emperor.[121] In another letter, Aurangzeb expresses his opinion regarding Shah Jahan's Central Asian policy, particularly towards the campaigns in Balkh, Bukhara, and Badakhshan.

There is a difference of opinion among modern historians regarding Shah Jahan's motives behind the campaign. Aurangzeb clearly mentions that Shah Jahan had a desire to keep this region under his direct control, as Central Asia had been the land of his dreams, the homeland of his ancestors. But unfortunately, due to various factors, he was unsuccessful in his attempts. Aurangzeb also failed to fulfil this dream and advised his sons to achieve the task, if possible.[122]

Some of the letters also reveal to an extent the minor details of the cultural climate of the country. For instance, one of the letters includes the comment that '*khichri biryani*' is a dish of winter;[123] in another letter, Aurangzeb forbids Shah Alam from celebrating *Nauroz* like the Iranians and asks him to keep his faith pure.[124] In a separate epistle, he quotes the advice of his mentor, Miyan Abdul Latif, forbidding him from meeting *faqirs*, because he believed *faqirs* had deviated from the path of the old religious mendicants.[125]

These remarks highlight his orthodox mindset. In one of his letters, Aurangzeb writes an anecdote showing his religious bias, when he refers to the killing of an unbeliever by a fanatic Muslim, as a result of God's help. However, the *qadi* (judge) had ordered *qisas* (compensation in return for committing murder) to be levied.[126] Aurangzeb's remarks suggest his misinterpretation of *shari'a* on an important religious issue.

The text demonstrates that the emperor was well-informed about all the private activities of his nobles; for instance, he writes about two nobles, Nawazish Khan and Shukurllah Khan:

> I was informed through some secret reports that Shukrullah Khan had reached the place and he spent his entire night in the house of Nawazish Khan enjoying liquor and dances. They indulged in all the prohibited activities. Efforts were made to avoid any interruption.[127]

It seems that despite the promulgation of the moral decrees issued by Aurangzeb, the nobles often paid no heed to them. His rules relating to *shari'a* had no practical effect. Rather, his sons had the habit of drinking wine. These letters also reveal that the emperor most likely did not have much objection to the habit of drinking, but a situation which alarmed him was Shukrullah Khan's visit to Nawazish Khan's house to attend such a party. He feared such clandestine revelry that flouted his rules would be seditious and undermine loyalty. Similarly, Ala al-Din Khilji also prohibited such parties, however, he allowed his nobles to consume alcohol privately.

An epistle mentions some financial matters of the Mughal Empire. There was a rule that once any financial grant was given to an official, it would have to be adjusted before asking for another grant. Aurangzeb wrote in a letter that a noble called Sarmast Khan was not properly trained, since he was not well aware of the rules and regulations.[128] The letter further suggests that many officers appointed to look after these matters could be bribed to overlook such objections. This corruption became one of the factors that facilitated the fall of the Mughal Empire. The nobility was morally corrupt; its slackness provided enemies of the state the opportunity to become more and more powerful.

One of the letters clearly states that Aurangzeb did not favour forced conversion, nor did he restrict the slowly increasing number of Hindu officials in the Mughal administration. He writes: 'Why do knowledgeable people leave truth and ambition before God and the Hindus are advised to embrace Islam without taking their consent.'[9][21] Judging from the *Tadhkirat al-Umara* of Kewal Ram (*c.* 1727 CE), *Umara-i-Hinud* of Sa'id Ahmad Khan and certain other sources, it appears that Hindus were freely employed by Aurangzeb and were given honourable ranks in the Mughal court.[130] Furthermore, some letters mention that the emperor wished to employ new officers and nobles so that they could perform a better job than the older ones. According to Aurangzeb, it was useless to increase the numbers of old nobility for the reason that they had lost their values.[131]

Since the purpose of all these compilations on *insha* were to provide model letters to train *munshi* aspirants, the compilers did not only pay much attention to presenting the letters in chronological order, but they often did irreparable damage to their historical worth by expunging the names of many of the correspondents and, in some cases, even deleting the dates and the names of places of their origin and destination.[132] Sometimes, the compiler mentions the title of a particular noble but does not provide a name. This could also be misleading because such titles were common and usually given to a number of nobles during different periods, for instance, Sa'adullah Khan, Amin Khan, etc.

However, besides the above-mentioned major works on *insha*, two prominent *munshis* of that period, Miyan Noor al-Haq Mushtaqi and Miyan Muhammad Sa'id, also compiled works of this kind in Sindh. Mushtaqi was a brilliant poet and an excellent prose writer too. The *Munshat-i-Miyan Noor al-Haq Mushtaqi* is a compendium of his prose and is also expounded with his poetry. The *Maktubat-i Muhammad Sa'id Munshi* is also a work of significant value. Unfortunately, both of these compilations are not extant.

Some of the studies of these books are by earlier scholars. From these it is apparent that the epistles in them were ill-arranged, yet the works nevertheless provided information on almost all plausible aspects of the Mughal administration in Sindh, as well as the social and political life in the region. They also proved to be a valuable source of information on the political situation prevalent in the territories bordering the province of Sindh and the adjoining regions of Iran and Afghanistan. Since these letters afford corroborative evidence to several historical facts, as well as being primary source material in their own right, they are very valuable, especially for writing an authentic history of seventeenth century Sindh, Multan and Qandahar.

CHAPTER 6

Conclusion

During Mughal rule in Sindh, historiography entered a new phase in South Asia and new developments took place. Literary activities that had long been stagnating due to the lack of peace in Sindh, now found a period of stability and growth. Political, religious, and social unrest revolved around ideas and concepts. This made the talent of the scholars and literati (scattered in far-off areas) an organised power. Their thinking and activities now found expression in regular and esteemed channels in society. The patronage of scholars and poets by the Mughals led to the amalgamation of different elements. Thus, when we come to the Mughal period, we find a qualitative change in historical writing.[1] The literature produced in Sindh at this time has a value of its own. It has to be cautiously tapped and systematically analysed, because it is an indispensable source to enable us to understand the broader patterns of Sindhi society.

While the Muslim period was one of progress and scholarly activities, the subject of history was not as yet recognised as an academic discipline (*'ilm*). It was viewed as a highly esteemed art form and a cornerstone of elite education, but beyond that was not regarded as being of any practical use. With the inception of the Muslim period, many erudite compilations by eminent scholars were produced very quickly under the patronage of the local rulers. These works are still considered the only source of history, culture, and society of this region, for over six centuries.

The impact of Mughal rule in Sindh, however, witnessed the emergence of new historiographical trends that gradually continued to strengthen and crystallise. Historiography during this period honed earlier trends and traditions in writing historical literature. Later, with the beginning of British colonial rule, history transformed into a full-fledged field of knowledge and a discipline of the arts and became a part of the syllabi in schools and colleges.

Under Muslim rule, historiography in Sindh became an integral part of the vibrant tradition of Indo-Persian historiography, which flourished in all the regions of India during the Mughal era. It witnessed the emergence of new trends, as hitherto there had been hardly one or two existing works of this genre.

In Sindh, the art of writing history was diligently developed by the educated elite who, in quest for employment and patronage, entered the service of the Mughals. These historians were men of the pen as well as the sword. They considered themselves as the true personifications of traditional values and their generations continued to live under the patronage of the glorious Mughals. As the transmitters as well as the consumers of their scholarly and literary productions, they reflected the mentality, interests, tastes, and concerns of their own class. Some of them, though, were not court historians, but individuals who pursued this subject by their own choice. Since they had the same social background and educational career as the Mughal elite, they had certain features and stylistic approaches to historical composition that were similar, especially regarding the traditions of the purpose and proper content of history and inserting couplets and religious quotations.

The Mughal period not only produced a prolific amount of historical literature, it was also significant for achieving definite advancement in historiographical traditions of medieval Sindh. We find a qualitative change in historical writings in this era. The tradition of writing historical records that was founded in Sindh, produced academia that is among the best anywhere in India. Most of this literature was in Persian.

Nevertheless, the quality of the language, the expression, and the style of writing gradually became defective when compared to the earlier classical works. It is evident that almost all historians concentrated on the political aspect of history and praised their patrons. Akbar persuaded the royal historiographers to compile an official history of the empire and this trend continued in the first ten years of Aurangzeb's reign.

The significance of historiography during the Mughal period can be assessed from the fact that the Mughal archives were placed at the authors' disposal. Their source material usually comprised eyewitness accounts of events. Chronicles, memoranda, reports about military campaigns, minutes prepared by officers, imperial decrees, and other official records, were carefully consulted. Although official historians drew heavily on the records of the daily proceedings of the imperial court, they seldom acknowledged the sources from which they borrowed any particular bit of information.

Historians would usually have the patronage of the ruler, or some other noble personage, or they would be seeking it hence they could not freely express their views and opinion regarding the prevailing conditions and were expected to record what their masters desired them to write, or what pleased them.

They were expected to glorify the achievements of their masters and often distorted facts. They tried their best to present their masters as benevolent, victorious, and just rulers, and pious defenders of the faith. The elitist nature of the learning and culture of the court made the official, or court historians more interested in matters relating to politics, conquests, or the rulers and nobility and they were not concerned with the lives of the rest of society, especially the lower classes. In fact, they hardly sought to rise above the divisions in the court and at least represent the interests of the entire nobility in their historical outlook.[2]

Consequently, the works we have on hand of the Mughal period in Sindh, are mainly court histories that share numerous aspects in their approach to history and yet differed on various issues. Since they were mostly members of the ruling elite, their attitude towards the conditions of the common people was not only one of disregard, but they were greatly apprehensive about the solidity and strength of the state machinery to function smoothly. They usually condemned uprisings by the natives of Sindh against the foreign rule and criticised the native feudals as a class.

The natives created much trouble for the ruling authorities, which often resulted in the disruption of Mughal authority in Sindh. In this framework, the historians tried to portray events as they perceived them and according to their own interests. That is why the same rules of evaluation cannot be applied to a study of each of them. Each historian needs to be understood and inferred in the context of his own environment and in the light of his own interests, perceptions, and ideals.

On the other hand, the influx of scholars from Persia and Central Asia provided an opportunity for the intermingling of different historical traditions, such as the Arab, Persian, Central Asian, etc. The historiographical traditions in Mughal Sindh are heavily influenced by Persian ones, whose approach was basically limited and dedicated to the rulers to the exclusion of all other sections of the public. Thus, the conceptual framework and scope of history drawn on the Persian model were ultimately narrow. However, it is indebted for much of its growth from the traditions set and trends established by their Central Asian predecessors, who had arduously instituted the historical foundation of the science of historiography.

The trait of highlighting the superiority of one's own or a favoured tribe, was an early Muslim or Arab tradition.[3] Pride in the clan and its heroic deeds were the main motives behind this tradition, which was followed by the Mughals too as we see in numerous historical works, such as the *Nusrat Nama-i-Tarkhan*, the *Beglar Nama*, the *Tarkhan Nama*, and the *Arghun Nama*.

The regular feature in the works of Mughal historians of tracing the genealogy of any specific ruler, or tribe, was an Arab trend.[4] This tradition was initially presented by the *akhbar* (the reports), and was recited by the *qusas* (the narrators) of Arab tribes, in order to glorify the tribes' heroism.[5] *Ansab*, or genealogy was of historical interest to the people of pre-Islamic Arabia and was significant because of their pride in tribal ancestry. The historians of the Mughal period also adopted this tradition in history writing. They further provided an enormous amount of geographical knowledge about the place they were writing about, which was another significant feature of Mughal historiography in Sindh, inspired by Arab historiographic traditions.

Al-Masudi (d. 956–957 CE), an Arab historian, geographer and explorer known as the 'Herodotus of the Arabs', introduced new trends in Arab Muslim historiography by adopting historico-geographical science and combining it with biographical and social commentary in his expansive history of the world, the *Muruj al-Dhahab* (Meadows of Gold).[6] Thus, despite the fact that Arab trends pertained to political, military, cultural, social, and economic activities of the common people, these found no place in the Persian style historiography of Sindh.

The Arghun and the Tarkhan rulers had already introduced the practice of history writing in Sindh and this tradition was continued by the Mughals, who employed reputed historians to write the official histories of their reign, in order to glorify their achievements and activities. Dr Gulfishan Khan writes:

> The native Persian speaking intelligentsia, from whose rank and files, the bureaucracy of the erstwhile regime was mainly recruited, despite the political upheavals continued to foster the tradition of scholarship and research with their agile pens. This traditional richness and cultural vibrancy of classical Persian, above all is reflected in the Indo-Persian literary and historical productions which witnessed new trends and new ideas.[7]

The main theme of all these political histories was dynastic and within the dynastic whole, each reign was treated as a unit. From the period of the Arghuns, till the period of the Mughal governors, the pattern of development in some elements of historiography is evident, specifically in terms of contents and the attitude of the historians toward the proper use of their sources of information and authentic evidence about historical data.

The growth of content is vertical rather than horizontal, which means the main focus of the histories remained concentrated on court activities, the lives and activities of the rulers, their campaigns, etc., and further vertical development in this field of reference was some additional information regarding related subjects like administration, imperial policies, and the composition of the ruling aristocracy. This feature of historiography still subsists in the works of modern historians on medieval India. The political histories are organised on a dynastic, or regal basis. Their contents are designed to follow the regal unit and the main emphasis of these works is the royal court and the political history of the era, such as the accession of rulers, wars, rebellions, etc. If we find glimpses of the socio-cultural and economic conditions during the reign of any particular ruler, or dynasty, it is because of the influence of modern European interest in this non-political perspective of history. This European trend emerged during the late nineteenth and early twentieth centuries.

Apart from political works, there was another type of compilation—the directories, or descriptions of the Mughal nobility. The *Dhakhirat al-Khawanin* of Shaykh Farid Bhakkari was the earliest work in this regard. It introduced a new dynamic genre to historical literature. For the first time, the author tries to analyse the composition of the ruling aristocracy in terms of the influence they wield. This and other works like it, encouraged modern historians to carry out in-depth studies on such significant features of history.[8] These works revealed many hidden facts and confirmed many facts that had been merely theories before they were discovered.

The utilisation of available source material and eyewitness accounts are techniques of historiography that developed in Mughal Sindh. Unfortunately, limited efforts were made by Mughal chroniclers to understand the basic framework, assumptions, attitudes, and viewpoints of previous historians before referring to their works. Generally, there is no conceptual framework or general explanation in the historical perspective presented by these chroniclers. Although most of the works were more or less generalised according to the fashion of the times, we do not observe any trace of the latter-day research methodology, which was introduced by Abu al-Fazl in the capital.

The chroniclers of Mughal Sindh considered historical events as singular occurrences, unrelated to any continuity, sequence of historic causality, or the outcome of prevailing socio-economic conditions. Consequently, their style of narration emphasises the individuality of the events, irrelevant to one another.

The historians of this period had a tacit theory that the causation of events depended upon human will, or human nature, primarily the ruler's will or nature. As most of the compilers of such works personally participated in some of the events or, as courtiers, were often eyewitnesses to most of the happenings they narrated, thus they would be cognizant of the element of the will of the king as a causative factor. In the same manner, they evaluated the causes of events of the distant, or recent past in terms of human will.

This characteristic of historical writing emphasised focusing on human decisions and action, which ultimately brought a great deal of realism to the historical narrative. Nevertheless, this outlook of treating history as narratives of various individual events limited analysis and precluded a wider historical perspective that could have suggested inter-relationship among the events as a whole.

The rulers' volition assumed a pivotal role in the whole approach and it was the beginning of treating the events of a reign as the expression of the rulers' will, or nature. As has already been discussed in the preceding chapter, medieval Indian historiography had a theological approach; that causation lay in the Divine Will and historical events were manifestations of that Will.

In this regard, the medieval Indian historical approach resembles the medieval European ecclesiastical approach. This conception of history applies God's Will to the past, present, and future and signifies that everything happens according to a well-designed plan, each event falling in place within the plan.[9]

During this period, historiography was a rapidly developing art and was associated with learned people of high- or low-profile collecting data and becoming custodians of significant and interesting information about the court. They received wide cooperation from different officials. In compiling their works, they collaborated with other historians too. They strove towards extending their historical perspective by including the accounts of the role and contribution of saints, poets, literati, and other notable members of society, in writing *malfuz*, *tadhkira*, and *insha* literature.

In fact, the Mughals, like the Safavids, were co-inheritors of the Mongol legacies, which they received through the Timurids and the Turkomans, of the tradition of compiling hagiographical and epistolography literature. Following these prevailing trends of non-political historical literature, Sindh very soon acquired a rich and highly developed discipline of compiling official as well as non-official historical accounts. Centuries later, when the British arrived in India, they did not feel inclined to change the prevailing model of the literary structure and chancellery practices at first.

A very significant genre of medieval historiography, the *tadhkira* extended beyond the classical hagiography (memoirs of the saints) and of lexicons and encyclopaedia. It too found its root in Sindh and quickly grew popular. It was a combination of biography and directory of the works of native poets, saints, scholars, nobles, literati, artists, etc. This non-political genre of historical literature, which included religious and poetical records, demanded methods different from those for political chronicles. It had to develop on the basis of the attitudes, objectives, and motivations of the author.[10]

The authors of such literature had a vision and approach quite different from official court historians. These studies covered the religious, political, and economic aspects of the lives of common people. *Tadhkira* literature emerged as an important genre of local history in the fourteenth century.[11] The authors preferred to give such literature more florid titles. However, we are led to believe that during the British period, *tadhkira* literature did not exist, at least not in its previous traditional form, but almost all the more recent Persian compilations, like the *Lubb i-Tarikh i-Sindh*, *Tazah Nawa'-i-Ma'arik*, and *A'inah-i-Jahan Numa* and others, include the biographical data of celebrated people, in the same way the originals depicted the contemporary socio-religious, cultural, and economic conditions.

Compiling biographies, which as a discipline was different from the science of historiography, increased to the extent that the eighteenth century can be regarded as an era of the proliferation of biographical literature (*tadhkira*).[12] Collection of autobiographies and biographical-memoirs, and the occasional personal memoir-cum-travelogue, became one of the most notable features of Mughal historiography not only in Sindh, but all over India. Muhammad Afzal Sarkhush (d. 1717 CE) wrote a hagiography of the Persian poets in Delhi, under the title of the *Kalimat al-Shuara* in 1682 CE, in which he provides biographical references of 169 Persian poets from the reign of Jahangir to that of Aurangzeb. Even though contemporary scholars have extensively studied the classic medieval hagiographies of the Sufi saints, the continued survival of *tadhkira* through the twentieth century has been largely ignored by scholarship.

There seems to be a peculiarly antithetical link between the study of scholars of a small number of medieval Sufi classics and the disregard of later examples of the *tadhkira* genre, whose numbers increased voluminously, with each passing century. The genre increasingly dealt with the lives and genealogy of saints instead of poets and nobility. On the other hand, the absolute admiration that the Persian, and later Urdu, mystic hagiography enjoyed previously, diminished with commercialisation and modernity in South Asia. After the introduction of printing, there grew an abundance of both new and old hagiographical literature. As the records of early Indian printed works confirm, with the onset of the twentieth century, the need for publications about the legends of the saints was felt by members of all of India's religious communities. Consequently, early Urdu printed hagiographical texts have received insufficient consideration from the literary circles of both the East and West.

As far as some *tadhkira* literature in Urdu is concerned, they are undoubtedly of a high literary craftsmanship. However, since these books are mainly read by common people, the text is often in a regional language, or otherwise written in a simplified style. If we disregard the stylistic quality (a feature that historically was very important in Persian literature), the significance of Urdu hagiography is evinced in its fame and popularity.

Printed editions of *tadhkira* literature, dealing with non-Indian, as well as Indian Sufi saints, appeared in huge numbers during the late nineteenth and early twentieth centuries. Some of these compilations, such as the *Hadiqat al-Awliya*, by Ghulam Sarwar Lahori (d. 1890 CE), attained a high degree of popularity all over India and ran into several editions. The *Maqasid al-Salihin* (Aims of Virtuous People), Muhammad Abdul Rahman of Kanpur's Urdu translation of the Persian *tadhkira* literature, titled the *Hikayat al-Salihin*, likewise rendered into many North Indian editions during the 1870s and afterwards.

On the other hand, it might be argued that the most popular works are in many respects the least rewarding. The great compendia (*tadhkira*) of saints of the nineteenth century are, by their nature, formulaic and often repetitive in the extreme. Every so often, they evince a sort of reformist trend and present the saint as a preacher and instructor, rather than a miracle worker, as he was depicted in medieval times. Be that as it may, there may still be found various hagiographies that continue to show the Sufi saint as a miracle worker in this extensive genre.

Dr Carl Ernst's view that *malfuzat* texts and hagiographies need to be judged according to different yardsticks compared to other genres, has led us to work out a methodology for evaluating the anecdotes that form a very large portion of this corpus. One may try to arrive at as close an approximation of the truth as possible. The historical reconstruction of truth of what happened in ages gone by is by no means an easy task. People's vision of what is the truth is inevitably influenced by loyalties, religion, superstitious beliefs, etc.

However, the historiography of Mughal Sindh represents a unique taste. There is variation in form, such as idiomatic, simple, arduous, or ornate in the prose and versification with sporadic use of indigenous words, maxims, and idiomatic expressions. It may be said that the trend that gradually developed in the later period of using a simple, concise, and straightforward style, was not as impressive as the rhetoric and ornate style of the classical Persian. It diminished the quality and excellence of language and suppressed the sophisticated and erudite aura of historiography. Yet on the other hand, it facilitated a factual narration and readers of average proficiency in the language could understand it.

Regarding language and dialect, during the British period there were examples of liberal use of English words in Persian historiography (e.g. the *Lubb i-Tarikh i-Sindh*) and in contemporary Urdu and even the regional literature of Pakistan that shows the massive influence of the colonial language. As for the local languages in the nineteenth century, there was an emerging trend of vocabulary from native dialects often used in Urdu to provide readers with more literary depth, interest, and intensity of emotion. On the other hand, Persian gradually lost its traditional elegance and refinement. Scholars continued the customary trend of showing their proficiency in Persian language in more than one way; in prose and poetry as well. The frequent embellishment of text with Persian couplets, added a literary dimension to books and readers appreciated the poetic infusion. At times, authors provided the reader with beautiful descriptions of the cultural and literary environment of the period. However, with the growing reading public, Persian gradually became irrelevant.

During the Mughal period, the appointment of different Mughal governors in Sindh not only provided an opportunity for Indian scholars and poets to introduce themselves in Sindh but also to share their literary contributions. Many Urdu-speaking poets and scholars came in contact with the native people of Sindh and inspired them with their works. Muhammad Sa'id Rahbar of Gwalior, Mir Jafar Ali Khan Benawa, Syed Fada'il Ali Khan Beqayd, Mohsin al-Din Shirazi, Imad al-Mulk Nawab Ghazi al-Din were some of them. Following this emerging trend of Urdu poetry, some Persian-speaking Sindhi poets such as Shaykh Waroo, Abdul Subhan Fa'iz Thattawi, Makhdum Muhammad Moin Beragi, and Mir Hyder al-Din Abu Turab Kamil also composed verses in Urdu.[13]

It is interesting to note that all the works, even those written by Hindu authors such as Kewal Ram's *Tadhkirat al-Umara*, continued the trend to begin their works with the traditional ascription to God. This trend was a traditional Muslim way of starting a work; a regular feature of Persian historiography from the first compilation entitled the *Chach Nama* in the early thirteenth century. Thereafter, usually a foreword or preface is given in which the authors mention the purpose and scope of the book.

The preface always starts in the name of Allah, followed by praise of the Holy Prophet (PBUH). The authors usually interpolated the text with a number of couplets and stanzas in praise of Allah and the Holy Prophet (PBUH) known as *hamd* and *na'at* respectively.

Another major trend of this period was the ample information about geography, topography, archaeology, and etymology besides the history of a region. For instance, in the *Mazhar-i-Shahjahani* of Yousuf Mirak, which is primarily a manual on the Mughal administration, there is a substantial detailed account of the environment. These accounts offer a lot of information about the social, cultural, and economic life of the people. For the first time, statistical data became a part of historical study in Sindh. The development of the ethnographic aspect of history, such as a detailed account of the *sarkars* of Sindh, is of great interest to students and scholars of history as well as sociology and anthropology of this province. These ethnographic descriptions reveal a picture of the economic rationalism of the period, as they tell us that the Sufi shrines were not only centres of religious matters, but also improved the local economic growth and social harmony.

Moreover, the accounts of the Mughal period are significant for the adaptation of the well-established *Hijra* calendar, which helped the authors to give the dates of events, but also place their accounts in chronological order. The chronicles of Sindh's previous history lack accuracy in recording dates and proper chronology of events. On the other hand, the historians of Mughal Sindh generally possessed a profound sense of chronological order. However, some of these accounts commit errors in designating dates, for instance, the *Tarikh-i-Masumi* and *Tarkhan Nama*. Another trend was a penchant to use lofty titles for their books, such as the *Nusrat Nama-i-Tarkhan*, or the *Tarikh-i Sind dar Zamana-i Arghun wa Tarkhan*, etc.

The compilation of encyclopaedic works was another prevailing historiographical trend in Mughal Sindh. The *Ma'lumat al-Aafaq* (c. 1702 CE) and the *Rushhat al-Fanun* (c. 1711 CE) are the works of such category written by Amin Al-Din Khan Hussain Harawi (d. 1715 CE), who was the son of Syed Abdul Mukarim Shahud and the grandson of Abu al-Qasim Namakin. His ancestors migrated from Herat and settled in India during the reign of Aurangzeb Alamgir. He was appointed as the governor of Thatta in 1701 CE. He possessed a fine taste in books and spent most of his time reading and other scholarly activities.

The *Ma'lumat al-Aafaq* deals with the subject of geography and discusses the wonders of the inhabited regions of the earth, which was said to be one-fourth of its total area, i.e. *ruba' maskun*.[14] The author collected bits of valuable information about India and completed this book in the year of Aurangzeb's death, in 1707 CE.[15]

The *Rushhat al-Fanun* is an encyclopaedia of sciences dealing with the traditional *chahardah 'ulum*. It comprises discussions on fourteen subjects and follows the pattern of the *Matla al-Uloom fi Majma al-Uloom*, which discusses the historical background of different sciences. A manuscript of the *Rushhat al-Fanun* is preserved in the Khuda Bakhsh Library of Patna. This book was completed in 1711–1712 CE.[16]

As we can see, there are a great number of male historians during this period, while females are distinctly lacking in this field, both among native scholars and foreign travellers, not only in Sindh, but India as a whole. However, Gulbadan Bano Begum (*c.* 1523–1603) Babar's daughter and half-sister to Humayun, compiled her memoirs on Humayun's period, titled the *Humayun Nama*, at the request of Akbar. We know that some European ladies also visited Sindh during Mughal rule[17] but unfortunately, there is no record left by them.

Besides historical literature in prose, some versified narratives in the form of *mathnawis*, were also introduced in Sindh in this period. A *mathnawi* is a long poem focusing mainly on one historical theme. For instance, Faizi composed a brief *mathnawi* on Akbar's conquest of Gujarat (India). It may be added that sometimes the poet lacked sufficient data to continue the 'epic'; in such cases the bard would take up the general theme of the event and amplify that.

The poetic literature produced during the reign of Akbar reflects the trends and traditions of the period. It fully reflects the trend of the imperial policy of religious syncretism and tolerance (*sulh-i-kul*). This literature sometimes could be more useful in studying the spirit of the age than prose literature, though it required a different method of critically evaluating it. On the other hand, we find some *mathnawis* composed during the Mughal period in Sindh overly romanticised and lacking in any useful historical facts, such as *Mazhar al-Aasar* and *Mazhar al-Anwar* of Shah Jahangir; Mir Masum Nami's *Husn-o-Naz*; Idraki Beglari's *Mathnawi Chanesar Nama*; and Muhammad Radai's *Ziba Nigar*. Amongst these, only *Mazhar al-Aasar* and *Mathnawi Chanesar Nama* are extant now.

The current study is primarily based on the political and non-political historical literature produced by the local authors in Sindh, but the accounts on Sindh available in other regional histories have to be carefully tapped and systematically analysed in order to obtain a clear picture of trends and issues in contemporary history writing.

Here I will mention some historical literature compiled outside Sindh during the Mughal rule that also includes accounts about the history of this region: *Gulshan-i-Ibrahimi* (Garden of Prophet Ibrahim) better known as the *Tarikh-i-Firishta* (History of Firishta) by Mohammad Qasim Hindu Shah; *Zafar al-Walih bi Muzaffar Waalih* (An Arabic History of Gujarat) by Abdullah Muhammad bin Omar al-Makki; *Mirat-i-Ahmadi* (Mirror of Ahmad) of Ali Muhammad; and *Mirat-i-Sikandari* (Mirror of Sikandar) of Sikandar ibn Muhammad. Then there are important histories of other regions as well: *Riyaz-us-Salatin* or the Garden of Kings (The History of Bengal) by Ghulam Husain Salim, and the *Baharistan-i-Shahi* and Haidar Malik's *Tarikh-i-Kashmir* (completed in 1621 CE). These books supplement some accounts relating to the history of Sindh; they depict the contemporary regional socio-cultural milieu and political environment. However, this literature has to be tapped cautiously and systematically analysed to verify historical information, but it is indispensable to our understanding of broader patterns of society. In fact, historical data should be collected on a regional basis, but interpreted on an all-India basis. This trend of compilation of regional histories in India remained popular after the downfall of Mughal rule.

British officials also encouraged the compilation of regional histories and as a result, an enormous amount of such work was produced during the British period on the different regions of India, such as the *Yadgar-i-Bahaduri* alias *Tarikh-i-Bahaduri* (History of Jaunpur) of Bahadur Singh; *Tarikh Gulzar-i-A'asifia* (History of Deccan) of Khawaja Ghulam Hussain Khan, alias Khan-i-Zaman; *Nishan-i-Hyderi* alias *Tipu Sultan* (History of Mysore) by Mir Hussain Khan Kirmani are essentially regional in scope.[18]

As has been discussed earlier, the Mughal period is significant for the abundance of the source material it produced to study the political history of medieval Sindh. There are a great many meticulous accounts of political matters and administrative achievements of the period, but practically nothing about the lives of common people. We may assume that historians preferred not to mention the sufferings of the common people, because this might negate the eulogistic remarks which they composed about their patron ruler. Rarely was there any reference to the general life and conditions of the lower classes of the people. And while there appear to be some fleeting observations on the social aspect of society in a few of the non-political works, the accounts of foreigners and travellers may be best for those looking to study the socio-economic and cultural history.

During the sixteenth and seventeenth centuries, a number of European travellers set out for India. Some of them, like Ralph Fitch, visited Sindh for searching commercial opportunities in terms of direct trade. Others, like William Hawkins and Thomas Roe came as ambassadors to represent their kings in the courts of the Mughal emperors. Reports compiled by these diplomats, along with the accounts by other non-English European travellers in India, are preserved in print form. Fitch provides a dry, straightforward description of events, whereas W. Glanius is more lurid in his recollection of how his expedition was ostensibly shipwrecked in Bengal and was forced out of hunger to dig up graves to eat flesh.[19]

These accounts were examined through the worldviews of European travellers and are therefore of limited use as sources for sixteenth or seventeenth century Indian history. Nonetheless, these accounts give us an idea of their impressions of the land and its people. They need to be studied to understand how travellers viewed Indian civilisation.

The early European wayfarers were part of a broader trend known as the European age of exploration. Spain and Portugal led the way in these ventures in the late fifteenth century. The pope designated that Spain could go westward and Portugal eastward to prevent conflict between these two Christian countries. Thus, the Portuguese set forth to make contact and establish trading posts with the legendary kingdoms of the East.

In 1498 CE, Vasco da Gama's fleet became the first Europeans to reach India by circuiting Africa around the Cape of Good Hope. Prior to da Gama's expedition, Europe already had overland commercial relations with India that had been going on for hundreds of years, through Arab traders and other mediators. By establishing direct commercial links with India, the Portuguese hoped to eradicate relying on intermediaries.

The British entered the process of exploration a century later. The British East India Company was set up in London, in 1600 CE, in order to encourage commercial ties between England and India. At this time, the Mughals were the dominant political power in north India. By the 1580s, the Mughal Empire controlled much of the Indo-Gangetic Plain, parts of the Deccan, and parts of modern-day Afghanistan.

The European travellers who visited north India came into contact with the Mughals and observed their empire that had spread out further than any other previous Indian dynasty. From the period of Akbar, we find elaborate and interesting accounts of Sindh in the writings of European travellers, such as Walter Payton (1613 CE), Nicholas Withington (1613–1614 CE), S. Manrique (1640–1641 CE), Niccolao Manucci (1659 CE), and Alexander Hamilton (1699 CE). These sixteenth century Western voyagers collected information on the various communities of Sindh, its fauna and flora, rivers, mountains, customs, and institutions. In addition, there are some official letters written by the factotum of the English factory in Sindh (1635–1662 CE) that shed substantial light on the contemporary commercial, social, and political conditions of Sindh.[20]

The travellers who visited Sindh may be categorised according to their professions, such as merchants, missionaries, spies, envoys, administrators, and adventurers. The first European that arrived in Sindh was a Portuguese. Unfortunately, most of the records of this traveller have been lost. Same is the case with a Dutch visitor. However, the accounts compiled by the Italian, Spanish, German, French, and British travellers, are extant. They are varied according to the pursuits and professions of the itinerants. The merchants noted their commercial interests and explored the land and sea routes. They highlighted the economic conditions and geography. The missionaries detail interesting accounts of a social and religious nature. The adventurers' memoirs include information about different aspects of the land and people.

The writings of foreign travellers display distinct features and characteristics. Their observations opened up a new aspect in the history writing of medieval India. They demonstrated a better judgement of the contemporary political conditions here than the native authors, since they had a wider experience from travelling over vast and varied regions of the world and having observed different cultures and societies. Generally, the local writers occupied the official posts and consequently, to some extent, their prejudices and interests tainted their writings. The accounts of the foreign travellers by and large were more pragmatic and relevant to their interests and free from the influence of the ruling authorities.

Undoubtedly, the tradition of factual narration and court histories in Sindh started with the Mughals. During this period, a substantial number of histories were compiled, and historians had no difficulty in tracing a record of this era; which was quite different to the situation regarding the pre-Mughal period. A historical record nominally existed, but it did not go beyond the affairs of the ruling class. Such a tendency provided a limited historical perspective for a substantial period of time.

The post-colonial period witnessed an admirable standard of historiography in English and other regional languages, but it did not widen the parameters of Persian historiography. The British officials tried to provide a literary refinement to history writing in Persian, but it did not substantially add to our knowledge of the past or its criticism.

In the initial stages of the British period, historiographical trends confirm that the Persian language and literature diminished in importance, even though the Indo-Persian intelligentsia was still well off then and enjoyed a good position in society. This indicates that the later political deprivation and impoverishment of the Muslim elite was not accompanied by a period of cultural decadence and mental stagnation for this native Persian-speaking intelligentsia. They had been the rank and file from whom the previous Mughal regime had recruited the bureaucracy. They continued to foster the tradition of scholarship and research with their agile pens, despite the political upheavals. However, Persian historical literature lost that richness and cultural vibrancy that it was heir to and witnessed new trends, challenges, and issues under the British-colonial regime.

The historical material produced under the Mughals has definite idiosyncrasies. Firstly, medieval Muslim chronicles had a strong religious bent and evinced racial pride. To some extent, these foreign immigrant historians considered the superiority of the Islamic faith and their racial legacy to be a patent fact. As a result, they usually referred to the natives using most uncomplimentary epithets. At times, it is contended that this was just a style of writing and no serious notice should be taken of their choice of words. But the manner of their writing surely reflects their psyche. Further, they didn't bother much about relating the life of the common people, their economic problems, and social behaviour.

The authors of the political chronicles, on the whole, compiled their works at the instance of the rulers and nobles, or dedicated them to these personages. Consequently, they obviously elevated their patrons to the highest levels, attributed all kinds of virtues to them and exaggerated their victories, particularly in the spheres of territorial and cultural achievements and in the suppression of native rebellions. Even their deeds of cruelty and atrocities have been portrayed as virtuous acts.

In the beginning, medieval historiography was based on works of political history and biographical memoirs. Then, increasingly, non-political aspects of history, such as the cultural influence of Mughal rule, literature and art, social and economic life, etc., began to grab the attention of historians.

Eventually, history was not confined to the accounts of kings and wars, but a narrative of matters concerning the people as well. This has now become a well-recognised aspect. But this concept took a long time to develop. There is now the conviction that history is a form of critical inquiry into the past and not merely a repetition of testimony and authority. The modern historiographers of medieval history try to probe into the reasons and background of human actions of the past. Unlike medieval historiographers, they seek not only religious motivation, but political, economic, social, and other causes as well and try to discover relationships and historical trends and developments. Lastly, modern historiography also utilizes footnotes, appendices, bibliographies, and at times, maps, in its study.

During the medieval period, the native scholars continued the previous trend and they too extensively contributed to writing historical literature during the Kalhora and subsequent periods. Several Persian works in poetry and prose were compiled, for instance *Tarikh-i-Abbasia* and *Tuhfat al-Tahirin* by Shaykh Azam; *Tuhfat al-Kiram*, *Maqalat al-Shuara*, and *Makli Nama* of Ali Sher Qani Thattawi; *Mayar-i Salikan-i Tariqat, Nama-i Nughdh* by Bagh Ali Khaif; *Guldasta i-Nawris Bahar*, a compilation of the letters of Munshi Miyan Abdul Rauf of Sewistan; *Nagiran-i-Sindh* of Pandit Mohan Lal, and *Lubb i-Tarikh-i-Kalhora*, etc.

After the Kalhora period, a number of Persian historical works were also compiled under the Talpur rulers. These included *Tarikh-i-Sindh* of Syed Mohibullah Bhakkari; *Fath Nama* and *Insha-i-Azim* by Mir Azim al-Din Thattawi; *Tarikh-i-Balochi* of Abdul Majeed Jokhyo; *Ahwal-i-Kalhora* of Mazhar Ali; *Fath Nama* of Mir Subedar Khan; and *Tadhkira Zibdat al-Ma'asirin* by Mir Hasan al-Hussaini. This literature enriched the Persian historiography in Sindh, which reached its glory and pinnacle. Nevertheless, these sources also include some non-political literature like *tadhkiras*, *insha*, and *manshoors* besides the political ones. They are equally important because they corroborate many historical events and so are referred to as important sources of the socio-cultural, religious, and economic development of the era.

Oral history was not unknown to the scholars of medieval Sindh. After the *Chach Nama* and the *Tarikh-i-Masumi*, the *Tuhfat al-Kiram* occupies the status of the third major compilation on the history of Sindh, which was written during the Kalhora period. A major portion of the work related to the history of the Soomra period, based on the folklore of Sindh, such as the story of Umar-Marui/Marvi, Moomal-Mahendra, Leela/Lilan-Chanesar, and Dalu Rai.

'The folklore of Sindh, like all other folklore is the result of an interaction of cultural, geographical, and religious factors and offers valuable historical evidence of cultural influence. Folklore was preserved orally for centuries by local *bhats* and *charans*'[21] that are mainly Hindu castes. They are traditionally employed to trace genealogies and are found mainly in the desert regions of India and Pakistan.

In fact, during the Kalhora period, people's minds were so suppressed in a feudal society that they did not have any collective idea of nationality. They hardly had any social, political, or other collective movements. They had no set economic and financial goals. They were ruled by monarchies and autocratic chieftains. Due to this reason, the great body of literature and poetry in a particular style has been handed down over the centuries that interpreted the feeling of patriotism that is particularly portrayed in the character of Marui/Marvi.

The British period in Sindh (1843–1947 CE), on the other hand, witnessed an admirable standard of historiography in English and other regional languages, but did not widen the parameters of historiography in the Persian language. In order to downplay the glory of Muslim rule, the British officials encouraged the compilation of regional histories and the ancient history of India. They also compiled gazetteers full of significant and miscellaneous information about different regions to aid their officers to understand the area and people they were administrating over.

This was the period when Persian, the long-flourishing and dominant official language of Sindh, was replaced by English and Sindhi. Persian soon lost its importance and prominence and gradually declined due to official contempt and negligence. It was no longer the language of the courts and administration and was supplanted by regional languages, such as Marathi, Bengali, Urdu, Sindhi, etc., all over the Indian sub-continent. This whole process of transforming official languages took two to three decades. During this period, some Persian work that was done was regarded as being very erudite and having literary and historical significance. The literary scene was dominated by British writers who recorded their observations and memoirs of their travels and stay in Sindh and other adjoining regions. This literature provides a brilliant record of the social, cultural, economic, and religious conditions of the inhabitants of this region.

This change gave a new shape to the historical writings and brought about a new era in the field of historiography all over India, including Sindh.

The compilation of sophisticated chronograms highlighting significant events was a major prevailing trend of the Mughal historiography in Sindh. It continued under the British, who were very fond of reading chronograms. Some Englishmen also composed some notable chronograms of their own, such as Thomas William Bale's *Miftah al-Tawarikh*, which was chronologically arranged and included other chronograms composed by the author's friends.[22] Monographs of important journeys and campaigns by British officials was another cultural trend that continued from the previous era. Compared to traditional monographs, these seem to be more 'travelogues' of a concise nature. These accounts are significant in their nature and outlook. However, unlike traditional historiographical material, they deal with the ethnographic aspect and usually included descriptions of different races, cities, and towns.

In fact, the Persian historical literature produced during the British era is, in many ways, far more genuine and accurate than that which was produced before it. It is more authentic because it is based on either the author's personal experience, or information collected from eyewitnesses of the time and is not biased in favour of a ruler, or patron. There is no trace of the mythical approach to the past in these works. Consequently, this historical literature has a value of its own and represents an excellent arrangement of facts.

The British colonial period in Sindh is rich in historical literature; there are contemporaneous histories and memoirs in English and Sindhi, written by a number of European as well as local Muslim and Hindu scholars. The list of chronicles includes numerous illustrious histories and translations of the previous works into English and Sindhi. These works brought a lot of unique and valuable information into the limelight, not only about the land and people, but of the neighbouring regions as well. This period was dominated mainly by British writers, but native writers also contributed significantly to the canon. The contemporary historical sources were written by the men of affairs, who personally witnessed the events outlined, and sometimes even took part in them.

This period is signified by the printing and publishing of many Persian, Sindhi, and English historical and literary books. Sir H. Bartle Frere, Chief Commissioner of Sindh (r. 1850–1859 CE), introduced the modern education system in this province and with it, a new era of development of the Sindhi language. Native and British officers translated Persian historical works of the past into Sindhi and English. These changes introduced new dimensions in the field of historiography and broadened its scope. Though the art of writing history adopted a new set of guidelines and theories during the nineteenth and twentieth centuries, unfortunately, these developments had no or very limited effect on Persian historiography. The official negligence left far-reaching effects on the Persian language in Sindh, as we see no significant compilation put together during this period.

In short, it may be said that the Mughal period in Sindh was a landmark in medieval historiography. From the very start, books on the history of Sindh were composed following the new model. The scope of historical literature was extensive and besides political history, included epistolography, biographical works, religious discourses, poetic compositions, etc. The richness and variety of historical literature compiled during the Mughal era, provided a unique understanding of the period and offered new perspectives for its study. The Mughal era was one of political strength, cultural progress, and intellectual zeal. The historical literature of this period reveals these trends. But still, this material requires different tools for examination, analysis, and synthesis.

It would certainly be unjust to expect that the historiography of the medieval period could stand the test of the twentieth century standards in terms of treatment, techniques, and approach, but if we judge from the viewpoint of what prevailed at that time, it was sophisticated and far ahead of its time.

From the mythological, theological, and legendary phase of oral ancient history under the Mughals in Sindh, writing the chronicles of the time emerged as a rational, secular, and authoritative phase. It possessed all the features of Perso-Arab traditions. Historical literature in Persian continued to be produced throughout the eighteenth century in Sindh, but, as Muslim political power declined following the collapse of Timurid-Mughal rule and subsequent rules of the Kalhoras and the Talpurs, patronage decayed, and simultaneously, Persian was supplanted by Sindhi and English by the mid-nineteenth century.

Notes

Introduction

1. E. Sreedharan, *A Textbook of Historiography, 500 BC to AD 2000* (New Delhi: Orient Longman Pvt. Ltd., 2004), p. 2.
2. R.G. Collingwood, *The Idea of History* (London: Oxford University Press, 1994), p. 1.
3. Ibid., p. 3.
4. John Van Antwerp Fine, *The Ancient Greeks: A Critical History*, reprint (USA: Harvard University Press, 1983), p. 309.
5. K. Rajayyan, *History in Theory and Method: A Study in Historiography* (New Delhi: Raj Publishers, 1982), p. 17
6. A.A. Duri, *The Rise of Historical Writing among the Arabs*, ed. and trans. by Lawrence I. Conrad (New Jersey: Princeton University Press, 1983), p. 12.
7. Syed Ali Ashraf, *The Quranic Concept of History* (Leicester: Islamic Foundation, 1980), pp. 8–12.
8. Hadith refers to the sayings and actions of Prophet Muhammad (PBUH).
9. Sirah refers to the biographical accounts of Prophet Muhammad (PBUH).
10. Jan Rypka, *History of Iranian Literature* (Holland: D. Reidel, 1968), p. 238.
11. Ibid., p. 5.
12. Also transliterated *Tazkera, Tazkirah*.
13. Christi A. Merrill, *Riddles of Belonging: India in Translation and Other Tales of Possession* (Fordham University Press, 2009), p. 61.
14. Roma Doctor, 'Sindhi Folklore: An Introductory Survey,' *Folklore* 96/2, (London: Taylor and Francis Ltd., 1985), p. 295.
15. Khan Bahadur Khudadad Khan, *Lubb i-Tarikh i-Sindh*, ed. Dr Nabi Bakhsh Khan Baloch, (Hyderabad: Sindhi Adabi Board, 1959), p. 48.
16. G.P. Singh, *Early Indian Historical Traditions and Archaeology* (New Delhi: D.K. Print World, 1994), p. 281.
17. See Ali bin Hamid bin Abi Bakar al-Kufi, *Fath Nama i-Sindh* alias *Chach Nama*, Preface, ed. Dr Umar bin Muhammad Daudpota (New Delhi: Majlis Maktubat-i-Farsi Hyderabad Deccan, 1939).
18. K.A. Nizami, *On History and Historians of Medieval India* (New Delhi: Munshiram Manoharlal, 1983), p. 43.
19. Abdul Baqi Nihawandi, *Ma'athir-i-Rahimi*, ed. M. Hidayat Hussain, vol. 2 (Calcutta: Asiatic Society Bengal, 1925), p. 733.

Chapter 1: Indian Historiography in Retrospect

1. R.C. Majumdar, B.V. Bhavan, and B.I. Simiti, *The History and Culture of the Indian People*, vol. 1 (London: G. Allen & Unwin, 1969), p. 37.

2. H.E. Barnes, *A History of Historical Writing*, 2nd revised ed. (New York: Dover Publications, 1963), p. 3.
3. E.H. Carr, *What is History?* (New York: Vintage Books, 1987), p. 136.
4. T.R. Sharma, *Historiography: A History of Historical Writings* (New Delhi: Concept Publishing Co., 2005), p. 13.
5. John Marincola (ed.), *A Companion to Greek and Roman Historiography* (India: Spi Publishers, 2010), pp. 27–8.
6. Proceedings, Punjab History Conference, Thirty-Sixth Session, 18–20 March 2004, Publication Bureau, Punjabi University, Patiala, p. 332.
7. T.R. Sharma, *Historiography*, p. 5.
8. Vandana Yadav, *History and Historiography: Trends and Practices* (New Delhi: Shree Publishers and Distributers, 2007), p. 4.
9. K.M. Ashraf (ed.), *Indian Historiography and Other Related Papers* (New Delhi: Sunrise Publications, 2006), p. 4.
10. H.E. Barnes, *A History of Historical Writing*, pp. 10–11.
11. R.G. Collingwood, *The Idea of History*, pp. 14–15.
12. Ibid., p. 17.
13. E. Sreedharan, *A Textbook of Historiography, 500 B.C. to A.D. 2000* (New Delhi: Orient Longman Pvt. Ltd., 2004), p. 7.
14. R.G. Collingwood, *The Idea of History*, p. 107.
15. K.M. Ashraf (ed.), *Indian Historiography and Other Related Papers*, p. 15.
16. D.K. Ganguly, *History and Historians of Ancient India* (New Delhi: Abhino Publishers, 1984), p. 4.
17. Ibid., p. 7.
18. Refer to Kader. D. Pathak, *Essentials of History and Historiography* (New Delhi: Swastik Publications, 2012), p. 202.
19. B. Sheikh Ali, *History: Its Theory and Method* (California: Macmillan, 1978), p. 360.
20. G.P. Singh, *Early Indian Historical Traditions and Archaeology*, p. 15.
21. Balkrishna Govind Gokhale, *Ancient India, History and Culture* (New Delhi: Asia Pub. House, 1959), p. 7.
22. V.S. Pathak, *Ancient Historians of India: A Study in Historical Biographies* (Jodhpur: Kusumanjali Book World, 1997), p. 26.
23. Amaresh Datta, *The Encyclopaedia of Indian Literature*, vol. 2, 15th ed. (New Delhi: Sahitya Akademi, 2005), p. 1181.
24. P. Thomas, *Epics, Myths and Legends of India*, 2nd ed. (Bombay: D.B. Taraporevala Sons and Co., 1961), p. 12.
25. Amaresh Datta, *The Encyclopaedia of Indian Literature*, p. 121.
26. F.E. Pargiter, *Ancient Indian Historical Traditions* (London: Oxford University Press, 1922).
27. D.K. Ganguly, *History and Historians in Ancient India*, p. 13.
28. Mohan Lal, *Encyclopaedia of Indian Literature: Sasay to Zorgot*, vol. 5 of *Encyclopaedia of Indian Literature* (New Delhi: Sahitya Akademi, 2006), p. 4609.
29. G.P. Singh, *Ancient Indian Historiography: Sources and Interpretations* (New Delhi: D.K. Print World, 2003), p. 7.
30. D.K. Ganguly, *History and Historians of Ancient India*, p. 28.
31. V.S. Pathak, *Ancient Historians of India*, p. 17.
32. Ibid., p. 114.
33. G.P. Singh, *Ancient Indian historiography*, p. 16.
34. E. Sreedharan, *A Textbook of Historiography*, p. 320.

35. Ibid., p. 338.
36. Also spelled *Buddhacharita*, in full *Buddhacarita-kavya-sutra* (Sanskrit: 'Poetic Discourse on the Acts of the Buddha').
37. Radhey Shyam Chaurasia, *History of Ancient India: Earliest Times to 1200 A.D.* (New Delhi: Atlantic Publishers, 2008), pp. 295–6.
38. V.S. Pathak, *Ancient Historians of India*, p. 30.
39. *Kavya* refers to the Sanskrit literary style used by the ancient Indian court poets flourished during the first half of the seventh century CE. This literary style is characterized by abundant usage of figures of speech, metaphors, similes, and hyperbole to create its emotional effects. The result is a short lyrical work, court epic, narrative, or dramatic work.
40. V.S. Pathak, *Ancient Historians of India*, p. 56.
41. G.P. Singh, *Early Indian Historical Traditions and Archaeology*, p. 199.
42. Ibid.
43. Tan Chung, ed., *Across the Himalayan Gap: An Indian Quest for Understanding China* (New Delhi: Indira Gandhi National Centre, 1998), p. 64.
44. Mohibbul Hasan, *Kashmir under the Sultans*, Reprint (Delhi: Aakar Books, 2005), p. 274.
45. Abu al-Qasim Firdausi (940–1020 CE) was a highly revered Persian poet. He composed the epic titled *Shah Nama*. It is the national epic of Iran and the Persian-speaking world.
46. B. Sheikh Ali, *History: Its Theory and Method*, p. 366.
47. Upinder Singh, *A History of Ancient and Early Medieval India: From the Stone Age to the 12th Century* (New Delhi: Dorling Kindersley, 2009), p. 27.
48. S.N. Sen, *Ancient Indian History and Civilization*, 2nd ed. (New Delhi: New Age Publishers, 1999), p. 204.
49. V.S. Pathak, *Ancient Historians of India*, p. 148.
50. K.M. Ashraf, ed., *Indian Historiography and Other Related Papers*, pp. 10–11.
51. Muhammad Ghulam Rasul, *The Origin and Development of Muslim Historiography* (Lahore: Sh. Muhammad Ashraf, 1976), p. 3.
52. K.D. Pathak, *Essentials of History and Historiography*, p. 181.
53. A.A. Duri, *The Rise of Historical Writing among the Arabs*, p. 50.
54. Jan Rypka, *History of Iranian Literature*, p. 238.
55. I.H. Siddiqui, *Indo-Persian Historiography up to the 13th Century* (Primus Books, 2010), p. 12.
56. E.G. Brown, *Literary History of Persia*, vol. I (London: Cambridge University Press, 1977), p. 275.
57. Tara Chand, *Influence of Islam on Indian Culture* (Allahabad: The Indian Press, 1936), p. 44.
58. Ahmad bin Yahya al Baladhuri, *Futuh al-Buldan*, Urdu trans. Syed Abul Khair Modudi (Karachi: Nafees Academy, 1982), p. 613.
59. James Wynbrandt, *A Brief History of Pakistan* (New York: Infobase Publishing, 2009), p. 43.
60. S.N. Sen, *Ancient Indian History and Civilization*, p. 594.
61. I.H. Qureshi, *The Muslim Community of the Indo-Pakistan Subcontinent (610–1947)*, Reprint (Karachi: University of Karachi, 1999), pp. 35–6; see Hakim Mohammed Said and Ansar Zahid Khan, *Al-Biruni: His Times, Life and Works* (Karachi: Hamdard Foundation, 1981).

62. Richard N. Frye, *The Golden Age of Persia*, Reprint (London: Weidenfeld & Nicolson, 1977), p. 162.
63. S. Gajrani, *History, Religion and Culture of India*, vol. I (New Delhi: Gyan Publishing House, 2004), p. 43.
64. Judith E. Walsh, *A Brief History of India* (New York: InfoBase Publishing, 2006), p. 69.
65. E. Sreedharan, *A Textbook of Historiography*, p. 342.
66. Refer to B. Sheikh Ali, *History: Its Theory and Method*, p. 78.
67. Ali bin Hamid bin Abi Bakr al-Kufi, *Fath Nama i-Sindh alias Chach Nama*, vol. 1, part. 1, Persian text ed. N.A. Baloch (Islamabad: Institute of Islamic History, Culture and Civilization, 1983).
68. Robert L. Canfield, ed., *Turko-Persia in Historical Perspective* (New York: Cambridge University Press, 1991), p. 107.
69. Peter Jackson, *The Delhi Sultanate: A Political and Military History* (Cambridge University Press, 1999), pp. 75 and 79.
70. Muhammad Yasin, *A Social History of Islamic India 1605–1748* (Lucknow: D.W. Publishers, 1958), p. 5.
71. Peter Jackson, *The Delhi Sultanate*, p. 179.
72. D. Daniel R. Woolf, *The Oxford History of Historical Writing: 1350–1750*, vol. III (New Delhi: Oxford University Press, 2011), p. 153.
73. T.R. Sharma, *Historiography*, p. 78.
74. V.N. Rao, David Shulman, and Sanjay Subrahmanyam, *Textures of Time: Writing History in South India 1600–1800* (New Delhi: Permanent Black, 2001), pp. 219–21.
75. Peter Hardy, *Historians of the Medieval India: Studies in Indo-Muslim Historical Writings* (London: Louzak & Co., 1960), p. 127.
76. Ibid., pp. 123–5.
77. Ibid., p. 119.
78. Ibid., p. 122.
79. Khawaja Abdul Malik Isami (b. 1311 CE) was a historian and court poet of Ala-ud-Din Bahman Shah, the founder of the Bahmani Sultanate, a Muslim state in the Deccan. He is best known for *Futuh-us-Salatin* (*c.* 1350 CE), a poetic history of the Muslim conquest of India. More details of his works follow in this chapter.
80. Ziya al-Din/Ziauddin Barani (1285–1359 CE) was a scholar and historian in the time of Mohammad Bin Tughluq and a friend of Amir Khusro. His famous works are *Tarikh-i-Ferozshahi* and *Fatawa-i-Jahandari*. More details of his works follow in this chapter.
81. S.M. Jaffar, *Some Cultural Aspects of Muslim Rule in India* (Peshawar: Muhammad Sadiq Khan Publishers, 1950), pp. 162–3.
82. The pioneer in history writing was Muhammad bin Mansur, also known as Fakhr-i-Mudabbir. He migrated from Ghazna to Lahore during the later Ghaznavid period. In Lahore he compiled *Shajra-i-Ansab*, the book of genealogies of the Prophet of Islam (PBUH), his companions, and the Muslim rulers, including the ancestors of Sultan Muizuddin Muhammad bin Sam (aka Sultan Shihabuddin Muhammad Ghori). The compiler wanted to present it to the sultan but the latter's assassination on his way from the Punjab to Ghazna in 1206, led him to append a separate portion as *muqadimma* (introduction) to it. This introduction narrates the life and military exploits of Qutub al-din Aibak from 1192 to 1206. This is the first history of the Ghorid conquest, the foundation of an independent Sultanate, and Aibak's reign compiled in India. It was in view of its importance that in 1927, the English scholar,

E. Denison Ross separated the *muqadimma* from the manuscript of *Shajra-i-Ansab* and published its critically edited text with his introduction (in English) under the title *Ta'rikh-i Fakhru'd-Din Mubarakshah* (London: Royal Asiatic Society, 1927).
83. See Minhaj-us-Siraj Juzjani, *Tabaqat-i-Nasiri*, vol. 1, trans. H.G. Raverty (Lahore: 1975). Minhaj al-Siraj Juzjani (b. 1193 CE), was a thirteenth century Persian historian born in the Ghorid capital city of Ferozkuh, which was located in Ghor province. Around 1230 CE Juzjani migrated to Delhi. Juzjani was the principal historian for the Mamluk Sultanate of Delhi during the unstable period after Iltutmish. Minhaj wrote of the Ghorid dynasty. He also wrote the *Tabaqat-i-Nasiri* (1260 CE) for Sultan Nasiruddin Mahmud of Delhi.
84. Yahya bin Ahmad Sirhindi, was a fifteenth century Indian chronicler who wrote *Tarikh-i-Mubarakshahi*, about the ruler Mohammad bin Tughluq.
85. Dr Khurram Qadir, 'Medieval Historiography of Muslim India: The Sultanate Period,' *Journal of the Pakistan Historical Society* 50, no. 3 (July–September 2002), p. 26.
86. On the pattern of Firdausi's *Shah Nama*.
87. Anil Chandra Banerji, *The State and Society in Northern India, 1206–1526* (K.P. Bagchi, 1982); Bhanwarlal Nathuram Luniya, *Life and Culture in Medieval India* (New Delhi: Kamal Prakashan, 1978), p. 72.
88. E.G. Brown, *Literary History of Persia*, vol. 3, p. 110.
89. Abu Nasar al-Utb'i, *Tarikh-i-Yamini*, ed. Ali and Sprenger (Delhi: 1847), extracts translated in Elliot and Dowson, vol. 2 (Allahabad, 1978).
90. Shams Siraj Afif, *Tarikh-i-Ferozshahi*, ed. Wilayat Hussain, Bibliotheca Indica (Calcutta, 1862).
91. N.K. Singh and A. Samiuddin, *Encyclopaedic Historiography of the Muslim World* (Delhi: Global Vision Publication House, 2003), p. 184.
92. Ziya al-Din Barani, *Tarikh-i-Ferozshahi*, Urdu trans. Moin al-Haque (Lahore: Urdu Science Board, 1991).
93. Ziya al-Din Barani, *Fatawa-i-Jahandari*, compiled by Dr Riaz Ahmad and trans. Prof. Atiq Ahmad (Islamabad: NIHCR, 2004).
94. Peter Hardy, *Historians of the Medieval India*, p. 104.
95. S.M. Waseem (ed.), *Development of Persian Historiography in India: From the Second Half of the 17th Century to the First Half of the 18th Century* (New Delhi: Kanishka Publishers, 2003), p. 28.
96. Jaswant Lal Mehta, *Advanced Study in the Study of Medieval India*, vol. 1, reprint (New Delhi: Sterling Publishers, 2009), p. 7; K.A. Nizami, *On History and Historians of Medieval India*.
97. Abu al-Qasim Muhammad Firishta, *Tarikh-i-Firishta*, Urdu trans. Abdul Hai Khawaja (Lahore: Book Talk, 1991), p. 232.
98. *The Gazetteer of India: History and culture*, vol. 2 (Publications Division, Ministry of Information and Broadcasting, 1973), p. 459.
99. Wahid Mirza, *The Life and Works of Amir Khusrau* (Lahore: University of the Punjab, 1962), p. 148.
100. Amir Khusro, *Khaza'in al-Futuh* (Aligarh: Allahabad University Press, 1927).
101. Salma Ahmed Farooqui, *A Comprehensive History of Medieval India: From Twelfth to the Mid-Eighteenth Century* (New Delhi: Pearson Education India, 2011), p. 8.
102. Peter Hardy, *Historians of the Medieval India*, p. 103.
103. Khawaja Abdul Malik Isami, *Futuh-us-Salatin*, ed. and trans. Agha Mahdi Husain, vol. 3 (Aligarh: 1977).

104. N.K. Singh and A. Samiuddin, *Encyclopaedic Historiography of the Muslim World*, p. 465.
105. Bhanwarlal Nathuram Luniya, *Some Historians of Medieval India* (New Delhi: Lakshmi Narain Agarwal, 1969), p. 99.
106. Mir Hassan Sijzi, *Fawa'id al-Fuad* (New Delhi: D.K. Print World, 1996).
107. Hamid Qalandar, *Khair al-Majalis*, ed. K.A. Nizami (Aligarh, 1959).
108. Mir Khurd, *Siyar al-Awliya* (New Delhi: Muhibb-i-Hind Press, 1885).
109. The eighth sultan of the Shah Mir dynasty in Kashmir.
110. Mohibbul Hasan, *Historians of Medieval India*, Urdu trans. Masroor Hashmi under the title of *Ahd-i-Wusta kay Moirrikheen* (New Delhi: Urdu Promotion Buru, 1985), p. 107.
111. Mohibbul Hasan, *Kashmir under the Sultans*, p. 1.
112. Mohibbul Hasan, *Historians of Medieval India*, p. 156.
113. N.K. Singh and A. Samiuddin, *Encyclopaedic Historiography of the Muslim World*, p. 951.
114. Mohibbul Hasan, *Historians of Medieval India*, p. 155.
115. Jan Rypka, *History of Iranian Literature*, pp. 444–5.
116. Peter Jackson, *The Delhi Sultanate*, p. 59.
117. Minhaj-us-Siraj Juzjani, *Tabaqat-i-Nasiri*, p. 391.
118. M. Tariq Awan, *History of India and Pakistan*, vol. 1 (Lahore: Ferozsons, 1994), p. 499.
119. Hijri calendar is associated with Hijra or the migration of the Muslims from Makkah to Madinah under the orders of Prophet Muhammad (PBUH). This is an event of great historical significance that took place in 622 CE.
120. Ishwari Prasad, *History of the Qaraunah Turks in India*, vol. 1 (Allahabad, 1936), p. 201.
121. N. Hanif, *Biographical Encyclopaedia of Sufis: South Asia* (New Delhi: Sarup and Sons, 2000), p. 277.
122. *Fiqh*, *hadith*, and *fatwa* are the three main forms in this regard.
123. See Ghazali, *Nishat al-Muluk*, trans. F.R.C. Bagley (London, 1962); Nizam al-Mulk Tusi, *Siyasat Nama*, trans. Herbert Darke (London, 1960).
124. Ishwari Prasad, *History of the Qaraunah Turks in India*, p. 206.
125. Carl W. Ernst, *Eternal Garden: Mysticism, History, and Politics at a South Asian Sufi Center* (New York: SUNY Press, 1992), p. 112.
126. Minhaj-us-Siraj Juzjani, *Tabaqat-i-Nasiri*, p. 51.
127. Anjum Rahmani, *Cultural Heritage of Pakistan* (Lahore Museum, 2000), p. 81.
128. K.A. Nizami, *On History and Historians of Medieval India*, p. 224.
129. Robert L. Canfield, *Turko-Persia in Historical Perspective* (New York: Cambridge University Press, 1991), p. 20.
130. Muhammad Ziauddin, 'Role of Persians at the Mughal Court: A historical study, during 1526–1717 AD' (PhD Thesis, University of Balochistan, 2005), p. 248.
131. Sukumar Ray, *Humayun in Persia* (Calcutta: Royal Asiatic Society of Bengal, 1948), p. 62.
132. Muhammad Ziauddin, 'Role of Persians at the Mughal Court,' p. 251.
133. Harbans Mukhia, *Historians and Historiography during the Reign of Akbar* (New Delhi: Vikas Publisher House, 1976), p. 14.
134. Peter Hardy, *Historians of the Medieval India*, p. 1.
135. Syed Abdullah, *Adabiyat-i-Farsi mein Hinduon ka hissa* (New Delhi: Anjuman Taraqqi Urdu, 1942), pp. 56–8.

136. Jaswant Lal Mehta, *Advanced Study in the History of Medieval India*, vol. 2, p. 45.
137. K.A. Nizami, *On History and Historians of Medieval India*, p. 7.
138. Ibid., p. 224.
139. Ibid., p. 1.
140. Harbans Mukhia, *Historians and Historiography during the Reign of Akbar*, p. 143.
141. K.A. Nizami, *On History and Historians of Medieval India*, p. 32.
142. Ibid., p. 34.
143. Mirza Hyder Dughlat, *Tarikh-i-Rashidi*, trans. Denison Ross (Patna, 1973), p. 152.
144. S.M. Waseem (ed.), *Development of Persian Historiography in India*, p. 34.
145. B. Sheikh Ali, *History: Its Theory and Method*, p. 371.
146. Transcendentalism is a form of philosophical idealism, which believes that society and its institutions; particularly those of organized religion or political parties—ultimately corrupts the purity of the individual. Transcendentalists have faith that people are at their best when they are truly 'self-reliant' and independent. It is only such pure individuals that can form a true community.
147. Fatalism is also a philosophical doctrine stressing the subjugation of all events or actions to fate.
148. S.M. Waseem (ed.), *Development of Persian historiography in India*, p. 37.
149. Abu al-Fazl Allami, *Akbar Nama*, vol. 1, trans. H. Beveridge (New Delhi: Low Price Publications, 1998), pp. 9–10.
150. See Abu al-Fazl Allami, *A'in-i-Akbari*, trans. H.F. Blochmann and H.S. Jarrett (Calcutta: Asiatic Society of Bengal, 1927).
151. Nabi Bakhsh Khan Baloch, *Sindh: Studies in Historical*, vol. 1 (Karachi: Kalhora Seminar Committee, 1996), p. 161.
152. K.M. Ashraf, ed., *Indian Historiography and Other Related Papers*, p. 31.

Chapter 2: Mughal Rule in Sindh: The Period of Origin and Development of Historiographical Trends

1. Aramaic is a family of languages (traditionally referred to as 'dialects') belonging to the Semitic group of nations. More specifically, it is a part of the Northwest Semitic sub-family, which also includes Canaanite languages such as Hebrew and Phoenician.
2. The Indus Valley Civilization was a Bronze Age civilization (3300–1300 BCE; mature period 2600–1900 BCE) in the north-western region of the Indian subcontinent, consisting mainly of what is now Pakistan. The civilization flourished on the banks of River Indus.
3. *Vedas*, *Puranas*, *Mahabharata*, and the *Ramayana* all are the Brahman Sanskrit religious literature, which are considered as the semi-historical sources for the history of ancient India.
4. K.S. Vaidyanathan, *Studies in Rig Veda (from Original Texts)* (India: K.V.S. Aiyer Indology Research Centre, 2000), p. 22.
5. Ibid., p. 24.
6. H. T. Lambrick, *Sindh: Before the Muslim Conquest* (Hyderabad: Sindhi Adabi Board, 1973), p. 69.
7. Sisir Kumar Das, *A History of Indian Literature, 500–1399: From Courtly to the Popular* (New Delhi: Sahitya Akademi, 2005), p. 259.

8. D.N. Majumdar, *Races and Cultures of India*, 4th ed. (New Delhi: Asia Publication House, 1961), p. 16.
9. *Balochistan Gazetteer*, vol. 6, pp. 34–5.
10. G.P. Singh, *Early Indian Historical Traditions and Archaeology*, p. 281; see Book LLC ed., *8th-Century History Books: Nihon Shoki, Chronicle of 754, Chach Nama, Historia Gentis Langobardorum, Royal Frankish Annals* (General Books LLC, 2010).
11. See Ali bin Hamid bin Abi Bakar al-Kufi, *Fath Nama i-Sindh* alias *Chach Nama*, Preface, ed. Dr Umar bin Muhammad Daudpota (New Delhi: Majlis Maktubat-i-Farsi Hyderabad Deccan, 1939).
12. Mir Ali Sher Qani Thattawi, *Tuhfat al-Kiram*, ed. S. Hussamuddin Rashidi, Urdu trans. Akhtar Ridwi, vol. 3 (Hyderabad: Sindhi Adabi Board, 1971), p. 12.
13. Nizam Al-Din Ahmad, *Tabaqat-i-Akbari*, Urdu trans. M. Ayyub Qadri (Lahore: Urdu Science Board, 1990), p. 632; Saeed Nafisi, *Tarikh Nazmwa Nasr dar Iran wadar Zaban-i-Farsi*, vol. 3, 2nd ed. (Tehran: Intisharat-i-Faroghi, 1944), p. 151.
14. Dr Zahuruddin Ahmad, *Pakistan mein Farsi Adab*, vol. 1 (Lahore, 1974), p. 280.
15. Saeed Nafisi, *Tarikh Nazmwa Nasr dar Iran wadar Zaban-i-Farsi* vol. 3, 2nd ed., p. 115.
16. Ali bin Hamid bin Abi Bakar al-Kufi, *Chach Nama*, pp. 7–8, 10, and 191.
17. Abu al-Hasan al-Mada'ini was a Muslim historian of Basra, whose work is the source for the main accounts of the Muslim conquest of Central Asia. It is said that he compiled a number of books on history, including accounts of the Arab conquest of Khurasan and Transoxiana, and biographies of the governors. The era of the great conquests had ended in 751 CE, just two years before his birth, so unlike other Arabs history writers, al-Mada'ini could gather and edit more realistic, vivid, and detailed stories about campaigns of this period. The conquest of Central Asia is the best documented of the early Muslim expansion.
18. Ahmad bin Yahya al Baladhuri, *Futuh al-Buldan*, pp. 424–5; Ahmad Ibn Yahya al-Baladhuri was a ninth century Persian historian. He was one of the most eminent middle-eastern historians of his age. He spent most of his life in Baghdad. He travelled in Syria and Iraq, compiling information for his major works. He is regarded as a reliable source for the history of the early Arabs and the history of Muslim expansion. His chief extant work is a condensation of a longer history, *Kitab Futuh al-Bulan* (Book of the Conquests of Lands). It tells of the wars and conquests of the Arabs from the seventh century, and the terms made with the residents of the conquered territories. It covers the conquests of lands from Arabia westward to Egypt, North Africa, and Spain and eastward to Iraq, Iran, and Sindh.
19. Ahmed Ibn Abi Yaqub Ibn Jaffer (Yaqubi), *Tarikh al-Yaqubi*, ed. M.T. Houtsma, vol. 1 (Leiden, 1883), pp. 50–5.
20. Ali bin Hamid bin Abi Bakar al-Kufi, *Chach Nama*, p. 38.
21. Abu Ja'far Muhammad b. Jarir al-Tabari (839–923 CE) was a prominent and influential Persian scholar, historian, and theologian. His most influential and best-known work is his historical chronicle titled *Tarikh al-Rusul wal-Muluk* (History of Prophets and Kings) that often has references to *Tarikh al-Tabari*.
22. Mannan Ahmed, 'The Long Thirteenth Century of the Chachnama,' *The Indian Economic and Social History Review* (Columbia University) 49, no. 4 (2012), p. 467.
23. Ali bin Hamid bin Abi Bakar al-Kufi, *Chach Nama*, pp. 14–17 and 21.
24. Shahpurshah Hormasji Hodivala, *Studies in Indo-Muslim History: A Critical Commentary on Elliot and Dowson's History of India as told by its own Historians,*

Foreword Sir Richard Burns, supplement, vol. 2, reprint (Bombay: Islamic Book Service, 1979), p. 83.
25. Ali bin Hamid bin Abi Bakar al-Kufi, *Chach Nama*, p. 11.
26. Mannan Ahmed, 'The Long Thirteenth Century of the Chachnama,' p. 467.
27. Ali bin Hamid bin Abi Bakar al-Kufi, *Chach Nama*, pp. 8–10.
28. Ibid., pp. 4, 6, 7, 346.
29. Ibid., p. 191.
30. Ibid., pp. 1–7.
31. Ibid., pp. 245–7.
32. Ibid., p. 459.
33. M.H. Panhwar, 'The Causes of Decline of Persian in Pakistan and Remedy' (presented in a Seminar at Hyderabad organized by the Iran Culture Centre, 1973).
34. D.N. Majumdar, *Races and Cultures of India*, p. 16.
35. Roma Doctor, 'Sindhi Folklore: An Introductory Survey,' p. 295.
36. Dr Nabi Bakhsh Khan Baloch, *Sindhi Boli aen Adab jee Tarikh*, 4th ed. (Jamshoro: University of Sindh, 1999), pp. 99–108.
37. Khan Bahadur Khudadad Khan, *Lubb i-Tarikh i-Sindh*, p. 48.
38. Dr Nabi Bakhsh Khan Baloch, *Sindhi Boli aen Adab jee Tarikh*, p. 187.
39. Syed Hussamuddin Rashidi, 'Nusrat Nama-i-Tarkhan,' *The Quarterly Mehran* (Jamshoro: Sindhi Adabi Board) no. 1–2 (1980), pp. 34–7.
40. Muhammad bin Bayazid Purani, *Nusrat Nama-i-Tarkhan*, ed. Dr Ansar Zahid Khan (Karachi: Institute of South and Central Asian Studies, 2000), p. 25.
41. Dr Ansar Zahid Khan, 'The Nusrat Nama-i-Tarkhan (Introduction),' *Journal of the Pakistan Historical Society* 45, no. 2 (April 1997), p. 118.
42. Makli Hill is one of the largest historical necropolises in the world which is located on the outskirts of Thatta, the capital of lower Sindh until the seventeenth century. Legends abound about its origin, but it is often believed that the cemetery grew around the shrine of a fourteenth-century Sarwa, Muhammad Hussain Abro. According to other sources however, the credit for establishing Makli as a holy place for worship and burial goes to the immigrant saint, poet, and scholar Shaikh Hammad Jamali and the then local Samma ruler, Jam Tamachi. The impressive royal mausoleums are divided into two major groups, those of the Samma (1352–1520 CE) and of the Tarkhan (1556–1592 CE) period. In total four historical periods are represented architecturally, namely the Samma, the Arghun, the Tarkhan, and the Mughal periods.
43. See the Introduction to *Nusrat Nama-i-Tarkhan* by Dr Ansar Zahid Khan.
44. Mir Ali Sher Qani Thattawi, *Tuhfat al-Kiram*, p. 611.
45. Dr Ansar Zahid Khan, *Nusrat Nama-i-Tarkhan*, Introduction, p. 129.
46. Mir Ali Sher Qani Thattawi, *Tuhfat al-Kiram*, p. 611.
47. Dr Ansar Zahid Khan, *Nusrat Nama-i-Tarkhan*, Introduction, p. 130.
48. Dr Mazhar Mahmud Shirani, 'Nusrat Namah-i-Tarkhan,' *The Quarterly Journal Fanun* (Lahore) 118 (September–December 2002), p. 329.
49. Muhammad bin Bayazid Purani, *Nusrat Nama-i-Tarkhan*, p. 22.
50. Shah Beg Arghan (r. 1520–1524 CE) was succeeded by his son Shah Hasan (r. 1524–1554 CE) who remained childless. Hasan became ill and incapable of ruling. After a civil war between him and Mirza Isa Tarkhan, the nobles made Mirza Isa Tarkhan ruler in 1554 CE. Shah Hasan died in 1556 CE.
51. Muhammad bin Bayazid Purani, *Nusrat Nama-i-Tarkhan*, p. 25
52. Ibid., p. 27.
53. Ibid., pp. 2, 5, 21, 286, 287, 333.

54. Ibid., p. 1.
55. Ibid., p. 26.
56. A chronogram is a sentence or inscription in which specific letters, interpreted as numerals, stand for a particular date when arranged. It was a well-known play on words used in medieval literature, mostly in poetic form.
57. Dr Muhammad Saleem Akhtar, 'Nusrat Nama-i-Tarkhan,' *Fikr wa Nazar, Quarterly Journal of Islamic Research Institute* (Islamabad) 39, no. 3 (July–September 2001), p. 192.
58. Muhammad bin Bayazid Purani, *Nusrat Nama-i-Tarkhan*, Annotation, p. 27.
59. Dr Muhammad Saleem Akhtar, 'Nusrat Nama-i-Tarkhan,' p. 193.
60. Dr Mazhar Mahmud Shirani, 'Nusrat Namah-i-Tarkhan,' p. 324.
61. Dr Ansar Zahid Khan, *Nusrat Nama-i-Tarkhan*, Introduction, p. 16.
62. Dr Bertold Spuler, 'Historiography in Muslim Persia,' *Journal of the Pakistan Historical Society* 6, part 4 (October–December 1958), p. 222.
63. Muhammad bin Bayazid Purani, *Nusrat Nama-i-Tarkhan*, p. 317.
64. Ibid., pp. 60–6.
65. Ibid., p. 222.
66. Mir Ali Sher Qani Thattawi, *Makli Nama*, ed. Syed Hussamuddin Rashidi (Hyderabad: Sindhi Adabi Board, 1967), p. 52.
67. Mir Ali Sher Qanai Thattawi, *Makli Nama*, Annotations, pp. 176–89.
68. Muhammad bin Bayazid Purani, *Nusrat Nama-i-Tarkhan*, p. 296.
69. Ibid., p. 257.
70. Ibid., p. 224.
71. Ibid., p. 60.
72. Ibid., p. 373.
73. Ibid., p. 291.
74. Ibid., p. 374.
75. See Yousuf Mirak, *Mazhar-i-Shahjahani*, ed. Syed Hussamuddin Rashidi (Hyderabad: Sindhi Adabi Board, 1962).
76. Dr Ansar Zahid Khan *Nusrat Nama-i-Tarkhan*, Introduction, pp. 112–13.
77. Muhammad bin Bayazid Purani, *Nusrat Nama-i-Tarkhan*, pp. 420–31.
78. Mir Masum Bhakkari, *Tarikh-i-Sindh* alias *Tarikh-i-Masumi*, ed. Dr Umar bin Muhammad Daudpota (Puna: Bahandarkar Oriental Institute, 1938), p. 110.
79. Muhammad bin Bayazid Purani, *Nusrat Nama-i-Tarkhan*, p. 215.
80. Ibid., p. 223.
81. Ibid., p. 230.
82. Ibid., p. 267.
83. Mir Masum Bhakkari, *Tarikh-i-Masumi*, pp. 111–12.
84. Zahiruddin Muhammad Babur, *Babur Nama*, Urdu trans. Mirza Hassan Beg (Karachi: Pakistan Historical Society, 2008), p. 178.
85. Muhammad bin Bayazid Purani, *Nusrat Nama-i-Tarkhan*, pp. 227–48.
86. Ibid., pp. 27–9.
87. Ibid., p. 333.
88. Raza Zadeh Shafaq, *Tarikh Adbiyat-i-Farsi*, edited and annotated (Tehran: 1337), p. 49; Jan Rypka, *History of Iranian Literature*, p. 155.
89. Muhammad bin Bayazid Purani, *Nusrat Nama-i-Tarkhan*, p. 333.
90. See, Muhammad Saleem Akhtar, 'Nusrat Nama-i-Tarkhan,' pp. 191–5.
91. See, Mazhar Mahmud Shirani, 'Nusrat Namah-i-Tarkhan,' pp. 322–30.

92. Mir Ali Sher Qani Thattawi, *Maqalat al-Shuara*, ed. Syed Hussamuddin Rashidi (Karachi: Sindhi Adabi Board, 1958), p. 774.
93. Ibid., p. 312.
94. Ibid., p. 42.
95. N.K. Singh and A. Samiuddin, *Encyclopaedic Historiography of the Muslim World*, p. 447.
96. Sadid al-Din Muhammad Awfi is one of the early immigrants from Central Asia. He was an eminent scholar and a prolific writer who composed masterpieces.
97. Ziauddin A. Desai, *Malfuz Literature: As a Source of Political, Social, and Cultural History of Gujarat and Rajasthan* (Patna: Khuda Bakhsh Oriental Library, 1991), p. 6.
98. Ibid., p. 7.
99. Amir Najm al-Din Hasan al-Sijzi was an important poet of the period of the Delhi Sultanate, whose work attracted the attention of literary figures and poets even outside of India. He was a contemporary and friend of Amir Khusro.
100. Professor Muhammad Aslam, *Malfuzati Adab ki Tarikhi Ehmiat* (Lahore: Idarah-i-Tahqiqat-i-Pakistan, 1995), p. 9.
101. Shaykh Muhammad Ikram, *Pakistan ka Saqafti Wirsa* (Lahore: Idara Saqafat-i-Islamia, 2001), p. 187.
102. K.A. Nizami, *On History and Historians of Medieval India*, pp. 188–9; see, Ahmad Moin Siyahposh, *Siraj al-Hidaya*, ed. Qazi Sajjad Hussain (New Delhi: ICHR, 1983).
103. Riazul Islam, *Sufism in South Asia: Impact on fourteenth century Muslim society* (Karachi: Oxford University Press, 2002), p. 2.
104. Its original text is still unpublished. The Sindhi translation of the *Tadhkirat al-Murad* is rendered by Dr Abdul Rasul Qadri, which was published by the Sindhi Adabi Board in 2006.
105. Ijazul Haque Quddusi, *Tarikh-i-Sindh*, vol. 1 (Lahore: Urdu Science Board, 1995), p. 168.
106. Shaykh Muhammad Azam Thattawi, *Tuhfat al-Tahirin*, ed. Badr Alam Durrani (Hyderabad: Sindhi Adabi Board, 1956), p. 20.
107. Ibid., p. 36.
108. Maulana Din Muhammad Wafa'i, *Tadhkirah Mashahir-i-Sindh* vol. 3 (Hyderabad: Sindhi Adabi Board, 1986), pp. 47–8.
109. Shaykh Hussain Safa'i Thattawi, *Tadhkirat al-Murad*, Original manuscript, p. 2; Shaykh Hussain Safa'i Thattawi, *Tadhkirat al-Murad*, Sindhi trans. Dr Abdul Rasul Qadri (Hyderabad: Sindhi Adabi Board, 2006), p. 15.
110. Shaykh Muhammad Azam Thattawi, *Tuhfat al-Tahirin*, p. 21.
111. Mir Ali Sher Qani Thattawi, *Tuhfat al-Kiram*, p. 580.
112. Shaykh Muhammad Azam Thattawi, *Tuhfat al-Tahirin*, p. 22.
113. Refer to Mubarak Ali, *Ulema, Sufis and Intellectuals* (Lahore: Fiction House, 2005), p. 181.
114. Abdul Rasul Qadri, *Tadhkirat al-Murad*, Sindhi trans., Introduction, p. 11.
115. Shaykh Hussain Safa'i Thattawi, *Tadhkirat al-Murad*, p. 2.
116. Abdul Rasul Qadri, *Tadhkirat al-Murad*, Sindhi trans., p. 35.
117. The Suhrawardiyya was a Sufi order founded by Sufi Zia Al-Din Abu (1097–1168 CE). It is a strictly Sunni order, guided by the Shafi'i school of Islamic law, and, like many such orders, traces its spiritual genealogy (*silsila*) to Hazrat Ali (RA), the fourth pious caliph of the Muslims.
118. Shaykh Hussain Safa'i Thattawi, *Tadhkirat al-Murad*, pp. 3–5.
119. Ibid., p. 7.

120. Ibid., pp. 33, 34, 40, 47, etc.
121. Ibid., pp. 18, 38, and 44.
122. Riazul Islam, *Sufism in South Asia*, p. 14.
123. Shaykh Hussain Safa'i Thattawi, *Tadhkirat al-Murad*, pp. 33–4.
124. Shaykh Muhammad Azam Thattawi, *Tuhfat al-Tahirin*, pp. 12–13.
125. Shaykh Hussain Safa'i Thattawi, *Tadhkirat al-Murad*, pp. 20–1.
126. Riazul Islam, *Sufism in South Asia*, p. 15.
127. Shaykh Hussain Safa'i Thattawi, *Tadhkirat al-Murad*, pp. 22–32.
128. Ibid., p. 13.
129. Ibid., p. 16.
130. Ibid., pp. 26, 34, 35, and 47.
131. Ibid., pp. 33–4.
132. *Tazia* is a replica of the tomb of Hazrat Hussain (RA), the martyred grandson of Prophet Muhammad (PBUH) that is carried in processions during the Shi'ite festival of the month of Muharram as mourning of the dead.
133. Shaykh Hussain Safa'i Thattawi, *Tadhkirat al-Murad*, pp. 38–40.
134. Dr Abdul Rasul Qadri, *Tadhkirat al-Murad*, Sindhi trans., Introduction, pp. 4–6.
135. Ibid., p. 7.
136. Mir Ali Sher Qani Thattawi, *Makli Nama*, p. 52.
137. Dr Mubarak Ali, *Ulema, Sufis and Intellectuals*, p. 198.
138. Riazul Islam, *Sufism in South Asia*, p. xx.
139. Ansar Zahid Khan, *History and Culture of Sind: A study of socio-economic organization and institutions during the 16th and 17th centuries* (Karachi: Royal Book Company, 1980), p. 344.
140. *Mathnawi* means 'rhyming couplets of profound spiritual meaning.' The *mathnawi* is a poetic collection of rambling anecdotes and stories derived from different Quranic sources and everyday tales. The stories are told to illustrate a point and each moral is discussed in detail.
141. *Ruba'i* (lit. quatrain) is a poetry style. It is used to describe a Persian quatrain, or its derivative form in English and other languages. The plural form of the word, *rubā'iyāt* (often Anglicized *rubaiyat*, is used to describe a collection of such quatrains.
142. Qazi Ahmad Miyan Akhtar Junagarhi, '*Rawzat al-Salatin*,' *Armughan-i-Ilmi* (Lahore) 1, part 2 (1955), p. 5.
143. Ibid., p. 11.
144. C.A. Storey, *Persian Literature: A Bio-bibliographical Survey*, vol. I, part 2, Reprint (England: Royal Asiatic Society of Great Britain and Ireland, 1989), p. 797.
145. Dr Syed Ali Raza Naqvi, *Tadhkirah Nawisi Farsi dar Hind wa Pakistan* (Tehran: Mo'assasa Matbu'at-i-Ilmi, 1968), p. 91.
146. Qazi Ahmad Miyan Akhtar Junagarhi, '*Rawzat al-Salatin*,' pp. 2–3.
147. Dr Syed Ali Raza Naqvi, *Tadhkirah Nawisi Farsi dar Hind wa Pakistan*, p. 92.
148. Fakhri Harawi, *Rawzat al-Salatin*, ed. Syed Hussamuddin Rashidi (Hyderabad: Sindhi Adabi Board, 1968), p. 69.
149. Ibid., p. 27.
150. C.A. Storey, *Persian Literature*, pp. 796–7.
151. Mir Masum Bhakkari, *Tarikh-i-Masumi*, p. 206.
152. Ibid.
153. Abdul Baqi Nehawandi, *Ma'athir-i-Rahimi*, p. 321.
154. Refer to Syed Ali Raza Naqvi, *Tadhkirah Nawisi Farsi dar Hind wa Pakistan*, p. 93; Qazi Ahmad Miyan Akhtar Junagarhi, '*Rawzat al-Salatin*,' p. 5.

155. Fakhri Harawi, *Rawzat al-Salatin*, pp. 49–50.
156. Muhammad Ziauddin, 'Role of Persians at the Mughal Court,' pp. 157–8.
157. See Fakhri Harawi, *Rawzat al-Salatin*.
158. Qazi Ahmad Miyan Akhtar Junagarhi, '*Rawzat al-Salatin*,' p. 16.
159. Fakhri Harawi, *Rawzat al-Salatin*, pp. 81–3.
160. Ibid., p. 193.
161. Ibid., pp. 83–4.
162. Ibid., pp. 85–6.
163. Ibid., pp. 101–5.
164. Ibid., pp. 96–8.
165. Ibid., p. 97.
166. Ibid., pp. 101–5.
167. Mir Masum Bhakkari, *Tarikh-i-Masumi*, pp. 141–206.
168. Mir Ali Sher Qani Thattawi, *Tuhfat al-Kiram*, p. 65.
169. Fakhri Harawi, *Rawzat al-Salatin*, p. 105.
170. Ibid., p. 59.
171. Khawaja Abdul Majeed Yazdani, *Tarikh-i Adabiyat Musalmanan-i Pakistan wa Hind* (Lahore: Punjab University, 1971), p. 602.
172. Nabi Hadi, *History of Indo-Persian Literature* (New Delhi: Iran Culture House, 2001), p. 167.
173. Ibid.
174. Fakhri Harawi, *Jawahir al-Aja'ib*, ed. Syed Hussamuddin Rashidi (Hyderabad: Sindhi Adabi Board, 1968), p. 71; Qazi Ahmad Miyan Akhtar Junagarhi, '*Rawzat al-Salatin*,' p. 28.
175. Refer to Syed Ali Raza Naqvi, *Tadhkirah Nawisi Farsi dar Hind wa Pakistan*, p. 98.
176. Ibid.
177. Fakhri Harawi, *Jawahir al-Aja'ib*, pp. 69–70.
178. Syed Ali Raza Naqvi, *Tadhkirah Nawisi Farsi dar Hind wa Pakistan*, p. 99.
179. Fakhri Harawi, *Jawahir al-Aja'ib*, p. 116.
180. Ibid., p. 115.
181. Ibid., p. 116.
182. Ibid., p. 115.
183. Fakhri Harawi, *Rawzat al-Salatin*, p. 103.
184. Ibid., p. 113.
185. Ibid., pp. 118–19.
186. Ibid., p. 119.
187. Ibid.
188. Syed Hussamuddin Rashidi, *Ahwal wa A'asar Fakhri Harawi* (Jamshoro: Sindhi Adabi Board, 1974), p. 71.
189. Ibid., pp. 122–3.
190. Ibid., pp. 120–2.
191. Ibid., pp. 132 and 137.
192. Ibid., pp. 133–5.
193. Ibid., pp. 136–7.
194. Fakhri Harawi, *Jawahir al-Aja'ib*, p. 136.
195. Ibid., p. 132.
196. Syed Ali Raza Naqvi, *Tadhkirah Nawisi Farsi dar Hind wa Pakistan*, p. 99.
197. Ansar Zahid Khan, *History and Culture of Sind*, p. 331.

Chapter 3: Political Literature/Chronicles

1. H.I. Sada Rangani, *Persian Poets of Sindh* (Hyderabad: Sindhi Adabi Board, 1987), p. 17.
2. Jan Rypka, *History of Iranian Literature*, pp. 441–2.
3. C.A. Storey, *Persian Literature*, pp. 120–2.
4. Refer to N.K. Singh and A. Samiuddin, *Encyclopaedic Historiography of the Muslim World*, p. 967.
5. Zahuruddin Ahmad, *Pakistan mein Farsi Adab*, p. 623.
6. Firishta was a historian in India, 1560–1620 CE. His name was Muhammad Qasim Hindu Shah and his patron was the ruler of Bijapur.
7. M.A. Rahim, *Social and Cultural History of Bengal*, vol. 2 (Karachi: Technical Printers, 1967), p. 29.
8. Mir Masum Bhakkari, *Tarikh-i-Masumi*, p. 3.
9. Refer to Syed Hussamuddin Rashidi, *Amin al-Mulk Nawab Mir Masum Bhakkari* (Hyderabad: Sindhi Adabi Board, 1979), p. 5.
10. M.H. Siddiqi, *History of the Arghuns and Tarkhans of Sind (1507–1593): An annotation of the relevant parts of Mir Masum's Tarikh-i-Sind with an Introduction and Appendices* (Jamshoro: Institute of Sindhology, 1972), p. 1.
11. S.H. Hodiwala, *Studies in Indo-Muslim History*, vol. 1, reprint, pp. 108–9.
12. Mir Masum Bhakkari, *Tarikh-i-Masumi*, p. 2.
13. This is a title and post given to the superior authority in the issues of Islam. It was the second most prominent official post after the *wazir* under the Mughals.
14. Mir Masum Bhakkari, *Tarikh-i-Masumi*, p. 131.
15. Refer to Arshad Islam, 'Tarikh-i-Masumi: An Appraisal of its Relevance to the History of Sindh,' *Journal the of Pakistan Historical Society* 47, no. 3 (July–September 1999), p. 40; Abdul Qadir Badayuni, *Muntakhib al-Tawarikh*, vol. 3, ed. Maulwi Muhammad Ali, (Calcutta: Asiatic Society Bengal, 1869), p. 366.
16. Shaykh Farid al-Din Bhakkari, *Dhakhirat al-Khawanin*, vol. 1, ed. Moin al-Haque (Karachi: Pakistan Historical Society, 1961), p. 201.
17. This is a rank which was given to the land holders or the Mughal officials under the *Mansabdari* system introduced by Akbar. The officer was to maintain a fixed number of soldiers for the Emperor whenever he needed them. *Yak Hazari* meant one thousand; *Panj Hazari* meant five thousand. Other officers having secretarial functions were also awarded such titles, but they weren't obliged to maintain soldiers.
18. Mir Masum Bhakkari, *Tarikh-i-Masumi*, p. 180.
19. Under the Mughal administration, provinces were divided into *sarkars* which were further subdivided into *parganas*. Each *pargana* consisted of several villages called *dih*.
20. Abdul Baqi Nihawandi, *Ma'athir-i-Rahimi*, pp. 131–2.
21. The *Amin al-Mulk* was the official who was stationed in different provinces and *parganas* by the Emperor to hold in trust the royal treasury located there, inform the Emperor of any lapse on behalf of the governor, and keep all records relating to revenue under his control.
22. Syed Hussamuddin Rashidi, *Amin al-Mulk Nawab Mir Masum Bhakkari*, p. 225.
23. Samsam al-Daula Shahnawaz Khan, *Ma'athir al-Umara*, Urdu trans. Muhammad Ayyub Qadiri, vol. 3 (Lahore: Markazi Urdu Board, 1968), p. 327.
24. Mir Masum Bhakkari, *Tarikh-i-Masumi*, p. 3.

25. In Islamic culture, an *Eidgah* or *Idgah* is an open-air mosque usually outside the city (or at the outskirts) for people to perform the Eid prayers.
26. Syed Hussamuddin Rashidi, *Amin al-Mulk Nawab Mir Masum Bhakkari*, pp. 530 and 542.
27. Ishwari Prasad, *The Life and Times of Humayun* (New Delhi: Orient Longmans, 1956), p. 402.
28. M.H. Siddiqi, 'Tarikh-i-Masumi: Date of its Compilation,' *Journal of Pakistan Historical Society, Karachi* xiv, part 3 (July 1966), p. 205.
29. Nizam al-Din Ahmad, *Tabaqat-i-Akbari*, p. 16.
30. See the chapters relating to the Soomras and the Sammas and that pertaining to Multan. Also see the chapters that deal with the Mughal conquest of Sindh. The reason for this similarity was that both of the authors used *Tarikh Tabaqat-i-Bahadurshahi* as their source and made extensive use of this work for the history of these periods.
31. Mir Masum Bhakkari, *Tarikh-i-Masumi*, p. 5.
32. Yahya bin Ahmad Sirhindi, *Tarikh-i-Mubarakshahi*, p. 168.
33. M. Saleem Akhtar, *Sindh under the Mughals: An Introduction to, Translation of and Commentary on the Mazhar-i-Shahjahani of Yusuf Mirak* (Islamabad: NIHCR, 1990), p. 127.
34. Mir Masum Bhakkari, *Tarikh-i-Masumi*, p. xxxvii.
35. M.H. Siddiqi, 'Tarikh-i-Masumi,' p. 201.
36. Mir Masum Bhakkari, *Tarikh-i-Masumi*, p. 3.
37. Yahya bin Ahmad Sirhindi, *Tarikh-i-Mubarakshahi*, p. 170.
38. Mir Masum Bhakkari, *Tarikh-i-Masumi*, p. 180.
39. Ibid., pp. 6–7.
40. Ahmad bin Yahya ibn Jabir Baladhuri, *Futuh al-Buldan*, (Cairo, 1932), p. 435; Ali bin Hamid bin Abi Bakar al-Kufi, *Chach Nama*, pp. 64–5.
41. Mir Masum Bhakkari, *Tarikh-i-Masumi*, p. 16; Ali bin Hamid bin Abi Bakar al-Kufi, *Chach Nama*, p. 44.
42. *Tarikh-i-Masumi*, pp. 18–19; *Chach Nama*, pp. 46–7.
43. Mir Masum Bhakkari, *Tarikh-i-Masumi*, pp. 29–30.
44. Abu al-Qasim Muhammad Firishta, *Tarikh-i-Firishta*, vol. 2, pp. 318–2.
45. Nizam al-Din Ahmad, *Tabaqat-i-Akbari*, p. 635.
46. Shahpurshah Hormasji Hodivala, *Studies in Indo-Muslim History*, p. 102.
47. Mir Masum Bhakkari, *Tarikh-i-Masumi*, pp. 62 and 73.
48. Elliot and Dowson, *History of Sindh as Told by Its Own Historians (The Muhammadan Period)* (Karachi: Karim Sons, 1976), p. 497.
49. Shahpurshah Hormasji Hodivala, *Studies in Indo-Muslim History*, p. 106.
50. Ibn Battuta, *The Travels of Ibn Battuta: A.D. 1325–1354*, ed. and trans. Sir Hamilton Alexander Rosskeen Gibb (New Delhi: Ashgate Publishing Ltd., 1971), p. 599.
51. Mir Masum Bhakkari, *Tarikh-i-Masumi*, pp. 62–3.
52. Ibid., p. 225.
53. Ibid., pp. 150 and 160.
54. Ibid., pp. 242–54.
55. Ibid., p. 243.
56. The *fawjdar* performed military, police, and judicial functions and also helped in revenue administration.
57. Shahpurshah Hormasji Hodivala, *Studies in Indo-Muslim History*, pp. 103–4.
58. Ibid., p. 257.
59. Ibid., p. xii.

60. Ibid., p. 50.
61. Mir Masum Bhakkari, *Tarikh-i-Masumi*, p. 257.
62. Abu al-Fazl Allami, *Akbar Nama*, trans. Beveridge, vol. 3, p. 1172 and notes.
63. Samsam al-Daula Shahnawaz Khan, *Ma'athir al-Umara*, vol. 3, p. 310.
64. Shahpurshah Hormasji Hodivala, *Studies in Indo-Muslim History*, p. 115.
65. Mir Masum Bhakkari, *Tarikh-i-Masumi*, pp. 129–30.
66. Ibid., p. 128.
67. Ibid., pp. 129–32.
68. J.N. Sarkar, *History of History Writing in Medieval India: Contemporary Historians* (New Delhi: Ratna Parkashan, 1977), p. 38.
69. Mir Masum Bhakkari, *Tarikh-i-Masumi*, p. 151.
70. Ibid., p. 237–41.
71. Ibid., p. 237.
72. Ibid., pp. 77, 180, and 249.
73. M. H. Siddiqi, *History of the Arghuns and Tarkhans of Sind (1507–1593)*, p. 6.
74. M. Saleem Akhtar, *Sindh under the Mughals*, p. 127.
75. C.A. Storey, *Persian Literature*, vol. 2, part 3, p. 654.
76. Shah Qasim Khan-i-Zaman was from the Beglar family of the Arghun tribe. His father Shah Qasim came to Sindh from Samarkand during the reign of Mirza Shah Hasan Arghun in 1522 CE. Khan-i-Zaman was famous for his valour and courage on the battlefield and was also a man of literary talents. When Jani Beg visited Agra to render his submission to Emperor Akbar, Khan-i-Zaman (Shah Qasim) accompanied him, and was received with favour, he was, afterwards nominated to an appointment in Sindh under Mirza Ghazi Beg Tarkhan.
77. Mir Ali Sher Qani Thattawi, *Maqalat al-Shuara*, p. 11; Yahya bin Ahmad Sirhindi, *Tarikh-i-Mubarakshahi*, pp. 216, 274, and 279; Maqbool Beg Badakhshani, ed., *Tarikh Ababiyat-i-Musalmanan-i-Pak o Hind*, vol. 2 (Lahore: Punjab University, 1971), p. 545; Syed Hussamuddin Rashidi, *Mirza Ghazi Beg Tarkhan aur us ki Bazm-i-Adab* (Karachi: Urdu Promotion Board, 1970), p. 761; H.I. Sada Rangani, *Persian Poets of Sindh*, p. 33.
78. Dr Zahuruddin Ahmad, *Pakistan mein Farsi Adab*, vol. 2, p. 515; Ahmad Munzawi, *Fehrist Mushtarik Nuskh Khatti Farsi Pakistan*, vol. 7 (Islamabad: Persian Research Centre for Iran and Pakistan, 1986), p. 771; Rahimdad Khan Maula'i Shayda'i, *Jannat al-Sindh*, (Hyderabad: Sindhi Adabi Board, 1985), p. 422.
79. Mir Ali Sher Qani Thattawi, *Maqalat al-Shuara*, p. 119.
80. Dr Zahuruddin Ahmad, *Pakistan mein Farsi Adab*, vol. 2, p. 515; Yahya bin Ahmad Sirhindi, *Tarikh-i-Mubarakshahi*, pp. 216 and 279; Saeed Nafisi, *Tarikh Nazmwa Nasr dar Iran wadar Zaban-i-Farsi*, p. 366.
81. Mir Ali Sher Qani Thattawi, *Maqalat al-Shuara*, p. 11; *Tuhfat al-Kiram*, p. 112.
82. Ibid., pp. 12 and 118; H.I. Sada Rangani, *Persian Poets of Sindh*, p. 33.
83. Idraki Beglari, *Beglar Nama*, ed. N.A. Baloch (Hyderabad: Sindhi Adabi Board, 1980), p. 265.
84. Idraki Beglari, *Mathnawi Chanesar Nama*, ed. Syed Hussamuddin Rashidi (Hyderabad: Sindhi Adabi Board, 1956), p. 2.
85. Idraki Beglari, *Beglar Nama*, p. 262.
86. Ibid., p. 263.
87. Idraki Beglari, *Mathnawi Chanesar Nama*, p. 5.
88. Syed Tahir Muhammad Nisyani Thattawi, *Tarikh-i-Baldah Thatta* alias *Tarikh-i-Tahiri*, Introduction by Dr Nabi Bakhsh Khan Baloch (Hyderabad: Sindhi Adabi Board,

1964), p. 7; Syed Mir Muhammad, *Tarkhan Nama* ed. Syed Hussamuddin Rashidi (Hyderabad: Sindhi Adabi Board, 1971), p. 13.
89. Idraki Beglari, *Beglar Nama*, pp. 3–4.
90. Ibid., pp. 5–6.
91. Ibid., p. 6.
92. Ibid., p. 25; Mir Ali Sher Qani Thattawi, *Tuhfat al-Kiram*, p. 276.
93. Idraki Beglari, *Beglar Nama*, p. 25.
94. Mir Ali Sher Qani Thattawi, *Tuhfat al-Kiram*, p. 276.
95. Idraki Beglari, *Beglar Nama*, pp. 31–2.
96. Ibid., p. 243.
97. Ibid., pp. 241–2.
98. Ibid., p. 220.
99. Ibid., p. 242.
100. Ibid., p. 99.
101. Ibid., p. 20.
102. Ibid., p. 116.
103. Ibid., pp. 46–7, 81–96, and 96–106.
104. Ibid., pp. 231–42.
105. M. Saleem Akhtar, *Sindh under the Mughals*, p. 128.
106. Zahuruddin Ahmad, *Pakistan mein Farsi Adab*, p. 521.
107. Idraki Beglari, *Beglar Nama*, p. 63.
108. Ibid., p. 116.
109. Ibid., p. 123.
110. Abu al-Fazl Allami, *Akbar Nama*, p. 358.
111. Idraki Beglari, *Beglar Nama*, p. 222.
112. Nabi Bakhsh Khan Baloch, *Sindh: Studies in Historical*, p. 193.
113. Mir Ali Sher Qani Thattawi, *Tuhfat al-Kiram*, p. 636.
114. Mir Ali Sher Qani Thattawi, *Maqalat al-Shuara*, p. 376.
115. Ibid., p. 836.
116. Syed Tahir Muhammad Nisyani Thattawi, *Tarikh-i-Tahiri*, p. 101.
117. Syed Hussamuddin Rashidi, *Mirza Ghazi Beg Tarkhan aur us ki Bazm-i-Adab*, p. 563.
118. Ibid., p. 8.
119. Mir Ali Sher Qani Thattawi, *Tuhfat al-Kiram*, p. 101
120. Mir Masum Bhakkari, *Tarikh-i-Masumi*, p. 76.
121. H.I. Sada Rangani, *Persian Poets of Sindh*, p. 50.
122. Syed Tahir Muhammad Nisyani Thattawi, *Tarikh-i-Tahiri*, pp. 8, 156, and 189.
123. Ibid., pp. 4–5.
124. Ibid., p. 242.
125. Ibid., p. 13.
126. An Arabic poem, usually in motorhome, that may be satirical, elegiac, threatening, or laudatory.
127. Syed Hussamuddin Rashidi, *Mirza Ghazi Beg Tarkhan aur us ki Bazm-i-Adab*, p. 577.
128. Ibid., pp. 576–8.
129. Syed Tahir Muhammad Nisyani Thattawi, *Tarikh-i-Tahiri*, p. 20.
130. Syed Hussamuddin Rashidi, *Mirza Ghazi Beg Tarkhan aur us ki Bazm-i-Adab*, p. 582.
131. Syed Tahir Muhammad Nisyani Thattawi, *Tarikh-i-Tahiri*, p. 23.
132. Shaykh Farid al-Din Bhakkari, *Dhakhirat al-Khawanin*, vol. 1, pp. 236–7.
133. Syed Tahir Muhammad Nisyani Thattawi, *Tarikh-i-Tahiri*, p. 23.
134. Ibid., p. 22.

135. Ibid., pp. 22–3.
136. Samsam al-Daula Shahnawaz Khan, *Ma'athir al-Umara*, p. 645.
137. Ibid., p. 11.
138. Ibid., p. 174.
139. Ibid., p. 12.
140. Ibid., p. 10.
141. Ibid., p. 23.
142. See Samsam al-Daula Shahnawaz Khan, *Ma'athir al-Umara* (annotations), pp. 282–3.
143. Syed Tahir Muhammad Nisyani Thattawi, *Tarikh-i-Tahiri*, p. 27.
144. Ibid., p. 24.
145. Ibid., pp. 224–50.
146. Ibid., pp. 256–8.
147. Ibid., pp. 161–3.
148. Ibid., p. 271.
149. Ibid., p. 20.
150. Ibid., p. 36.
151. Ibid., p. 257.
152. Ibid., p. 36.
153. M. Saleem Akhtar, *Sindh under the Mughals*, p. 129.
154. Syed Tahir Muhammad Nisyani Thattawi, *Tarikh-i-Tahiri*, p. 166.
155. Ibid., p. 225.
156. Ibid., pp. 42–5.
157. Elliot and Dowson, *History of India as Told by Its Own Historians*, p. 266.
158. H.T. Sorley, *Shah Abdul Latif of Bhit: His Poetry, Life and Times*, reprint (Karachi, 1966), p. 166.
159. Dr Nabi Bakhsh Khan Baloch, *Sindh: Studies in Historical*, p. 190.
160. Syed Tahir Muhammad Nisyani Thattawi, *Tarikh-i-Tahiri*, pp. 100–1.
161. Ibid., p. 76.
162. Ibid., p. 156.
163. Yahya bin Ahmad Sirhindi, *Tarikh-i-Mubarakshahi*, p. 275.
164. Mir Ali Sher Qani Thattawi, *Maqalat al-Shuara*, p. 837.
165. See annotations, pp. 315 and 325.
166. Nabi Bakhsh Khan Baloch, *Sindh: Studies in Historical*, pp. 184–5.
167. Syed Tahir Muhammad Nisyani Thattawi, *Tarikh-i-Tahiri*, p. 92; Syed Mir Muhammad, *Tarkhan Nama*, p. 46.
168. F.C. Danvers, *The Portuguese in India Being a History of the Rise and Decline of Their Eastern Empire*, vol. 1, reprint (W.H. Allen & Company Limited, 1894), p. 99.
169. Abu al-Fazl Allami, *Akbar Nama*, vol. 2, p. 277.
170. Syed Tahir Muhammad Nisyani Thattawi, *Tarikh-i-Tahiri*, pp. 282–3.
171. Ibid., p. 45.
172. Sikandar bin Muhammad Manju, *Mirat-i-Sikandari* (The History of Gujarat), trans. Abu al-Fazl Lutfullah, reprint, (New Delhi: 1990), p. 239.
173. Mir Ali Sher Qani Thattawi, *Tuhfat al-Kiram*, p. 145.
174. Ibid., pp. 126–50.
175. Syed Tahir Muhammad Nisyani Thattawi, *Tarikh-i-Tahiri*, pp. 32–5.
176. Ibid., p. 133.
177. Ibid., p. 40.
178. Ibid., pp. 141–5.
179. Ibid., p. 136.

180. In fact, limited polygamy, having four wives as per orthodox interpretations of the Quranic verse was prevalent among all sections of Muslim society.
181. Syed Tahir Muhammad Nisyani Thattawi, *Tarikh-i-Tahiri*, p. 53.
182. M. Saleem Akhtar, *Sindh under the Mughals*, p. 133.
183. See, Felix Tauer, in Jan Rypka, *History of Iranian Literature*, p. 426.
184. M. Saleem Akhtar, *Sindh under the Mughals*, p. 133.
185. Mir Ali Sher Qani Thattawi, *Tuhfat al-Kiram*, p. 393.
186. Syed Hussamuddin Rashidi, *Tadhkirah-i-Amir Khani* (Hyderabad: Sindhi Adabi Board, 1961), p. 8.
187. Yousuf Mirak, *Mazhar-i-Shahjahani*, p. 114.
188. Ibid., pp. 121–2.
189. Ibid., p. 156.
190. Ibid., p. 158.
191. Ibid., p. 154.
192. Ibid., pp. 160–1.
193. Ibid., pp. 161–2.
194. Ibid., p. 162.
195. Ibid., p. 257.
196. Ibid., p. 39.
197. Ibid., p. 100.
198. M. Saleem Akhtar, *Sindh under the Mughals*, p. 92.
199. Yousuf Mirak, *Mazhar-i-Shahjahani*, p. 17.
200. The provinces under the Mughals were subdivided into *sarkars* which were further divided into a number of *parganas* or districts.
201. See, Yousuf Mirak, *Mazhar-i-Shahjahani*, pp. 3–22.
202. Ibid., pp. 23–32.
203. Ibid., pp. 33–54.
204. Ibid., pp. 55–81.
205. Ibid., pp. 82–8.
206. Ibid., pp. 89–181.
207. Ibid., pp. 182–93.
208. Ibid., pp. 194–247.
209. M. Saleem Akhtar, *Sindh under the Mughals*, p. 252.
210. See, Nizam al-Mulk Tusi, *Siyasat Nama*, ed. Abbas Iqbal (Tehran: Intisharat-i-Asatir, 1993).
211. See, Diyaal-Din Barani, *Fatawa-i-Jahandari*, ed. Dr Riaz Ahmad, trans. Prof. Atiq Ahmad (Islamabad: NIHCR, 2004).
212. Yousuf Mirak, *Mazhar-i-Shahjahani*, p. 135.
213. Ibid., pp. 145 and 162–3.
214. Ibid., p. 247.
215. Ibid., p. 156.
216. See, Idraki Beglari, *Beglar Nama*.
217. Yousuf Mirak, *Mazhar-i-Shahjahani*, pp. 90, 34–5, 89–90, 216–17.
218. Ibid., p. 242.
219. Ibid., pp. 180–1.
220. Ibid., p. 190.
221. Ibid., p. 193.
222. Samsam al-Daula Shahnawaz Khan, *Ma'athir al-Umara*, vol. 1, p. 195.
223. Shaykh Farid al-Din Bhakkari, *Dhakhirat al-Khawanin*, vol. 2, pp. 369–70.

NOTES

224. Yousuf Mirak, *Mazhar-i-Shahjahani*, p. 156.
225. Syed Hussamuddin Rashidi, *Tadhkirah-i-Amir Khani*, p. 177.
226. Yousuf Mirak, *Mazhar-i-Shahjahani*, p. 242.
227. M. Saleem Akhtar, *Sindh under the Mughals*, p. 132.
228. Ibid., pp. 183–5.
229. The officers who dealt with the amount spent on household. They checked the accounts of the household expenses of people for the purposes of exacting taxes.
230. M. Saleem Akhtar, *Sindh under the Mughals*, pp. 17–20.
231. Shaykh Farid al-Din Bhakkari, *Dhakhirat al-Khawanin*, vol. 1, pp. 198–9; 204–5.
232. Yousuf Mirak, *Mazhar-i-Shahjahani*, pp. 154–9.
233. Ibid., p. 158.
234. Ibid., p. 40.
235. Ibid., p. 41.
236. Abu al-Fazl Allami, *A'in-i-Akbari*, pp. 173–7.
237. Yousuf Mirak, *Mazhar-i-Shahjahani*, p. 135.
238. Zahuruddin Ahmad, *Pakistan mein Farsi Adab*, p. 525.
239. Syed Hussamuddin Rashidi, *Tadhkirah-i-Amir Khani*, p. 170.
240. Yousuf Mirak, *Mazhar-i-Shahjahani*, p. 247.
241. Syed Mir Muhammad, *Tarkhan Nama*, pp. 3–4.
242. C.A. Storey, *Persian Literature*, p. 655; Elliot and Dowson, *History of Sindh as Told by Its Own Historians*, p. 300.
243. Nabi Hadi, *History of Indo-Persian Literature*, p. 278; Zahuruddin Ahmad, *Pakistan mein Farsi Adab*, p. 528.
244. Syed Abdul Qadir, *Hadiqat al-Awliya*, ed. Syed Hussamuddin Rashidi (Hyderabad: Sindhi Adabi Board, 1971), p. 65.
245. Mir Ali Sher Qani Thattawi, *Tuhfat al-Kiram*, p. 528.
246. Mir Masum Bhakkari, *Tarikh-i-Masumi*, p. 216.
247. Syed Mir Muhammad, *Tarkhan Nama*, p. 35.
248. Ibid., p. 55.
249. Ibid.
250. Abdul Baqi Nihawandi, *Ma'athir-i-Rahimi*, p. 325; Mir Masum Bhakkari, *Tarikh-i-Masumi*, pp. 212–13.
251. Syed Mir Muhammad, *Tarkhan Nama*, p. 69; Mir Masum Bhakkari, *Tarikh-i-Masumi*, pp. 247–8; Abdul Baqi Nihawandi, *Ma'athir-i-Rahimi*, pp. 244–5.
252. Arshad Islam, 'The Tarkhan Nama,' *Pakistan Journal of History and Culture* (Islamabad: NIHCR) 14, no. 1 (January–June 1993), p. 72.
253. Nabi Hadi, *History of Indo-Persian Literature*, p. 278.
254. Mir Ali Sher Qani Thattawi, *Tuhfat al-Kiram*, p. 188.
255. Syed Mir Muhammad, *Tarkhan Nama* (Preface).
256. Refer to Arshad Islam, 'The Tarkhan Nama,' p. 70.
257. Syed Mir Muhammad, *Tarkhan Nama*, p. 3.
258. Ibid., pp. 3–4.
259. Ibid., p. 1.
260. Ibid., pp. 1–3.
261. Ibid., p. 4.
262. Syed Mir Muhammad, *Tarkhan Nama*, pp. 21–2.
263. Zahuruddin Ahmad, *Pakistan mein Farsi Adab*, p. 528.
264. Syed Mir Muhammad, *Tarkhan Nama*, pp. 1–3, 19, 93, 95.
265. Ibid., p. 90.

266. Arshad Islam, 'The Tarkhan Nama,' p. 73.
267. Syed Mir Muhammad, *Tarkhan Nama*, pp. 52–4.
268. Ibid., pp. 59–61.
269. Ibid., pp. 65–6.
270. Ibid., pp. 97–8.
271. Ibid., pp. 27, 32, and 34.
272. Shaykh Farid al-Din Bhakkari, *Dhakhirat al-Khawanin*, vol. 2, pp. 23–5; Mir Ali Sher Qani Thattawi, *Tuhfat al-Kiram*, vol. 3, pp. 129, 164–165, and 310.
273. Syed Mir Muhammad, *Tarkhan Nama*, p. 4.
274. Ibid., p. 5.
275. Ibid., p. 95.
276. Ibid., p. 98.
277. Ibid., p. 93.
278. A chronogram is a sentence or inscription in which specific letters, interpreted as numerals, stand for a particular date when rearranged. The word, meaning 'time writing', derives from the Greek words *chronos* (χρόνος 'time') and *gramma* (γράμμα, 'letter').
279. Ibid., p. 83.
280. Ibid., p. 60.
281. Ibid., p. 49.
282. Ibid., p. 35.
283. Mir Masum Bhakkari, *Tarikh-i-Masumi*, p. 107.
284. Zahiruddin Muhammad Babur, *Babur Nama*, p. 350.
285. Shahpurshah Hormasji Hodivala, *Studies in Indo-Muslim History*, pp. 125–6.
286. Ibid., p. 11.
287. Mir Masum Bhakkari, *Tarikh-i-Masumi*, pp. 107–8; Abdul Baqi Nihawandi, *Ma'athir-i-Rahimi*, pp. 286–7.
288. Sidi Ali Reis, *Safar Namah Sidi Ali Reis*, trans. A. Vambery under the title of *The Travels and Adventures of the Turkish Admiral Sidi Ali Reis* (London: Luzac, 1899), p. 37.
289. Syed Tahir Muhammad Nisyani Thattawi, *Tarikh-i-Tahiri*, pp. 218–22; Idraki Beglari, *Beglar Nama*, pp. 136–42.
290. Abu al-Qasim Muhammad Firishta, *Tarikh-i-Firishta*, vol. 2, p. 323; Abdul Baqi Nihawandi, *Ma'athir-i-Rahimi*, vol. 2, p. 348; Mir Masum Bhakkari, *Tarikh-i-Masumi*, pp. 256–7.
291. Syed Mir Muhammad, *Tarkhan Nama*, pp. 18 and 21.
292. I received a manuscript of this work from Professor Dr G.M. Lakho, which he received from Abu Said Ghulam Mustafa Qasimi.
293. Zahuruddin Ahmad, *Pakistan mein Farsi Adab*, p. 251.
294. Ahmad Munzawi, *Fehrist warah'i Kitab ha'i Farsi*, vol. 1 (Tehran, 1995), pp. 659–61.
295. Elliot and Dowson, *History of Sindh as Told by Its Own Historians*, p. 485.
296. Nabi Hadi, *History of Indo-Persian Literature*, p. 425.
297. Zahuruddin Ahmad, *Pakistan mein Farsi Adab*, pp. 251–2.
298. Ibid., p. 251–3.
299. Syed Mir Muhammad, *Tarkhan Nama*, p. 4.
300. S.M. Abdullah, *A Descriptive Directory of Persian Urdu and Arabic Manuscripts in the Punjab University Library*, vol. 1 (Lahore: Punjab University, 1942), p. 12.

301. Ghulam Muhammad Lakho, 'Intikhab-i-Muntakhib: Sind ji Tarikh jo Hik Wadhik Ma'akhidh (Intikhab-i-Muntakhib: A Great Source of Sindh's History),' *The Quarterly Mehran* (Jamshoro: Sindhi Adabi Board) no. 1 (1986), p. 117.
302. Nabi Hadi, *History of Indo-Persian Literature*, p. 425.
303. Ibid.; Zahuruddin Ahmad, *Pakistan mein Farsi Adab*, p. 256.
304. Refer to Ghulam Muhammad Lakho, 'Intikhab-i-Muntakhib,' p. 121.
305. Zahuruddin Ahmad, *Pakistan mein Farsi Adab*, p. 554.
306. Mir Ali Sher Qani Thattawi, *Tuhfat al-Kiram*, pp. 729–30.
307. Ibid., p. 736.
308. Muhammad Abdul Ghafoor, *The Calligraphers of Thatta* (Karachi: Centre of Central and West Asian Studies, UOK, 1968), p. 61.
309. Nurul Hasan Ansari, *Farsi Adab ba Ehd-i-Aurangzeb* (Delhi: Indo-Persian Society, 1969), p. 469.
310. *Tarikh Adbiyat i-Musalmanan i-Pakistan wa Hind, (1526–1707)*, vol. 4; C.A. Storey, *Persian Literature: A Bio-bibliographical Survey* vol. 3, part 2 (Psychology Press, 1999), p. 542.
311. Yahya bin Ahmad Sirhindi, *Tarikh-i-Mubarakshahi*, p. 487.
312. Zahuruddin Ahmad, *Pakistan mein Farsi Adab*, pp. 554–6.
313. Refer to Nurul Hasan Ansari, *Farsi Adab ba Ehd-i-Aurangzeb*, p. 470.
314. Yahya bin Ahmad Sirhindi, *Tarikh-i-Mubarakshahi*, p. 488.
315. Hem Chandra Ray, *The Dynastic History of Northern India (Early Medieval Period)*, vol. 1, 2nd ed. reprint (New Delhi: Munshiram Manoharlal Publishers, 1931), p. 31.
316. Ghulam Muhammad Lakho, 'Intikhab-i-Muntakhib,' p. 142.
317. Ibid., p. 105.
318. Ibid., p. 113.
319. Ibid., p. 113.
320. Ibid., p. 116.
321. Ibid., p. 118.
322. Ibid., p. 119.
323. Ibid., p. 120.
324. Ibid., p. 125.
325. Yahya bin Ahmad Sirhindi, *Tarikh-i-Mubarakshahi*, p. 788; Zahuruddin Ahmad, *Pakistan mein Farsi Adab*, p. 251.

Chapter 4: *Tadhkira* and *Malfuz* Literature

1. Jamal Malik, *Islam in South Asia: A Short History* (Leiden: Koninklijke Brill NV, 2008), p. 61.
2. Esra Ekin, *Mustafa Ali's Epic Deeds of Artists* (Leiden: Koninklijke Brill NV, 2011), p. 113.
3. Jan Rypka, *History of Iranian Literature*, p. 453.
4. Ibid., p. 119.
5. The biographies of the transmitters of *hadiths* were termed as the *asm'a al-rijal*. Traditionalists undertook the painstaking labour of investigating the authenticity of their informers and thus the science of *asm'a al-rijal* had come to its full bloom by the third century AH.
6. Syed Ali Raza Naqvi, *Tadhkirah Nawisi Farsi dar Hind wa Pakistan*, p. 81.
7. Jan Rypka, *History of Iranian Literature*, p. 452.

8. K.A. Nizami, *On History and Historians of Medieval India*, p. 32.
9. Jan Rypka, *History of Iranian Literature*, p. 452.
10. Muhammad Aslam, *Malfuzati Adab ki Tarikhi Ehmiat*, pp. 12–16.
11. Annemarie Schimmel, *Islam in the Indian Subcontinent* (Leiden: E. J. Brill, 1980), p. 29.
12. Ali Sher Qani Thattawi, *Tuhfat al-Kiram*, p. 654.
13. Tahera Aftab, *Inscribing South Asian Muslim Women: An Annotated Bibliography & Research Guide* (Leiden: Brill NV, 2008), p. 107.
14. Ali Sher Qani Thattawi, *Maqalat al-Shuara*, p. 843.
15. Nabi Hadi, *History of Indo-Persian Literature*, p. 21.
16. Syed Abdul Qadir, *Hadiqat al-Awliya*, p. 6.
17. Mir Ali Sher Qani Thattawi, *Tuhfat al-Kiram*, pp. 635–6.
18. Mir Ali Sher Qani Thattawi, *Maqalat al-Shuara*, p. 424.
19. Syed Abdul Qadir, *Hadiqat al-Awliya*, p. 69.
20. Refer to Abdul Jabbar Junejo, 'Syed Abdul Qadir b. Syed Muhammad Nasarpuri: the author of Hadiqat al-Awliya,' *The Quarterly Mehran* (Jamshoro: Sindhi Adabi Board) (1988), p. 200.
21. Ibid., pp. 201–2.
22. *Tafsir* (lit. transliteration or interpretation) is an explanation of holy text generally of Holy Quran.
23. Abdul Jabbar Junejo, 'Syed Abdul Qadir b. Syed Muhammad Nasarpuri,' p. 204.
24. Syed Abdul Qadir, *Hadiqat al-Awliya*, p. 12.
25. Ibid., p. 13.
26. Ibid., pp. 71–2.
27. Ibid., p. 157.
28. Ibid., p. 232.
29. Ibid., p. 137.
30. Ibid., p. 11.
31. Ibid., p. 240.
32. Shaykh Farid al-Din Bhakkari, *Dhakhirat al-Khawanin*, vol. 1, p. 163.
33. Syed Abdul Qadir, *Hadiqat al-Awliya*, p. 77.
34. Mir Ali Sher Qani Thattawi, *Maqalat al-Shuara*, pp. 201–2.
35. Syed Abdul Qadir, *Hadiqat al-Awliya*, p. 11.
36. Ibid., p. 18.
37. Ibid., p. 79.
38. Ibid., p. 21.
39. Ibid., p. 26.
40. Ibid., p. 27.
41. Annemarie Schimmel, *A History of Indian Literature: Sindhi Literature*, vol. 9, part 1 (Germany: Otto Harrassowitz Verlag, 1974), p. 11.
42. R. Burhanpuri, *Burhanpur kay Sindhi Awliya* (Karachi, 1957), p. 52.
43. Syed Abdul Qadir, *Hadiqat al-Awliya*, p. 53.
44. Ibid., p. 56.
45. Ibid., p. 232.
46. Mohan Lal, *Encyclopaedia of Indian Literature: Sasay to Zorgot*, p. 4209.
47. Syed Abdul Qadir, *Hadiqat al-Awliya*, pp. 7–8.
48. According to the Bible the equivalent of Hazrat Khizar is the 'wandering Jew'.
49. Ibid., p. 137.
50. Ibid., p. 126.

51. Syed Abdul Qadir, *Hadiqat al-Awliya*, p. 81.
52. Ibid., pp. 203–4.
53. Abdul Ghafoor bin Hyder Sewistani, *Tadhkira Mashayikh-i-Sewistan*, Preface by G.M. Lakho, ed. Syed Hussamuddin Rashidi (Jamshoro: Committee Jashn-i-Lal Shahbaz, 2010), pp. 15–16.
54. Abdul Ghafoor bin Hyder Sewistani, *Tadhkira Mashayikh-i-Sewistan*, p. 21.
55. Ibid., p. 15.
56. Zahuruddin Ahmad, *Pakistan mein Farsi Adab*, vol. 4 (Lahore: Idara Tehqiqat-e-Pakistan, UOP, 1990) p. 657.
57. Abdul Ghafoor bin Hyder Sewistani, *Tadhkira Mashayikh-i-Sewistan*, p. 21.
58. Ibid., p. 24.
59. Ibid.
60. Zahuruddin Ahmad, *Pakistan mein Farsi Adab*, pp. 560–1.
61. Khan Bahadur Khudadad Khan, *Lubb i-Tarikh i-Sindh*, p. 314.
62. Abdul Ghafoor bin Hyder Sewistani, *Tadhkira Mashayikh-i-Sewistan*, p. 16.
63. Ibid., pp. 15–16.
64. Ibid., p. 19.
65. Jan Rypka, *History of Iranian Literature*, p. 82.
66. Abdul Ghafoor bin Hyder Sewistani, *Tadhkira Mashayikh-i-Sewistan*, Persian text, pp. 24–5.
67. Ibid., pp. 63–5.
68. Syed Tahir Muhammad Nisyani Thattawi, *Tarikh-i-Tahiri*, p. 48.
69. Abdul Ghafoor bin Hyder Sewistani, *Tadhkira Mashayikh-i-Sewistan*, p. 35.
70. Ibid., pp. 27–8.
71. Ibid., pp. 28–9.
72. Ibid., pp. 30–1.
73. Ibid., p. 453.
74. Ibid., p. 454.
75. Yahya bin Ahmad Sirhindi, *Tarikh-i-Mubarakshahi*, p. 369.
76. Zahuruddin Ahmad, *Pakistan mein Farsi Adab*, p. 530.
77. Nabi Hadi, *History of Indo-Persian Literature*, p. 174; Yahya bin Ahmad Sirhindi, *Tarikh-i-Mubarakshahi*, pp. 369–70.
78. Shaykh Farid al-Din Bhakkari, *Dhakhirat al-Khawanin*, vol. 3, p. 39.
79. Zahuruddin Ahmad, *Pakistan mein Farsi Adab*, p. 530; Shaykh Farid al-Din Bhakkari, *Dhakhirat al-Khawanin*, vol. 2, p. 14.
80. Shaykh Farid al-Din Bhakkari, *Dhakhirat al-Khawanin*, vol. 1, p. 239 and vol. 3, p. 67.
81. Zahuruddin Ahmad, *Pakistan mein Farsi Adab*, p. 529.
82. Shaykh Farid al-Din Bhakkari, *Dhakirat al-Khawanin*, vol. 1, p. 6.
83. Refer to Dr Muhammad Mehdi Tavassoli, 'Shaykh Farid Bhakkari' (Proceedings of the Seminar on *Zaban wa Adabiyat-i-Farsi dar Sindh* organized by the Department of Persian, University of Karachi, 2003), p. 94.
84. Shaykh Farid al-Din Bhakkari, *Dhakirat al-Khawanin*, vol. 1, p. 6.
85. Ibid., p. 200.
86. Ali Sher Qani Thattawi, *Tuhfat al-Kiram*, p. 395.
87. *Wakil* was the highest minister at the imperial court but without any office or department under him.
88. Zahuruddin Ahmad, *Pakistan mein Farsi Adab*, p. 529.
89. Ibid., p. 533.

90. Shaykh Farid al-Din Bhakkari, *Dhakhirat al-Khawanin*, vol. 1, p. 200.
91. *Ilm al-Kalam* (lit. the study of 'speech' or 'words') is the Islamic philosophical discipline of seeking theological principles through dialectic. *Kalam* in Islamic practice relates to the discipline of seeking theological knowledge through debate and argument.
92. Maulana Din Muhammad Wafa'i, *Tadhkirah Mashahir-i-Sindh*, vol. 1, 95.
93. Shaykh Farid al-Din Bhakkari, *Dhakhirat al-Khawanin*, vol. 2, 352.
94. Nizam al-Din Ahmad, *Tabaqat-i-Akbari*, vol. 2, p. 446.
95. Shaykh Farid al-Din Bhakkari, *Dhakhirat al-Khawanin*, vol. 2, p. 216.
96. In the empire of the Indian Mughals, the minister in charge of the military department was termed as the *Bakhshi-i-kul*, *Mir Bakhshi*, or *Bakhshi-i-Mumalik*.
97. Shaykh Farid al-Din Bhakkari, *Dhakhirat al-Khawanin*, vol. 2, pp. 342–3.
98. The general of the Mughal army under Jahangir, who initially quelled Shah Jahan's rebellion and later joined Shah Jahan because of Nur Jahan's intrigues and Mahabat Khan, is best known for his coup against Jahangir in 1626 CE.
99. Nizam al-Din Ahmad, *Tabaqat-i-Akbari*, vol. 2, p. 122.
100. Shaykh Farid al-Din Bhakkari, *Dhakhirat al-Khawanin*, vol. 1, p. 3.
101. Shaykh Farid al-Din Bhakkari, *Dhakhirat al-Khawanin*, vols. 1, 2, and 3.
102. Shaykh Farid al-Din Bhakkari, *Dhakhirat al-Khawanin*, vol. 1, pp. 19 and 176.
103. Ibid., p. 202.
104. Shaykh Farid al-Din Bhakkari, *Dhakhirat al-Khawanin*, vol. 1, p. 72; Shaykh Farid al-Din Bhakkari, *Dhakhirat al-Khawanin*, vol. 2, pp. 20 and 72.
105. Shaykh Farid al-Din Bhakkari, *Dhakhirat al-Khawanin*, vol. 1, p. 139.
106. Shaykh Farid al-Din Bhakkari, *Dhakhirat al-Khawanin*, vol. 2, p. 151.
107. Abu al-Fazl, *A'in-i-Akbari*, vol. 1, p. 321.
108. See Kewal Ram, *Tadhkirat al-Umara*, ed. Moin al-Haque and Ansar Zahid Khan, vols. 1 and 2 (Karachi: Pakistan Historical Society, 1986); see, Samsam al-Daula Shahnawaz Khan, *Ma'athir al-Umara*.
109. Refer to Shaykh Farid al-Din Bhakkari, *Dhakhirat al-Khawanin*, vol. 1 (Introduction), p. 11.
110. Ibid., p. 529.
111. Ibid., p. 260.
112. Shaykh Farid al-Din Bhakkari, *Dhakhirat al-Khawanin*, vol. 2, pp. 228 and 260.
113. Ibid., p. 458.
114. Ibid., pp. 75–7.
115. Ibid., pp. 166–7.
116. Ibid., pp. 144–5.
117. Ibid., pp. 151–2.
118. Ibid., p. 387.
119. Ibid., p. 47.
120. Ibid., p. 73.
121. In the nineteenth regal year of Akbar, he divided the *khalisah* lands into 182 units. It was expected that each unit would produce a crore (ten million) *dam*. Hence, the officers in charge of these units were called *karoris*.
122. Shaykh Farid al-Din Bhakkari, *Dhakhirat al-Khawanin*, vol. 1, pp. 139, 142, 168, 207, and 209; Shaykh Farid al-Din Bhakkari, *Dhakhirat al-Khawanin*, vol. 2, pp. 14, 26, 96, 163, 209, 256, and 407; vol. 3, pp. 26, 36, 37, 83, 140, etc.
123. Shaykh Farid al-Din Bhakkari, *Dhakhirat al-Khawanin*, vol. 2, p. 212.
124. Shaykh Farid al-Din Bhakkari, *Dhakhirat al-Khawanin*, vol. 1, p. 199.

125. Ibid., p. 204.
126. Shaykh Farid al-Din Bhakkari, *Dhakhirat al-Khawanin*, vol. 2, p. 223.
127. The term *wahdat al-wujood* was coined by the famous Sufi Ibn Arabi for a goal to be achieved in mysticism which roughly means Divine harmony or unity.
128. Shaykh Farid al-Din Bhakkari, *Dhakhirat al-Khawanin*, vol. 2, p. 401.
129. Ibid., p. 322.
130. Nizam al-Din Ahmad, *Tabaqat-i-Akbari*, vol. 2, p. 829.
131. *Urs* (lit. wedding) is the death anniversary of a Sufi saint in South Asia, usually held at the saint's *dargah* (shrine or tomb).
132. Shaykh Farid al-Din Bhakkari, *Dhakhirat al-Khawanin*, vol. 2, pp. 321–3.
133. Ibid., p. 222.
134. Annemarie Schimmel, *Mystical Dimensions of Islam*, 35th Anniversary edition (University of North Carolina Press, 2011), p. 398.
135. Shaykh Farid al-Din Bhakkari, *Dhakhirat al-Khawanin*, vol. 3, p. 55.
136. Shaykh Farid al-Din Bhakkari, *Dhakhirat al-Khawanin*, vol. 1, p. 205.
137. Ziauddin A. Desai, *The Dhakhirat ul-Khawanin of Shaikh Farid Bhakkari* (New Delhi: Idara Adbiyat-i-Dilli, 2009), p. xxiv.
138. Shaykh Farid al-Din Bhakkari, *Dhakhirat al-Khawanin*, vol. 1, pp. 94, 135, 155, 197; Shaykh Farid al-Din Bhakkari, *Dhakhirat al-Khawanin*, vol. 2, pp. 21, 164, etc.
139. Ibid., vol. 1, p. 1.
140. Ahmad Munzawi, *Fehrist Mushtarik Nuskh Khatti Farsi Pakistan*, vol. 11, p. 912.
141. Syed Abdul Qadir, *Hadiqat al-Awliya*, p. 14.
142. Shah Abdul Karim Bulri (1536–1623 CE) was a famous *Sufi* poet of the Sindhi language from Matiari, Sindh. He was the great-grandfather of the famous poet Shah Abdul Latif Bhittai.
143. Syed Abdul Qadir, *Hadiqat al-Awliya*, p. 24.
144. Ibid., p. 9.
145. Ibid., p. 15.

Chapter 5: *Insha* Literature (Epistolography)

1. Jan Rypka, *History of Iranian Literature*, p. 315.
2. Anders Pettersson, *Literary History: Towards a Global Perspective: Notions of literature across time and cultures*, vol. 1 (Berlin, 2006), p. 237.
3. K.A. Nizami, *On History and Historians of Medieval India*, p. 17.
4. N.K. Singh and A. Samiuddin, *Encyclopaedic Historiography of the Muslim World*, p. 191.
5. Refer to M.R. Waldman, *Toward a Theory of Historical Narrative: A Case Study in Perso-Islamicate Historiography* (Ohio State University Press, 1980), p. 44.
6. See, Ain al-Mulk Abdullah bin Mahru, *Insha-i-Mahru*, ed. Shaykh Abdul Rashid (Lahore: Research Society of Pakistan, 1965); N.K. Singh and A. Samiuddin, *Encyclopaedic Historiography of the Muslim World*, p. 443.
7. K.A. Nizami, *On History and Historians of Medieval India*, p. 18.
8. Syed Nurul Hasan and Satish Chandra, *Religion, state, and society in medieval India: Collected works of S. Nurul Hasan* (New Delhi: Oxford University Press, 2005), p. 301.
9. Jaswant Lal Mehta, *Advanced Study in the History of Medieval India*, vol. 3, *Medieval Indian Society and Culture*, reprint (New Delhi: Sterling Publishers, 1990), p. 21.

10. N.K. Singh and A. Samiuddin, *Encyclopaedic Historiography of the Muslim World*, p. 892.
11. J.N. Sarkar, *Mughal Polity* (New Delhi: Idara Adbiyat-i-Dilli, 1984), p. 21.
12. Manik Lal Gupta, *Sources of Mughal History, 1526 to 1740* (New Delhi: Atlantic Publishers, 1989), p. 51.
13. Waheed Qureshi, 'Insha Literature in Persian: A critical study,' (PhD Thesis, University of the Punjab, 1952), p. 181; K.A. Nizami, *On History and Historians of Medieval India*, pp. 19–20.
14. See, Ain al-Mulk Abdullah bin Mahru, *Insha-i-Mahru*, pp. 233–4.
15. Syed Hussamuddin Rashidi, 'Historical and Political Epistles of Sindh,' Sindhi trans. G.M. Lakho, *The Quarterly Mehran* (Hyderabad: Sindhi Adabi Board) no. 1 (1987), p. 81.
16. M. Saleem Akhtar, 'The Contribution of Sindh in the Development of Historical Epistolography: A bio-bibliographical survey,' *Pakistan Journal of History and Culture* (Islamabad: NIHCR) VII, no. 1 (January–June 1986), p. 7.
17. The details about his origin and family background have been provided in Chapter 4, under the account of his son Yousuf Mirak, the author of *Mazhar-i-Shahjahani*. See M. Saleem Akhtar, 'Mir Abu Al-Qasim Namakin: A critique of his career and achievements,' *Pakistan Journal of History and Culture* (Islamabad: NIHCR) V, no. 1 (January–June 1984), p. 15.
18. Samsam al-Daula Shahnawaz Khan, *Ma'athir al-Umara*, vol. 3, p. 73.
19. Shaykh Farid al-Din Bhakkari, *Dhakhirat al-Khawanin*, vol. 1, p. 198.
20. Syed Hussamuddin Rashidi, *Tadhkirah-i-Amir Khani*, pp. 9 and 66.
21. M. Saleem Akhtar, 'The Contribution of Sindh in the Development of Historical Epistolography,' p. 7.
22. Abu al-Fazl, *Akbar Nama*, vol. 3, pp. 39, 123, 101, and 182.
23. M. Saleem Akhtar, *Sindh under the Mughals*, p. 96.
24. Syed Hussamuddin Rashidi, *Tadhkirah-i-Amir Khani*, pp. 19–20.
25. Samsam al-Daula Shahnawaz Khan, *Ma'athir al-Umara*, p. 76.
26. Yousuf Mirak, *Mazhar-i-Shahjahani*, pp. 115–16; Syed Hussamuddin Rashidi, *Tadhkirah-i-Amir Khani*, p. 43.
27. Ibid., p. 120.
28. Syed Hussamuddin Rashidi, *Tadhkirah-i-Amir Khani*, p. 52.
29. Syed Hussamuddin Rashidi, *Mirza Ghazi Beg Tarkhan aur us ki Bazm-i-Adab*, p. 596.
30. Momin Mohiuddin, *The Chancellery and Persian Epistolography under the Mughals: From Babur to Shah Jahan (1526–1658)* (Calcutta: Iran Society, 1971), p. 173.
31. Syed Hussamuddin Rashidi, *Mirza Ghazi Beg Tarkhan aur us ki Bazm-i-Adab*, p. 597.
32. Syed Hussamuddin Rashidi, *Tadhkirah-i-Amir Khani*, pp. 67–8.
33. Mir Syed Abu al-Qasim Namakin, *The Munshat-i-Namakin*, ed. Ishtiaq Ahmad Zilli (New Delhi: Manohar Publishing House, 2007), p. 403.
34. Ibid., p. 3.
35. Ibid., p. 2.
36. Ibid.
37. Momin Mohiuddin, *The Chancellery and Persian Epistolography under the Mughals*, pp. 173–4.
38. Syed Hussamuddin Rashidi, *Tadhkirah-i-Amir Khani*, 65.
39. Refer to Momin Mohiuddin, 'Munshat-i-Namakin; A unique collection of historical documents,' *Journal of the Pakistan Historical Society* 8, part 2 (April–June 1960), p. 90.

40. Mir Syed Abu al-Qasim Namakin, *The Munshat-i-Namakin*, p. 108.
41. Ibid., pp. 29–126.
42. Ibid., pp. 124–6.
43. Ibid., pp. 7–23.
44. Ibid., p. 91–2.
45. Ibid., p. 126.
46. Ibid., pp. 29–32; 55–6; 38–42; 66–9.
47. Ibid., pp. 134–44.
48. Dr Riazul Islam, *A Calendar of Documents on Indo Persian Relations (1500–1750)*, vol. 1, no. 418 (Karachi: Institute of Central and West Asian Studies, 1979), p. 97.
49. Khafi Khan, *Muntakhib al-Lubab*, ed. Elliot and Dowson, vol. 1 (Lahore: Sang-e-Meel Publications, 2006), p. 161.
50. Abu al-Fazl, *Akbar Nama*, vol. 2, pp. 149–50.
51. G.L. Lewis, *Fathnamas*, Encyclopaedia of Islam, new edition, vol. 2 (Leiden, 1964), p. 839.
52. Ziya al-Din Barani, *Tarikh-i-Feroz Shahi*, pp. 14–361.
53. Mir Syed Abu al-Qasim Namakin, *The Munshat-i-Namakin*, pp. 15–17.
54. Ibid., pp. 66–9.
55. Ibid., pp. 63–5.
56. Ibn Hasan, *The Central Structure of the Mughal Empire and its Practical Working up to the year 1657* (New Delhi: Munshiram Manoharlal, 1970), p. 256.
57. Mir Syed Abu al-Qasim Namakin, *The Munshat-i-Namakin*, pp. 38–42.
58. It is said that Isfandyar Kayani and the Achaemenid King Artaxerxes, son of Xerxes, also known as Longimanus by the Greeks are the same person.
59. Momin Mohiuddin, 'Munshat-i-Namakin,' p. 174.
60. Ibid., p. 175.
61. Ibid., pp. 175–6.
62. Ibid., p. 176.
63. Ibid., p. 177.
64. Ibid., p. 177.
65. Mir Syed Abu al-Qasim Namakin, *The Munshat-i-Namakin*, pp. 331–402.
66. Ibid., pp. 333–5.
67. Ibid., pp. 376–7.
68. Ibid., pp. 34–7.
69. Abu al-Fazl, *Akbar Nama*, p. 197.
70. P. Saran, *The Provincial Government of the Mughals (1526–1658)* (New Delhi: Asia Pub. House, 1973), p. 328.
71. I.H. Qureshi, *The Administration of the Mughal Empire* (Karachi: University of Karachi, 1966), p. 87.
72. Mir Syed Abu al-Qasim Namakin, *The Munshat-i-Namakin*, pp. 49–51.
73. Ibid., pp. 15 and 18.
74. H.H. Dodwelli, *The Cambridge History of India: British India 1497–1858*, vol. 5 (Cambridge University Press Archive, 1929), p. 583.
75. C.A. Storey, *Persian Literature*, vols. 3–4, p. 234.
76. Abu al-Fath Qabil Khan, *Aadab-i-Alamgiri*, ed. Chaudhry, vol. 2 (Lahore: Research Society of Pakistan, 1971), p. 964.
77. Ibid., p. 5.
78. Mir Ali Sher Qani Thattawi, *Tuhfat al-Kiram*, p. 674.
79. Mir Ali Sher Qani Thattawi, *Maqalat al-Shuara*, p. 43; *Tuhfat al-Kiram*, p. 675.

80. Abu al-Fath Qabil Khan, *Aadab-i-Alamgiri*, vol. 2, p. 964.
81. Ibid., pp. 853–4.
82. Ibid., pp. 959–61.
83. Ibid., p. 847.
84. Saqi Musta'id Khan, *Ma'athir-i-Alamgiri*, trans. Jadunath Sakar (Calcutta, 1947), p. 15.
85. Muhammad Kazim, *The Alamgir Nama*, ed. Maulwi Khadim Hussain and Abdul Hayi (Calcutta, 1868), pp. 751–2.
86. Abu al-Fath Qabil Khan, *Aadab-i-Alamgiri*, vol. 2, pp. 836–40.
87. Mir Ali Sher Qani Thattawi, *Maqalat al-Shuara*, p. 43.
88. Nurul Hasan Ansari, *Farsi Adab ba Ehd-i-Aurangzeb*, p. 369.
89. Abu al-Fath Qabil Khan, *Aadab-i-Alamgiri*, vol. 2, pp. 877, 878, and 881.
90. Mir Ali Sher Qani Thattawi, *Tuhfat al-Kiram*, p. 675.
91. Abu al-Fath Qabil Khan, *Aadab-i-Alamgiri*, vol. 1, p. 19.
92. Ibid., p. 18.
93. Ibid., p. 18.
94. Ibid., p. 19.
95. Refer to M. Saleem Akhtar, 'The Contribution of Sindh in the Development of Historical Epistolography,' p. 9.
96. Abu al-Fath Qabil Khan, *Aadab-i-Alamgiri*, vol. 2, pp. 833–78.
97. Ibid., pp. 965–78.
98. Dr Waheed Qureshi, 'Insha Literature in Persian,' p. 180.
99. Abu al-Fath Qabil Khan, *Aadab-i-Alamgiri*, vol. 2, pp. 19, 1152, and 1287.
100. Ibid., pp. 981–1131.
101. C.A. Storey, *Persian Literature*, vols. 3–4, pp. 323–4.
102. Abu al-Fath Qabil Khan, *Aadab-i-Alamgiri*, vol. 2, p. 39.
103. Ibid., p. 57.
104. Ibid., p. 102.
105. Ibid., pp. 38–48.
106. Ibid., pp. 837–40.
107. Ibid., p. 833.
108. Ibid., p. 842.
109. Ibid., p. 843.
110. Ibid., p. 847–8.
111. Ibid., p. 954.
112. Syed Ashraf Khan Hussaini, *Raqa'im-i-Kara'im*, ed. Syed Muhammad Azizuddin Hussaini, Preface (New Delhi: Idara Adbiyat-i-Dilli, 1990).
113. Samsam al-Daula Shahnawaz Khan, *Ma'athir al-Umara*, vol. 1, p. 303.
114. Syed Hussamuddin Rashidi, *Tadhkirah-i-Amir Khani*, pp. 171–4.
115. Samsam al-Daula Shahnawaz Khan, *Ma'athir al-Umara*, vol. 1, p. 307.
116. Mir Ali Sher Qani Thattawi, *Maqalat al-Shuara*, p. 166.
117. Nurul Hasan Ansari, *Farsi Adab ba Ehd-i-Aurangzeb*, p. 370.
118. Syed Ashraf Khan Hussaini, *Raqa'im-i-Kara'im*, p. 64.
119. Ibid., p. 66.
120. Ibid., p. 14.
121. Ibid., p. 10.
122. Ibid., p. 58.
123. Ibid., p. 29.
124. Ibid., p. 59.

125. Ibid., p. 60.
126. Ibid., p. 2.
127. Ibid., p. 7.
128. Ibid., pp. 12–13.
129. Ibid., p. 19.
130. See, Kewal Ram, *Tadhkirat al-Umara*.
131. Syed Ashraf Khan Hussaini, *Raqa'im-i-Kara'im*, p. 19.
132. M. Saleem Akhtar, 'The Contribution of Sindh in the Development of Historical Epistolography,' p. 13.

Chapter 6: Conclusion

1. Mohibbul Hasan, *Historians of Medieval India*, p. vii.
2. Harbans Mukhia, *Historians and Historiography during the Reign of Akbar*, p. 170.
3. Franz Rosenthal, *A History of Muslim Historiography* (Leiden: E.J. Brill, 1952), p. 87.
4. A.A. Duri, *The Rise of Historical Writing among the Arabs*, p. 45.
5. Ibid., p. 23.
6. I.H. Siddiqui, *Indo-Persian Historiography up to the 13th Century*, pp. 4–5.
7. Gulfishan Khan, 'New Trends in Indo-Persian Historiography during the Eighteenth Century,' pp. 72–3.
8. See Iqtidar Alam Khan, 'The Nobility under Akbar and the Development of his Religious Policy 1560–1580,' *Journal of the Royal Asiatic Society* 100 no. 1 (January 1968), pp. 29–36; Athar Ali, *The Mughal Nobility under Aurangzeb* (New Delhi: Oxford University Press, Incorporated, 2001).
9. R.G. Collingwood, *The Idea of History*, p. 55.
10. K.A. Nizami, *On History and Historians of Medieval India*, p. 3.
11. Jamal Malik, *Islam in South Asia*, p. 61.
12. Gulfishan Khan, 'New Trends in Indo-Persian Historiography during the Eighteenth Century,' p. 56.
13. Ijazul Haque Quddusi, *Tarikh-i-Sindh*, pp. 380–1.
14. Ansar Zahid Khan, *History and Culture of Sind*, p. 345.
15. Nabi Hadi, *History of Indo-Persian Literature*, p. 78.
16. Ijazul Haque Quddusi, *Tarikh-i-Sindh*, p. 363.
17. Raghunath Rai, *Themes in World History*, 5th ed. (New Delhi: FK Publications, 2011), p. 181.
18. C.A. Storey, *Persian Literature*, pp. 648–712.
19. See, W. Glanius, *A Relation of an Unfortunate Voyage to the Kingdom of Bengala* (London, 1682).
20. Mubarak Ali, *The English Factory in Sindh* (Lahore: Fiction House, 2005), p. 75.
21. Ref. Roma Doctor, *Sindhi Folklore: An Introductory Survey*, vol. 96, no. 2 (London: Taylor and Francis Ltd., 1985), p. 223.
22. Mohammad Wahid Mirza, *The Life and Works of Amir Khusrau*, p. 509.

Selected Bibliography

Primary Sources

Abdul Qadir, Syed. *Hadiqat al-Awliya*. Edited by Syed Hussamuddin Rashidi. Hyderabad: Sindhi Adabi Board, 1971.
Afif, Shams Siraj. *Tarikh-i-Firuzshahi*. Edited by Wilayat Hussain, Bibliotheca Indica. Calcutta: 1862.
Ahmad, Nizam al-Din. *Tabaqat-i-Akbari*. Urdu translation by M. Ayyub Qadri. Lahore: Urdu Science Board, 1990.
al Baladhuri, Ahmad bin Yahya Ibn Jabir. *Futuh al-Buldan*. Urdu translation by Syed Abul Khair Modudi. Karachi: Nafees Academy, 1982.
al-Kufi, Ali bin Hamid bin Abi Bakar. *Fath Nama i-Sindh* alias *Chach Nama*. Preface and edited by Dr Umar bin Muhammad Daudpota. New Delhi: Majlis Maktubati-Farsi Hyderabad Deccan, 1939.
Allami, Abu al-Fadl. *Akbar Nama*. Translated by H. Beveridge. 3 vols. Delhi: Low Price Publications, 1998.
———. *A'in-i-Akbari*. Translated by H. Blochmann and H. S. Jarrett. Calcutta: Asiatic Society of Bengal, 1927.
al-Mudabbir, Fakhar. *Shajara-i-Ansab-i-Mubarakshahi*. Edited by Denson Ross. London: 1927.
al-Tabari, Muhammad b. Jarir. *Tarikh al-Rusul wal-Muluk* (History of the Prophets and Kings). Edited and translated Ehsan Yar-Shater. New York: The State University of New York Press, 1999.
al-Utb'i, Abu Nasar. *Tarikh-i-Yamini*. Edited by Ali and Springer. New Delhi: 1847.
Babur, Zahiruddin Muhammad. *Babur Nama*. Urdu translation by Mirza Hassan Beg. Karachi: Pakistan Historical Society, 2008.
Badayuni, Abdul Qadir. *Muntakhib al-Tawarikh*. Edited by Maulwi Muhammad Ali. Vol. III. Calcutta: Asiatic Society Bengal, 1869.
Barani, Diya al-Din. *Fatawa-i-Jahandari*. Compiled by Dr Riaz Ahmad and translated by Prof. Atiq Ahmad. Islamabad: NIHCR, 2004.
———. *Tarikh-i-Firuzshahi*. Urdu translation by Dr Moin al-Haque. Lahore: Urdu Science Board, 1991.
Beglari, Idraki. *Beglar Nama*. Edited by Dr N. A. Baloch. Hyderabad: Sindhi Adabi Board, 1980.
———. *Mathnawi Chanesar Nama*. Edited by Syed Hussamuddin Rashidi. Hyderabad: Sindhi Adabi Board, 1956.
Bhakkari, Mir Masum. *Tarikh-i-Sindh* alias *Tarikh-i-Masumi*. Edited by Dr Umar bin Muhammad Daudpota. Puna: Bahandarkar Oriental Institute, 1938.
Bhakkari, Shaykh Farid al-Din. *Dhakhirat al-Khawanin*. Edited by Dr Moin al-Haque. Vol. I, II, and III. Karachi: Pakistan Historical Society, 1961.
bin Mahru, Abdullah. *Insha-i-Mahru—Munsha'aat e 'Ainuddin 'Ainul Mulk*. Edited by Shaykh Abdul Rashid. Lahore: Research Society of Pakistan, 1965.
Dughlat, Mirza Hyder. *Tarikh-i-Rashidi*. Translated by Denison Ross. Patna: 1973.
Firishta, Abu al-Qasim Muhammad. *Tarikh-i-Firishta*. Urdu translation by Abdul Hai Khawaja vol II. Lahore: Book Talk, 1991.
Ghazali. *Nishat al-Muluk*. Translated by F. R. C. Bagley. London: 1962.
Harwi, Fakhri. *Jawahir al-Aja'ib*. Edited by Syed Hussamuddin Rashidi. Hyderabad: Sindhi Adabi Board, 1968.
———. *Rawdat us-Salatin*. Edited by Syed Hussamuddin Rashidi. Hyderabad: Sindhi Adabi Board, 1968.
Hussaini, Syed Ashraf Khan. *Raqa'im-i-Kara'im*. Preface and edited by Syed Muhammad Azizuddin Hussaini. New Delhi: Idara Adbiyat-i-Dilli, 1990.

SELECTED BIBLIOGRAPHY

Ibn Batuta. *The Travels of Ibn Batuta:* A.D. *1325–1354.* Edited and translated by Sir Hamilton Alexander Rosskeen Gibb. New Delhi: Ashgate Publishing Ltd., 1971.
Isami, Khawaja Abdul Malik. *Futuh-us-Salatin.* Edited and Translated by Agha Mahdi Husain. 3 vol. Aligarh: 1967–77.
Juzjani, Minhaj-us-Siraj. *Tabaqat-i-Nasiri.* Translated by Maj. H. G. Raverty. Vol. I. Lahore: 1975.
Kazim, Munshi Muhammad. *The Alamgir Nama.* Edited by Maulwi Khadim Hussain and Abdul Hayi. Calcutta: 1868.
Khusro, Amir. *Khaza'in al-Futuh.* Aligarh: Allahabad University Press, 1927.
Qalandar, Hamid. *Khair al-Majalis.* Edited by K. A. Nizami. Aligarh: 1959.
Ram, Kewal, *Tadhkirat al-Umara,* ed. Dr S. Moin al-Haque and Dr Ansar Zahid Khan. 2 vols. Karachi: Pakistan Historical Society, 1986.
Khan, Khafi. *Muntakhib al-Lubab.* Edited by Elliot and Dowson. Vol. I. Lahore: Sang-i-Meel Publications, 2006.
Khan, Abu al-Fath Qabil. *Aadab-i-Alamgiri.* Edited by Chaudhry. 2 vols. Lahore: Research Society of Pakistan, 1971.
Khan, Khan Bahadur Khudadad. *Lubb i-Tarikh i-Sindh.* Edited by Dr Nabi Bakhsh Khan Baloch. Hyderabad: Sindhi Adabi Board, 1959.
Khan, Samsam al-Dawla Shahnawaz. *Ma'athir al-Umara.* Urdu translation by Muhammad Ayyub Qadiri. 3 vols. Lahore: Markazi Urdu Board, 1968.
Khan, Saqi Musta'id. *Ma'athir-i-Alamgiri.* Translated by Jadunath Sarkar. Calcutta: 1947.
Manju, Sikandar bin Muhammad. *Mirat-i-Sikandari* (The History of Gujrat). Translated by Abu al-Fadl Lutfullah, reprint. New Delhi: 1990.
Mir Khurd. *Siyar al-Awliya.* New Delhi: Muhibb-i-Hind Press, 1885.
Mirak, Yousuf. *Mazhar-i-Shahjahani.* Edited by Syed Hussamuddin Rashidi. Hyderabad: Sindhi Adabi Board, 1962.
Muhammad, Syed Mir *Tarkhan Nama.* Edited by Syed Hussamuddin Rashidi. Hyderabad: Sindhi Adabi Board, 1971.
Nihawandi, Abdul Baqi. *Ma'athir-i-Rahimi.* Edited by M. Hidayat Hussain. Vol. II. Calcutta: Asiatic Society Bengal, 1925.
Namakin, Mir Syed Abu al-Qasim. *The Munshat-i-Namakin.* Edited by Ishtiaq Ahmad Zilli. New Delhi: Manohar Publishing House, 2007.
Nisyani, Syed Tahir Muhammad. *Tarikh-i-Baldah Thatta* alias *Tarikh-i-Tahiri.* Introduction by Dr Nabi Bakhsh Khan Baloch. Hyderabad: Sindhi Adabi Board, 1964.
Purani, Muhammad bin Bayazid. *Nusrat Nama-i-Tarkhan.* Edited by Dr Ansar Zahid Khan. Karachi: Institute of South and Central Asian Studies, 2000.
Reis, Sidi Ali. *Safar Namah Sidi Ali Reis.* Translated by A. Vambery as *The Travels and Adventures of the Turkish Admiral Sidi Ali Reis.* London: Luzac, 1899.
Sijzi, Mir Hassan. *Fawa'id al-Fuad.* New Delhi: D. K. Print World, 1996.
Sirhindi, Yahya bin Ahmad. *Tarikh-i-Mubarakshahi.* Urdu translation by Dr Aftab Asghar. Lahore: 1986.
Sewistani, Abdul Ghafoor bin Hyder. *Tadhkira Mashayikh-i-Sewistan.* Edited by Syed Hussamuddin Rashidi. Jamshoro: Committee Jashn-i-Lal Shahbaz, 2010.
Thattawi, Mir Ali Sher Qani. *Makli Nama.* Annotated and edited by Syed Hussamuddin Rashidi. Hyderabad: Sindhi Adabi Board, 1967.
_____. *Maqalat al-Shuara.* Edited by Syed Hussamuddin Rashidi. Jamshoro: Sindhi Adabi Board, 1958.
_____. *Tuhfat al-Kiram.* Edited by S. Hussamuddin Rashidi and Urdu translation by Akhtar Ridwi. Vol. 3, ed. I. Hyderabad: Sindhi Adabi Board, 1971.
Thattawi, Shaykh Hussain Safa'i. *Tadhkirat al-Murad.* Sindhi translation by Dr Abdul Rasul Qadri. Hyderabad: Sindhi Adabi Board, 2006.
Thattawi, Shaykh Muhammad Azam. *Tuhfat al-Tahirin* Edited by Badr Alam Durrani. Hyderabad: Sindhi Adabi Board, 1956.
Tusi, Nizam al-Mulk. *Siyasat Nama.* Translated by Herbert Drake. London: 1960.
Yaqubi, Ahmed bin Abi Yaqub bin Jafar. *Tarikh-i-Yaqubi.* Edited by M. T. Houtsma. Vol. I. Leiden: 1883.

The Gazetteer of India: History and culture. Vol. 2. Publications Division, Ministry of Information and Broadcasting, 1973.

Original Manuscripts

Thattawi, Shaykh Hussain Safa'i. *Tadhkirat al-Murad* (Arabic).
Thattawi, Shaykh Abdul Shakoor. *Intikhab-i-Muntakhib.*

Secondary Sources

Abdul Ghafoor, Dr Muhammad. *The Calligraphers of Thatta.* Karachi: Centre of Central and West Asian Studies, UOK, 1968.
Abdullah, S. M. *A Descriptive Directory of Persian Urdu and Arabic Manuscripts in the Punjab University Library*. Vol. I. Lahore: Punjab University, 1942.
Aftab, Dr Tahira. *Inscribing South Asian Muslim Women: An Annotated Bibliography & Research Guide.* Leiden: Brill NV, 2008.
Akhtar, Dr M. Saleem. *Sindh under the Mughals: An Introduction to, Translation of and Commentary on the Mazhar-i-Shahjahani of Yousuf Mirak.* Islamabad: NIHCR, 1990.
Ali, Athar. *The Mughal Nobility under Aurangzeb.* New Delhi: Oxford University Press, Incorporated, 2001.
Ali, B. Sheikh. *History: Its Theory and Method.* California: Macmillan, 1978.
Ali, Dr Mubarak. *The English Factory in Sindh.* Reprint. Lahore: Fiction House, 2005.
―――――. *Ulema, Sufis and Intellectuals.* Reprint. Lahore: Fiction House, 2005.
Ashraf, K. M., ed. *Indian Historiography and Other Related Papers.* New Delhi: Sunrise Publications, 2006.
Awan, M. Tariq. *History of India and Pakistan.* Vol. I. Lahore: Ferozsons, 1994.
Baloch, Dr Nabi Bakhsh Khan. *Sindh: Studies in Historical.* Vol. I. Karachi: Kalhora Seminar Committee, 1996.
Benarji, Anil Chandra. *The State and Society in Northern India, 1206–1526.* K. P. Bagchi, 1982.
Barnes, H. E. *A History of Historical Writing.* 2nd rev. ed. New York: Dover Publications, 1963.
Beg, Mirza Kaleech. *A History of Sindh.* 2 vols. 2nd ed. Karachi: Scinde Classics, 1982.
Book LLC. ed. *8th-Century History Books: Nihon Shoki, Chronicle of 754, Chach Nama, Historia Gentis Langobardorum.* Royal Frankish Annals. General Books LLC, 2010.
Brown, E. G. *Literary History of Persia.* 3 vols. London: Cambridge University Press, 1977.
Canfield, Robert L. ed. *Turko-Persia in Historical Perspective.* New York: Cambridge University Press, 1991.
Carr, E. H. *What is History?* New York: Vintage Books, 1987.
Chand, Tara. *Influence of Islam on Indian Culture.* Allahabad: The Indian Press, 1936.
Chaurasia, Radhey Shyam. *History of Ancient India: Earliest Times to 1000 A.D.* New Delhi: Atlantic Publishers, 2008.
Chung, Tan., ed. *Across the Himalayan Gap: An Indian Quest for Understanding China.* New Delhi: Indira Gandhi National Centre, 1998.
Collingwood, R. G. *The Idea of History.* London: Oxford University Press, 1994.
Das, Sisir Kumar. *A History of Indian Literature, 500–1399: from courtly to the popular.* New Delhi: Sahitya Akademi, 2005.
Datta, Amaresh. *The Encyclopaedia of Indian Literature.* Vol. II, 15th ed. New Delhi: Sahitya Akademi, 2005.
Davies, S. *Archives and Manuscripts: contents and use: using the sources.* 3rd ed. UK: Aberystwyth University Press, 2008.
Danvers, F. C. *The Portuguese in India Being a History of the Rise and Decline of Their Eastern Empire.* Vol. I, reprint. W. H. Allen & Company Limited, 1894.
Desai, Ziauddin A. *The Dhakhirat al-Khawanin of Shaikh Farid Bhakkari.* Introduction. Delhi: Idara Adbiyat-i-Dilli, 2009.
―――――. *Malfuz Literature: As a source of political, social, and cultural history of Gujarat and Rajasthan.* Patna: Khuda Bakhsh Oriental Library, 1991.

SELECTED BIBLIOGRAPHY 245

Doctor, Roma. 'Sindhi Folklore: An Introductory Survey'. *Folklore* (London: Taylor and Francis Ltd.) 96, no. 2 (1985).
Dodwelli, H. H., *The Cambridge History of India: British India 1497–1858*. Vol. V. Cambridge University Press Archive, 1929.
Duri, A. A. *The Rise of Historical Writing among the Arabs*. Edited and translated by Lawrence I. Conrad. New Jersey: Princeton University Press, 1983.
Ekin, Esra. *Mustafa Ali's Epic Deeds of Artists*. Leiden: Koninklijke Brill NV, 2011.
Elliot, H. M., and John Dowson. *History of India as told by its own historians, (The Muhammadan Period)*. With a foreword by Sir Richard Burns. Supplement, 3 vols. Reprint. Bombay: Islamic Book Service, 1979.
Elphinston, Moundstuart. *The History of India*. Vol. V. London: John Murray, 1841.
Farooqui, Salma Ahmed. *A Comprehensive History of Medieval India: From Twelfth to the Mid-Eighteenth Century*. New Delhi: Pearson Education India, 2011.
Beg, Mirza Kaleech. *The Chach Nama: An ancient history of Sind*. Lahore: Vanguards Book Ltd., 1985.
Frye, Richard N. *The Golden Age of Persia*. Reprint. London: Weidenfeld and Nicolson, 1977.
Gajrani, S. *History, Religion and Culture of India*, Vol. I. New Delhi: Gyan Publishing House, 2004.
Ganguly, D. K. *History and Historians of Ancient India*. New Delhi: Abhino Publishers, 1984.
Garewal, J. S. *Medieval India: History and Historians*. Amritsar: Guru Nanak University, 1975.
Glanius, W. *A Relation of an Unfortunate Voyage to the Kingdom of Bengala*. London: 1682.
Gokhale, Balkrishna Govind. *Ancient India, History and Culture*. New Delhi: Asia Pub. House, 1959.
Gupta, Manik Lal. *Sources of Mughal History, 1526 to 1740*. New Delhi: Atlantic Publishers, 1989.
Hadi, Nabi. *History of Indo-Persian Literature*. New Delhi: Iran Culture House, 2001.
Hanif, N. *Biographical Encyclopaedia of Sufis: South Asia*. New Delhi: Sarup and Sons, 2000.
Hardy, Peter. *Historians of the Medieval India: Studies in Indo-Muslim historical writings*. London: Louzak & Co., 1960.
———. *Some Studies in Pre- Mughal Muslim Historiography*. New Delhi: 1997.
Hasan, Mohibbul. *Kashmir under the Sultans*. Reprint. New Delhi: Aakar Books, 2005.
Hodivala, Shahpurshah Hormasji. *Studies in Indo-Muslim History: a critical commentary on Elliot and Dowson's History of India as told by its own historians*. Vol. I, reprint. Lahore: Islamic Book Service, 1979.
Ibn Hasan. *The Central Structure of the Mughal Empire and its Practical Working up to the year 1657*. New Delhi: Munshiram Manoharlal, 1970.
Jackson, Peter. *The Delhi Sultanate: A Political and Military History*. Cambridge University Press, 1999.
Jaffar, S. M. *Some Cultural Aspects of Muslim Rule in India*. Peshawar: Muhammad Sadiq Khan Publishers, 1950.
Khan, Dr Ansar Zahid. *History and Culture of Sind: A study of socio-economic organization and institutions during the 16th and 17th centuries*. Karachi: Royal Book Company, 1980.
Lal, Mohan. *Encyclopaedia of Indian Literature: Sasay to Zorgot*. Vol. V of *Encyclopaedia of Indian Literature*. New Delhi: Sahitya Akademi, 2006.
Lambrick, H.T. *Sindh: Before the Muslim Conquest*. Hyderabad: Sindhi Adabi Board, 1973.
Lewis, G. L. *Fathnamas, Encyclopaedia of Islam*. New ed., vol. II. Leiden: 1964.
Luniya, Bhanwarlal Nathuram. *Some Historians of Medieval India*. New Delhi: Lakshmi Narain Agarwal, 1969.
———. *Life and Culture in Medieval India*. New Delhi: Kamal Prakashan, 1978.
Majumdar, D. N. *Races and Cultures of India*. 4th edition. New Delhi: Asia Publication House, 1961.
Majumdar, R. C., B. V. Bhavan, and B. I. Simiti. *The History and Culture of the Indian People*. Vol. I. London: G. Allen & Unwin, 1969.
Malik, Jamal, *Islam in South Asia: A short history*. Leiden: Koninklijke Brill NV, 2008.
Marincola, John. ed. *A Companion to Greek and Roman Historiography*. India: Spi Publishers, 2010.
Mehta, Jaswant Lal. *Advanced Study in the History of Medieval India*. 3 vols. Reprint. New Delhi: Sterling Publishers, 2009.
Mirza, Dr Wahid. *The Life and Works of Amir Khusrao*. Lahore: University of the Punjab, 1962.
Mohiuddin, Dr Momin. *The Chancellery and Persian Epistolography under the Mughals: From Babur to Shah Jahan (1526–1658)*. Calcutta: Iran Society, 1971.

Mukhia, Harbans. *Historians and Historiography during the Reign of Akbar.* New Delhi: Vikas Publisher House, 1976.
Najeebabadi, Akbar Shah. *The History of Islam.* Vol. II. Lahore: Darrussalam, 2001.
Nizami, Khaliq Ahmad. *On History and Historians of Medieval India.* New Delhi: Munshiram Manoharlal, 1983.
Nurul Hasan, Syed., and Satish Chandra. *Religion, State, and Society in Medieval India: Collected Works of Syed Nurul Hasan.* New Delhi: Oxford University Press, 2005.
Pargeter, F. E. *Ancient Indian Historical Traditions.* London: 1922.
Pathak, Kader D. *Essentials of History and Historiography.* New Delhi: Swastik Publications, 2012.
Pathak, V. S. *Ancient Historians of India: A Study in Historical Biographies.* Jodhpur: Kusumanjali Book World, 1997.
Pettersson, Anders. *Literary History: Towards a Global Perspective: Notions of literature across time and cultures.* Vol. I. Berlin: 2006.
Prasad, Ishwari. *History of the Qaraunah Turks in India.* Vol. I. Allahabad: 1936.
_____. *The Life and Times of Humayun.* New Delhi: Orient Longmans, 1956.
Qureshi, I. H. *The Administration of the Mughal Empire.* Karachi: University of Karachi, 1966.
_____. *The Muslim Community of the Indo-Pakistan Subcontinent (610–1947).* Reprint. Karachi: University of Karachi, 1999.
Rahim, M. A. *Social and Cultural History of Bengal.* Vol. II. Karachi: Technical Printers, 1967.
Rahmani, Anjum. *Cultural Heritage of Pakistan.* Lahore Museum, 2000.
Rai, Dr Raghunath. *Themes in World History.* 5th ed. New Delhi: FK Publications, 2011.
Rao, V. N. Shulman, D. and, S. Subrahmanyam. *Textures of Time: Writing History in South India 1600–1800.* New Delhi: 2001.
Rasul, Muhammad Ghulam. *The Origin and Development of Muslim Historiography.* Lahore: Sh. Muhammad Ashraf, 1976.
Ray, Hem Chandra. *The Dynastic History of Northern India (Early Medieval Period).* Vol. I, 2nd ed., reprint. New Delhi: Munshiram Manoharlal Publishers, 1931.
Ray, Sukumar. *Humayun in Persia.* Calcutta: Royal Asiatic Society of Bengal, 1948.
Riazul, Dr Islam. *A Calendar of Documents on Indo Persian Relations (1500–1750).* Vol. I, no. 418. Karachi: Institute of Central and West Asian Studies, 1979.
_____. *Sufism in South Asia: Impact on fourteenth century Muslim society.* Karachi: Oxford University Press, 2002.
Rosenthal, Franz. *A History of Muslim Historiography.* Leiden: E. J. Brill, 1952.
Rypka, Jan. *History of Iranian Literature.* Holland: D. Reidel, 1968.
Sada Rangani, Dr H. I. *Persian Poets of Sindh.* Hyderabad: Sindhi Adabi Board, 1987.
Said, Hakim Mohammed, and Ansar Zahid Khan. *Al-Biruni: His Times, Life and Works.* Karachi: Hamdard Foundation, 1981.
Saran, P. *The Provincial Government of the Mughals (1526–1658).* New Delhi: Asia Pub. House, 1973.
Sarkar, Jagadish Narayan. *Mughal polity.* New Delhi: Idara Adbiyat-i-Dilli, 1984.
_____. *History of History Writing in Medieval India: Contemporary Historians.* New Delhi: Ratna Parkashan, 1977.
Schimmel, Annemarie. *A History of Indian Literature: Sindhi Literature.* Vol. IX, Part-1. Germany: Otto Harrassowitz Verlag, 1974.
_____. *Islam in the Indian Subcontinent.* Leiden: E. J. Brill, 1980.
_____. *Mystical Dimensions of Islam.* Thirty-fifth Anniversary ed. University of North Carolina Press, 2011.
Sen, S. N. *Ancient Indian History and Civilization.* New Delhi: New Age International, 1999.
Sharma, T. R. *Historiography: A History of Historical Writings.* New Delhi: Concept Publishing Co., 2005.
Siddiqui, Dr M. H. *History of the Arghuns and Tarkhans of Sind, 1507–1593: An annotated translation of the relevant parts of Mir Masum's Tarikh-i-Sind, with an Introduction and Appendices.* Introduction. Jamshoro: Institute of Sindhology, 1972.
Siddiqui, Iqtidar Hussain. *Indo-Persian Historiography up to the 13th Century.* Primus Books, 2010.

Singh, G. P. *Ancient Indian Historiography: Sources and Interpretations*. New Delhi: D. K. Print World, 2003.
_____. *Early Indian Historical Traditions and Archaeology*. New Delhi: D. K. Print World, 1994.
_____. *The Evolution of Historiographical Tradition in Ancient and Medieval India*. New Delhi: D. K. Print World, 2011.
Singh, N. K., and A. Samiuddin. *Encyclopaedic Historiography of the Muslim World*. New Delhi: Global Vision Publication House, 2003.
Singh, Upinder. *A History of Ancient and Early medieval India: From the Stone Age to the 12th Century*. New Delhi: Dorling Kindersley, 2009.
Sorley, H. T. *Shah Abdul Latif of Bhit: His Poetry, Life and Times*. Reprint. Karachi: 1966.
Sreedharan, E. *A Textbook of Historiography, 500 B.C. to A.D. 2000*. New Delhi: Orient Longman Pvt. Ltd., 2004.
Storey, C. A. *Persian Literature (A Bio-Bibliographical Survey)*. Vol. I. London: Royal Asiatic Society of Great Britain and Ireland, 1989.
_____. *Persian Literature*. Vol. 3. Psychology Press, 1999.
Thomas, Paul. *Epics, Myths and Legends of India*. 2nd ed. Bombay: D. B. Traporevala Sons and Co., 1961.
Vaidyanathan, K. S. *Studies in Rig Veda (from Original Texts)*. India: K. V. S. Aiyer Indology Research Centre, 2000.
Waldman, M. R. *Toward a Theory of Historical Narrative: A Case Study in Perso-Islamicate Historiography*. Ohio State University Press, 1980.
Walsh, Judith E. *A Brief History of India*. New York: InfoBase Publishing, 2006.
Waseem, S. M., ed. *Development of Persian historiography in India: from the second half of the 17th century to the first half of the 18th century*. New Delhi: Kanishka Publishers, 2003.
Woolf, D. Daniel R. *The Oxford History of Historical Writing: 1350–1750*. Vol. III. New Delhi: Oxford University Press, 2011.
Wynbrandt, James. *A Brief History of Pakistan*. New York: Infobase Publishing, 2009.
Yadav, Vandana. *History and Historiography: Trends and Practices*. New Delhi: Shree Publishers and Distributers, 2007.
Yasin, Muhammad. *A Social History of Islamic India 1605–1748*. Lucknow: D. W. Publishers, 1958.

Books in Persian

Asghar, Dr Aftab. *Tarikh Nawisi-i-Farsi dar Hind wa Pakistan: Timurian-i-Buzurgaz Babur ta Aurangzeb* (Persian Historiography in Indo-Pak: Great Timurids, from Babur to Aurangzeb). Lahore: Culture Centre Islamic Republic of Iran, 1985.
Munzawi, Ahmad. *Fehrist Mushtarik Nuskh Khatti Farsi Pakistan* (Directory of Persian Manuscripts in Pakistan). Vols. VII and XI. Islamabad: Persian Research Centre for Iran and Pakistan, 1986.
_____. *Fehrist warah'i Kitab ha'i Farsi* (Directory of Books in Persian). Vol. I. Tehran: 1995.
Nafisi, Saeed. *Tarikh Nazmwa Nasr dar Iran wadar Zaban-i-Farsi* (History of Prose and Poetry in Iran and Persian Language). Vol. III, 2nd ed. Tehran: Intisharat-i-Faroghi, 1944.
Naqvi, Dr Syed Ali Rada. *Tadhkirah Nawisi Farsi dar Hind wa Pakistan* (Compilation of Persian Biographical Dictionaries in India and Pakistan). Tehran: Mo'assasa Matbu'at-i-Ilmi, 1968.
Safa, Dr Zabihullah. *Tarikh Adbiyat-i-Iran* (History of Iranian Literature). Vol. III, 2nd ed. Tehran: Tehran University Press, 1353.
Shafaq, Rada Zadeh. *Tarikh Adbiyat-i-Farsi* (History of Persian Literature). Edited and annotated. Tehran: 1337.

Books in Urdu

Abdullah, Dr Syed. *Adabiyat-i-Farsi mein Hinduon ka hissa* (Contribution of the Hindus towards Persian Literature). New Delhi: Anjuman Taraqqi Urdu, 1942.
Ahmad, Dr Zahuruddin. *Pakistan mein Farsi Adab* (Persian Literature in Pakistan). Vol. I. Lahore: 1974.
_____. *Pakistan mein Farsi Adab*. Vol. IV. Lahore: Idara Tehqiqat-e-Pakistan, UOP, 1990.

Ansari, Dr Nurul Hasan. *Farsi Adab ba Ehd-i-Aurangzeb* (Persian Literature During the Reign of Aurangzeb). New Delhi: Indo-Persian Society, 1969.

Aslam, Prof. Muhammad. *Malfuzati Adab ki Tarikhi Ehmiat* (Historical Significance of the Malfuz Literature). Lahore: Idarah-i-Tahqiqat-i-Pakistan, 1995.

Badakhshani, Maqbool Beg., ed. *Tarikh Adabiyat-i-Musalmanan-i-Pak o Hind.* Vol. II. Lahore: Punjab University, 1971.

Burhanpuri, R. *Burhanpur kay Sindhi Awliya* (The Sindhi saints of Burhanpur). Karachi: 1957.

Hasan, Mohibbul. *Historians of Medieval India.* Urdu translation by Masroor Hashmi as *Ahd-i-Wusta kay Moirrikheen.* New Delhi: Urdu Promotion Buru, 1985.

Ikram, Shaykh Muhammad. *Pakistan Ka Saqafti Wirsa* (Cultural heritage of Pakistan). Lahore: Idara Saqafat-i-Islamia, 2001.

Quddusi, Ijazul Haque. *Tarikh-i-Sindh.* Vols. I and II. Lahore: Urdu Science Board, 1995.

Rashidi, Syed Hussamuddin. *Mirza Ghazi Beg Tarkhan aur us ki Bazm-i-Adab.* Karachi: Urdu Promotion Board, 1970.

Yazdani, Khawaja Abdul Majeed. *Tarikh-i Adabiyat Musalmanan-i Pakistan wa Hind.* 3 vols. Persian Literature (Part-1) Lahore: Punjab University, 1971.

Books in Sindhi

Baloch, Dr Nabi Bakhsh Khan. *Sindhi Boli aen Adab jee Tarikh* (The history of Sindhi language and literature). 4th ed. Jamshoro: University of Sindh, 1999.

Rashidi, Syed Hussamuddin. *Amin al-Mulk Nawab Mir Masum Bhakkari.* Hyderabad: Sindhi Adabi Board, 1979.

_____. *Galhiun Goth watanjoon* (Villagers' Talks). Karachi: Anjuman Tarikh-i-Sindh, 1981.

_____. *Tadhkirah-i-Amir Khani.* Hyderabad: Sindhi Adabi Board, 1961.

Shayda'i, Rahimdad Khan Maula'i. *Jannat al-Sindh.* Hyderabad: Sindhi Adabi Board, 1985.

Wafa'i, Maulana Din Muhammad. *Tadhkirah Mashahir-i-Sindh* (Description of the Dignitaries of Sindh). Edited by S. Hussamuddin Rashidi. 3 vols. Hyderabad: Sindhi Adabi Board, 1986.

Unpublished PhD Thesis

Ziauddin, Dr Muhammad. 'Role of Persians at the Mughal Court: A Historical Study, during 1526–1717 AD'. PhD Thesis, University of Balochistan, 2005.

Qureshi, Dr Waheed. 'Insha Literature in Persian: A Critical Study'. PhD Thesis, University of the Punjab, 1952.

Periodicals and Reference Material

Articles in English

Ahmed, Mannan. '*The Long Thirteenth Century of the Chachnama.*' *The Indian Economic and Social History Review* (Columbia University) 49, no. 4 (2012).

Akhtar, Dr M. Saleem. 'Mir Abu al-Qasim Namakin: A critique of his career and achievements.' *Pakistan Journal of History and Culture* (Islamabad: National Institute of Historical and Cultural Research) 5, no. 1 (January–June 1984).

_____. 'The Contribution of Sindh in the Development of Historical Epistolography: A bio-bibliographical survey.' *Pakistan Journal of History and Culture* (Islamabad: NIHCR) 7, no. 1 (January–June 1986).

Al-Da'mi, Dr M. A. 'Major Trends of Arab Historiography.' *The Quarterly 'Historicus Journal of Pakistan Historical Society* 41, no. 2 (July 1993).

Habibullah, B. M. 'Re-evaluation of the Literary Sources of Pre-Mughal History.' *Journal of Islamic Culture* (Hyderabad) 15 (1941).

Hardy, P. 'Is the Chachnamah Intelligible to the Historian as Political Theory?' In *Sindh through the Centuries,* edited by Dr Hamida Khuhro. Karachi: Oxford University Press, 1981.

SELECTED BIBLIOGRAPHY

Islam, Dr Arshad. 'Tarikh-i-Masumi: An Appraisal of its Relevance to the History of Sindh.' *Journal of Pakistan Historical Society* 47, no. 3 (July–September 1999).

―――――. 'The Tarkhan Nama.' *Pakistan Journal of History and Culture* (Islamabad: NIHCR) 14, no. 1 (January–June 1993).

Islam, Dr Riazul. 'A Survey in Outline of the Mystic Literature of the Sultanate Period.' *Journal of Pakistan Historical Society* 3–4, no. 3 (1955).

Keshavmurthy, P. 'Finitude and the Authorship of Fiction: Muhammad 'Awfi's Preface to his Chronicle, Lubab al-Albab (The Piths of Intellects).' *Arab Studies Journal* 19 (2011).

Khan, Dr Ansar Zahid. 'The Nusrat Nama-i-Tarkhan.' *Journal of Pakistan Historical Society* 45, no. 2 (April 1997).

Khan, Dr Gulfishan. 'New Trends in Indo-Persian Historiography during the Eighteenth Century.' *The Quarterly Historicus, Journal of Pakistan Historical Society* 58, nos. 3 and 4 (July–December 2010).

Khan, Iqtidar Alam 'The Nobility under Akbar and the Development of his Religious Policy 1560–1580.' *Journal of the Royal Asiatic Society* 100, no. 1 (January 1968).

Mohiuddin, Momin. 'Munshat-i-Namakin: A unique collection of historical documents.' *Journal of Pakistan Historical Society* 8, part 2 (April–June 1960).

Panhwar, M. H. 'The Causes of Decline of Persian in Pakistan and Remedy.' Paper presented in a Seminar at Hyderabad organized by the Iran Culture Centre, 1973.

Qadir, Dr Khurram 'Medieval Historiography of Muslim India: The Sultanate Period.' *Journal of the Pakistan Historical Society* 50, no. 3 (July–September 2002).

Spuler, Dr Bertold. 'Historiography in Muslim Persia.' *Journal of Pakistan Historical Society* 6, part 4 (October–December 1958).

Articles in Urdu

Akhtar, Dr M. Saleem. 'Nusrat Nama-i-Tarkhan.' *Fikr wa Nazar The Quarterly Journal of Islamic Research Institute* (Islamabad) 39, no. 3 (July–September 2001).

Junagarhi, Qadi Ahmad Miyan Akhtar. 'Rawdat us-Salatin.' *The Quarterly Armughan-i-Ilmi* (Lahore) 1, part. 2 (1955).

Shirani, Dr Mazhar Mahmud, 'Nusrat Namah-i-Tarkhan.' *The Quarterly Journal Fanun* (Lahore) 118 (September–December 2002).

Articles in Persian

Tavassoli, Dr Muhammad Mehdi. 'Shaykh Farid Bhakkari.' Proceedings of the Seminar on *Zaban Adabiyat-i-Farsi dar Sindh* (Persian Language and Literature in Sindh) organized by the Department of Persian, University of Karachi, 2003.

Articles in Sindhi

Lakho, Dr Ghulam Muhammad. 'Intikhab-i-Muntakhib: Sind ji Tarikh jo Hik Wadhik Ma'akhidh (Intikhab-i-Muntakhib: A Great Source of Sindh's History).' *The Quarterly Mehran* (Jamshoro: Sindhi Adabi Board) no. 1 (1986).

Junejo, Dr Abdul Jabbar, 'Syed Abdul Qadir b. Syed Muhammad Nasarpuri: the author of Hadiqat al-Awliya.' *The Quarterly Mehran* (Jamshoro: Sindhi Adabi Board) no. 1 (1988).

Rashidi, Syed Hussamuddin. 'Historical and Political Epistles of Sindh.' Sindhi trans. Dr G. M. Lakho, *The Quarterly Mehran* (Jamshoro: Sindhi Adabi Board) no. 1 (1987).

―――――. 'Nusrat Nama-i-Tarkhan.' *The Quarterly Mehran* (Jamshoro: Sindhi Adabi Board) nos. 1–2 (1980).

Index

A

A'in-i-Akbari, 34, 38, 39, 88, 125, 160, 177, 187
Aadab-i-Alamgiri, 171, 181–5
Abbasid(s), 13, 14, 16, 28, 87, 127, 144
Abi-Sufyan, Muawiyah bin, 15
Afghani, Syed Mohib, 151
Afif, Shams Siraj, 19, 21, 22, 23, 29
Ahkam-i-Alamgiri, 188, 189
Ahmad, Nizam al-Din, 86, 89, 132, 133, 157, 159
Aibak, Qutub al-Din, 16
Akbar Nama, 38, 83, 85, 87, 93, 129, 135, 174, 175, 177, 180
Akbar, Emperor, 32, 33, 35, 37, 38, 75, 76, 79, 80, 82, 83, 84, 86, 88, 90, 91, 96, 98, 99, 101, 102, 111, 116, 122, 127, 134, 136, 138, 143, 156, 157, 159, 160, 163–5, 169, 170–7, 194, 203, 205
Akhyana, 6, 7, 8, 10
Alamgir, Emperor, 34, 39, 135, 170, 189, 202
Al-Baladhuri, 43, 44, 88
Al-Biruni, 15
al-Fazl, Abu, 34, 37, 38, 87, 91, 99, 111, 125, 160, 162, 163, 169, 174, 180, 197
Ali, Syed Mir, 63, 64
Al-Kufi, Ali bin Hamid bin Abi Bakar, 43–6
Al-Masudi, 196
Amal-i-Salih, 132, 160
Ansab, 13, 196
Arghun(s), 47–9, 50, 51, 53–9, 67, 69, 70–3, 75, 76, 85–7, 89, 93, 95, 96, 99, 101–7, 110, 111, 114, 121, 126–9, 130–3, 138, 139, 148, 196, 202
Arghun, Mirza Beg, 105
Arghun, Mirza Shah Hassan, 53, 54, 70, 95, 96, 101, 104, 105, 111, 131–3
Ashvaghosha, 10
Ataki, Muhammad Yousuf, 134, 135
Awfi, Muhammad, 43, 60, 77, 142, 143
Awliya, Nizam al-Din, 61, 62, 84
Ayyam al-Arab, 13

B

Babur Nama, 133

Babur, Emperor, 32, 35, 49, 55–8, 83, 84, 115, 133, 139, 143
Badshah Nama, 128, 132
Balban, Ghiyas al-Din, 22, 152
Banabhatta, 10
Barani, Ziya al-Din, 19, 20, 22, 23, 29, 120, 125, 147
Bardai, Chand, 11
Bayan al-A'arifin, 166
Beg, Mirza Jani, 59, 90, 91, 95, 96, 99, 101, 110, 122, 127, 129, 131–3, 136, 138, 145, 157
Beglar Nama, 55, 81, 82, 86, 93–9, 100, 104, 107, 110, 129, 148, 196
Beglar, Khan-i-Zaman Shah Qasim, 93, 95, 96, 99, 102, 204
Beglari, Idraki, 47, 55, 93, 95, 96, 99, 107, 110, 121, 129, 203
Bhakkari, Mir Muhammad Masum Shah, 54–8, 70, 73, 82–9, 90–3, 104, 107, 110, 120, 124, 129, 132, 133, 157, 162, 163, 165, 172, 203
Bhakkari, Shaykh Farid, 124, 131, 147, 156, 157, 160, 197
Bhittai, Shah Abdul Latif, 151
Bhrigvangiras(es), 6, 8, 9
Bilhana, 10
Brahmanas, 7, 8, 9
Buddhist, 5, 9, 10, 12
Burhan al-Din, Qazi, 151
Buzurg, Syed Mir, 128

C

Chach Nama, 17, 42–7, 86–8, 107, 108, 201, 208
Chanesar Nama, 47, 94, 107, 203

D

Dabistan-i-Herat, 31
Dalil al-Dhakirin, 167
Debal, 15, 88
Dehlvi, Shaykh Abdul Haque Muhaddith, 125, 144
Dehlvi, Shaykh Nasir al-Din Chiragh, 26
Dhakhirat al-Khawanin, 131, 132, 147, 156, 157, 160–4, 166, 197
Dhikr-i Kharab-i Delhi, 21
Dittah, Qazi, 151

251

Diwan(s), 14, 24, 81, 85, 137, 162, 169
Diwan-i-Ruba'iyat, 85
Dodha, Shaykh, 151

F

Fatawa-i-Jahandari, 22, 23, 120, 125
Fath Nama-i-Chittor, 177, 181
Fath Nama-i-Sindh, 17, 43, 54
Fawa'id al-Fuad, 26, 61
Firdausi, 12, 25, 44, 49, 50, 52, 58, 98, 119
Firishta, Muhammad Qasim, 19, 83, 87, 89, 132, 133, 204
Futuh al-Buldan, 15, 43, 86, 88
Futuhat-i-Alamgiri, 34
Futuh-us-Salatin, 25, 27

G

Gathas, 6, 7
Ghadhi, Syed Salaar, 151
Ghori, Shihab al-Din Muhammad, 11, 16

H

Habib al-Siyar, 56, 72, 86, 90, 135
Hadiqat al-Awliya, 144–9, 152, 166, 200
Hadith, 13, 42, 67, 93, 97, 142, 146, 163
Haji Mah Begum, 75, 76, 127
Hamd, 21, 202
Hammira Mahakavya, 11
Harawi, Fakhri, 69, 70–2, 74, 75, 77, 79, 143
Harawi, Nizam al-Din Ahmad, 38
Harshacharita, 10
Harshavardhana, 10
Historiography, 1, 2, 3, 4, 8, 9, 10–19, 20, 21, 24, 25, 27–9, 30, 31, 33–8, 44–7, 51–3, 140, 141, 193–9, 201, 206–9, 210, 211
Humayun, Emperor, 32, 56, 57, 70, 73, 74, 84, 85, 88, 101, 110, 115, 116, 127, 132, 143, 164, 169, 171, 175, 203
Hyder, Abdul Ghafoor bin, 151, 153

I

Idrees, Qazi, 151
Imran, Shaykh Channa, 151
Insha(s), 17, 25, 35, 59, 60, 72, 116, 137, 140, 168, 169, 170, 171, 174–7, 19, 180, 181, 184, 187, 192, 198, 208
Insha-i-Abu al-Fazl, 169, 175, 176
Intikhab-i-Muntakhib (*Intikhab Nama*), 82, 134, 136, 137, 138
Isami, Khawaja Abdul Malik, 19, 25, 27, 30

Iskandaria, Makhdum, 151
Isnad, 13, 18, 20,
Itihasa, 6, 7, 8

J

Jahangir, Emperor, 85, 102, 103, 116, 122, 123, 138, 158, 159, 160, 162, 165, 170, 172, 174, 199
Jahaniyan, Syed Jalal al-Din Bukhari Makhdum, 61
Jain, 5, 9, 11
Jalal, Syed Miyan, 151
Jami Fatawa-i-Purani, 48
Jawahir al-Aja'ib, 69, 74–9
Jayanaka, 11, 12
Juzjani, Minhaj-us-Siraj, 19, 43

K

Kalhana, 4, 11, 12, 26
Kalimat al-Shuara, 199
Kavya, 10
Khair al-Majalis, 26, 29, 37
Khan, Mirza Shah Muhammad Beg Adil, 103, 104, 105
Khilji, Alauddin, 11, 20
Khulasat al-Hayat, 155
Khusro, Amir, 19, 24, 25, 58, 145, 168

L

Lahori, Abdul Hamid, 128
Lahori, Mufti Ghulam Sarwar, 144, 200
Lakha, Haji Sadr, 151
Lubab al-Albab, 43, 60, 142, 143
Lubb-i Tarikh i-Sindh, 152, 201

M

Ma'athir-i-Rahimi, 70, 83, 90, 93, 133, 175
Ma'dan al-Ma'ani, 61
Ma'lumat al-Aafaq, 202, 203
Maghazis, 13
Mahabharata, 5, 6, 7, 8, 40, 41, 42
Mahmud (of Ghazni), 15, 21, 25, 118
Mahru, Ain al-Mulk, 19, 25, 60, 169, 171
Makli Nama, 54, 153, 208
Makran, 15, 43
Maktubat-i-Allami, 169, 176
Malfuzat(s), 17, 26, 29, 35, 37, 59, 61, 62, 65, 66, 140, 143, 144, 166, 200
Manaqib, 21
Manaqib-i Sultan Muhammad, 21

INDEX

Manaqib-i-Ala'i, 21
Manaqib-i-Sultan Ghiyas al-Din Tughluq Shah, 21
Manasollasa, 10, 11
Maqalat al-Shuara, 48, 73, 93, 100, 136, 145, 189, 208
Mathnawi(s), 19, 24, 51, 52, 58, 69, 72, 80, 85, 94, 98, 104, 173, 203
Mazhar-i-Shahjahani, 55, 82, 98, 115, 116, 118, 120–3, 125, 126, 173, 202
Mirak, Yousuf, 55, 115, 117, 118, 120, 121, 122, 124, 173, 202
Mongol(s), 16, 20, 25, 31, 43, 50, 52, 90, 127, 198
Muhammad, Syed Mir, 126, 128, 129, 130, 132, 133, 135
Munshat-i-Mahru, 60, 171
Munshat-i-Namakin, 116, 170, 171, 173, 175—9, 180, 181, 188
Muntakhib al-Tawarikh, 34, 87, 129, 134, 137, 138
Muqaddima, 51, 64, 135
Muruj al-Dhahab, 196

N

Na'at, 21, 202
Nafa'is al-Ma'asir, 35, 143
Nakhrij, Shaykh, 151
Namakin, Mir Abu al-Qasim, 115, 116, 124, 157, 162, 170–4, 179, 188, 202
Nanda, Jam Nizam al-Din, 53, 54, 66, 89, 109, 110, 111
Nandi, Sandhyakar, 10
Narasamsis, 6, 7
Nava-Sahasanka-Charita, 11
Nisyani, Syed Tahir Muhammad, 55, 100, 102, 104, 110
Nizami, Hassan, 23, 52, 98, 119
Nusrat Nama-i-Tarkhan, 47–9, 50, 52, 53, 55–9, 86, 107, 108, 196, 202

P

Padmagupta, 11
Prithviraj Raso, 11
Prithviraj, 11
Prithviraja Vijaya, 11
Puran(i), 48, 49, 55, 57, 58, 92, 131
Purana(s), 5, 6, 7, 8, 40, 42
Purani, Syed Mir Muhammad Bayazid, 48, 49, 52, 54, 57

Q

Qalandar, Lal Shahbaz, 145, 146, 150–5
Qalandar, Makhdum Uthman, 151

Qasida(s), 13, 21, 46, 72, 75, 76, 85, 102, 145, 167
Qasim, Muhammad bin, 15, 44, 46, 88, 136
Qiran-us-Sa'dain, 24
Qizwini, Ala al-Dawla, 143

R

Rahmat, Makhdum, 80
Rajatarangini, 4, 11, 12, 26, 27
Ramacharitam, 10
Ramayana, 5, 6, 7, 8, 10, 40, 42
Rampala, King, 10
Ramz wa Ishara ha'i Alamgiri, 170
Raqa'im-i-Kara'im, 170, 171, 173, 187–9, 190
Rashidi, Syed Hussamuddin, 54, 59, 71, 74, 75, 78, 79, 94, 116, 125, 126, 134, 135, 145–7, 150, 152, 153, 172, 173
Rawzat al-Salatin, 69, 70–8, 143
Rig Veda, 6, 7, 41
Risala-i Fat'hiya, 166
Risala-i-Tahlilha, 63
Riyaz-us-Salatin, 39, 204
Ruqqat-i-Abu al-Fazl, 169
Ruqqat-i-Alamgiri, 188
Rushhat al-Fanun, 202, 203

S

Sachal Sarmast, 151
Safavid, Shah Abbas, 90, 176
Safavid, Shah Ismail, 70, 74, 76, 133, 139
Safavid, Shah Tahmasp, 89
Samarqandi, Daulat Shah, 77, 143
Samma(s), 46, 47, 49, 51, 53, 54, 63, 66, 87–9, 104–6, 109, 110, 127
Samudragupta, 4
Sanda'i, Shaykh Ahmad, 151
Sangam, 12
Sanskrit, 5, 6, 7, 11, 26, 27, 40, 42, 44
Saqi Nama, 85
Shah Jahan, Emperor, 48, 60, 80, 115, 117, 118, 122, 125, 127, 128, 131, 134, 136, 138, 155, 158, 159, 160, 161, 163, 165, 184, 186, 187, 190
Shah Nama, 12, 21, 25, 49, 58, 97, 98
Shah, Fakhar al-Mudabbir Mubarak, 19
Shah, Khawr, 82
Shahjahan Nama, 34
Shajara-i-Ansab-i-Mubarakshahi, 19
Shajrah Sadat-i-Purani, 48, 49
Shikoh, Dara, 35, 186, 187
Shirazi, Shah Murad, 62–7, 145
Shirazi, Syed Mir Muhammad bin Jamal bin Jalal al-Din Hussaini, 55

INDEX

Shujat-i-Alamgiri, 188
Sijzi, Mir Hassan, 26, 61
Sindhuraja, 11
Sirah, 13, 142
Siraj al-Hidaya, 61
Sirhindi, Shaykh Ahmad, 63
Sirhindi, Yahya bin Ahmad, 19, 20, 23, 29, 63
Siyar al-Auliya, 26
Siyar us-Salatin, 145
Someshvara, 10
Soomra(s), 46, 47, 87, 104–7, 109, 110–13, 135, 138, 208
Suri, Nayachandra, 11
Suta(s), 8, 9

T

Tabaqat-i-Akbari, 38, 39, 83, 85, 86, 88, 90, 93, 159, 160
Tabaqat-i-Nasiri, 43, 86, 87
Tabaqat-i-Shahjahani, 155
Tadhkira Mashayikh-i-Sewistan, 140, 151, 153, 166
Tadhkira(s), 17, 35, 37, 59, 65, 72, 137, 140, 142, 144, 148, 166, 167, 208
Tadhkirat al-Awliya, 142, 144, 147
Tadhkirat al-Murad, 62, 63, 65, 66
Taj al-Ma'athir, 23
Tarikh al-Hind, 15
Tarikh i-Sind, 54
Tarikh Mazhar-i-Shahjahani, 82
Tarikh Tabaqat-i-Bahadurshahi, 38, 86, 87, 88
Tarikh-i-Alfi, 82
Tarikh-i-Ferozshahi, 21, 22, 23, 86, 87, 147, 152
Tarikh-i-Firishta, 83, 88, 204
Tarikh-i-Humayuni, 129, 135, 147, 203
Tarikh-i-Kashmir, 27, 34, 204
Tarikh-Ilchi-i-Nizamshahi, 82
Tarikh-i-Masumi, 48, 70, 81–3, 85–8, 90, 92, 93, 98, 104, 107, 110, 111, 129, 130, 133–5, 139, 202, 208
Tarikh-i-Shahjahani, 157
Tarikh-i-Tahiri, 81, 82, 86, 94, 98, 99, 100, 103, 104, 109, 110–12, 114, 129, 132, 133, 148, 154
Tarjumat al-Ahadith al-Arba'in fi Nasihat al-Muluk wa'i Salatin, 125
Tarkhan Nama, 48, 55, 82, 86, 111, 114, 126, 128, 129, 130–5, 196, 202
Tarkhan(s), 47–9, 50, 51, 54, 55–9, 71, 75, 79, 84, 85, 87, 91, 93, 95–9, 101, 103–7, 110, 111, 114, 122, 125–9, 130–9, 144, 145, 157, 159, 162, 172, 173, 196

Tarkhan, Mirza Ghazi Beg, 59, 96, 97, 99, 101, 102, 104–7, 110, 112, 129, 131, 132, 146, 157, 159, 172, 173
Tarkhan, Mirza Jani Beg, 59, 90, 91, 95, 96, 99, 101, 105, 110, 122, 127, 129, 131, 132, 133, 136, 145, 146, 157
Tarkhan, Mirza Muhammad Salih, 96, 98, 126–8, 131
Thattawi, Mir Ali Sher Qani, 100, 131, 145, 208
Thattawi, Muhammad Hussain Safa'i, 62, 63
Thattawi, Mulla Ahmad Nasrullah, 82
Thattawi, Mulla Ahmad, 155, 157, 158
Thattawi, Qazi Mahmud, 144, 147
Thattawi, Shaykh Abdul Shakoor, 134–7
Thattawi, Shaykh Muhammad Azam, 66
Thattawi, Syed Abdul Qadir bin Syed Hashim, 145
Topin, Shaykh, 151
Tughluq, Sultan Feroz Shah, 21, 26, 60, 62, 74
Tughluq, Sultan Muhammad bin, 21–6, 29, 30, 60, 89, 147, 152, 155
Tuhfat al-Kiram, 48, 53, 63, 73, 100, 112, 114, 131, 135, 136, 145, 208
Tuhfat al-Tahirin, 63, 66, 208
Tuzuk-i-Baburi, 57
Tuzuk-i-Jahangiri, 34, 159, 160

U

Umar, Hazrat, 15, 28
Umayyad(s), 14, 15, 16, 44, 88
Upanishads, 7

V

Vamsas, 5
Vedas, 6, 7, 8, 40, 41
Vedic, 5, 6, 7, 8, 9, 10, 41
Vikramaditya VI, 10
Vikramankabhyudaya, 11
Vikramankadeva Charita, 10
Vyasa, 7

Y

Yamin al-Barakat, 167

Z

Zakariya, Shaykh Baha al-Din, 64–6, 144, 147, 157, 163, 178
Zinat al-Kuttab, 168